Guide to Wireless Communications

Mark Ciampa

Australia • Canada • Mexico • Singapore • Spain • United Kingdom • United States

Guide to Wireless Communications

by Mark Ciampa

Acquisitions Editor:
Will Pitkin

Product Manager:
Laura Hildebrand

Editorial Assistant:
Nick Lombardi

Associate Product Manager:
Tim Gleeson

Marketing Manager:
Jason Sakos

Production Editor:
Karen Jacot

Photo Research Editor:
Abby Reip

Development Editor:
Deb Kaufmann

Cover Design:
Janet Lavine

Compositor:
GEX Publishing Services

Printed in the United States of America

2 3 4 5 6 7 8 9 BH 06 05 04

For more information, contact Course Technology, 25 Thomson Place, Boston, Massachusetts, 02210.

Or find us on the World Wide Web at: www.course.com

ISBN 0-619-12000-2

BRIEF

Contents

TABLE OF
Contents

Preface

The hottest topic in the computer world today can be summed up in a single word: *wireless*. Everywhere you turn you see evidence of this exciting new technology. Students are carrying wireless notebook computers across campus and surfing the Internet as they go. Salespeople are receiving up-to-the-minute inventory figures on the displays of their digital telephones. Business executives are sending and receiving e-mails on hand-held personal digital assistants as they move through the office building. Wireless communications seem to be happening everywhere.

Although wireless is the hottest computer topic today, it is also perhaps the least understood of the new technologies. How can data signals be sent and received through the air? What are the limitations of wireless communications? How do you set it up and use it? Because wireless technology is rapidly becoming a primary means of business communication, it is important for people in the computer industry to understand how to use it today and determine how it can be used tomorrow.

This book is designed to provide you with the necessary tools to help you become part of this revolutionary change in communications and networking. *Guide to Wireless Communications* is designed to give you a "behind-the-scenes" technical view of how wireless communications work, as well as give you direct experience with today's major wireless technologies. Each chapter in the book contains hands-on projects that cover many aspects of wireless communications. In addition, projects that show how to install and use the latest wireless technology are also included. These projects are designed to make what you learn come alive through actually performing the tasks. Besides the hands-on projects, each chapter gives you experience through realistic case projects that put you in the role of a wireless technology consultant who works in different scenarios helping solve the problems of clients. Every chapter also includes review questions to reinforce your knowledge while preparing you to use and support wireless technology.

The book is divided into four parts. Part One (chapters 1-3) covers how wireless communications works. **Chapter 1**, "Introduction to Wireless Communication," defines wireless communications and helps you see how wireless communications are used today. This chapter explains how these technologies compare with each other and gives real-life illustrations of how this technology is being used today as well as showing its advantages and disadvantages. In **Chapter 2**, "How Wireless Works," you learn the technology behind wireless communication and how data can be sent and received over the air.

Chapter 3, "Understanding Radio Frequency Communications," digs deeper into this primary means of data transmission.

Part Two (chapters 4–7) deals with the wireless technologies used in personal area networks. **Chapter 4**, "Infrared," looks at wireless infrared technologies while **Chapter 5**, "Bluetooth," helps you learn how this exciting new technology functions and how it will change the way in which devices communicate between themselves.

Part Three (chapters 6 and 7) deals with wireless technologies used in local area networks. In **Chapter 6** you will explore low-speed wireless local area networks, namely those that transmit at 15 Mbps or less. **Chapter 7**, "High Speed WLANs and WLAN Security," looks at WLANs with speeds up to 108 Mbps and also discusses how to make WLAN transmissions secure.

Part Four (chapters 8–10) covers wireless technologies that are found in wide area networks and gives an overview of wireless communications in business. In **Chapter 8**, "Digital Cellular Telephony," you learn how cell phones are used to send and receive data transmission and what changes are just ahead for this technology. "Fixed Wireless" is the topic of **Chapter 9.** This chapter explains the technologies used to transmit data over long distances of up to 35 miles. The last chapter, **Chapter 10**, "Wireless Communications in Business," covers the advantages and disadvantages of wireless communications and how to build a wireless infrastructure.

The book concludes with two appendixes: one on the history of wireless communications, and one that provides summary charts on the various wireless technologies you've learned about in the book.

FEATURES

To ensure a successful learning experience, this book includes the following pedagogical features:

- **Chapter Objectives:** Each chapter in this book begins with a detailed list of the concepts to be mastered within that chapter. This list provides you with a quick reference to the contents of that chapter, as well as a useful study aid.
- **Illustrations, Photographs, and Tables:** Numerous illustrations, photographs and tables aid you in understanding wireless communications technology, design, and setup.
- **End of Chapter Material:** The end of each chapter includes the following features to reinforce the material covered in the chapter:
  - **Chapter Summaries:** Each chapter's text is followed by a summary of the concepts it has introduced. These summaries provide a helpful way to recap and revisit the ideas covered in each chapter.
  - **Key Terms List:** A list of all new terms in the chapter, along with their definitions.

- **Review Questions:** To test knowledge of the chapter, the review questions cover the most important concepts of the chapter.
- **Hands-on Projects:** Although it is important to understand the theory behind wireless technology, nothing can improve upon real-world experience. To this end, along with theoretical explanations, each chapter provides numerous hands-on projects aimed at providing you with research and implementation experience.
- **Case Projects:** Located at the end of each chapter is a multipart case project. In this extensive case example, as a consultant at the fictitious The Baypoint Group, you implement the skills and knowledge gained in the chapter through real-world research, implementation, and troubleshooting.
- **Optional Team Case Project:** Each chapter concludes with an optional team case project that enables you to work in a small group of students to solve a real-world problem or to extensively research a topic. These projects give you experience working as a team member, which is a common format used by many businesses and corporations.

Text and Graphic Conventions

Wherever appropriate, additional information and exercises have been added to this book to help you better understand what is being discussed in the chapter. Icons throughout the text alert you to additional materials. The icons used in this textbook are as follows:

Tips are included from the author's experience that provide extra information about how to attack a problem or what to do in certain real-world situations.

The Note icon is used to present additional helpful material related to the subject being described.

Each Hands-on Project in this book is preceded by the Hands-on icon and a description of the exercise that follows.

Case project icons mark the case project. These are more involved, scenario-based assignments. In this extensive case example, you are asked to implement independently what you have learned.

Optional case projects for teams icons indicate special projects that students can tackle as a group and that often require extra research and group decision making, which simulates the team environment stressed in many organizations.

Instructor's Materials

The following supplemental materials are available when this book is used in a classroom setting. All of the supplements available with this book are provided to the instructor on a single CD-ROM.

Electronic Instructor's Manual. The Instructor's Manual that accompanies this textbook includes:

- Additional instructional material to assist in class preparation, including suggestions for lecture topics, suggested lab activities, tips on setting up a lab for the hands-on assignments, and alternative lab setup ideas in situations where lab resources are limited.
- Solutions to all end-of-chapter materials, including the Review Questions, Hands-on Projects, Case and Optional Team Case assignments.

ExamView Pro 3.0. This textbook is accompanied by ExamView®, a powerful testing software package that allows instructors to create and administer printed, computer (LAN-based), and Internet exams. ExamView includes hundreds of questions that correspond to the topics covered in this text, enabling students to generate detailed study guides that include page references for further review. The computer-based and Internet testing components allow students to take exams at their computers, and also save the instructor time by grading each exam automatically.

PowerPoint presentations. This book comes with Microsoft PowerPoint slides for each chapter. These are included as a teaching aid for classroom presentation, to make available to students on the network for chapter review, or to be printed for classroom distribution. Instructors, please feel at liberty to add your own slides for additional topics you introduce to the class.

Read This Before You Begin

TO THE STUDENT

This book helps you understand wireless communications and how to install, use, and manage the most popular wireless technologies. Every chapter is designed to present you with easy-to-understand information about wireless technologies to help you plan and implement these systems in different environments. Each chapter of the book ends with review questions, hands-on projects, case assignments, and team case assignments that are written to be as realistic as the work you will soon be performing on the job. Your instructor can provide you with answers to the review questions and additional information about the hands-on projects.

Internet assignments. Some projects require Internet access for information searches. These projects will help train the student in using this resource as a prospective network administrator.

Wireless technologies. To complete the projects and assignments in the book, the students will need access to different wireless technologies. These technologies include infrared, Bluetooth, and wireless local area networks. Infrared capabilities are standard equipment on almost all notebook computers and personal digital assistants (PDAs). Bluetooth devices can be easily added to a notebook computer that contains a PC Card slot. Wireless local area network technology can also be added to any notebook computer or PDA that has a PC Card slot along with using an access point. To maximize the learning experience, it is recommended that you have one or more access points that can be dedicated for classroom use. In addition, each student should have a computer with a wireless NIC adapter installed. Although it is not required, it is desirable for each access point to be connected to a wired Ethernet network in order that the full advantages of a wireless network can be experienced.

System requirements. The recommended software and hardware configurations are as follows:

Notebook Computer

- Portable notebook computer with Type II or Type III PC Card slot
- Windows 95, Windows 98, Windows ME, Windows NT, Windows 2000 or Windows XP operating system
- Netscape Navigator 5.0+ or Internet Explorer 4.0+ browser installed
- Minimum Pentium 133 MHz processor
- Minimum 32 MB of RAM
- VGA monitor

- Mouse or pointing device
- Wireless NIC adapter
- PC Card Type II Bluetooth adapter
- Infrared port
- Hard disk drive
- At least one high density 3.5-inch floppy disk drive
- Internet access (recommended but not required for selected research assignments)

Personal Digital Assistant

- Hand-held PDA device using StrongARM or similar Intel-type processor
- Minimum 32MB RAM
- Infrared port
- PC Card Type II slot
- Pocket PC 2002 or Windows CE 3.x operating system

Access Point

- Cisco Aironet 340 access point

ACKNOWLEDGMENTS

An author may write the words, but a team creates a book. And the team that worked on this book was one of the very best. Reviewers Peggy Mooney, Tracy Stinson, and Terry Zlatnicky provided many helpful criticisms and comments, while Technical Editor Andy Faulkner helped identify technical errors. Product Manager Laura Hildebrand was fantastic at keeping the project on track and answering all my questions. Developmental Editor Deb Kaufmann was again outstanding at correcting my mistakes and making excellent suggestions. The Academic Computing staff at Volunteer State Community College was great in helping me solve wireless technology problems. And the entire Course Technology staff was always very helpful and worked very hard to create the finished product. To all of these I extend my sincere thanks.

And finally, I want to thank my family—my wife Susan and my sons Brian and Greg. Their constant interest in the project and their support, patience, and love helped see me through another book. I could not have done it without them.

DEDICATION

To my wife Susan and my sons Brian and Greg

PHOTO CREDITS

Figure 1-2	Bluetooth headset	Courtesy of Ericsson Inc.
Figure 1-6	Personal Digital Assistant	Courtesy of Hewlett-Packard Company
Figure 1-9	Access point and wireless NIC	Courtesy of 3Com Corporation
Figure 2-6	Infrared wireless device	Copyright © 2001 NEC Computers Inc. All rights reserved
Figure 3-13	Large diameter antenna	© 2001 PhotoDisc
Figure 6-1	NIC	Courtesy of 3Com Corporation
Figure 6-2	PCI wireless NIC	Courtesy of 3Com Corporation
Figure 6-3	PC Card wireless NIC with retractable antenna	Courtesy of 3Com Corporation
Figure 6-4	PC Card wireless NIC	Courtesy of 3Com Corporation
Figure 6-5	CF Card wireless NIC	Courtesy of Symbol Technologies
Figure 6-6	Access point	Courtesy of 3Com Corporation
Figure 9-5	Remote wireless bridge	Courtesy of Solectek Corporation
Figure 9-6	FSO link head	Courtesy of Terabeam Corporation
Figure 9-18	Pizza box antenna	Courtesy of Alan Herrell LemurZone Design, Phoenix, Arizona

CHAPTER

1

INTRODUCTION TO WIRELESS COMMUNICATIONS

After reading this chapter and completing the exercises you will be able to:

- Explain how the major wireless technologies are used today
- Describe the applications used in wireless technology
- List and explain the advantages of wireless technology
- List and explain the disadvantages of wireless technology

Seldom do information technology (IT) professionals all agree on anything. Each one has his or her own opinion on which software is the best, which brand of personal computer is superior, and which operating system should be found on every computer. However, there is something that all IT professionals today do agree on: the tremendous impact of wireless communications technology on the world. Wireless is poised to become the next major event in the history of technology.

Wireless communications will revolutionize how we live. Just as personal computers in the 1980s forever altered how we work and the Internet in the 1990s dramatically changed how we acquire information, the spread of wireless technologies in the 2000s will have an even greater and more far-reaching effect. Using wireless communications to send and receive messages, browse the Internet, and access corporate databases from any location in the world using a cell phone or handheld device will become commonplace and will transform how we work and play. A wide array of devices ranging from computers, digital cameras, laser printers, and even refrigerators will be able to communicate without wires. Users will always be able to be in touch with the digital resources that they need no matter where they may find themselves. The IT industry and consumer marketplace are already seeing dramatic changes based on wireless technologies. It is truly becoming a new wireless world.

How Wireless Technology Is Used

It is unfortunate that the term *wireless* is used to describe all types of devices and technologies that are not connected by a wire. A garage door opener, a television remote control, a portable telephone, and a pager all can be called "wireless," since these devices do not have wires, but that is the extent of what they share in common. Because the term wireless today is sometimes used to refer to any device that has no wires, users tend to be puzzled about the exact meaning of wireless communications. For the purposes of this book, **wireless communications** is defined as the transmission of user data without the use of wires. "User data" may include e-mail messages, spreadsheets, and telephone voice messages. A day in the life of a typical couple, Joseph and Ann Kirkpatrick, reveals something of today's wireless landscape.

SWAP

Joseph and Ann get ready for a typical day. Before Ann leaves for the office she must first print a copy of a spreadsheet that she finished working on late last night. Because there are several computers in their house, Ann has set up a wireless computer network. This network is based on the **Shared Wireless Access Protocol (SWAP).** This protocol defines a set of specifications for wireless data and voice communications around the home. Devices can be as far as 150 feet (45 meters) apart and can send and receive data up to 10 million bits per second (megabits or Mbps). The devices that can be part of the network include not only computer equipment but also cordless telephones and home entertainment equipment. SWAP was established by the **HomeRF Working Group**, which is made up of over 50 different companies from the personal computer, consumer electronics, communications, and software industries.

Ann sits down at the desktop computer upstairs and retrieves the spreadsheet. She then selects the Print command. A device called a **wireless home networking adapter** is connected to the computer. This adapter upstairs sends the data over radio waves to the computer downstairs that also has a home networking adapter as well as a laser printer connected to it. This wireless network is ideal for the Kirkpatricks. They can have all of their home computing and electronic devices connected together without the expense of installing cable and can share printers, files, and even Internet connections. Figure 1-1 illustrates the home wireless network.

Runners in the Boston Marathon cover the 26.2-mile course with tiny wireless transponder chips clipped to their shoelaces. The chips are used to track the times of all runners and also to e-mail updates to friends and relatives regarding the runners' progress.

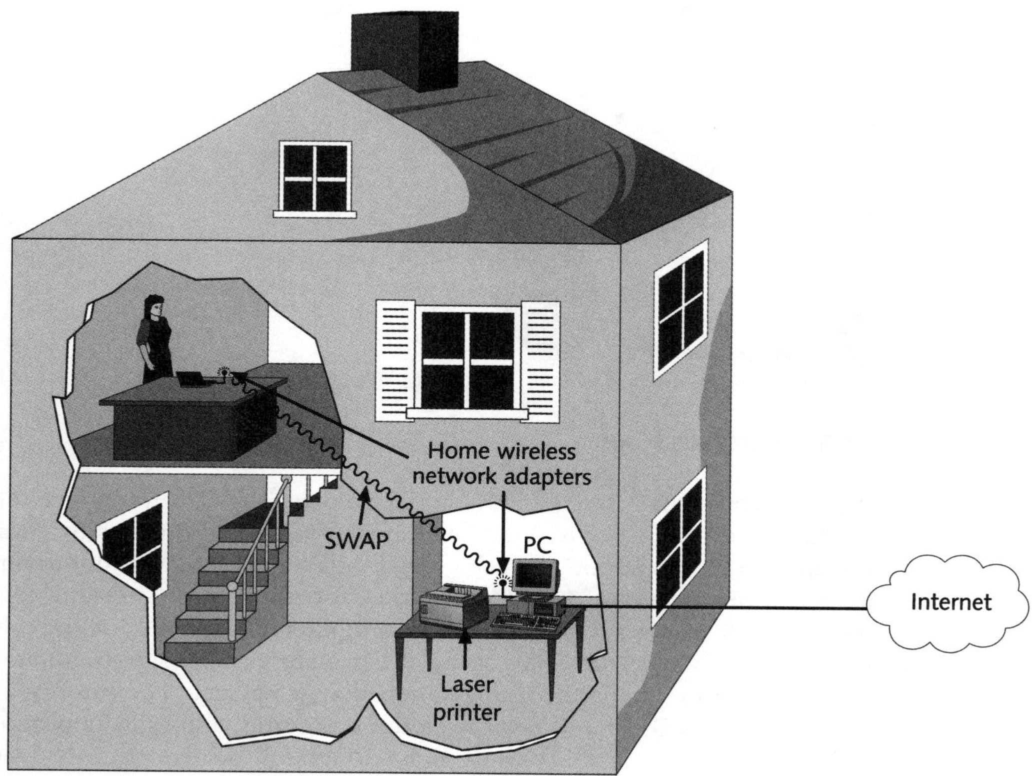

Figure 1-1 Home wireless network

Bluetooth

Joseph and Ann both work for Federated Package Express (FPE), a package delivery service. When a customer wants to send a package, they telephone the local FPE call center. An FPE customer service representative receives the call using a telephone headset that conforms to the **Bluetooth** wireless standard. This device is illustrated in Figure 1-2. Bluetooth devices communicate using small radio transceivers called **radio modules** built onto microprocessor chips. Each Bluetooth device uses a **link manager**, which is special software that helps identify other Bluetooth devices, creates the links with them, and sends and receives data. A Bluetooth device can transmit data at up to 1 Mbps over a distance of 33 feet (10 meters). Bluetooth can send data through physical barriers, like walls, to one or many different devices all at the same time. These devices don't even have to be aimed at each other. Over 1,500 different computer, telephone and peripheral vendors have agreed to create products based on the Bluetooth standard.

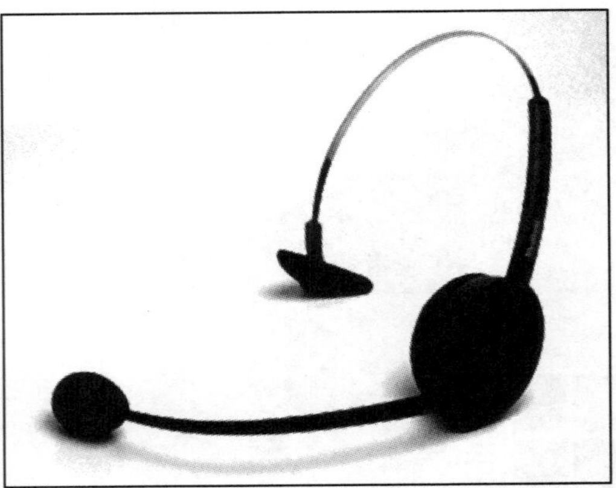

Figure 1-2 Bluetooth headset

As the customer service representative walks into her cubicle to answer the phone, several things instantly occur. Her Bluetooth headset automatically establishes a connection with the telephone. She can immediately start talking without having to pick up the telephone receiver. In addition, the notebook computer she is carrying automatically synchronizes with her desktop computer. The address list and calendar on the notebook computer, which she changed last night at home, are transmitted to the desktop computer and the information is immediately updated. The automatic connection between various Bluetooth devices creates a **piconet**, also called a **personal area network (PAN)**. A piconet is two or more Bluetooth devices that are sending and receiving data with each other. The customer service representative answers the call while she is moving around her cubicle without being tethered by telephone wires. She then sits down and enters the pick-up information on her computer. Figure 1-3 illustrates a Bluetooth wireless network.

Figure 1-3 Bluetooth network

Bluetooth is named after the 10th century Danish King Harald Bluetooth, who was responsible for unifying Scandinavia.

Satellite

After the pick-up information has been entered into the computer, the data is then transmitted to a satellite circling the earth. In satellite communications, a device called a **repeater** is located in a satellite. A repeater simply "repeats" the signal to another location. An earth station transmits to the satellite at one frequency band and the satellite regenerates and transmits ("repeats") the signal back to earth at another frequency. The transmission time needed to repeat a signal from one earth station to another is approximately 250 milliseconds. This is illustrated in Figure 1-4.

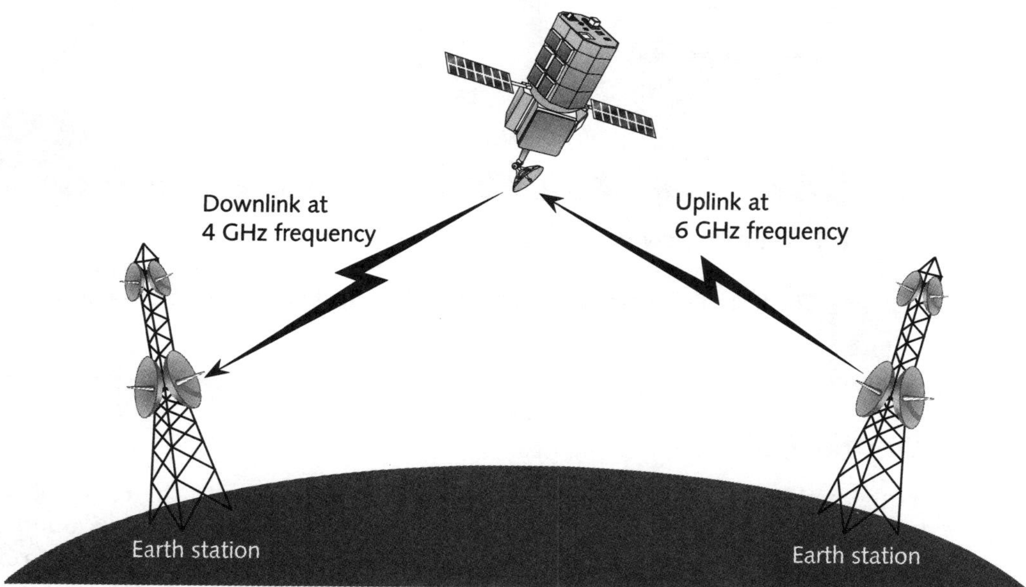

Figure 1-4 Satellite frequency transmission

Federated Package Express contracts with a vendor that provides international satellite communications. Although trucking companies have used satellite systems to track the location of fleets of trucks for several years, Federated is one of the first companies to use this system to relay customer data directly to its trucks.

Joseph Kirkpatrick drives a delivery truck for FPE. Joseph's truck is equipped with a smart wireless computer terminal that is embedded into the hub of the steering wheel of his van. The satellite transmits the pick-up order to the terminal in Joseph's van. The satellite can also send time-sensitive information, such as route alerts to warn of traffic delays or changes in pick-up schedules. Even remote diagnostics on the van can be performed and transmitted back to Federated through the satellite. The satellite network that Federated uses is illustrated in Figure 1-5.

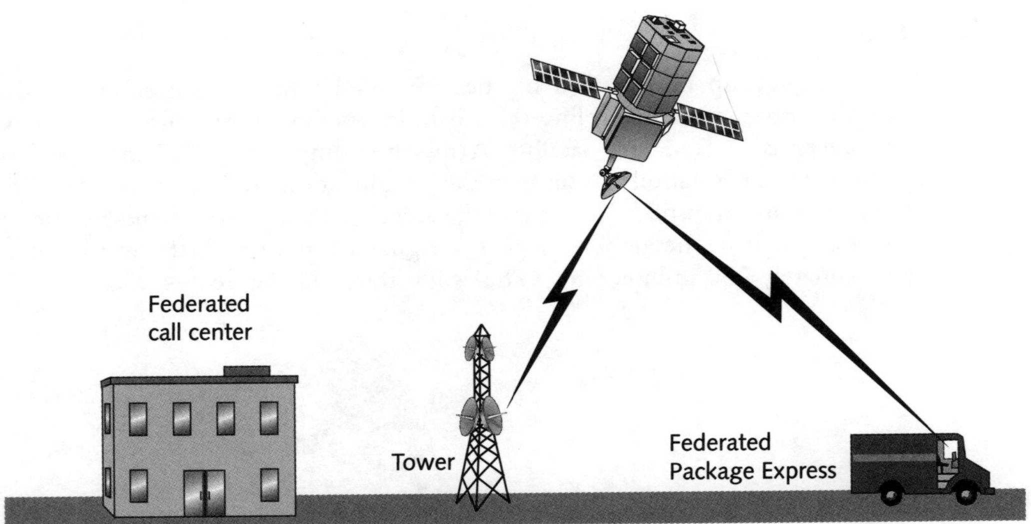

Figure 1-5 Satellite network

The first satellite was called SPUTNIK, launched by the Soviet Union in 1957.

2G Digital Cellular

As the pick-up order is transmitted through the satellite onto the terminal in the van, Joseph swings onto the highway and reaches the address in about 15 minutes. Joseph leaves the van carrying his **Personal Digital Assistant (PDA)**, which is a hand-held computing device, shown in Figure 1-6. Joseph walks into the building to retrieve the package. The sender has already filled out a form called a waybill that includes the sender's information as well as the recipient's name, address, and other information. A unique, 12-digit tracking number is printed on the waybill along with a bar code that corresponds to the tracking number. Using his PDA, which includes a barcode scanner and keyboard, Joseph scans the barcode on the waybill and then types in the destination of the package, the type of service delivery (such as Priority or Standard Overnight), and the delivery deadline. The PDA then prints out a special detailed routing label that contains all of this information, which Joseph affixes to the package before placing it in the back of the truck.

Figure 1-6 Personal Digital Assistant (PDA)

The information Joseph enters on his PDA is immediately transmitted back to the terminal in his van using wireless digital cellular technology. The data from Joseph's PDA is actually transmitted to a cellular tower which then re-transmits the data back to the van. This technology is based on a standard known as **second generation (2G)** technology. 2G sends data at rates of up to 14 thousand bits per second (kilobits per second or Kbps). Federated is looking forward to the new **third generation (3G)** technology, which will allow data to be transmitted up to 2 Mbps. 3G will also "harmonize" all of the different specifications used around the world into one universal standard. However, 3G may not be widely available for some time, so Federated is planning to upgrade to the interim technology known as **2.5G**, which has a bandwidth of up to 384 Kbps.

In a moving automobile the maximum 3G bandwidth would be only 128 Kbps.

As Joseph steps into the van, the information from the PDA has been transmitted to the terminal in his van and he's ready to return to Federated with a load of packages. The digital cellular network is illustrated in Figure 1-7.

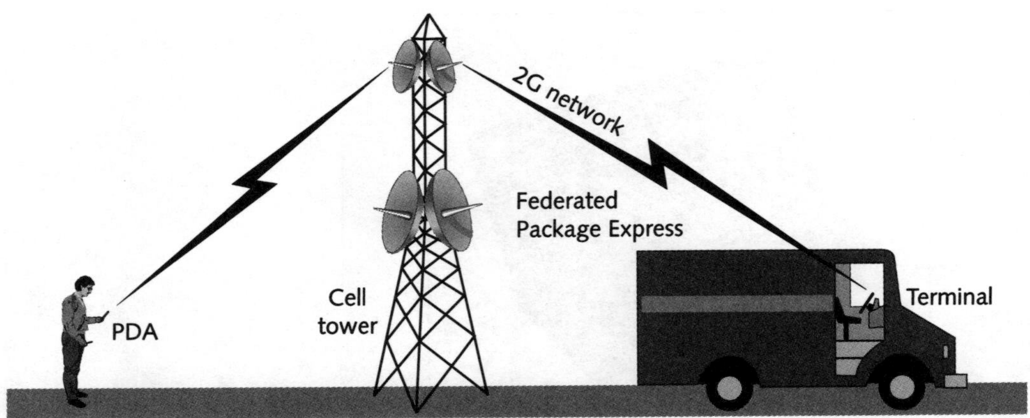

Figure 1-7 Digital cellular network

Wireless Local Area Network

Joseph pulls his van into the FPE distribution warehouse where packages are unloaded and sorted for delivery. There is a large amount of important data contained in the terminal on his van. As soon as Joseph pulls his van up to the unloading dock, the terminal in his van begins communicating with the computer network in the warehouse through a **wireless local area network (WLAN)**. A WLAN is identical to a standard LAN except that the devices are not connected by wires. The WLAN is based on the **Institute of Electrical and Electronic Engineers (IEEE) 802.11b** networking standard. This standard specifies that WLAN computers can transmit at up to 11 Mbps at a distance of up to 375 feet (112 meters). Federated Package Express is in the process of updating their WLAN to the **IEEE 802.11a** standard, which increases the bandwidth to 54 Mbps. The transmission of data from Joseph's terminal in his van, which includes all of the important information regarding each pick up, is completed before the first package is unloaded from his truck. See Figure 1-8.

Joseph's wife Ann, who also works for Federated, uses WLANs at her office. Ann does not have a desktop computer in her cubicle on which to work. Instead, Federated provides their employees with portable notebook computers that they use while traveling, at home, and in the office. None of the notebook computers in the office are connected to the local area network by cables. Instead, a WLAN is used.

Each computer on the WLAN has a **wireless network interface card** installed. This card performs the same basic functions and looks similar to a traditional network interface card (NIC) except that it does not have a cable that connects it to a jack in the wall. Instead, the wireless NIC has an antenna built into it.

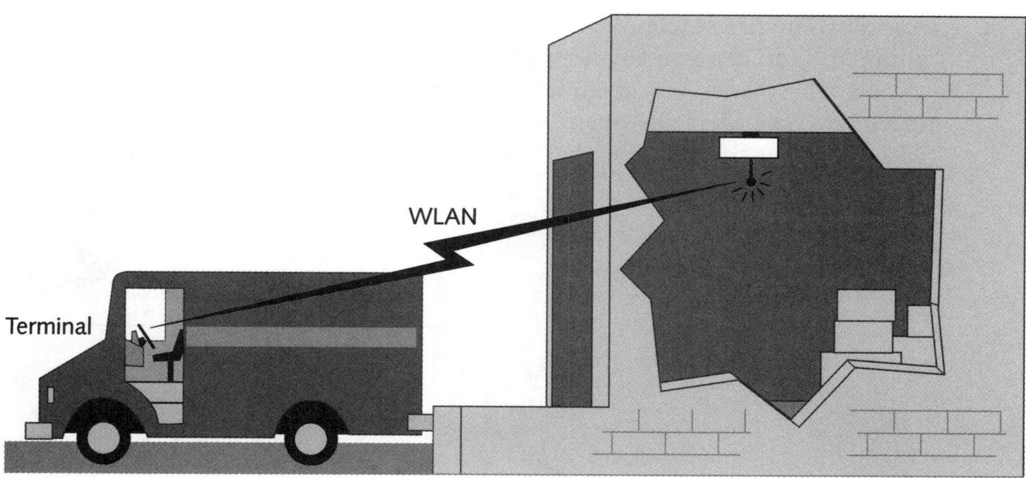

Figure 1-8 WLAN warehouse network

The wireless NIC sends its signals through radio waves to an **access point (AP)**. The access point receives the signals and transmits signals back to the wireless NIC. A cable to the regular local area network (LAN) also connects to the access point. Through the access point, the wireless devices can communicate with all of the devices that are connected to the wired network, such as file servers, printers, and even other access points (and the wireless devices connected to them). The access point is fixed in one place, although it can be moved when necessary, while the computing devices with wireless NICs have the freedom to move around. An AP and wireless NIC are illustrated in Figure 1-9.

Figure 1-9 Access point and wireless NIC

Ann turns on her notebook at her desk, and then establishes a connection with the access point. Ann can perform any network activity as if she was connected to the network with a cable. She carries her notebook down the hall to the conference room for her next meeting. Once there she opens the laptop and it's still connected to the network, along with the other five staff members' laptops. Figure 1-10 illustrates the office WLAN.

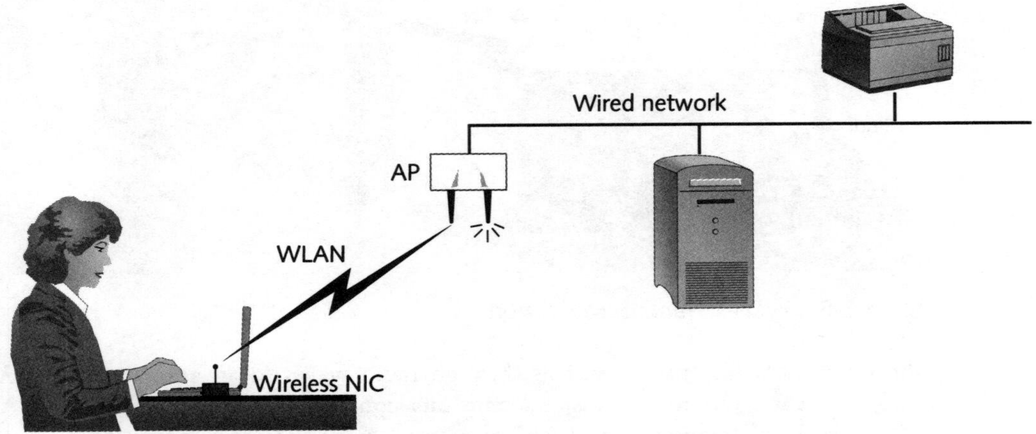

Figure 1-10 Office WLAN

Fixed Broadband Wireless

Federated's main office is located downtown, while the warehouse is situated in a small industrial park, and the call center is at the edge of town. Through the years Federated has tried a variety of connections to link the main office, warehouse, and call center. Initially they used telephone modems, but these soon proved to be too slow. Next, expensive transmission lines were leased from the local telephone company. **Integrated Services Digital Networks (ISDN)**, which transmit at 256 Kbps, were soon replaced with **T-1** lines, which transmit at 1.544 Mbps. However, these lines cost several thousand dollars per month. Technologies such as **cable modems**, which use a television cable connection, and **digital subscriber lines (DSL)**, which use special telephone lines, were generally only available in residential areas.

Recently, Federated started using **fixed broadband wireless**. Fixed broadband wireless uses wireless transmissions for data communications. A small custom antenna is located on the roof of each building that is to be connected. The signal is transmitted to the antenna of the receiving building which can be as far as 35 miles (56 kilometers) away. The transmission speed can be as high as 1 billion bits per second (gigabits or Gbps) for receiving data (downloads) and 512 Kbps for sending data (uploads), with a substantial reduction in cost.

Federated Package Express has an antenna on each of its three buildings in the area.

Once the data is transmitted from Joseph's van to the network in the warehouse, that data is sent to the main office by using fixed broadband wireless. This is illustrated in Figure 1-11.

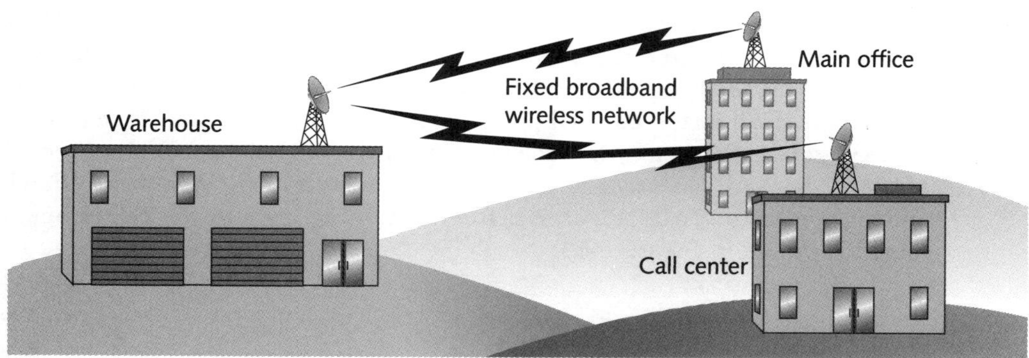

Figure 1-11 Fixed broadband wireless network

WAP

As Joseph's van is unloaded, he takes his afternoon break. Joseph pulls out his digital cellular telephone in order to surf the Internet. He can do this because his cell phone is based on the **Wireless Application Protocol (WAP)**. WAP provides a standard way to transmit, format, and display Internet data for devices like cell phones. With traditional computers, software known as a **Web browser** runs on a local computer to display Internet data. The Web browser software makes a request from the World Wide Web file server for a Web page. That page is transmitted back to the Web browser in **Hypertext Markup Language (HTML)**, which is the standard language for displaying content on the Internet. This model is illustrated in Figure 1-12.

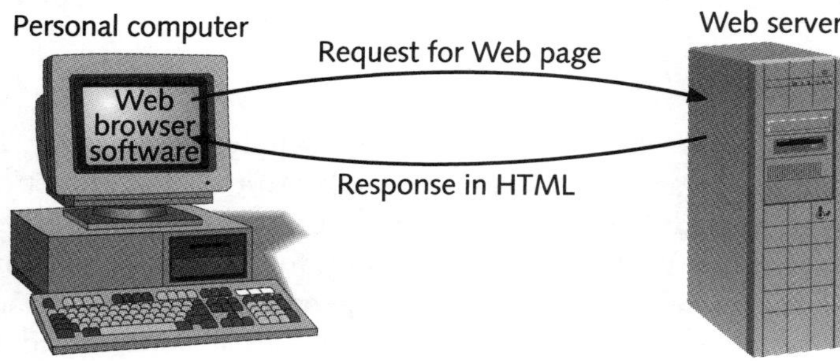

Figure 1-12 Browsing the World Wide Web

When a Web server sends a Web page back to a PC, it is only sending HTML code; the Web browser is responsible for interpreting that code and displaying the results on the screen.

WAP follows this standard Internet model with a few variations. A WAP cell phone runs a tiny browser program (called a **microbrowser**) that uses **Wireless Markup Language (WML)** instead of HTML. WML is designed to display text-based Web content on the small screen of a cell phone. However, since the Internet standard is HTML, a **WAP gateway** (sometimes called a **WAP proxy**) must translate between WML and HTML. The WAP gateway takes the Web page sent from the Web server in HTML code and changes it to WML language before forwarding it on to the cell phone. This WAP model is shown in Figure 1-13.

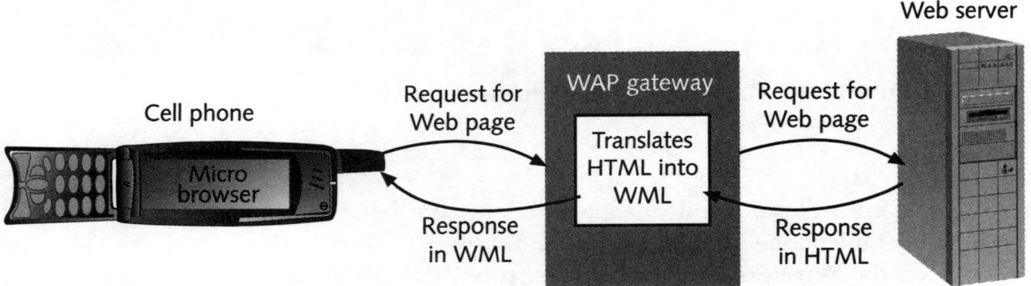

Figure 1-13 WAP communications

Joseph uses his cell phone to connect to a Web server. The cell phone connects to the nearest cell tower, which connects to the local telephone company, which then calls his local Internet provider, which completes the connection to the Web server. The images are sent back to Joseph in HTML format to the WAP gateway, which extracts only the necessary text data, converts it to WML, and sends it to his cell phone display.

The Wireless Landscape

The Kirkpatrick's typical day is obviously built around wireless technology. Table 1-1 summarizes these technologies, as shown in Figure 1-14. Most of these functions could not have been completed—much less attempted—without wireless technology. It's clear that wireless communication is no longer reserved only for high-end users. Instead, it has become a standard means of communication for people in many occupations and circumstances. As new wireless communications technologies are introduced, they will become even more integral to our lifestyle and will continue to change how we live.

Table 1-1 Wireless technologies

Wireless Technology	Transmission Distance	Speed
SWAP	150 feet (45 meters)	10 Mbps
Bluetooth	33 feet (10 meters)	1 Mbps
Satellite	Worldwide	250 milliseconds
2G digital cellular	Nationwide	14 Kbps
2.5G digital cellular	Nationwide	384 Kbps
3G digital cellular	Nationwide	2 Mbps
WLAN 802.11b	375 feet (112 meters)	11 Mbps
WLAN 802.11a	300 feet (90 meters)	54 Mbps
Fixed broadband wireless	35 miles (56 kilometers)	1 Gbps
WAP	Nationwide	384 Kbps

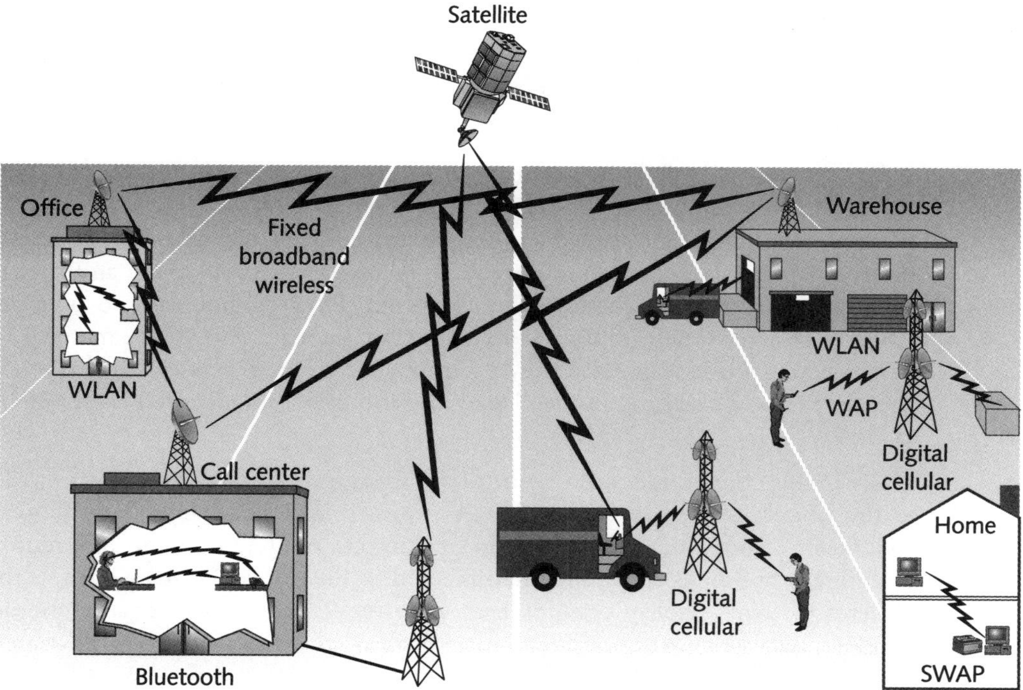

Figure 1-14 The wireless landscape

Just as the number of wireless devices will dramatically increase, so will the number of job opportunities to support this new technology. Positions such as wireless engineers, wireless local area network managers, and wireless technical support personnel will be needed to build wireless networks and assist wireless users. The job market for these new careers is already exploding across the country.

The prospects for the future reveal nothing short of exponential growth in this area. It is estimated that there will be over 1 billion users of wireless technology by the year 2003.

A team of anthropologists recently studied wireless device usage among people in nine major cities around the world. They noted several cultural differences in how wireless products were perceived. In Stockholm, wireless phone devices become an extension of users' personalities. In Paris, users are more concerned about how the phone looks than the underlying technology or what it can do. In London, shy people find wireless devices help them overcome their shyness and encourage them to reach out to others. In Japan, wireless usage helps citizens hurdle social barriers. And in the U.S., there's concern about information overload from being available 24 hours a day.

Wireless Applications

Wireless applications can be found in any industry whose employees need the mobility and freedom to conduct business without being confined to a specific location. Several of the leading industries are illustrated here.

Education

Wireless technology is an ideal application for colleges and schools. Teachers can create classroom presentations on the notebook computer in their office and then carry that computer with them right into the classroom. They do not have to plug and unplug cables to attach to the campus network. Instead, their notebook automatically makes the wireless connection as soon as they walk into the room. Teachers can also send handouts directly to students sitting in the classroom who have brought their own wireless devices to class.

The wireless connection also frees students from having to go to a specific computer lab or the library to get on the computer network. They can access the school network "wirelessly" from almost any location on campus. As they move to different classrooms in different buildings they remain connected to the network. Many schools that require students to own a laptop computer are now requiring that those same computers have wireless network connections. This wireless education model makes computing resources available to students from anywhere and at anytime.

Wireless technology translates into a cost savings for colleges as well. Traditional classrooms now become fully accessible computer labs without the expense of additional wiring and infrastructure. And colleges no longer have to consider the expense of adding open computer labs for students, since everyone can access the resources from anywhere on campus.

Military

The U.S. military has created a Universal Handset, a 1.5 lb. device that will be delivered to over 300,000 soldiers. It allows military personnel in the field to communicate through a variety of methods using wireless technologies. Using cellular and satellite communications, soldiers can talk, access the Internet, and receive full-motion video through their Universal Handset. Military personnel can also connect with other wireless devices using the Bluetooth wireless protocol, or to a WLAN using the IEEE 802.11b standard. The military is currently working on preventing an enemy from eavesdropping or jamming the signal.

Business

Wireless technologies have changed how business is conducted. No longer are meetings routinely held in conference rooms where employees are away from the data they need to help make decisions. With wireless technologies, employees can bring their wireless notebook computers to the conference room and remain connected to the network and their data without worrying about patch cables or free ports. They have access to their data, which allows them to make business decisions whenever and wherever the need arises.

Wireless technologies allow businesses to create an office where the traditional infrastructure doesn't already exist. Typically, an office space must be wired with computer cables for network connections and telephone wires for telephones. With wireless technologies such as WLAN and Bluetooth, that expensive cabling infrastructure is necessary no longer. This means that an office can be created in a very short period of time with minimum expense. For example, a hotel conference room that may not have the infrastructure to support a wired network can quickly be turned into a wireless networked office environment.

Entertainment

Managing spectators attending a sporting event or concert can be a daunting task. Each attendee has a ticket, and there are special passes for the press and team officials. However, tickets can be lost, stolen, or even counterfeited. Attempting to identify a stolen or counterfeit ticket as thousands of spectators are waiting to be admitted to the event is almost an impossible task. Several large arenas and stadiums are now turning to wireless systems to facilitate this process.

Event tickets are printed with a unique barcode that is then scanned at the venue's point of entry using hand-held or integrated turnstile hardware, which is connected to a wireless network. The network instantly validates the ticket and then sends a signal back to the turnstile that either allows or bars the entry of the patron into the arena. Not only does this prevent the use of counterfeit tickets, but it also can be used to identify stolen tickets.

The wireless point-of-entry turnstiles can also give a real-time look at traffic flow. It helps the venue more effectively manage their manpower and to help determine where additional people are needed. Data about who is entering at which gate can even be used by advertisers to tailor their marketing efforts.

In addition, wireless technologies are changing the entertainment experience itself. In several major stadiums, wireless transmissions are available to any fan in the stadium with a wireless device like a notebook computer or PDA. This allows fans to instantly access game statistics. They can also view instant replays of the event they are attending, or even replays from other games around the country. In some stadiums, fans can use their wireless devices to order concessions and have them delivered to their seats.

Travel

Because wireless technology creates mobility, the travel industry was one of the first to embrace wireless technologies. Wireless global positioning systems (GPS) and emergency roadside assistance have become standard features on many automobiles sold today. Satellite radio transmission of over 150 music stations solves the problem of losing a station outside of its transmission range.

Airport terminals are likewise turning to wireless technologies. Many large airport terminals transmit wireless signals that passengers can pick up on their wireless notebook computers or PDAs while waiting for their flights. For a nominal fee, they can surf the Internet or read e-mail.

Even the airplanes themselves are becoming wireless. Several large airlines are providing wireless capabilities to passengers on flights. Like their earth-bound counterparts, these passengers can access the Internet or view their corporate data from their seats at 30,000 feet.

A car rental firm uses the global positioning system (GPS) and a cellular telephone system to track drivers who rent their cars. If any driver is tracked by the GPS as speeding, then a fine of $150 per incident is automatically charged against their credit card. One driver was recently charged $450 for speeding across seven different states.

Construction

Although at first glance the construction industry may not seem to be a prime candidate for wireless technologies, in reality it benefits greatly. This is due to the fact that each construction phase must be completed before the next can begin. For example, if the concrete footings for a new building cannot be poured, then the entire project must be put on hold. This often means idle construction employees, not to mention the need to reschedule, possibly at a moment's notice. In addition, construction employees may often have to travel to several different job sites in one day. This makes paperwork management a difficult task. Pay sheets must be manually filled out by several different foremen and dropped off at the office late at night. Payroll clerks often wrestle the next day with scrawled or illegible notes and are unable to contact the foreman on the job for clarification.

Wireless technology is a real plus to the construction industry. Foremen can enter time sheet information on a notebook computer and have it immediately transmitted to the main office. Information from the job site, such as a tardy subcontractor or a problem with materials, can be instantly relayed back to the main office for rescheduling of workers to other sites to prevent idle time.

In addition, construction equipment such as bulldozers and earth graders are being fitted with wireless terminals in order to turn them into "smart" equipment. A global positioning system on a bulldozer can provide location information accurate to within feet. The exact location of the bulldozer and where it will dig can be transmitted to a terminal on the bulldozer, which displays a color-coded map to guide the operator as it digs. Also, smart equipment can be connected through wireless transmissions back to the home office, which tracks engine hours and equipment location. The equipment can also be connected into the engine's diagnostic system, sending an alert when maintenance items like the oil needs to be changed.

Warehouse Management

Managing a warehouse stocked with inventory can be a nightmare. New products arrive continuously and must be inventoried and stored. When products are shipped out of the warehouse, they must be located and then transferred to the correct loading dock so they can be placed on the right truck. A mistake in any one of these steps can result in a warehouse stocked with products that it cannot locate, in irate customers receiving the wrong items, or in a store running out of goods to sell.

Implementing wireless technology is key for many warehouse operations. Forklift trucks in the warehouse are outfitted with a wireless computer device. Employees can also be given portable wireless devices. Warehouse management system (WMS) software can manage all of the activities from receiving through shipping. And since this network is tied into the front office computer system, managers can have statistics that are current at any given moment.

Pallet loads arriving from other locations come with bar-coded pallet labels. The bar coding includes product identification numbers, product code dates or expiration dates, originating plants and lines of manufacture, and sequentially assigned serial numbers. As pallets arrive, a forklift truck operator scans the barcode label with his portable wireless device. This device sends the data to the wireless network where the warehouse software immediately designates a storage location for the pallet and relays the information back to the computer on the forklift truck. A bar code is immediately printed and fixed to the pallet. The forklift operator then transports the pallet to a storage location in the warehouse. A bar code label suspended from the ceiling for floor locations or attached to a rack face identifies every storage location. The operator scans that bar code to confirm that the pallets are being put in the correct location before depositing the load.

In the front office, orders are received and entered into the computer that connects to the WLAN in the warehouse. The WMS software manages order picking, balances workloads, and selects pick sequences for lift truck operators. The dock control module then releases orders for picking. A forklift operator locates the correct storage location, scans the bar code of the pallet, and then ferries it to the shipping dock to be loaded onto a truck.

Health Care

Administering medication in a hospital setting is one of the major problem areas for the health care industry. It is estimated that incorrectly dispensed medication results in hundreds of thousands of medical emergencies annually. Typically, medication printouts are posted at the medication area. As medications are given, they are crossed off the list and initialed. However, since the paper record cannot always be updated immediately, there is a possibility that a patient could get an extra dose of medication before an order for a new or changed medication is processed. This also forces duplicate documentation. Nurses first check the medication printout to determine the medication to be given. Then, they document on paper that the medication was actually given and later enter the data on the computers.

However, wireless point-of-care computer systems allow medical staff to access and update patient records immediately. Many hospitals are using notebook computers on mobile carts or hand-held PDAs with barcode scanners and a wireless connection. Health care professionals can document a patient's medication administration immediately in the computer as they move from room to room without connecting and disconnecting cables. Nurses first identify themselves to the computer system by scanning their own personal bar-coded ID badge. The patient's bar-coded armband is then scanned and all medications that are currently due for that particular patient are brought up on the screen. The medications to be administered are sealed in bar-coded pouches. Nurses scan this barcode before opening the package. An alert immediately appears on the screen if the wrong medication or incorrect amount is identified. After administration, the nurse indicates through the wireless network that the medication has been given, essentially electronically signing the distribution form. A hard copy can be printed out as needed.

The system immediately verifies that medication is being administered to the correct patient in the correct dosage, which eliminates potential errors and documentation inefficiencies. The documentation process now takes place at the bedside where care is delivered, which improves accuracy. In addition, all hospital personnel now have real-time access to the latest medication and patient status information.

Select medical groups are now beginning to provide their physicians with a PDA, printer, and prescription writing software. It is intended to reduce errors associated with illegible handwritten prescriptions.

Wireless Advantages and Disadvantages

As with any new technology, there are advantages and disadvantages to be considered. Wireless communications are no exception.

Advantages

There are many advantages to using wireless technology, including mobility, ease of installation and lower cost, increased reliability, and more rapid disaster recovery.

Mobility

The freedom to move about without being tethered by wires is certainly the primary advantage of a wireless configuration. Mobility enables users to stay in contact with the network no matter where they may roam. Many occupations that require workers to be mobile, such as police officers and inventory clerks, are finding that wireless communications are becoming vital to them.

Today's changing business environment allows even more workers to take advantage of the mobility afforded by wireless technology. An increasingly mobile workforce is one characteristic of the business world of today. Many employees spend large portions of their time away from the office. Because of this, they are being equipped with notebook computers and other portable devices. However, these employees still need immediate access to the company network. WLANs fit well in this work environment, giving mobile workers the freedom they need but still allowing them to access the network resources that they need. With a wireless network, workers can access information from almost anywhere.

Another characteristic of the business world of today is "flatter" organizations. Much of an employee's work is done in teams that cross functional and organizational boundaries. This means that today's workers' productivity occurs in team meetings away from their desks. Yet the need for immediate access to network resources still exists even while these meetings are taking place. WLANs are again the solution to the problem. They give team-based workers the ability to access the network resources that they need while collaborating in a team environment.

Easier and Less Expensive Installation

Installing network cabling in older buildings can be a difficult and costly task. These buildings were built with no thought of running computer wiring in each room. Thick masonry walls and plaster ceilings are difficult to drill holes through and snake cabling around. Sometimes an older building may have asbestos that would have to first be completely removed before any new cabling could be installed. And often there are restrictions on modifying older facilities that have an historical value.

In these instances a wireless LAN would be the ideal solution. Historical buildings would be preserved, dangerous asbestos would not be disturbed, and difficult drilling could be avoided by using a wireless system. And of course, eliminating the need to install cabling will result in a significant cost savings.

Wireless networks also make it easier for any office—in either an old or new building—to be modified with new cubicles or furniture. No longer does the design for a remodeled office first have to consider the location of the computer jack in the wall when relocating furniture. Instead, the focus can be on creating the most effective work environment for the employees.

Also, the time to install network cabling is generally significant. Installers must pull wires through the ceiling and then drop cables down walls to network outlets. This can usually take days or even weeks to complete. During that time employees must somehow continue their work in the midst of the construction zone, which is often difficult to do. Using a wireless LAN eliminates any such disruption because there are no cables to be installed.

Increased Reliability

Network cable failures are perhaps the most common source of network problems. Moisture from a leak during a thunderstorm or a coffee spill can erode metallic conductors. A user who shifts the computer on his desk may break the network connection. A cable splice that is done incorrectly can cause problems that result in unexplainable errors and are very difficult to identify. Using wireless technology eliminates these types of cable failures and increases the overall reliability of the network.

Disaster Recovery

Accidents happen every day: fires, tornados, and floods can occur with little if any warning. Any business that is not prepared to recover from these or other disasters will find itself quickly out of business. A documented disaster recovery plan is vital to every business if they are to quickly get back on their feet after a calamity.

Because the computer network is such a vital part of the daily operation of a business, the ability to have the network up and working after a disaster is critical. Many businesses are turning to WLANs as a major piece of their disaster recovery plan. Laptop computers with wireless NICs and access points are kept in reserve along with backup network servers. In the event of a disaster, the office can be quickly relocated. No consideration has to be given to a building that has adequate network wiring, for this wiring will not be used. Instead, the network servers are installed in the building along with the access points, and the laptop computers are distributed to the resettled employees. The network can be immediately up and running in order for business to return to normal as soon as possible.

Disadvantages

Along with the many advantages of wireless technology, there are likewise disadvantages and concerns, including health risks, radio signal interference, and security concerns.

Health Risks

Wireless devices contain radio transmitters and receivers that emit radio frequency (RF) energy. Typically, these wireless devices emit low levels of RF while being used. It is well documented that high levels of RF can produce biological damage through heating effects (this is how a microwave oven is able to cook food). However, it is not known if lower levels of RF can cause adverse health effects. Although some research has been done to address these questions, no clear picture of the biological effects of this type of radiation has emerged to date.

Most wireless devices also emit very low levels of RF energy when in the stand-by mode. However, these levels are considered non-significant and do not appear to have health consequences.

In the United States, the Food and Drug Administration (FDA) and the Federal Communications Commission (FCC) set policies and procedures for some wireless devices such as cellular telephones. The latest FDA update stated that "the available science does not allow us to conclude that (wireless devices) are absolutely safe, or that they are unsafe." However, the report went on to say that "the available scientific evidence does not demonstrate any adverse health effects associated with the use of (wireless devices)." At the present time, no scientific studies have revealed health problems associated with the absorption of low-level RF energy on the human body.

The FCC and FDA, along with the Environmental Protection Agency (EPA), established RF exposure safety guidelines for wireless phones in 1996. Before a wireless phone is available for sale to the public, it must be tested by the manufacturer and certified that it does not exceed specific limits. One of the limits is expressed as a Specific Absorption Rate (SAR). SAR relates to the measurement of the rate of absorption of RF energy by a wireless phone user. The FCC requires that the SAR of handheld wireless phones not exceed 1.6 watts per kilogram, averaged over one gram of tissue.

Questions regarding safety have been raised about hand-held mobile phones, the kind that have a built-in antenna that is positioned close to the user's head during normal telephone conversation. These types of mobile phones are of concern because of the short distance between the phone's antenna—the primary source of the RF—and the person's head. The safety of "cordless phones," which have a base unit connected to the telephone wiring in a house and which operate at far lower power levels and frequencies, has not been questioned.

Thus, the available science does not permit a conclusion that wireless mobile devices are absolutely safe, or that they are unsafe. However, there is currently nothing to demonstrate any adverse health effects associated with the use of mobile wireless devices. Although there is no evidence regarding any health risks associated with using any wireless device, it is always wise to be aware of the concern and to monitor ongoing scientific research.

Radio Signal Interference

Because wireless devices operate using radio signals, there is the potential for two types of signal interference. Signals from other devices can disrupt what a wireless device is trying to transmit, or the device may itself be the source of interference for other devices.

For example, there are several different types of devices that transmit a radio signal that may interfere with a WLAN. These devices include microwave ovens, elevator motors, photocopying machines, certain types of outdoor lighting systems, theft protection devices, and cordless telephones. These may cause errors to occur in the transmission between a wireless device and an access point. In addition, both Bluetooth and WLAN 802.11b devices operate within the same radio frequency. This may result in interference between the devices.

Interference is nothing new for a computer data network. Even when using cables to connect network devices, interference from fluorescent light fixtures and electric motors can sometimes disrupt the sending and receiving of data. The solution for wireless devices is the same as that for standard cabled network devices: locate the source of the interference and eliminate it. This usually is solved by moving a photocopying machine or microwave oven across the room or to another room. In addition, many wireless devices have the ability to identify that an error has occurred in the transmission and can re-transmit the data as necessary.

Outside interference from AM or FM radio stations, TV broadcast stations, or other large-scale transmitters cannot occur since these stations and WLANs operate at different frequencies and power levels.

Security

Because a wireless device transmits radio signals over a broad area, security becomes a major concern. It is possible for an intruder to be lurking in the parking lot with a notebook computer and wireless NIC in order to intercept the signals from a wireless network. Because much of a business' network traffic may contain sensitive information, this is a real concern for many users.

However, some wireless technologies can provide added levels of security. A special coded number can be programmed into every authorized wireless device, which must transmit the special number prior to gaining access to the network; otherwise it is denied access. A list of approved wireless devices can also be programmed in advance. Only those devices on the list will be allowed access. As a further protection, data transmitted between the access point and the wireless device can also be encrypted or encoded in such a way that only the recipient can decode the message. If an unauthorized user were to intercept the radio signals being transmitted, he or she could not read the messages being sent.

Chapter Summary

- Wireless communications have become commonplace today and are becoming the standard in the business world. Remote wireless Internet connections and entire wireless computer networks are appearing on the scene and will dramatically impact the way business is conducted.
- Wireless networks and devices are found in all different circles of life today. Home users can implement SWAP to connect different devices, while Bluetooth can connect devices over a short distance. WAP is used for cell phones to display text-based Internet information, and WLANs are becoming a fixture of business networks. Fixed broadband wireless is used to transmit data at distances up to 35 miles (56 kilometers), while satellite transmissions can send signals around the world. Digital cellular networks are used to transmit data between devices at up to 2 Mbps.
- WLAN applications are found in a wide variety of industries and organizations, including the military, education, business, entertainment, the travel industry, construction, warehouse management, and health care.
- Mobility, or the freedom to move without being connected to the network by a cable, is the primary advantage of a WLAN. Other advantages include easier and less expensive installation, increased network reliability, and support for disaster recovery.
- There are some disadvantages to a WLAN. Radio signal interference, security, and health risks are sometimes considered as disadvantages.

Key Terms

2G (second generation) — A digital cellular technology that sends data at up to 14 Kbps.

2.5G — A digital cellular technology that sends data at a maximum of 384 Kbps.

3G (third generation) — A digital cellular technology that sends data at up to 2 Mbps and will harmonize all of the different specifications used around the world into one universal standard.

access point (AP) — A device that receives the signals and transmits signals back to wireless network interface cards (NICs).

Bluetooth — A wireless standard for devices to transmit data at up to 1 Mbps over a distance of 33 feet.

cable modems — A technology used to transmit data over a television cable connection.

digital subscriber lines (DSL) — A technology used to transmit data over a telephone line.

fixed broadband wireless — Data transmissions that use antennas between sites up to 35 miles apart.

HomeRF Working Group — A group of over 50 different companies from the personal computer, consumer electronics, communications, and software industries that established the SWAP standard.

Hypertext Markup Language (HTML) — The standard language for displaying content on the World Wide Web.

Institute of Electrical and Electronic Engineers (IEEE) 802.11a — A standard that allows WLAN computers to transmit up to 54 Mbps.

Institute of Electrical and Electronic Engineers (IEEE) 802.11b — A standard that allows WLAN computers to transmit up to 11 Mbps over a distance of 375 feet.

Integrated Services Digital Networks (ISDN) — A technology that transmits data over telephone lines at a maximum of 256 Kbps.

link manager — Special software in Bluetooth devices that helps identify other Bluetooth devices, creates the links between them, and sends and receives data.

microbrowser — A tiny browser program that runs on a WAP cell phone.

personal area network (PAN) — See piconet.

Personal Digital Assistant (PDA) — A hand-held computer device often used for taking notes, making records, and communicating with other devices.

piconet — Two or more Bluetooth devices that are sending and receiving data with each other.

radio module — A small radio transceiver built onto microprocessor chips that are embedded into Bluetooth devices and enable them to communicate.

repeater — A device commonly used in satellite communications that simply "repeats" the signal to another location.

Shared Wireless Access Protocol (SWAP) — A set of specifications for wireless data and voice communications around the home that can include computer equipment, cordless telephones, and home entertainment equipment.

SWAP — See Shared Wireless Access Protocol.

T-1 — A technology to transmit data over special telephone lines at 1.544 Mbps.

WAP — See Wireless Application Protocol.

WAP gateway — A device that translates HTML to WML so that it can be displayed on a WAP cell phone; also called a WAP proxy.

WAP proxy — A device that translates HTML to WML so that it can be displayed on a WAP cell phone; also called a WAP gateway.

Web browser — Software that runs on a local PC and makes a request from the World Wide Web file server for a Web page.

Wireless Application Protocol (WAP) — A standard for transmitting, formatting, and displaying Internet data for devices like cell phones.

wireless communications — The transmission of user data without the use of wires.

wireless home networking adapter — A device that connects to a home computer to transmit and receive data over radio waves.

wireless local area network (WLAN) — A local area network that is not connected by wires but instead uses wireless technology.

Wireless Markup Language (WML) — A language for displaying Internet content on WAP cell phones.

wireless network interface card — A network interface card (NIC) installed in a computer that performs the same functions as a standard NIC, except that it does not have a cable that connects it to the network, and it includes an antenna for wireless communication.

WML — See Wireless Markup Language.

Review Questions

1. The Shared Wireless Access Protocol (SWAP) is designed for use in the ________________.
   a. home
   b. office
   c. car
   d. satellite
2. Bluetooth devices communicate using small radio transceivers called a ________________ that is built onto microprocessor chips.
   a. receiver
   b. transponder
   c. radio module
   d. link manager
3. ________________ provides a standard way to transmit, format, and display Internet data on cell phones.
   a. WLAN
   b. WAP
   c. HTML
   d. WML

4. SWAP devices can be as far as 150 feet apart and can send and receive data up to ________________ million bits per second (Mbps).
   a. 2
   b. 10
   c. 100
   d. 1000
5. Each Bluetooth device uses a ________________ which is special software that helps identify other Bluetooth devices.
   a. frame
   b. link manager
   c. repeater
   d. bridge
6. Bluetooth can send data through physical barriers, like walls. True or false?
7. A Bluetooth device can transmit data at up to 1 Mbps over a distance of 33 feet (10 meters). True or false?
8. A wireless network interface card performs the same functions and looks identical to a traditional network interface card (NIC) card. True or false?
9. An earth station transmits to a satellite at one frequency and the satellite regenerates and transmits the signal back to earth at another frequency. True or false?
10. Eliminating installation costs is a disadvantage of a WLAN. True or false?
11. The automatic connection between various Bluetooth devices creates a network called a(n) ________________.
12. The new third generation (3G) technology will allow data to be transmitted at a maximum speed of ________________ Mbps.
13. The wireless NIC sends its signals through invisible radio waves to a(n) ________________.
14. ________________ uses wireless transmissions for data communications as much as 35 miles apart.
15. "WAP" stands for ________________ Access Protocol.
16. Explain the role of an access point (AP) in a WLAN.
17. Explain how a WAP cell phone works to send and receive Internet data.
18. Explain how a WLAN can be used in a classroom.
19. Tell how wireless networks can reduce installation time.
20. Explain how a wireless network can aid in a disaster recovery.

HANDS-ON PROJECTS

1. Write a one-page paper outlining the differences and similarities between SWAP and Bluetooth. Use the Internet as well as material from SWAP and Bluetooth vendors. Include their advantages and disadvantages. When would you use SWAP instead of Bluetooth, and vice versa? What limitations have kept Bluetooth from gaining more market share? Will SWAP ever replace IEEE 802.11b WLANs?
2. Research the differences between HTML and WML. How are they similar? How are they different? Be sure to include information about WML "decks" and "cards." What type of WAP browsers are available to display WML? Write a one-page paper on your findings.
3. Locate a school, hospital, manufacturing plant, warehouse, or other business that is switching to wireless devices. Interview appropriate people to determine why they are making the change. Ask what benefits and drawbacks they considered. Write a one-page paper on your findings.
4. Because a wireless device transmits radio signals over a broad area, security becomes a major concern. What are the security concerns with using a WLAN? Why are some experts claiming that the security built into an IEEE 802.11b WLAN is insufficient? What other options are available? Write a one-page paper that addresses these concerns. Use the Internet and information from vendors as additional resources.
5. Using the Internet, find the latest information about health concerns using wireless technologies. What studies are currently underway? What issues are under concern? What are the official positions of the FCC, the FDA, and the EPA? Write a one-page paper about your findings.

CASE PROJECTS

You are employed by The Baypoint Group (TBG), a company of 50 consultants that assists organizations and businesses with issues involving network planning, design, implementation and problem solving. You have recently been hired by TBG to work with one of their new clients, Vincent Medical Associates, concerning their wireless needs.

Each day Vincent Medical health technicians stop at the offices of local physicians to pick up blood samples for testing. These samples are delivered to the Vincent Medical facilities where the tests are performed and the results are then faxed or telephoned back to the physician's office.

1. Vincent Medical is interested in expanding their office space into a temporary area of the building until the new renovation work is completed. They do not want to spend money installing network cabling for their computers since they will be there only a short period of time. Vincent Medical has asked you to make a presentation to their office manager regarding the use of a WLAN. Create a presentation to deliver to the service about WLANs. Be sure to cover the following points:
   - Mobility
   - Ease and cost of installation
   - Easier network modifications
   - Increased network reliability
   - Radio signal interference
   - Security
2. After your presentation, the physicians have two concerns. The first regards health risks and what impact a wireless system would have on their employees. The second issue regards radio signal interference from X-ray machines and other medical equipment. Create another presentation that looks at the issues of health risks with WLANs along with interference issues.
3. Vincent Medical is also interested in providing its health technicians with another means of communication besides pagers and analog cellular telephones. They would like them to receive their pick-up information from the company's Web server. They have asked your opinion regarding using WAP with cellular telephones or wireless PDAs. Prepare to present your recommendations to Vincent Medical's management team.

Optional Teams Case Project

A syndicated magazine is writing an article about Bluetooth technology and has asked TBG for information. Form a team of two or three consultants and research Bluetooth technology. Specifically pay attention to the future of Bluetooth. Provide information regarding its problems and concerns by some vendors. Also provide estimates regarding how you envision Bluetooth will be used in home, office, and personal applications.

CHAPTER

2

HOW WIRELESS WORKS

After reading this chapter and completing the exercises you will be able to:

- Explain how network data is represented using binary notation
- List and explain the two types of wireless transmission
- Describe the different ways in which data can be transmitted by radio waves

Consider for a moment a wireless cellular telephone that is in your pocket or on your desk. If you were to take that telephone apart, you would find an array of pieces: a microphone, a loudspeaker, resistors, capacitors, and a variety of other parts. Yet much more than that single telephone is needed to complete a call. Consider some of the other elements involved: the cellular towers and all of the equipment that manages your call as you move from one cellular region to another, and equipment at the telephone company's central office that directs your call to the correct recipient. And suppose you were calling someone overseas—what additional equipment, such as satellites or underwater cables, might be used?

The number of parts that make up a modern communications system is truly mind-boggling. Making sense of it all can often be confusing simply because of the sheer number of components that are involved. How can we begin to understand how it all works?

One approach is the "bottom-up" method. This approach looks first at the individual elements or components that make up a system, and then it ties them all together to show how it all works. This chapter uses the bottom-up approach to set the foundation for our exploration of wireless communications and networks. First, you will learn how data is represented and then you will see how the various types of wireless signals are used to transmit data. Next, we'll delve a little deeper into how radio data is transmitted.

How Data Is Represented

When exploring wireless data communications, a first good step is to see how the data itself is represented. Digital data for wireless communications is represented in the same way as standard computer data. But let's back up a little and review how numbers are represented as we know them in the decimal system.

Consider for a moment the number 639. This number can be defined as follows:

6	3	9
100s	10s	1s

6 *100s* + 3 *10s* + 9 *1s* = 639

The number 639 is six 100s plus three 10s plus nine 1s. This way of representing numbers is based on the **decimal** or **Base 10 number system**. It's known as the Base 10 number system because the number 10 is the base number. This number 10 is increased by one power as you move from one column to the next (right to left). The rightmost column is the 10^0 (or 1s) position, the next column is the 10^1 (or 10s) position, and so on. Consider again the number 639 in decimal:

6	3	9
10^2	10^1	10^0
(100s)	(10s)	(1s)

6 10^2s + 3 10^1s + 9 10^0s = 639

The digits used to represent a number in the decimal number system are 0, 1, 2, 3, 4, 5, 6, 7, 8, and 9. Whenever more than 9 needs to be represented, the number in the column to the left is increased by one. Consider adding 1 to 639. It is represented as follows:

6	4	0
10^2	10^1	10^0
(100s)	(10s)	(1s)

6 10^2s + 4 10^1s + 0 10^0s = 640

No additional digits besides 0–9 are needed to represent any number in decimal.

The decimal number system is ideal for humans to use. This is because humans have ten fingers for counting that correspond to the base number of 10 in decimal. However, the decimal number system is not good for a computer or for data transmissions. Computers and transmission equipment are better suited for a base of 2 instead of 10. This is because these devices are electrical.

An electrical current has only two states: on and off. Since computers and data transmission equipment are electrical devices, and electricity has two states, these devices use the **Base 2** or the **binary number system**. Binary uses a base number of 2 instead of

10. The only digits used to represent a number in binary are the digits 0 and 1. Consider how the following numbers are represented in binary:

2^3 (8)	2^2 (4)	2^1 (2)	2^0 (1)	
0	0	0	0	= 0
0	0	0	1	= 1
0	0	1	0	= 2
0	0	1	1	= 3
0	1	0	0	= 4
0	1	0	1	= 5
0	1	1	0	= 6
0	1	1	1	= 7
1	0	0	0	= 8

Any number can be represented in binary by only using the digits 0 and 1. The digits 0 and 1 are known as **bits** (BInary digiTS). Eight binary digits grouped together form a **byte**.

However, what about storing letters of the alphabet or symbols like a dollar sign? The solution is that every character or symbol is assigned an arbitrary number based on a specific coding scheme. One of these arbitrary coding schemes uses the numbers from 0 to 255 and is called the **American Standard Code for Information Interchange (ASCII)**. Table 2-1 shows part of the ASCII code. The upper case letter "A", for example, has been assigned the number 65 in ASCII. To store the letter "A", it is first converted to its ASCII (decimal) equivalent (65) and then that number is stored as a byte (8 bits) in binary code (01000001).

In addition to letters of the alphabet and symbols, numbers are also stored based on the ASCII code. However, the number 47 is not stored as its binary equivalent (00101111). Instead, the ASCII value of the digit 4, which is 52, is stored as one byte (00110100) and the digit 7 (ASCII 55) is stored as another byte (00110111).

One of the limitations of ASCII is that there are not enough codes for all the symbols used by foreign languages. Another coding scheme called Unicode can represent 65,535 different characters because it is 16 bits in length instead of only 8 bits.

Table 2-1 Partial ASCII code table

Decimal Value	Character Represented
48	0
49	1
50	2
51	3
52	4
53	5
54	6
55	7
56	8
57	9
58	:
59	;
60	<
61	=
62	>
63	?
64	@
65	A
66	B
67	C
68	D
69	E
70	F

WIRELESS SIGNALS

Traditional wired communications use copper wires or fiber optic cables to send and receive data. Wireless transmissions, of course, do not use these or any other visible media. Instead, they travel on waves.

All forms of electromagnetic energy, from gamma rays to radio waves, travel through space in waves. Light from a flashlight and heat from a fire move through space as a special type of wave known as electromagnetic waves. These waves require no special medium for movement. They travel freely through space at the speed of light, or 186,000 miles per second. Figure 2-1 illustrates the electromagnetic spectrum.

2

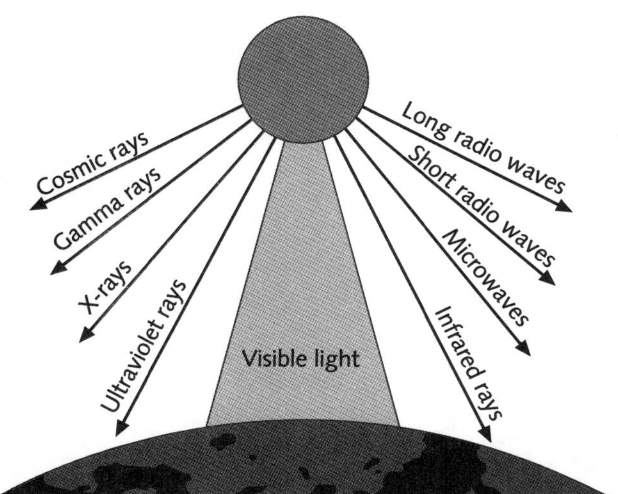

Figure 2-1 Electromagnetic spectrum

There are two basic types of waves by which wireless signals are sent and received: infrared light and radio waves.

Infrared Light

Flashes of light have been used for centuries to transmit information. Bonfires set on top of hills were used in early America to relay messages. Ocean vessels sent signals from ship to shore using light. Even Alexander Graham Bell in 1880 demonstrated an invention called the photophone, which used the concept of light waves to transmit voice information. Transmitting modern computer or network data using light follows the same basic principle.

Because computers and data communication equipment use binary code, it is easy to transmit information with light. Just as binary code uses only two digits (0 and 1), light has only two properties (off and on). To send a "1" in binary code could result in a light quickly flashing on; to send a "0", the light would remain off. For example, the letter "A" (ASCII 65 or 01000001) could be transmitted by light as "off-on-off-off-off-off-off-on." This is illustrated in Figure 2-2.

What type of light should be used to transmit these signals? To transmit data by visible light flashes, such as a strobe light, would be very unreliable. This is because other lights could be mistaken for the transmission signal or another bright light could "wash out" the light flashes. Visible light could not be used for reliable data transmissions.

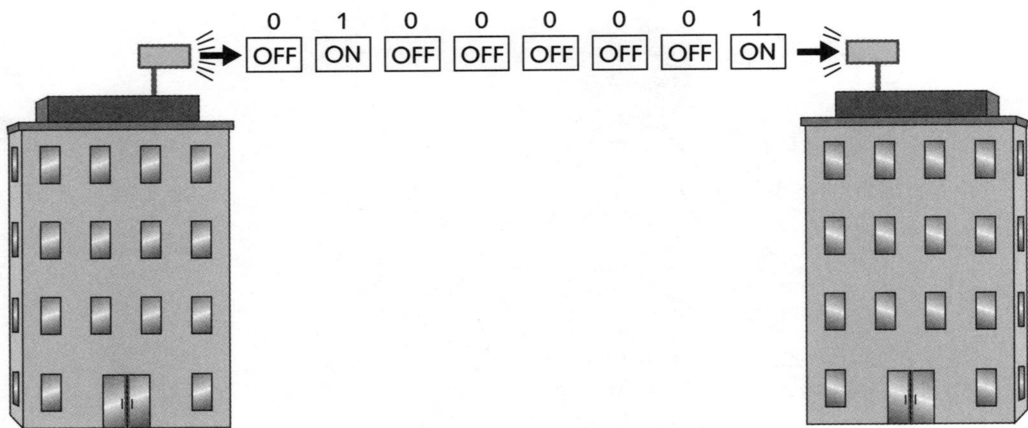

Figure 2-2 Light transmission

However, visible light is only one type of light. All the different types of light that travel from the sun to the earth make up the **light spectrum.** Visible light is just a small part of that entire spectrum. Some of the other energies of the spectrum, such as x-rays, ultraviolet rays, and microwaves, are invisible to the human eye. **Infrared light**, although invisible, has many of the same characteristics as visible light because it is next to visible light on the light spectrum. Infrared light is a better candidate for data transmission.

Each wavelength within the spectrum of visible light represents a particular color. This is because the differing wavelengths of light waves will bend different amounts when passed through a prism, which produces different colors. The colors that visible light produces are red (R), orange (O), yellow (Y), green (G), blue (B), indigo (I), and violet (V). Visible light is sometimes referred to as ROYGBIV.

Infrared wireless systems require that each device have two components: an **emitter** that transmits a signal, and a **detector** that receives the signal (these two components are sometimes combined into one device). An emitter is usually a laser diode or a light-emitting diode. Infrared wireless systems send data by the intensity of the light wave instead of "on-off" signals of light. To transmit a "1" the emitter increases the intensity of the current and sends a "pulse" using infrared light. The detector senses the higher intensity pulse of light and produces a proportional electrical current. This is seen in Figure 2-3.

Infrared wireless transmission can be either directed or diffused**.** A **directed transmission** requires that the emitter and detector be directly aimed at one another (called **line of sight**), as seen in Figure 2-4. The emitter sends a narrowly focused beam of infrared light. The detector has a small receiving or viewing area. A television remote control device uses directed transmission.

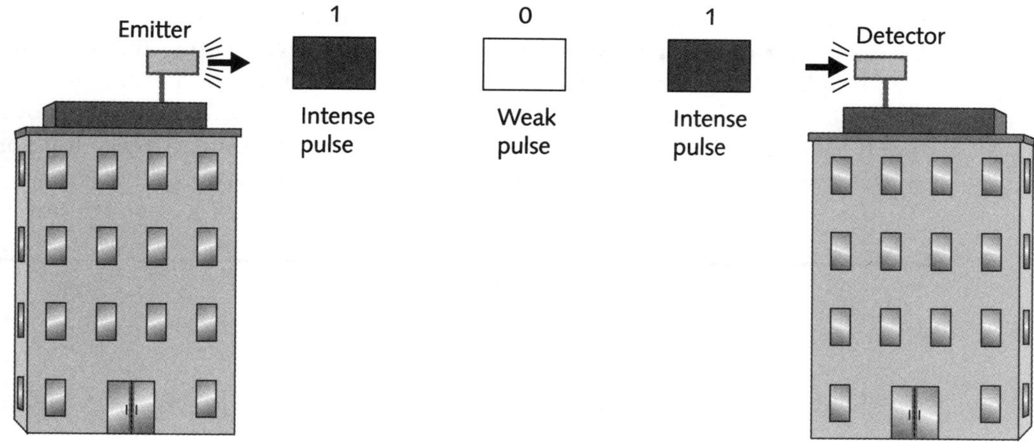

Figure 2-3 Light pulses

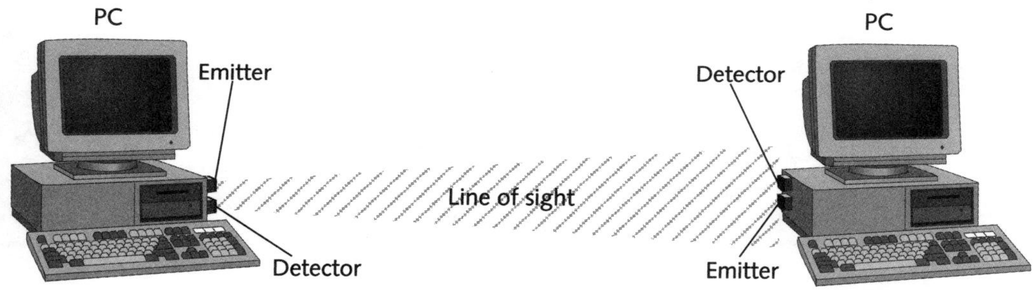

Figure 2-4 Directed transmission

A **diffused transmission** relies on reflected light. The emitters on diffused transmissions have a wide-focused beam instead of a narrow beam. The emitter is pointed at the ceiling of a room and uses it as the reflection point. When the emitter transmits an infrared signal it bounces off the ceiling and fills the room with the signal. The detectors are also pointed at the same reflection point and can detect the reflected signal, as seen in Figure 2-5.

Infrared wireless systems have several advantages. Infrared light neither interferes with other communications signals nor is it affected by other signals. Also, because infrared light does not penetrate walls, the signals are kept inside a room. This makes it impossible for someone elsewhere to "listen in" on the transmitted signal.

However, there are several serious limitations to infrared wireless systems. The first limitation involves the lack of mobility. Directed infrared wireless systems use a line of sight principle, which makes it impossible for mobile users to use it since the alignment between the emitter and the detector would have to be continuously adjusted. The second limitation is the range of coverage. Directed infrared systems, which require line of sight, cannot be placed in an environment where there is the possibility that anything could get in the way of the infrared beam (imagine someone standing in front of your remote while you are trying to change TV channels). This means devices using infrared transmissions must be placed close enough to one another to eliminate the possibility of something moving between them. Due to the angle of deflection, diffused infrared can cover a range of only 50 feet (15 meters). Also, because diffused infrared requires a reflection point, it can be used only indoors. These restrictions limit the range of coverage.

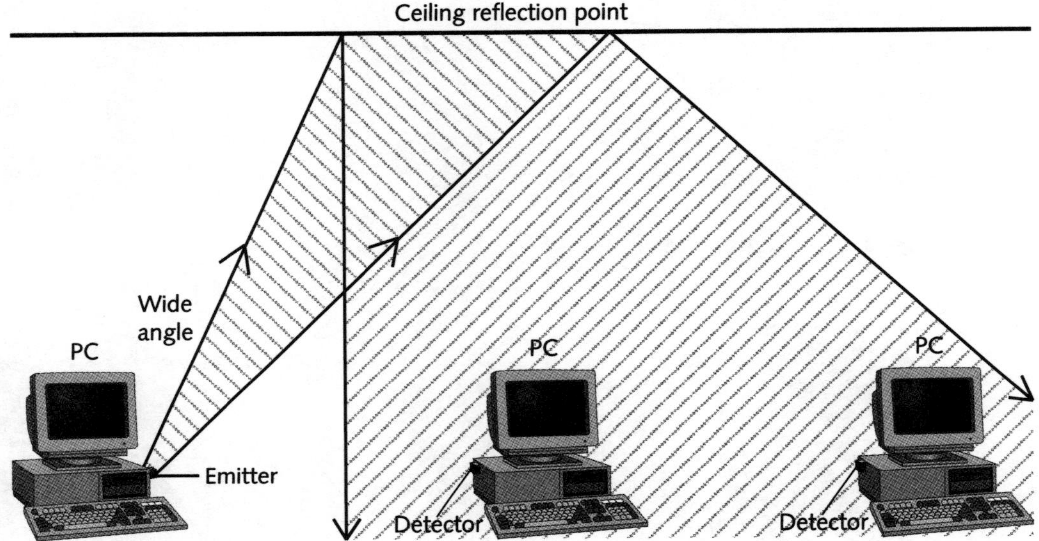

Figure 2-5 Diffused transmission

The final limitation of an infrared system is the speed of transmission. Diffused infrared can send data at only up to 4 Mbps. This is because the wide angle of the beam loses energy as it reflects. The loss of energy results in a weakening signal. The weak signal cannot be transmitted over long distances nor does it have sufficient energy to maintain a high transmission speed. This results in a lower data rate.

Because of these limitations, infrared wireless systems are generally used in specialized applications, such as data transfers between notebook computers, digital cameras, handheld data collection devices, PDAs, electronic books, and other similar mobile devices. A device using an infrared wireless system is illustrated in Figure 2-6.

There are specialized wireless local area networks that are based on the infrared method of transmitting data signals. These are used in situations where radio signals would interfere with other equipment, such as in hospital operating rooms, or when security is a concern, such as in secure government buildings.

Figure 2-6 Infrared wireless device

Infrared light, like other types of electromagnetic waves such as visible light and heat, has limitations regarding its movement. Light waves, for example, cannot penetrate through materials like wood or concrete, and heat rays are absorbed by most objects, including human skin (we feel these waves as heat). Thus, the distance that light and infrared waves can travel is limited. This is illustrated in Figure 2-7.

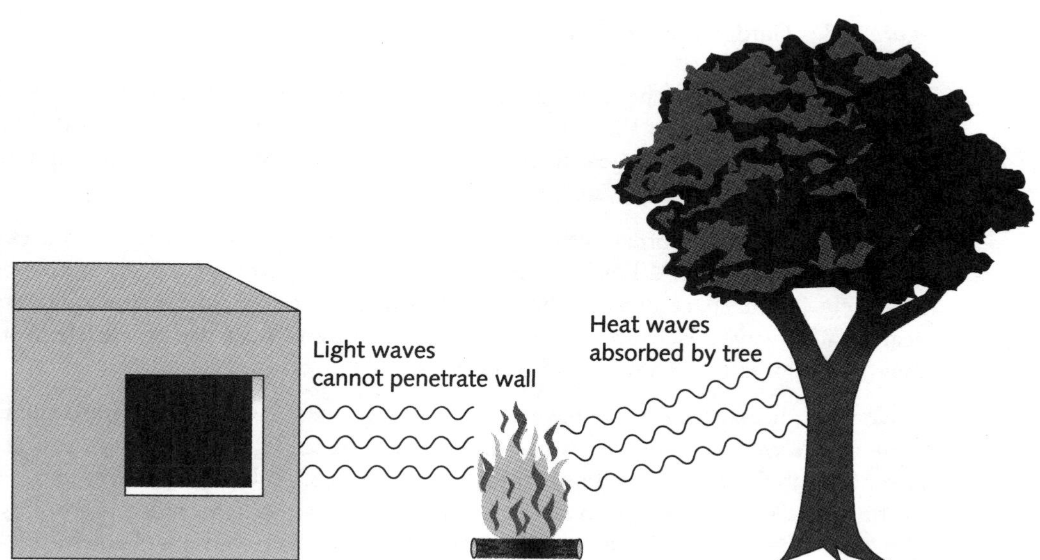

Figure 2-7 Limitations of light and heat waves

Is there a wave in the electromagnetic spectrum that does not have the distance limitations of light or infrared? The answer is yes: radio waves.

Radio Waves

The second means of transmitting a wireless signal is by using radio transmission. Radio waves provide the most common and effective means of wireless communications today. To understand the basics of radio waves, imagine that you are standing out in your yard with a garden hose in your hand watering the lawn. As you move your hand up and down, the water will create what looks like waves that move up and down, as seen in Figure 2-8.

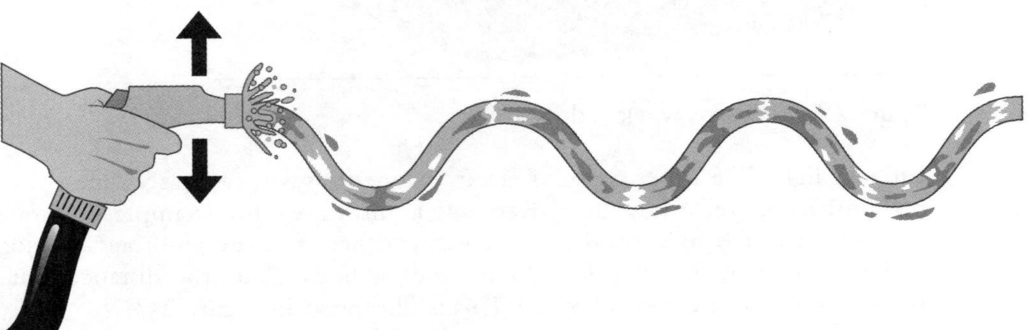

Figure 2-8 Garden hose waves

The waves created by the garden hose are similar to electromagnetic waves. You will recall that energy travels through space in electromagnetic waves. Infrared light, visible light from a flashlight, and heat from a fire move through space as electromagnetic waves. These waves require no physical medium for movement.

Another type of electromagnetic wave that travels in this fashion is called a **radiotelephony (radio) wave**. When an electric current passes through a wire, it creates a magnetic field in the space around the wire. As this magnetic field radiates or moves out, it creates radio waves. Because radio waves, like light and heat waves, are electromagnetic waves, they radiate outward in all directions.

However, radio waves do not have some of the limitations that light and heat waves do. Unlike heat waves, radio waves can travel great distances. Radio waves can also penetrate nonmetallic objects, whereas light waves cannot. Visible light waves and heat waves can be seen and felt, but radio waves are invisible. These characteristics are illustrated in Figure 2-9. Because of these characteristics, radio waves are an excellent means to transmit data without wires.

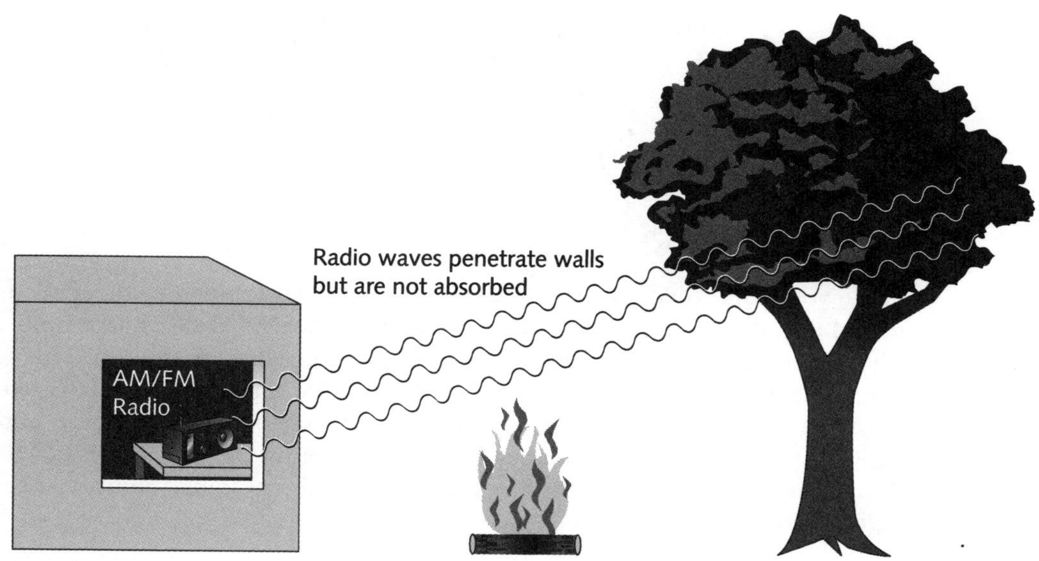

Figure 2-9 Radio waves without boundaries

How Radio Data Is Transmitted

Radio waves can be used to transmit data over long distances without the need for wires. To understand the method by which these waves can transport data requires an understanding of several different concepts.

Analog and Digital

Consider again standing out in your yard with a garden hose watering the lawn. As you move your hand up and down, the water will create what looks like waves that move up and down. The waves are continuous as long as the water is turned on. These waves represent an analog signal. An **analog signal** is a continuous signal with no "breaks" in it. This means that no individual element of an analog signal can be uniquely identified from another element of the signal. Figure 2-10 illustrates an analog signal. Audio, video, and even light are all examples of analog signals. A video signal carrying the latest movie release in a theater, or an audio signal that contains a song, is a continuous flow that doesn't start and stop until the movie or song is over.

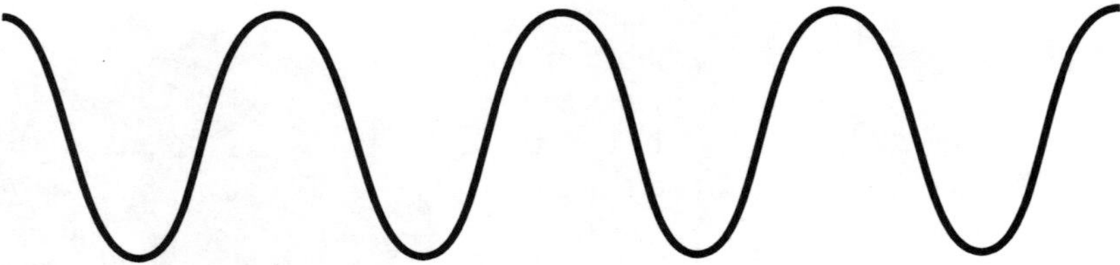

Figure 2-10 Analog signal

Suppose you were to take your thumb and place it over the end of the garden hose for a second and then remove it. Water would stop flowing (while your thumb was over the hose) and then would squirt out (when you moved your thumb). This is seen in Figure 2-11. This on-off activity is similar to a digital signal. A **digital signal** consists of data that is discrete or separate, as opposed to an analog signal, which is continuous. A digital signal has numerous starts and stops throughout the signal stream. Morse code with its series of dots and dashes is an example of a digital signal. Figure 2-12 illustrates a digital signal.

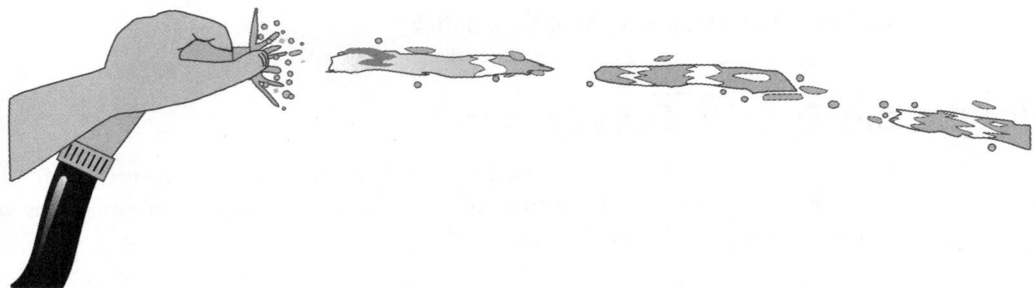

Figure 2-11 Squirting garden hose

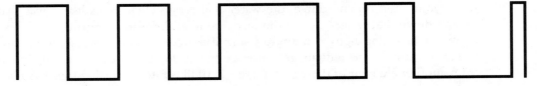

Figure 2-12 Digital signal

Computers operate using digital signals. If analog data, such as a video image or an audio sound, needs to be stored on the computer, it must be converted to a digital format before it can be stored and interpreted by the computer.

Various techniques are used to convert analog signals to digital signals. For example, with audio, a "snapshot" of the sound is sampled at the rate of 44,100 times per second and then each snapshot is stored in a digital format. Computers will also compress the data through other techniques to minimize the total amount of storage space needed.

When a digital signal needs to be transmitted over an analog medium, such as when a computer needs to send digital signals over an analog telephone line or TV cable, a device known as a **modem** (for MOdulator/DEModulator) is used. Changing a signal from analog to digital or vice versa is known as **modulation.** A modem converts the distinct digital signals from a computer into a continuous analog signal for transmission. Then, a modem will reverse the process by receiving an analog signal and converting it back into digital.

Frequency

Think about standing in your yard with a garden hose watering the lawn once again. If you move your hand up and down slowly while holding the hose you will create long waves, as seen in Figure 2-13. If you move your hand up and down rapidly, the waves become shorter, as seen in Figure 2-14. Depending on how fast you move your hand the waves will vary, from several inches to several feet in height.

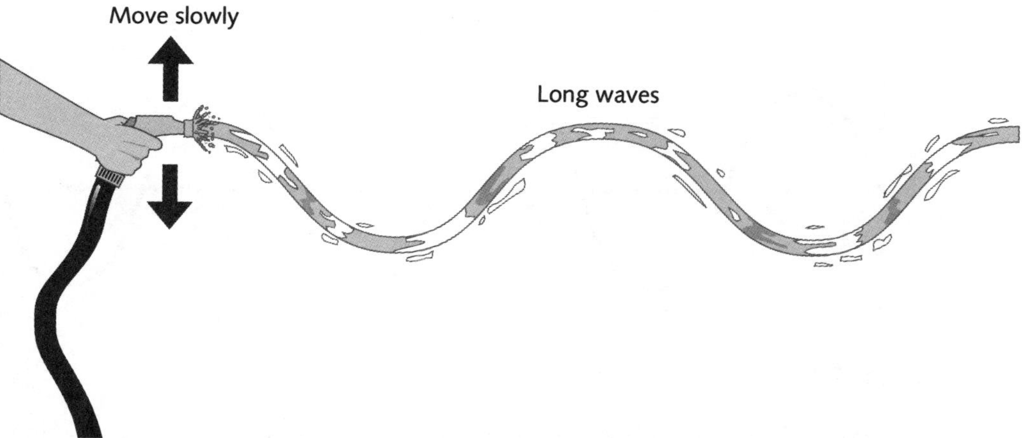

Figure 2-13 Long waves

The same is true with radio waves. The rate at which an event occurs (like moving the garden hose up and down) will result in a different number of radio waves being created. This is a radio wave's **frequency**. That is, how *frequently* an event occurs can create different *frequencies.* The changing event that creates the different radio frequencies (such as moving your hand up and down and back to center in our example) is a **cycle**.

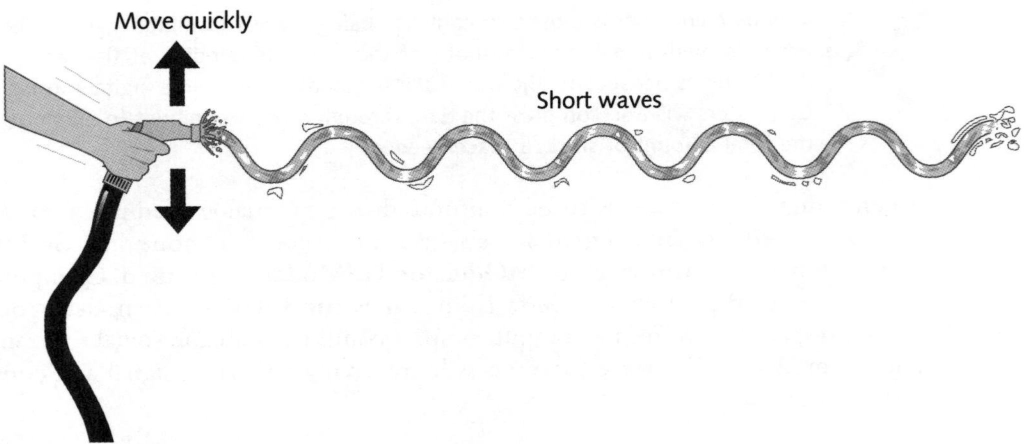

Figure 2-14 Short waves

Radio transmissions send what is known as a **carrier signal**. This signal can change based on the electrical pressure (**voltage**) and the direction of the signal. Changing signals are illustrated by an up-and-down wave called an **oscillating signal** or a **sine wave**. This is illustrated in Figure 2-15.

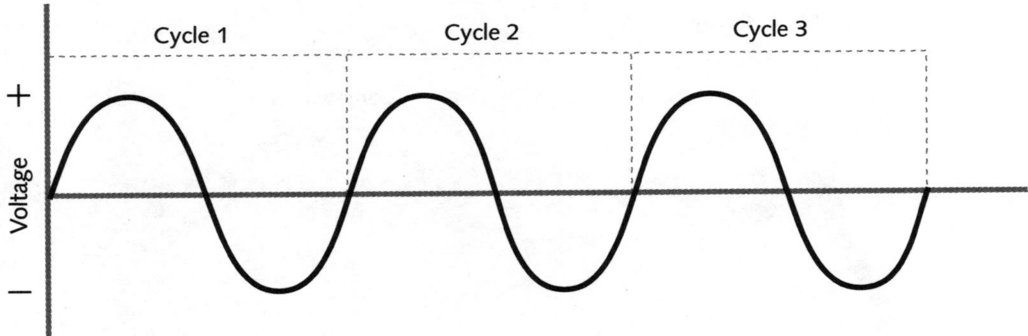

Figure 2-15 Sine wave

Notice in Figure 2-15 that the wave starts at zero, moves up to the maximum voltage (+), then down to the minimum voltage (-), and finally returns back to its starting point (0) before beginning all over again. Whenever the wave completes its trip and returns back to the starting point it has finished one cycle. Frequency is the number of times that a wave completes a cycle.

In Figure 2-16, two different frequencies are illustrated. Notice that the lower frequency and the higher frequency still alternate to the same maximum and minimum voltage. A change in voltage does not create a change in frequency. Instead, a change in frequency is a result of how long it takes to reach the maximum, fall back to the minimum, and then return to neutral to complete a cycle.

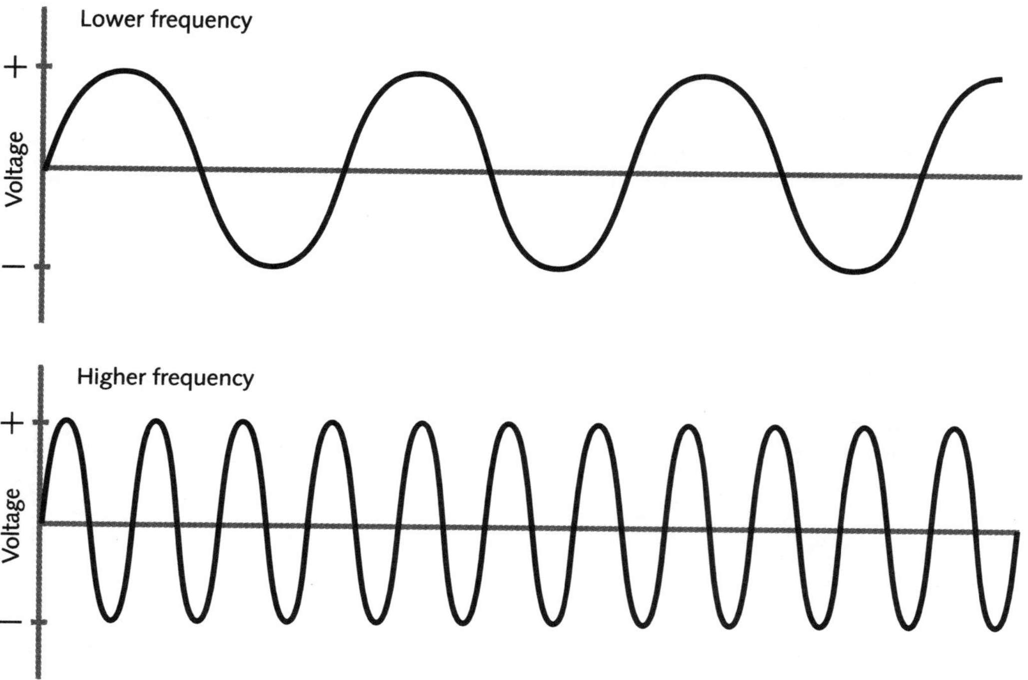

Figure 2-16 Lower and higher frequencies

In electrical terms, the cycle produces what is known as an alternating current (AC) because it flows between positive (+) and negative (-). AC is the type of current that runs to the electrical outlets in a house. Direct current (DC) is found in batteries. With DC, the current flows only from one terminal (+) to the other (-) and does not alternate.

Frequencies are measured in the number of cycles per second. Today the term **hertz (Hz)** is used instead of "cycle." A radio wave measured as 710,000 Hz means that its frequency is 710,000 cycles per second. Because of the high number of cycles required, metric prefixes are generally used when referring to frequencies. A **kilohertz (KHz)** is a thousand hertz, a **megahertz (MHz)** is a million hertz, and a **gigahertz (GHz)** is one billion hertz. The wave measured as 710,000 Hz would more properly be listed as 710 KHz.

Frequency is an important part of music also. The key of A is 440 Hz and middle C is 263 Hz.

Radio waves can be transmitted and received using an antenna. An **antenna** is a copper wire, or similar device, that has one end in the air and the other end connected through a receiver or transmitter to the ground or a grounded device. When transmitting, the radio waves strike this wire (the length of an antenna should be about ¼ of the wavelength). This will set up an electrical pressure (voltage) along the wire, which will cause a small electrical current to flow into it. The voltage causes a movement back and forth of the electricity in the antenna at the same frequency as the radio waves. Broadcasting or sending out radio waves is accomplished by forcing the electricity in the antenna to move at the same frequency as the radio waves. To pick up transmitted radio signals, an antenna is also used. The electricity in this receiving antenna moves back and forth in response to the radio signals reaching it. The motion causes a voltage that leads from the antenna into the receiver. This is seen in Figure 2-17.

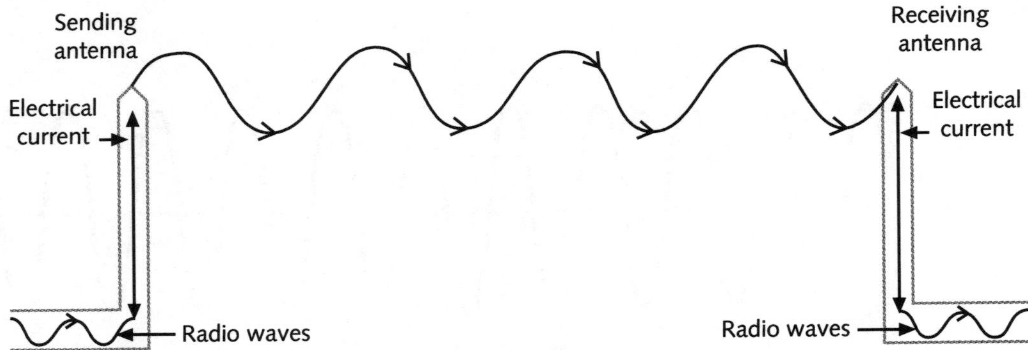

Figure 2-17 Radio antennas transmit and receive

Transmission Speed

There are several different terms that are used when referring to the transmission speed of radio waves. When data is transmitted using radio waves, the measure of speed is usually **bits per second (bps)**, or the number of bits that can be transmitted per second.

Another term used in measuring the speed of radio transmission is baud rate. You will recall that radio transmissions send out a carrier signal and this signal can change. A **baud** is a change in that signal. Changing signals are illustrated by a sine wave. The **baud rate** is the number of times that a signal changes per second.

It is not uncommon for bps and baud rate to be used interchangeably, although the terms are not synonymous. This confusion dates back to early computer modems. Modems developed in the late 1980s had speeds of 2400, 4800, and 9600 bps. With these early modems, whenever a binary 1 was transmitted the signal changed, and whenever a binary 0 was transmitted the signal changed (you will recall that with the binary system only 1s and 0s are needed). For example, to transmit the letter "A" (65 ASCII or 01000001) it would take 8 signal changes, one for each bit. Thus, the number of bits transmitted per signal change (baud) was 1, so the terms "bps" and "baud" were used interchangeably.

However, with later modems it became possible to have a change in signal (baud) represent more than 1 bit. A signal can actually change in several different ways. Taking advantage of these different changes could result in two bits each being assigned to four different signal changes. This is illustrated in Table 2-2.

Table 2-2 Bit representation of four signal changes

Signal Change (Baud)	Bits Represented
Signal W	00
Signal X	01
Signal Y	10
Signal Z	11

Thus, instead of the letter "A" (01000001) requiring 8 signal changes, it only requires 4 signals (X-W-W-X). A signal transmitting at 28,800 bps would have a baud rate of 14,400. The ability to have a signal represent two bits is known as a **dibit**. When a signal can represent three bits, it is called a **tribit**. A tribit can result in a signal transmitting at 28,800 bps to have a baud rate of only 9,600. If 16 different signals could be used, then 4 bits per signal could be represented (known as a **quadbit**). These different signaling techniques are summarized in Table 2-3.

Table 2-3 Signaling techniques

Name	Number of Signals Needed	Number of Bits per Signal
Standard	1	1
Dibit	4	2
Tribit	8	3
Quadbit	16	4

Another term used when referring to transmission speeds is **bandwidth**. Although this term is often used to refer to the maximum data transmission capacity, strictly speaking bandwidth is defined as the range of frequencies that can be transmitted. It is the difference between the higher frequency and the lower frequency. Suppose a transmission for voice could be sent between 3,400 Hz and 300 Hz. The difference between the two frequencies (3,400 Hz - 300Hz) is 3,100 Hz, the bandwidth of this transmission.

Analog Modulation

The carrier signal sent by analog radio transmissions is simply a continuous electrical signal. This signal itself carries no information. How then can data be transmitted by an analog carrier signal? There are three types of modulations, or changes, to the signal that can be made to enable it to carry information: the height of the signal, the frequency of the signal, and the relative starting point.

The height, frequency, and relative starting point of a signal are sometimes called the "three degrees of freedom."

Amplitude Modulation (AM)

The height of a carrier wave is known as the **amplitude**. This is illustrated in Figure 2-18 with a typical sine wave. The height of the carrier can be changed so that a higher wave represents a 1 bit while a lower wave represents a 0 bit. This is known as **amplitude modulation (AM)**. Figure 2-19 illustrates the letter "A" (ASCII 65 or 01000001) being transmitted by amplitude modulation. Notice that the highest peaks of the carrier wave represent a 1 bit while the lower waves represent a 0 bit.

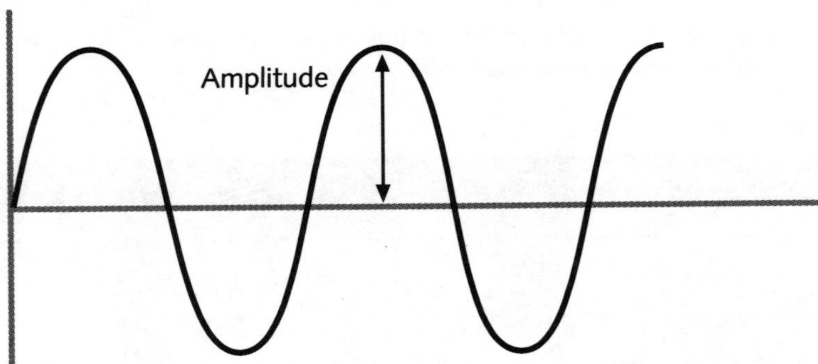

Figure 2-18 Amplitude

Amplitude modulation is most frequently used by broadcast radio stations. However, AM is often susceptible to interference from outside sources, such as lightning, and is not generally used for data transmissions.

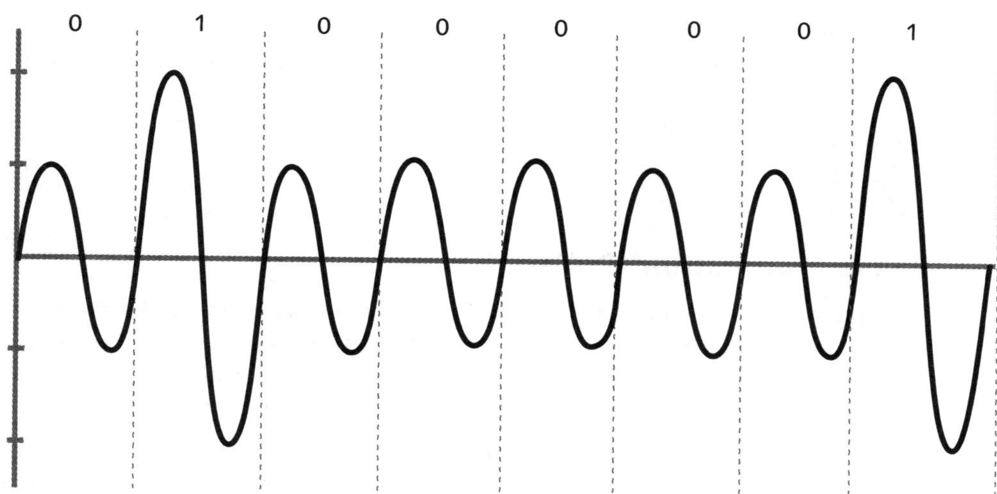

Figure 2-19 Amplitude modulation (AM)

Frequency Modulation (FM)

As amplitude modulation varies the height of the signal, **frequency modulation (FM)** changes the number of waves used to represent one cycle. When using frequency modulation, the number of waves needed to represent a 1 bit are more than the number of waves needed to represent a 0 bit. Figure 2-20 illustrates the letter "A" (ASCII 65 or 01000001) being transmitted by frequency modulation. Notice that the number of waves to represent a 1 bit are double that of the number of waves to represent a 0 bit.

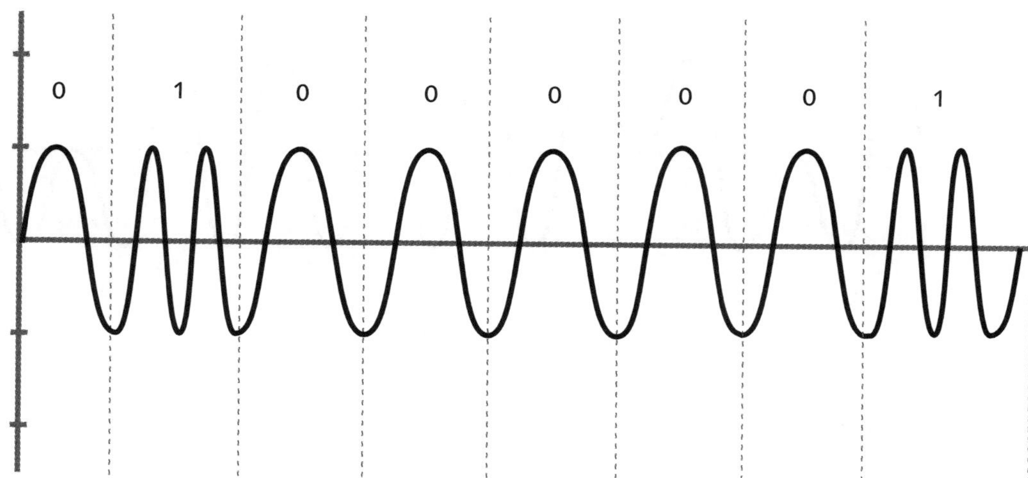

Figure 2-20 Frequency modulation (FM)

Like amplitude modulation, frequency modulation is often used by broadcast radio stations. However, unlike AM, FM is not as susceptible to interference from outside sources.

FM stations broadcast between 88 MHz and 108 MHz, while AM stations transmit between 535 KHz and 1,700 KHz.

Phase Modulation (PM)

In contrast to AM, which changes the height of the wave, and FM, which increases the number of waves per cycle, **phase modulation (PM)** changes the starting point of the cycle. This change only takes place when the bits being transmitted change from a 1 bit, to a 0 bit, or vice versa. The change in starting point indicates that a different bit is now being sent.

Figure 2-21 illustrates the letter "A" (ASCII 65 or 01000001) being transmitted by phase modulation. Notice that whenever a bit being transmitted changes from 1 to 0 (or 0 to 1), the starting point of the wave changes. For example, after the first 0 bit is represented by a "normal" carrier wave cycle, the next bit is a 1 bit. However, instead of this being indicated by another "normal" carrier wave cycle where the signal advances into the positive range (goes up on the sine wave), it instead starts by going down into the negative range. The change in starting point (going down instead of going up) represents a change in the bit being transmitted (0 to 1).

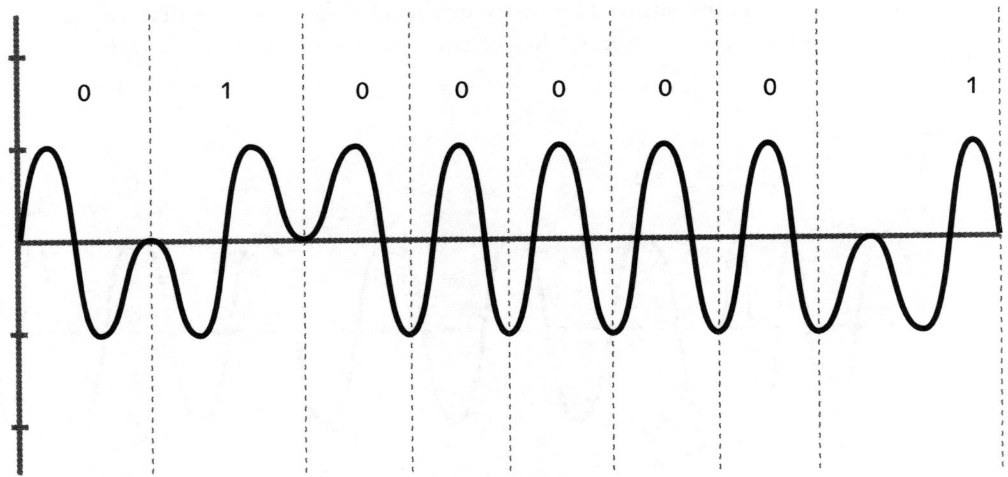

Figure 2-21 Phase modulation (PM)

In our example, the change in the starting point is the complete opposite of what is being sent, or 180 degrees. Phase modulation can change the starting point from various angles, as Figure 2-22 illustrates. There are eight different starting points of a carrier signal (0 degrees-180 degrees, 45 degrees-225 degrees, 90 degrees-270 degrees, 135 degrees-335 degrees), with each dot in the figure representing a different signal starting point. You will recall that with a tribit, 8 different signals are needed. Using phase modulation with 180 degree angles can result in 8 different signals. However, when phase modulation is combined with amplitude modulation, a total of 16 different signals can be created, as seen in Figure 2-23. Each dot in the figure represents a different signal. This technique is used in quadbit and is called **quadrature amplitude modulation (QAM)**.

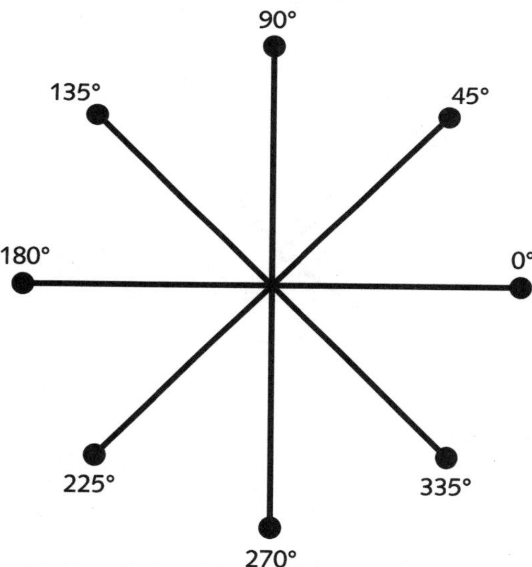

Figure 2-22 Phase modulation angles

Although radio broadcasts use either amplitude modulation (AM) or frequency modulation (FM), television broadcasts actually use AM, FM, and phase modulation (PM). Television video uses amplitude modulation, the sound uses frequency modulation, and the color information uses phase modulation.

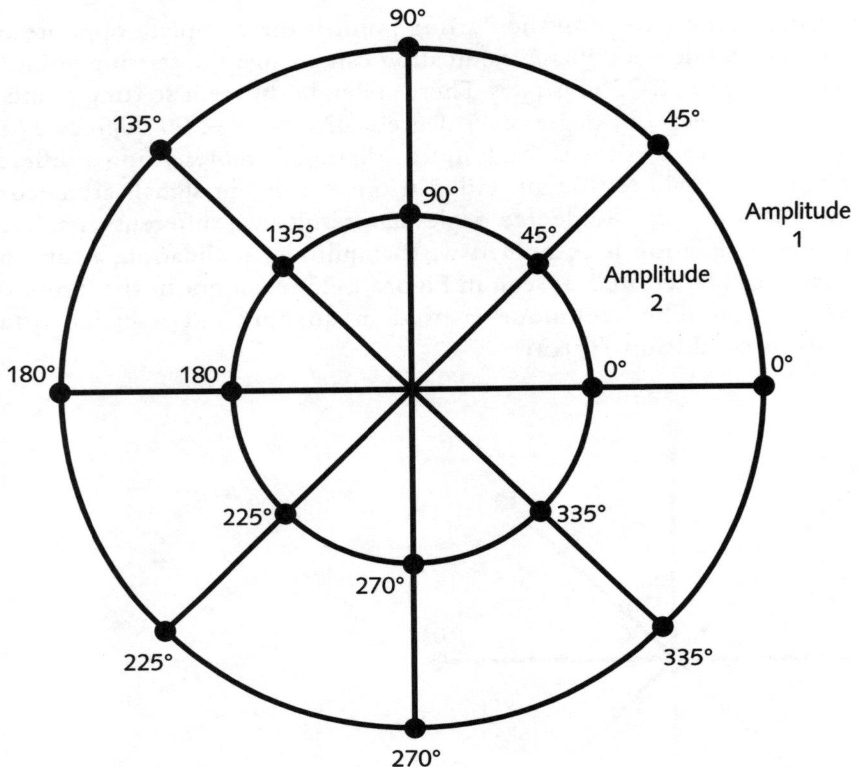

Figure 2-23 Phase modulation angles and amplitude

Digital Modulation

Although analog modulation can be used for data communications, most modern wireless systems use digital modulation. In an analog system, the carrier signal is continuous, and amplitude, frequency, and phase changes also occur continuously. With a digital system, on the other hand, the changes are distinct using binary signals. There are four primary advantages of digital modulation over analog modulation:

- It makes better use of the bandwidth
- It requires less power to transmit
- It performs better when the signal is being interfered with by other signals
- Its error-correcting techniques are more compatible with other digital systems

With digital modulation, like analog modulation, there are three types of modulations, or changes, to the signal that can be made to enable it to carry information: the height, the frequency, or the relative starting point of the signal.

Binary Signals

Recall that with an analog signal the carrier wave alternates between the positive and negative voltage in a continuous cycle; that is, it doesn't stop. A binary signal likewise alternates between positive and negative voltage. However, unlike the analog signal, the binary signal starts and stops.

There are three different types of binary signaling techniques that can be used. The **return-to-zero (RZ)** technique calls for the voltage to increase to represent a 1 bit, and no voltage for transmitting a 0 bit. This is illustrated in Figure 2-24. Notice that the voltage is reduced to zero before the end of the period for transmitting a 1 bit.

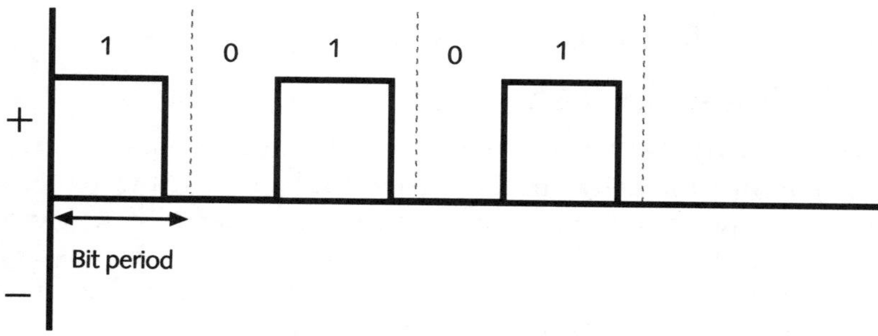

Figure 2-24 Return-to-zero (RZ)

The second technique is known as the **non-return-to-zero (NRZ)**. With NRZ, the voltage signal remains at high for the entire length of the bit period. Like RZ, there is no voltage for transmitting a 0 bit. This is illustrated in Figure 2-25.

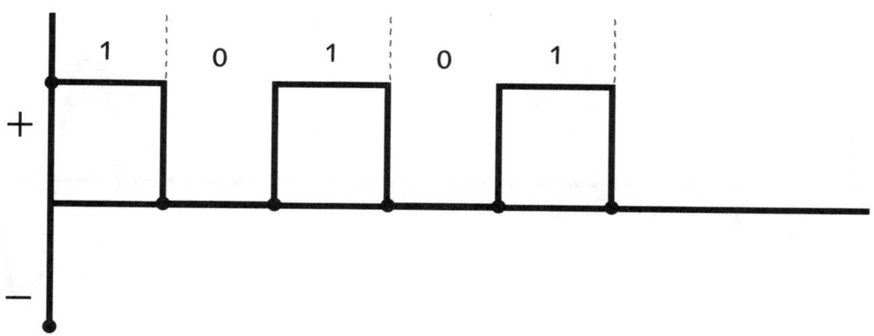

Figure 2-25 Non-return-to-zero (NRZ)

The final technique, **polar non-return-to-zero (polar NRZ)**, increases the voltage to represent a 1 bit but drops the voltage to a negative amount to represent a 0 bit. Polar NRZ is illustrated in Figure 2-26.

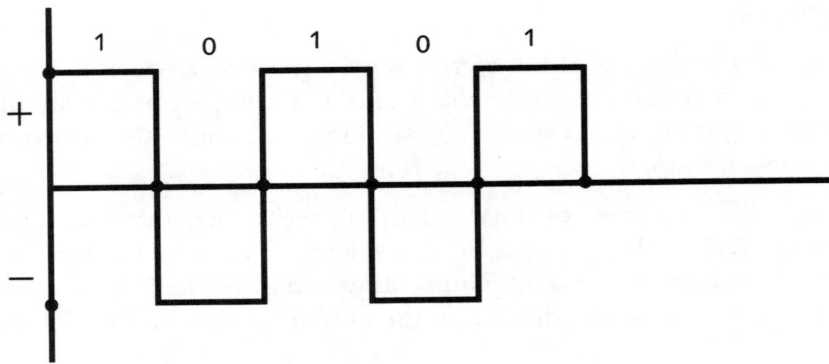

Figure 2-26 Polar non-return-to-zero (polar NRZ)

Amplitude Shift Keying (ASK)

Amplitude shift keying (ASK) is a binary modulation technique similar to amplitude modulation, in that the height of the carrier can be changed to represent a 1 bit or a 0 bit. However, instead of both a 1 bit and a 0 bit having a carrier signal, as with amplitude modulation, ASK uses NRZ coding. This means that a 1 bit has a carrier signal (positive voltage) while a 0 bit has no signal (zero voltage). Figure 2-27 illustrates the letter "A" (ASCII 65 or 01000001) being transmitted by ASK.

Digital binary modulation is still shown as a standard sine wave.

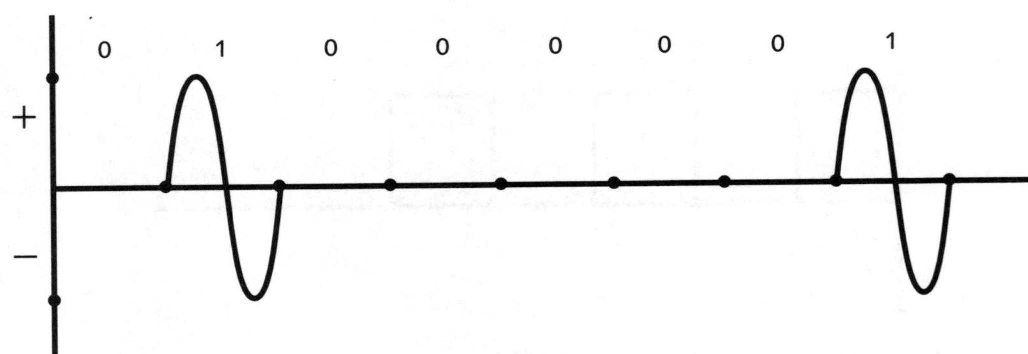

Figure 2-27 Amplitude shift keying (ASK)

Frequency Shift Keying (FSK)

Similar to frequency modulation, **frequency shift keying (FSK)** is a binary modulation technique that changes the frequency of the carrier signal. Because it is sending a binary signal, the carrier signal does start and stop. Figure 2-28 illustrates the letter "A" (ASCII 65 or 01000001) being transmitted by frequency shift keying.

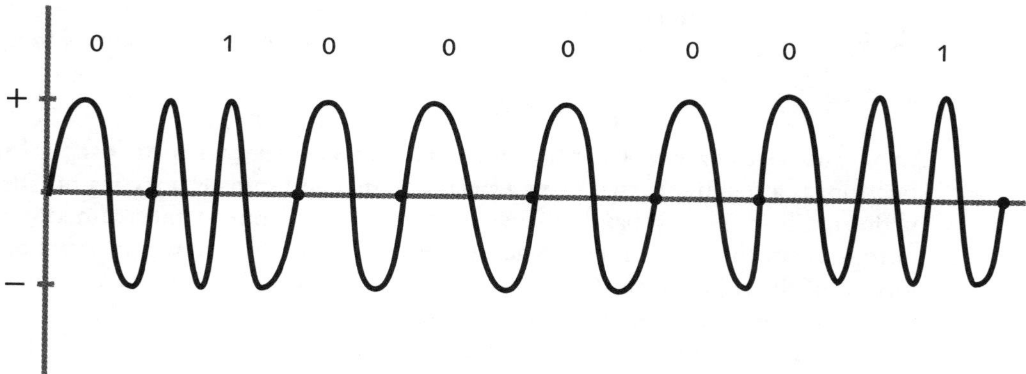

Figure 2-28 Frequency shift keying (FSK)

Phase Shift Keying (PSK)

Phase shift keying (PSK) is a binary modulation technique similar to phase modulation. The difference is that the PSK signal starts and stops because it is a binary signal. Figure 2-29 illustrates the letter "A" (ASCII 65 or 01000001) being transmitted by phase shift key.

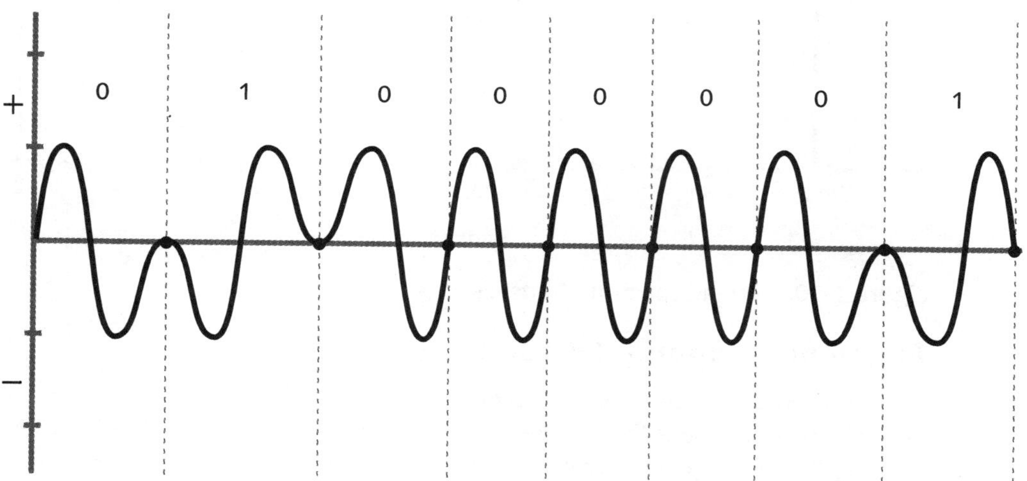

Figure 2-29 Phase shift keying (PSK)

Spread Spectrum

Radio signals are by nature **narrow-band transmissions.** This means that they transmit on one radio frequency or a very narrow spectrum of frequencies. Broadcast radio stations, for example, tell their listeners to "tune to 90.3" because this is the frequency on which they broadcast. Narrow-band transmissions are vulnerable to outside interference from another signal. A single interfering signal at or near the broadcast frequency can easily render the radio signal inoperable, much as an accident can stop all traffic on a one-lane road.

Broadcast radio stations work effectively with narrow-band transmissions because each station is allowed to transmit on only one frequency in one specific area.

An alternative to narrow-band transmissions is **spread spectrum transmission**. Spread spectrum is a technique that takes a narrow signal and spreads it over a broader portion of the radio frequency band, as seen in Figure 2-30. Spread spectrum transmission is more resistant to outside interference, because any interference would affect only a small portion of the signal instead of impacting the entire signal. Although an accident in one lane of an eight-lane freeway is inconvenient, there are still seven other lanes by which traffic can move around it and keep going. Spread spectrum likewise results in less interference and fewer errors.

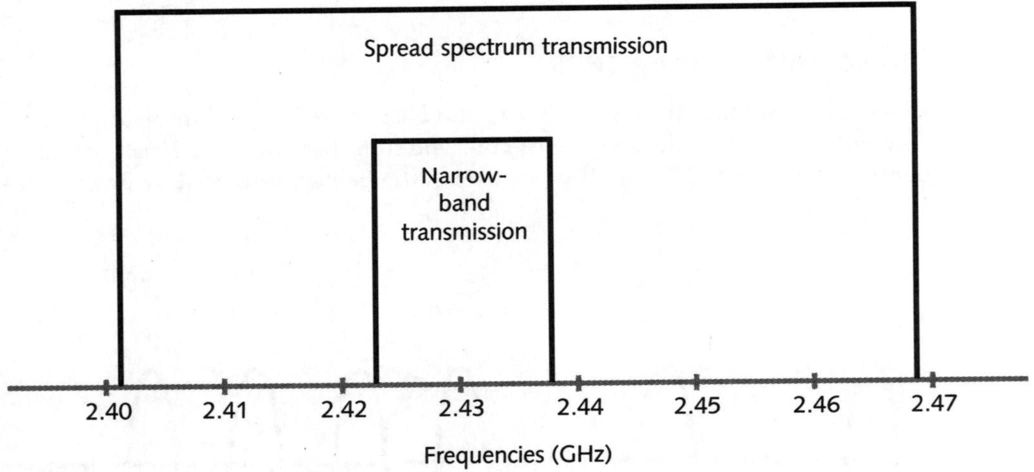

Figure 2-30 Spread spectrum transmissions

Frequency Hopping Spread Spectrum (FHSS)

Spread spectrum transmission uses two different methods to spread the signal over a wider area. The first method is **frequency hopping spread spectrum (FHSS)**. Instead of sending on just one frequency, frequency hopping uses a range of frequencies and will change frequencies during the transmission. With FHSS, a short burst is transmitted at one frequency, then a short burst is transmitted at another frequency, etc., until the transmission is completed.

Hedy Lamarr, a well-known film actress during the 1940s, and George Antheil, who had experience synchronizing the sounds of music scores with motion pictures, originally conceived the idea of frequency hopping spread spectrum during the early part of World War II. Their goal was to keep the Germans from jamming the radios that guided U.S. torpedoes against German warships. Lamarr and Antheil received a U.S. patent in 1942 for their idea.

Figure 2-31 shows how an FHSS transmission starts by sending a burst of data at the 2.44 GHz frequency for 1 microsecond. Then the transmission switches to the 2.41 GHz frequency and transmits for the second microsecond. At the third microsecond the transmission takes place at the 2.42 GHz frequency. This continual switching of frequencies takes place until the entire transmission is complete. The sequence of changing frequencies is called the **hopping code**. In Figure 2-31, the hopping code is 2.44-2.41-2.42-2.40-2.43. The receiving station must also know the hopping code in order to correctly receive the transmission.

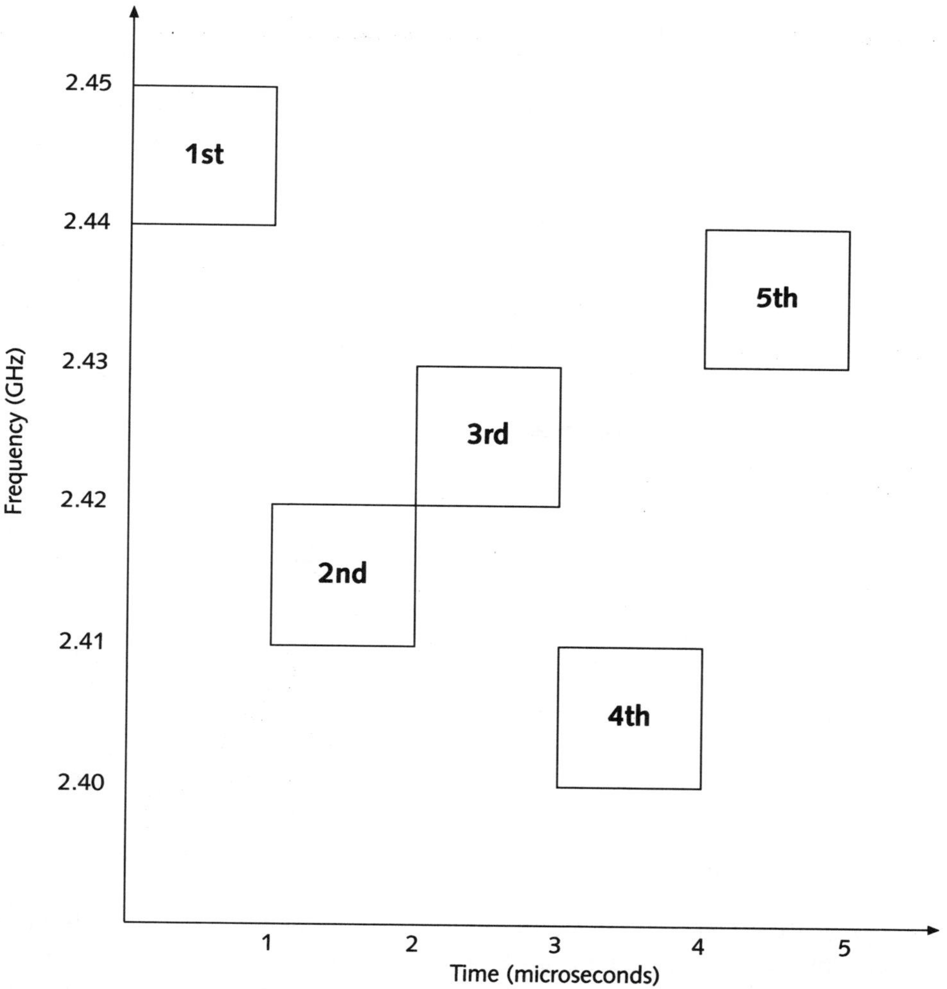

Figure 2-31 FHSS transmission

While transmitting with FHSS, if interference is encountered on a frequency, that part of the signal will be retransmitted on the next frequency, as established in the hopping code. Figure 2-32 shows that the second transmission received interference, so it was retransmitted on the frequency that would normally carry the third transmission. All other transmissions are then on the next frequency of the hopping code.

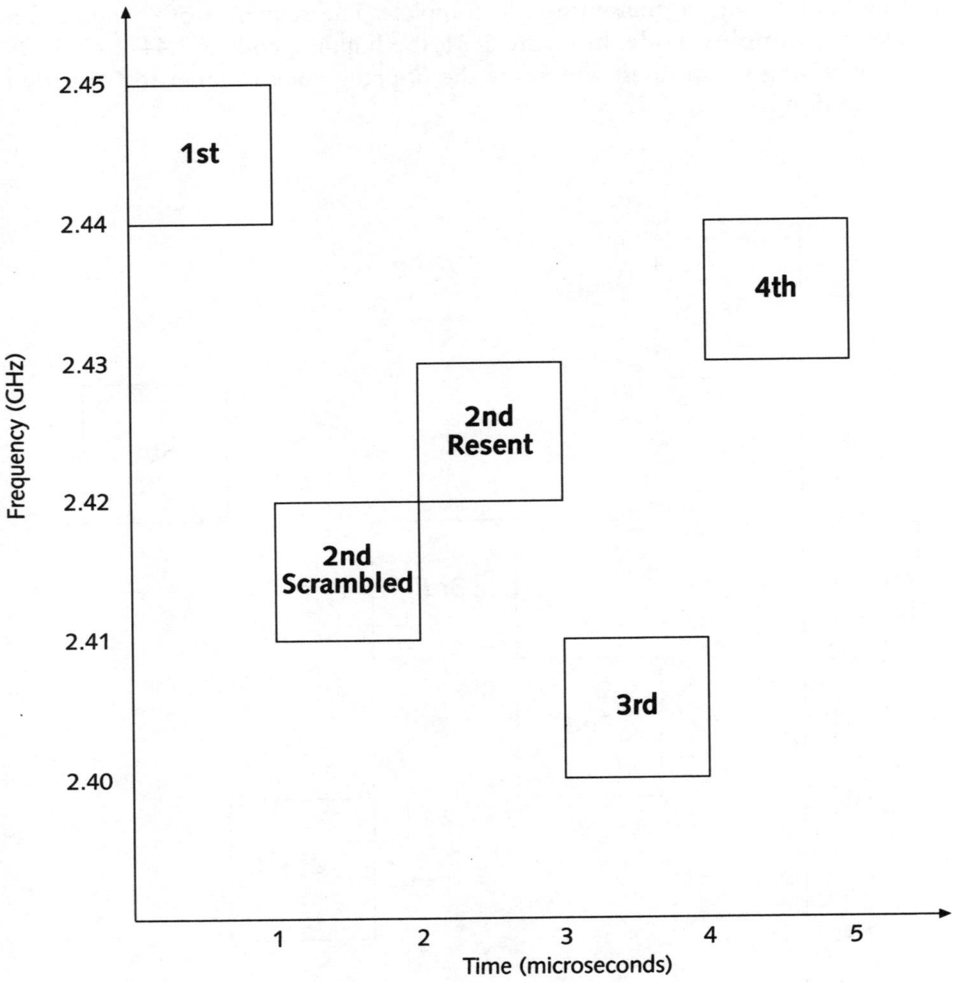

Figure 2-32 FHSS error correction

Frequency hopping can reduce the impact of interference from other radio signals. An interfering signal will affect the FHHS signal only when both are transmitting at the same frequency at the same time. Because FHHS transmits short bursts over a wide range of frequencies, the extent of any interference will be very small and can be easily corrected by error checking. In addition, FHSS signals have a minimal interference on other signals. To an unintended receiver, FHSS transmissions appear to be of a very short duration and again can be easily corrected by error checking.

There are a variety of devices that use FHSS. Several of these devices are consumer-oriented products, because FHSS devices are generally less expensive to manufacture. Home wireless local area network products, which have a low transmission rate and limited transmission distance, and portable telephones, typically use FHSS.

Direct Sequence Spread Spectrum (DSSS)

The other type of spread spectrum technology is **direct sequence spread spectrum (DSSS)**. DSSS uses an expanded redundant code to transmit each data bit. Figure 2-33 shows three original data bits to be transmitted: 1, 0, and 1 (top of figure). However, instead of transmitting these three bits, a different sequence of bits is substituted, as seen in the middle line of the figure. This bit pattern is called the **chipping code**. In Figure 2-33, the chipping code is 1001. That means instead of sending a 1 bit, the chipping code of a 1 (1001) is substituted instead. The inverse of that code (0110) is substituted for the 0 data bit to be transmitted. Instead of sending a 0 bit, the chipping code of a 0 (0110) is substituted instead.

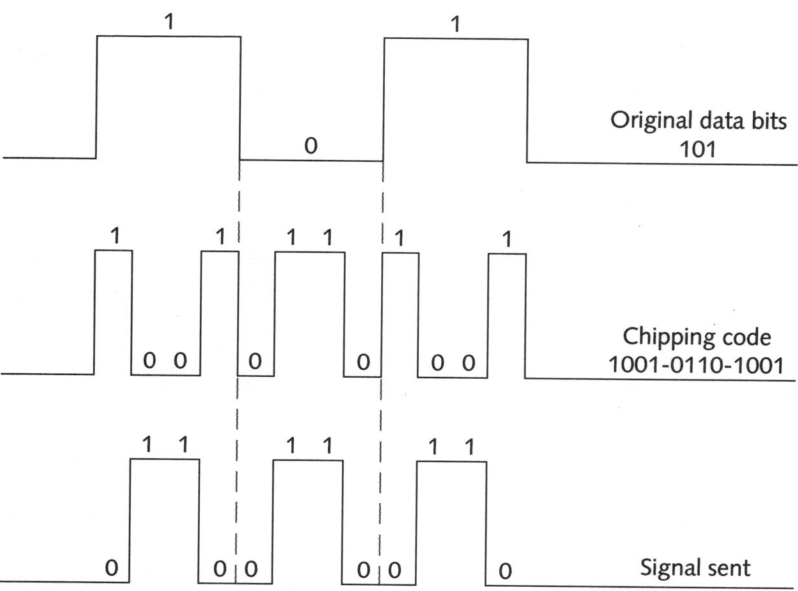

Figure 2-33 DSSS transmission

The term "chipping code" is used because a single radio bit is commonly referred to as a "chip."

The last step is to add the original data bit to the chipping code, as seen in the bottom line of Figure 2-33, to create the signal that is actually sent. If a 1 bit is to be transmitted, then a 1 is added to each bit of the chipping code:

Bit to be transmitted is 1				
Chipping code for 1:	1	0	0	1
Value to add to chipping code:	1	1	1	1
Signal sent	0	1	1	0

If a 0 data bit is to be transmitted, then a 0 is added to each bit of the chipping code:

Bit to be transmitted is 0				
Chipping code for 0:	0	1	1	0
Value to add to chipping code:	0	0	0	0
Signal sent	0	1	1	0

The adding of the chipping code and the value to add to the chipping code is accomplished by the Boolean operation of exclusive or (XOR).

Although it may appear that 0-1-1-0 would be sent for all 0 and 1 bits to be transmitted, that is not the case. When the bits to be transmitted are consecutive 1 bits, an extra 0 is placed between them in the chipping code so that it becomes [1001][0][1001], which would result in a transmitted code of [0-1-1-0]-[1]-[0-1-1-0].

There are several advantages to using DSSS with a chipping code. If there is interference in the transmission when sending only one bit, it would have to be resent, which takes time. However, if there is interference when sending the chipping code, statistical techniques embedded in the receiving device can recover the original data without the need for retransmission. Another advantage is that if the DSSS signal is picked up by an unintended device, the signal will appear as low-powered "noise" and will be rejected. Perhaps the greatest advantage of sending several bits with DSSS instead of just one is security. If an eavesdropper intercepts the signal of the original data bit, it would be a simple task to read the message. A chipping code would make reading the message more difficult—if not impossible—to read.

Devices that use DSSS are typically higher-end products because they are more expensive to manufacture, but also have advantages over FHSS. High-end office-based wireless local area networks use DSSS, along with products to connect networks between several buildings in a campus setting such as schools, large corporations, manufacturing plants, and convention centers.

Chapter Summary

- Humans typically use the decimal or Base 10 number system. However, the decimal number system is not good for a computer or for data transmissions. Because these are electrical devices, and electricity has two states, these devices instead use the binary or Base 2 number system. Binary uses a base number of 2 instead of 10 and the only digits used to represent a number in binary are the digits 0 and 1. Every character or symbol that is stored or transmitted is assigned an arbitrary number based on a specific coding scheme.
- One of these arbitrary coding schemes uses the numbers from 0 to 255 and is called the American Standard Code for Information Interchange (ASCII). To store a character, it is first converted to its ASCII (decimal) equivalent and then that number is stored as a byte in binary code.
- Whereas traditional wired communications use copper wires or fiber optic cables to send and receive data, wireless transmissions do not use these or any other visible media. Instead, they travel on electromagnetic waves. There are two basic types of waves by which wireless signals are sent and received: infrared light and radio waves. Infrared light, next to visible light on the light spectrum, has many of the same characteristics as visible light.
- Infrared wireless transmission can be either directed or diffused. A directed transmission sends a narrowly focused beam of infrared light to the receiver. A diffused transmission relies on reflected light. The second means of transmitting a wireless signal is by using radio transmission. Radio waves provide the most common and effective means of wireless communications today. However, radio waves do not have the limitations that other types of waves do.
- Radio transmissions send a carrier signal. This signal can change based on the electrical pressure (voltage) and the direction of the signal. Changing signals are illustrated by an up-and-down wave called a sine wave. The carrier signal sent by analog radio transmissions is simply a continuous electrical signal and itself carries no information.
- There are three types of modulations, or changes, to the signal that can be made to enable it to carry information: the height of the signal, the frequency of the signal, and the relative starting point. The height of the carrier can be changed so that a higher wave represents a 1 bit while a lower wave represents a 0 bit. This is known as amplitude modulation (AM). Frequency modulation (FM) changes the number of waves used to represent one cycle. Phase modulation (PM) changes the starting

point of the cycle. With digital modulation, like analog modulation, there are three types of modulations, or changes, to the signal that can be made to enable it to carry information: the height of the signal, the frequency of the signal, or the relative starting point.

- Amplitude shift keying (ASK) changes the height of the carrier to represent a 1 bit or a 0 bit. A 1 bit has a carrier signal (positive voltage) while a 0 bit has no signal (zero voltage). Frequency shift keying (FSK) is a binary modulation technique that changes the frequency of the carrier signal. Phase shift keying (PSK) is a binary modulation technique similar to phase modulation. The difference is that the PSK signal starts and stops because it is a binary signal.
- Radio signals are by nature narrow-band transmissions, which means that they transmit on one radio frequency or a very narrow spectrum of frequencies. An alternative to narrow-band transmissions is spread spectrum transmission. Spread spectrum is a technique that takes a narrow signal and spreads it over a broader portion of the radio frequency band.
- Spread spectrum transmission uses two different methods to spread the signal over a wider area. The first method is frequency hopping spread spectrum (FHSS). Instead of sending on just one frequency, frequency hopping uses a range of frequencies and will change frequencies during the transmission. The other type of spread spectrum technology is direct sequence spread spectrum (DSSS). DSSS uses an expanded redundant code to transmit each data bit.

Key Terms

American Standard Code for Information Interchange (ASCII) — An arbitrary coding scheme that uses the numbers from 0 to 255.

amplitude — The height of a carrier wave.

amplitude shift keying (ASK) — A binary modulation technique whereby 1 bit has a carrier signal while a 0 bit has no signal.

amplitude modulation (AM) — A change in the height of the cycle.

analog signal — A continuous signal.

antenna — A copper wire, rod, or similar device that has one end up in the air and the other end connected to the ground through a receiver.

bandwidth — The range of frequencies that can be transmitted.

Base 2 number system — See binary number system.

Base 10 number system — See decimal number system.

baud — A change in a carrier signal.

baud rate — The number of times that a carrier signal changes per second.

binary number system — A numbering system commonly used by computers that has a base number of 2 and uses the digits 0 and 1.

bit — A binary digit; an electronic 0 or a 1 based on the binary number system.

bits per second (bps) — The number of bits that can be transmitted per second.

byte — Eight binary digits (bits).

carrier signal — A transmission over a radio frequency that carries no useful information.

chipping code — A bit pattern used in a DSSS transmission. The term "chipping code" is used because a single radio bit is commonly referred to as a "chip."

cycle — An oscillating sine wave that completes one full series of movements.

decimal number system — A numbering system that has a base number of 10 and uses the digits 0-9.

detector — A diode that receives a light-based transmission signal.

dibit — A signal that represents two bits.

diffused transmission — A light-based transmission that relies on reflected light.

digital signal — Data that is discrete or separate.

direct sequence spread spectrum (DSSS) — A spread spectrum technique that uses an expanded, redundant code to transmit each data bit.

directed transmission — A light-based transmission that requires the emitter and detector to be directly aimed at one another.

emitter — A laser diode or a light-emitting diode that transmits a light-based signal.

frequency — A measurement of radio waves that is determined by how frequently a cycle changes.

frequency hopping spread spectrum (FHSS) — A spread spectrum technique that uses a range of frequencies and changes frequencies during the transmission.

frequency modulation (FM) — A change of the number of waves used to represent one cycle.

frequency shift keying (FSK) — A binary modulation technique that changes the frequency of the carrier signal.

gigahertz (GHz) — One billion hertz.

hertz (Hz) — The number of cycles per second.

hopping code — The sequence of changing frequencies used in FHSS.

infrared light — Light that is next to visible light on the light spectrum that has many of the same characteristics as visible light.

kilohertz (KHz) — One thousand hertz.

light spectrum — All the different types of light that travel from the sun to the earth.

line of sight — The direct alignment as required in a directed transmission.

megahertz (MHz) — One million hertz.

modem (MOdulator/DEModulator) — A device used to convert digital signals into an analog format, and vice versa.

modulation — The process of changing a carrier signal.

narrow-band transmissions — Transmissions that send on one radio frequency or a very narrow portion of the frequencies.

non-return-to-zero (NRZ) — A binary signaling technique that increases the voltage to represent a 1 bit, but provides no voltage for a 0 bit.

oscillating signal — A wave that illustrates the change in a carrier signal.

phase modulation (PM) — A change in the starting point of a cycle.

phase shift keying (PSK) — A binary modulation technique that changes the starting point of the cycle.

polar non-return-to-zero (Polar NRZ) — A binary signaling technique that increases the voltage to represent a 1 bit, but drops to negative voltage to represent a 0 bit.

quadbit — A signal that represents four bits.

quadrature amplitude modulation (QAM) — A combination of phase modulation with amplitude modulation to produce 16 different signals.

radio wave (radiotelephony) — An electromagnetic wave created when an electric current passes through a wire and creates a magnetic field in the space around the wire.

return-to-zero (RZ) — A binary signaling technique that increases the voltage to represent a 1 bit, but the voltage is reduced to zero before the end of the period for transmitting the 1 bit, and there is no voltage for a 0 bit.

sine wave — A wave that illustrates the change in a carrier signal.

spread spectrum transmission — A technique that takes a narrow signal and spreads it over a broader portion of the radio frequency band.

tribit — A signal that represents three bits.

voltage — Electrical pressure.

REVIEW QUESTIONS

1. The Base 10 number system is also known as ________________.
   a. octal
   b. decimal
   c. binary
   d. hexadecimal
2. With the Base 10 number system, the base number 10 is increased by ________________ power(s) as you move from one column to the next (right to left).
   a. one
   b. two
   c. three
   d. ten
3. The only digits used to represent a number in binary are the digits ________________.
   a. 1–10
   b. 2, 4, 6, and 8

c. 1, 2, 4, 6, and 8
d. 0 and 1

4. The reason computers and electronic transmission equipment use binary is:
   a. They are electrical devices and electricity has two states.
   b. Base 2 is too difficult to use.
   c. Base 10 was developed before binary.
   d. Binary is the next step above quadecimal.
5. Eight binary digits grouped together form a ________________.
   a. byte
   b. bit
   c. binary
   d. 2x quad
6. The arbitrary coding schemes for the numbers from 0 to 255 is called the American Standard Code for Information Interchange (ASCII). True or false?
7. Letters of the alphabet and symbols are stored based on the ASCII code, but not numbers. True or false?
8. Infrared light, although invisible, has many of the same characteristics as visible light. True or false?
9. Infrared wireless systems require that each device needs to have only one component: either an emitter that transmits a signal, or a detector that receives the signal. True or false?
10. Infrared wireless systems send data by the intensity of the light wave instead of "on-off" signals of light. True or false?
11. Infrared wireless transmission can be either directed or ________________.
12. Radiotelephony or radio travels in waves known as ________________ waves.
13. Unlike a digital signal, a(n) ________________ signal is a continuous signal with no "breaks" in it.
14. Changing a signal is known as ________________.
15. The changing event that creates the different radio frequencies is a(n) ________________.
16. Explain how a radio antenna works when transmitting a signal.
17. Explain the difference between bps, baud, and baud rate.
18. Explain the difference between amplitude modulation, frequency modulation, and phase modulation.
19. What is quadrature amplitude modulation (QAM) and how does it work?
20. List and describe the three different types of binary signaling techniques.

HANDS-ON PROJECTS

1. Locate an ASCII chart on the Internet or in a book. Using the letters of your first and last name, look up the ASCII value for each of these letters. The values will range from 65 to 122. Note that there is a difference between uppercase and lowercase letters. After having determined the ASCII value, convert each value to binary code. Because all ASCII values are between 0-255, the number of bits needed to represent any ASCII code is eight. The binary equivalents are:

27	26	25	24	23	22	21	20
(128)	(64)	(32)	(16)	(8)	(4)	(2)	(1)

   For example, the name "Li Smith" contains the ASCII value of uppercase "L," which is 76, and the binary equivalent of "L" is 010001100.
2. Telephone dial-up modems are fading in popularity among home computer users, and digital subscriber line (DSL) modems are becoming the transmission method of choice. Using the Internet, research DSL. Explain how each type of connectivity works (*Hint*: different frequencies over a telephone line). How can a telephone line be used when a DSL connection is active but cannot be used when a standard data dial-up modem is being used? Determine the top speeds for cable broadband and ADSL and DSL G.lite. What are the advantages and disadvantages of each?
3. TV remote controls were some of the first devices to use infrared signals generated by light-emitting diodes. However, TV remote controls date back to 1950 when Zenith introduced the first remote control, the Lazy Bones. Using the Internet and printed sources, trace the development of the TV remote control as one of the pioneers of infrared technology. Explain how other technologies, such as radio frequency and ultrasonics, were proposed but rejected. What are the capabilities and limitations of today's infrared remotes?
4. Using the information obtained from Hands-on Project 1, take the first letter of your first name in binary and draw a sine wave of how it would appear in each of the following modulations:
   - Amplitude modulation (AM)
   - Frequency modulation (FM)
   - Phase modulation (PM)
5. Amplitude modulation (AM), frequency modulation (FM), and phase modulation (PM) all have strengths and weaknesses. Research these three types of modulations and develop a chart indicating the advantages, disadvantages, and how each modulation is currently being used. Also, include a list of at least two devices that use the technology.

Case Project

The Baypoint Group (TBG), a company of 50 consultants who assist organizations and businesses with issues involving network planning and design, has again hired you as a consultant. One of their oldest clients, Woodruff Medical Group, needs your help.

Woodruff Medical has been approached by a vendor who is trying to sell them an infrared wireless local area network for their office. Although none of the networking equipment will be around any sensitive medical equipment, the vendor has convinced the office manager that "stray infrared signals" could "leak out" of the third-floor office area into the x-ray lab on the ground floor.

1. Prepare a PowerPoint presentation outlining how infrared and radio wireless transmissions work. This will be presented to the office manager and the local area network manager, one of whom is not technically inclined while the other individual has a strong technology background. Be sure to list the advantages and disadvantages of both. The presentation should contain at least 12 slides.
2. After listening to your presentation, the office manager has several questions. One of the questions involves wireless transmission speeds. The office manager has a "good 14,400 baud" dial-up data modem at home and wants to know how its transmission speed compares with that of an infrared WLAN. He also says that baud and bps are the same, because when his Windows 3.11 computer asks for information about his modem it wants him to enter the baud rate. This time the office manager wants a written report instead of a presentation. Write a one-page summary regarding different transmission speeds. Be sure to include information about the difference between bps, baud, baud rate, and bandwidth. Also, show how bps is not always identical to baud.

Optional Team Case Project

A local community college has contacted The Baypoint Group for information about modulation for a networking class, and TBG has passed this request on to you. Form a team of two or three consultants and research AM, FM, PM, ASK, FSK, and PSK. Specifically pay attention to how they are used as well as their strengths and weaknesses. Provide an opinion regarding which technology will become the dominant player in the future of wireless.

CHAPTER

3

UNDERSTANDING RADIO FREQUENCY COMMUNICATIONS

After reading this chapter and completing the exercises you will be able to:

- List the components of a radio system
- Describe how different factors affect the design of a radio system
- Tell why standards are beneficial and list the major telecommunications standards organizations
- Explain the radio frequency spectrum

Radio frequency (RF) communications is the most common type of wireless communications. Unlike light-based communications, such as infrared, RF communications can travel long distances and are not always impeded by surrounding objects. Radio communications is also a mature technology, with the first radio transmission taking place over 100 years ago. (To learn more about the history of wireless communications, see the Appendix of this book.)

RF communications can also be very complicated. This chapter attempts to "demystify" RF communications. The first part of the chapter explores the different components that are necessary for radio frequency communications. Then we look at the issues regarding the design and performance of an RF system, concluding the chapter by exploring the national and international organizations that create and enforce radio frequency standards, along with an examination of the radio frequency spectrum.

COMPONENTS OF A RADIO SYSTEM

Several components are essential for communicating using RF. These components are common to all radio systems, even though the function and purpose of the radio systems may vary. These components include filters, mixers, amplifiers, and antennas.

Filter

A **filter** is a component that is used to either accept or block a radio frequency signal, much like an oil filter on a car engine that will block large contaminants from reaching the engine but allow the oil itself to pass through. A radio filter will either pass or reject a signal based on its frequency. The block diagram symbol for a filter is illustrated in Figure 3-1.

The block diagram symbols are universal and are commonly used to illustrate radio frequency as well as microwave components.

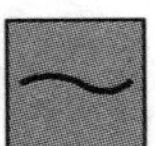

Figure 3-1 Filter symbol

There are three types of RF filters. The first is a **low-pass filter**. With a low-pass filter a maximum frequency threshold is set. All signals below that maximum threshold are allowed to pass through, as seen in Figure 3-2.

Figure 3-2 Low-pass filter

The second type of filter is a **high-pass filter**. Instead of setting a maximum frequency threshold level, as with a low-pass filter, a minimum frequency threshold is set with a high-pass filter. All signals that are above the minimum threshold are allowed to pass through, while those below the minimum threshold are blocked. This is illustrated in Figure 3-3.

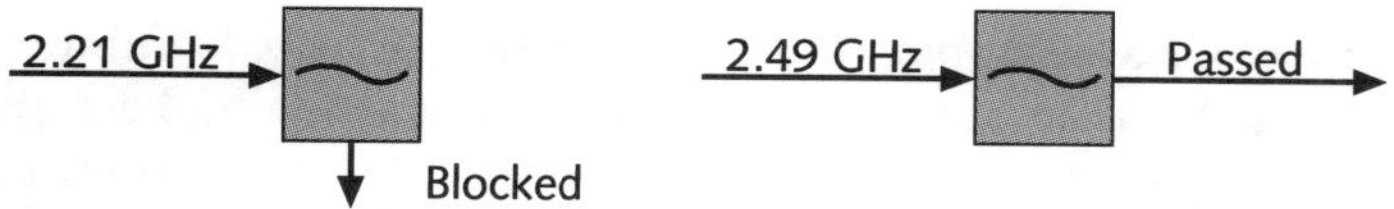

Figure 3-3 High-pass filter

A **bandpass** filter is the third type of RF filter. Instead of setting either a minimum or maximum frequency threshold, a bandpass filter sets a **passband**, which is both a minimum and maximum threshold. Signals that fall within the passband are allowed through the bandpass filter. This is seen in Figure 3-4.

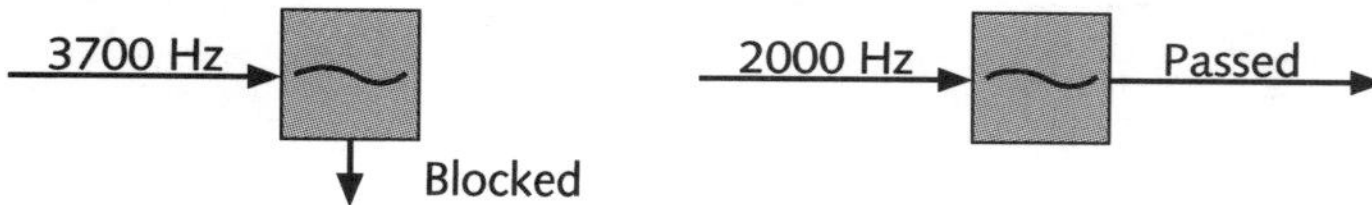

Figure 3-4 Bandpass filter

The function of a filter can be seen in Figure 3-5, which is a functional block diagram of a radio transmitter. The input data is what needs to be sent, and may be in the form of audio, video, or data. The transmitter takes the input data and modulates the signal (through analog modulation or digital modulation) by changing the amplitude, frequency, or phase of the sine wave (review Chapter 2, if necessary, to refresh your memory on RF signal modulation). The resulting output from the modulation process is known as the **intermediate frequency (IF)** signal. This IF signal is between 10 MHz and 100 MHz. The IF signal is then filtered through a bandpass filter to remove any undesired high or low frequency signals. In this example, the output from the modulator was 8 MHz to 112 MHz. This signal was then put through a filter to produce a signal of 10 MHz to 100 MHz.

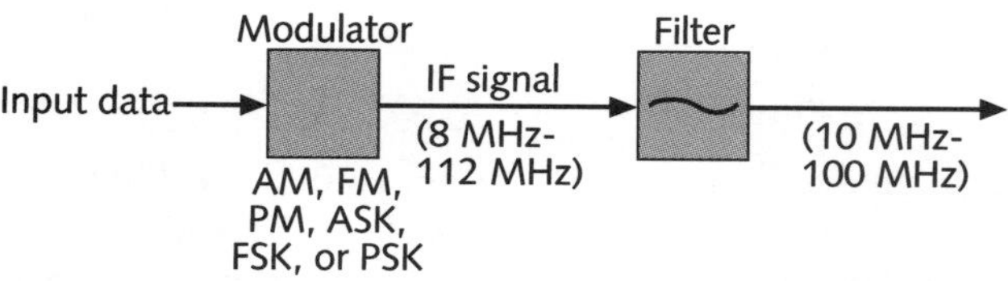

Figure 3-5 Filter function in a radio transmitter

Mixer

The purpose of a **mixer**, whose symbol is seen in Figure 3-6, is to combine two radio frequency inputs to create a single output. The single output is the highest sum and the lowest difference of the frequencies. In Figure 3-7, the input signal is 300 Hz to 3400 Hz and the frequency mixed in is 20,000 Hz.

Figure 3-6 Mixer symbol

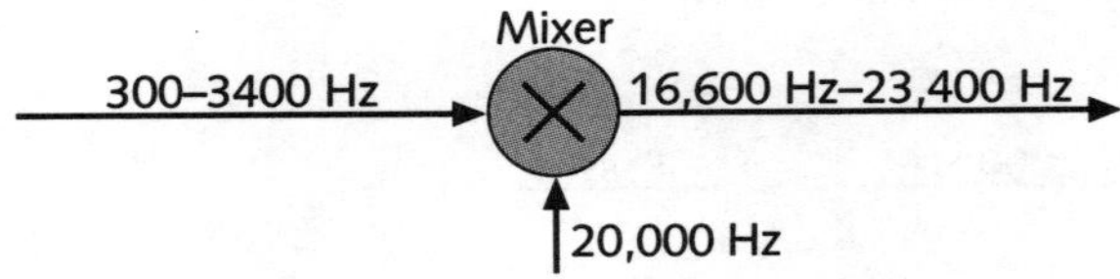

Figure 3-7 Mixer output

The mixer adds the input frequencies to the mixed-in frequency to produce the sums:

20,000 Hz	20,000 Hz
+ 300 Hz	+3,400 Hz
20,300 Hz	23,400 Hz

In this example, 23,400 Hz is the highest sum. The mixer also determines the lowest difference between the input frequencies and the mixed-in frequency, for example:

20,000 Hz	20,000 Hz
- 300 Hz	-3,400 Hz
19,700 Hz	16,600 Hz

In this example, the lowest difference frequency would be 16,600 Hz. Therefore, the output from the mixer would be a frequency from 16,600 Hz to 23,400 Hz. The sum and the differences are known as the **sidebands** of the frequency carrier. These serve as buffer spaces around the frequency of the transmitted signal to shield it from "stray" signals that may invade the frequency. One way to illustrate this is by considering AM radio signals. AM broadcast radio is confined to a frequency range of 535 KHz to 1605 KHz. In an AM broadcast radio signal, the sidebands are typically 7.5 KHz wide, so a radio station on the AM dial requires about 15 KHz of bandwidth. This is illustrated in Figure 3-8.

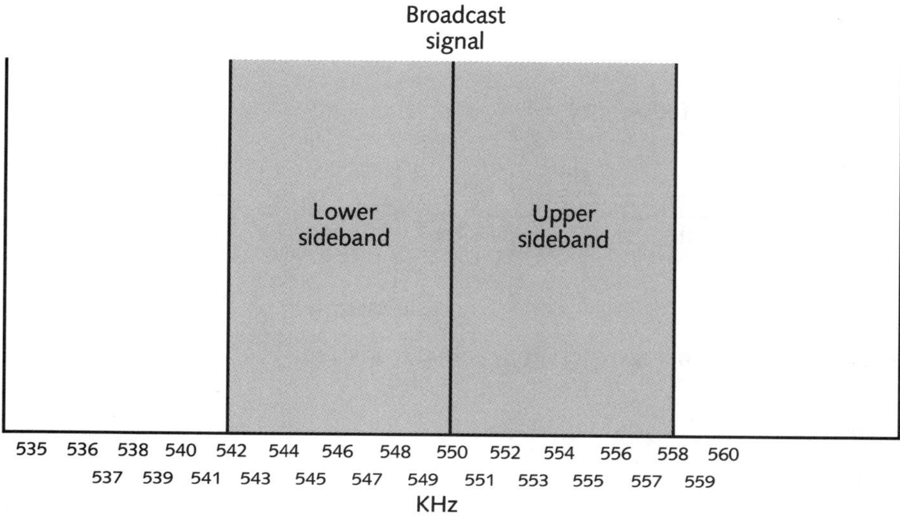

Figure 3-8 AM radio sidebands

Mixers are used to convert an input frequency to a desired output frequency. Figure 3-9 illustrates how a mixer functions in a radio transmitter. The transmitter takes the input data and modulates the signal to produce an IF signal. In this example, the output from the modulator was 8 MHz to 112 MHz. This signal was then put through a bandpass filter to produce the desired IF signal of 10 MHz to 100 MHz. This IF signal then becomes the input to the mixer along with the desired frequency of 800 MHz. This creates a signal with a frequency of 700 MHz to 900MHz. This output is then typically run through another bandpass filter to remove any stray frequencies.

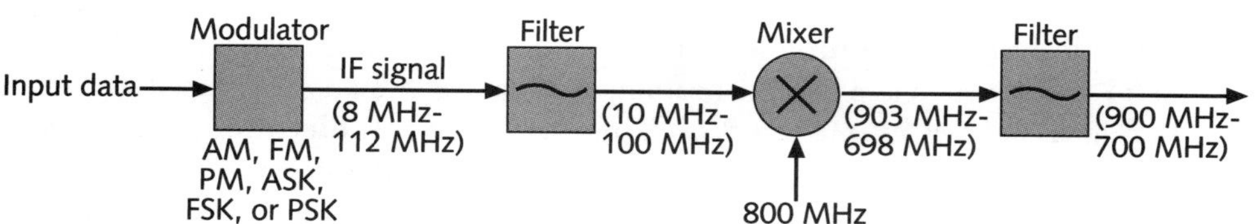

Figure 3-9 Mixer function in a radio transmitter

Amplifier

An **amplifier** increases a signal's intensity or strength. The symbol for an amplifier is seen in Figure 3-10. Amplifiers are critical in radio wireless receivers and transmitters. In the radio transmitter illustration in Figure 3-11, the amplifier boosts the power of the signal received from the filter before it is transmitted.

Figure 3-10 Amplifier symbol

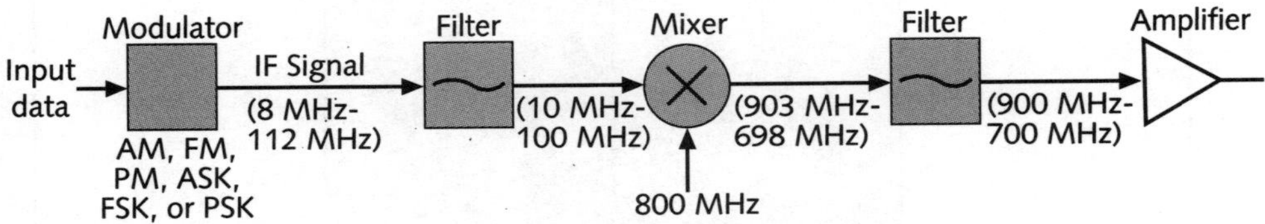

Figure 3-11 Amplifier function in a radio transmitter

Antenna

You will recall that the purpose of an antenna in a radio transmitter is to convert a signal generated by a transmitter into an electromagnetic wave and send that wave into space. An antenna is used on a receiver to pick up as much of that signal as possible. When transmitting, the transmitter forces electrical energy into the antenna wire and pushes it back and forth, creating an electrical pressure (voltage) along the wire. The voltage causes a back and forth movement of the electricity in the antenna at the same frequency as the radio waves. This creates a magnetic field that surrounds the antenna. As that magnetic field radiates out, it will travel through space and strike the receiving antenna. When it does, the magnetic field creates the same electrical pressure on the receiving antenna. Thus the signal is sent through space.

There are different types of antennas, depending upon the desired spread of the signal being transmitted. A television or radio station, as well as cellular telephones, want the signal to spread out over the landscape, reaching as many viewers and listeners as possible. An **omnidirectional antenna** sends out the signal in a uniform pattern in all directions. Other radio systems, such as a satellite beaming a signal back to an earth-based station, require that the signal radiates in one direction. These are known as **directional antennas**. The **gain** of an antenna is the measure of the directional intensity of an antenna pattern. An omnidirectional antenna has a low gain, while a directional antenna has a high gain. This is illustrated in Figure 3-12.

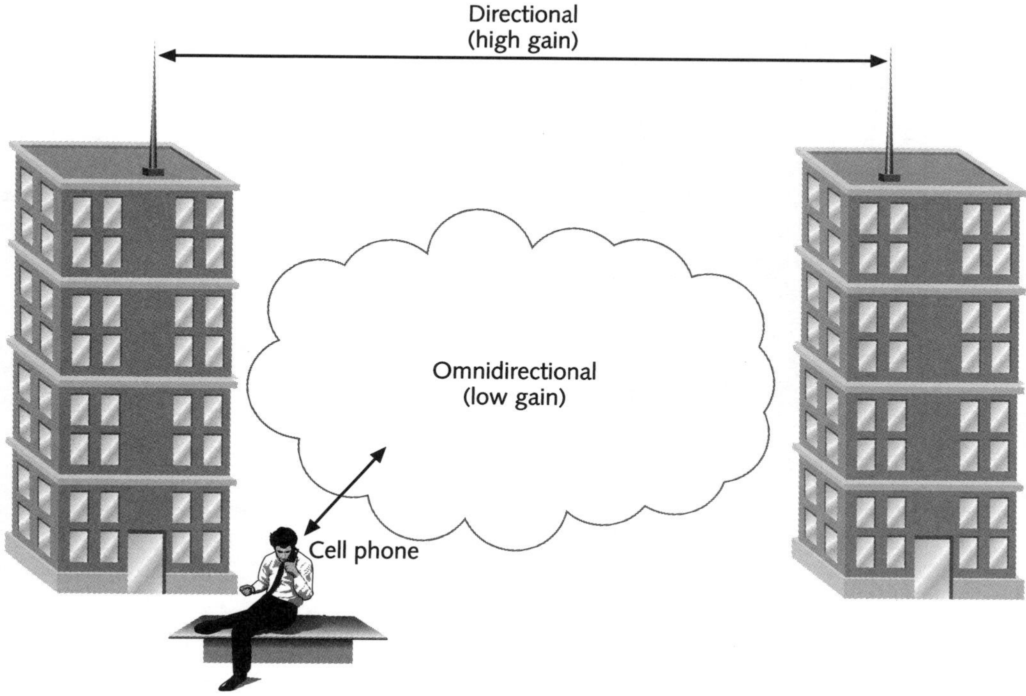

Figure 3-12 Antenna gains

The size of an antenna depends upon two main factors. The first is the frequency of the RF signal. Antennas that receive a low frequency signal need to be larger in diameter than an antenna that receives a higher frequency because of the wavelength. The second factor is the gain. A high-gain antenna needs to be larger than a low-gain antenna. For example, a hand-held global positioning system (GPS) device requires an antenna that is only several inches square and can be built into the device. Its small size is due to the fact that the signal it receives is a low-gain signal at a high frequency. Figure 3-13 illustrates a large-diameter antenna.

The block diagram symbol for an antenna is seen in Figure 3-14. Adding the antenna symbol completes the radio transmitter block diagram, which is illustrated in Figure 3-15.

A radio receiver uses all the same components as a radio transmitter but in reverse order. Figure 3-16 is a functional diagram of a radio receiver. The antenna receives the electromagnetic waves that are then sent to the filter, which eliminates the unwanted high and low frequencies but passes on the desired frequencies. The amplifier then boosts the weak signal that was received by the antenna. Next the mixer converts the RF signal that was received down to a lower frequency (the IF). The IF signal is then passed on to another filter and then is amplified before the demodulator extracts the output data from the signal. Table 3-1 lists these major components of a radio and illustrates the block diagram figures.

Figure 3-13 Large diameter antenna

Figure 3-14 Antenna symbol

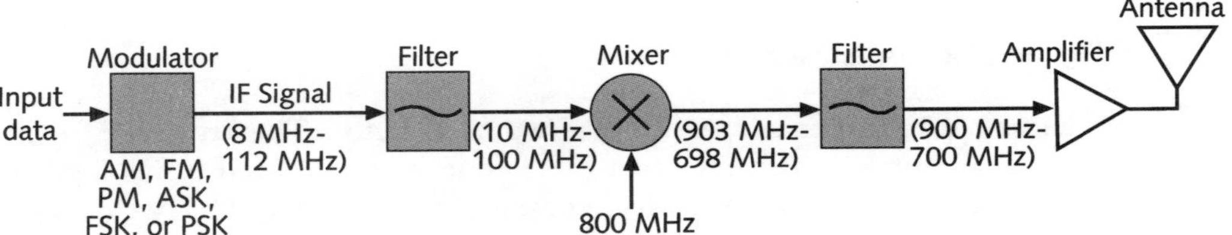

Figure 3-15 Antenna function in a radio transmitter

Table 3-1 Radio components and their symbols

Component Name	Function	Block Diagram Symbol
Filter	Accept or block RF signal	
Mixer	Combine two radio frequency inputs to create a single output	
Amplifier	Boost signal strength	
Antenna	Send or receive electromagnetic wave	

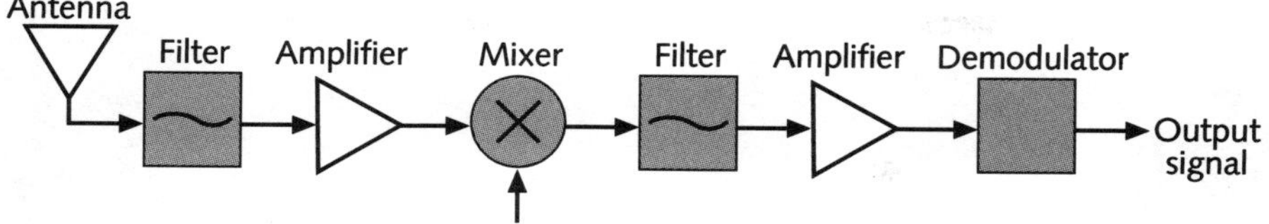

Figure 3-16 Radio receiver functions

The IF signal from the mixer in a radio receiver is about 100 MHz.

Design of a Radio System

Although filters, mixers, amplifiers, and antennas are all necessary components for a radio system, the list does not stop there. There are other design considerations that must be taken into account when creating a radio system, including multiple access, transmission direction, switching, and signal strength.

Multiple Access

The number of radio frequencies is not unlimited. Because there are only a limited number of frequencies available, conserving the use of frequencies is important. One way to conserve is by sharing a frequency among several individual users. Instead of giving each user his or her own frequency, it is possible to "divide" one frequency among multiple users, which reduces the number of frequencies needed. This is illustrated in Figure 3-17.

Multiple access has been used for several years with large computer systems to share a single communications line in order to reduce transmission costs. A device receives the signals from several difference sources, combines them into one signal, and transmits that signal over a single communications line.

There are several methods that allow multiple access, the most significant of which in terms of wireless communications are Frequency Division Multiple Access (FDMA), Time Division Multiple Access (TDMA), and Code Division Multiple Access (CDMA).

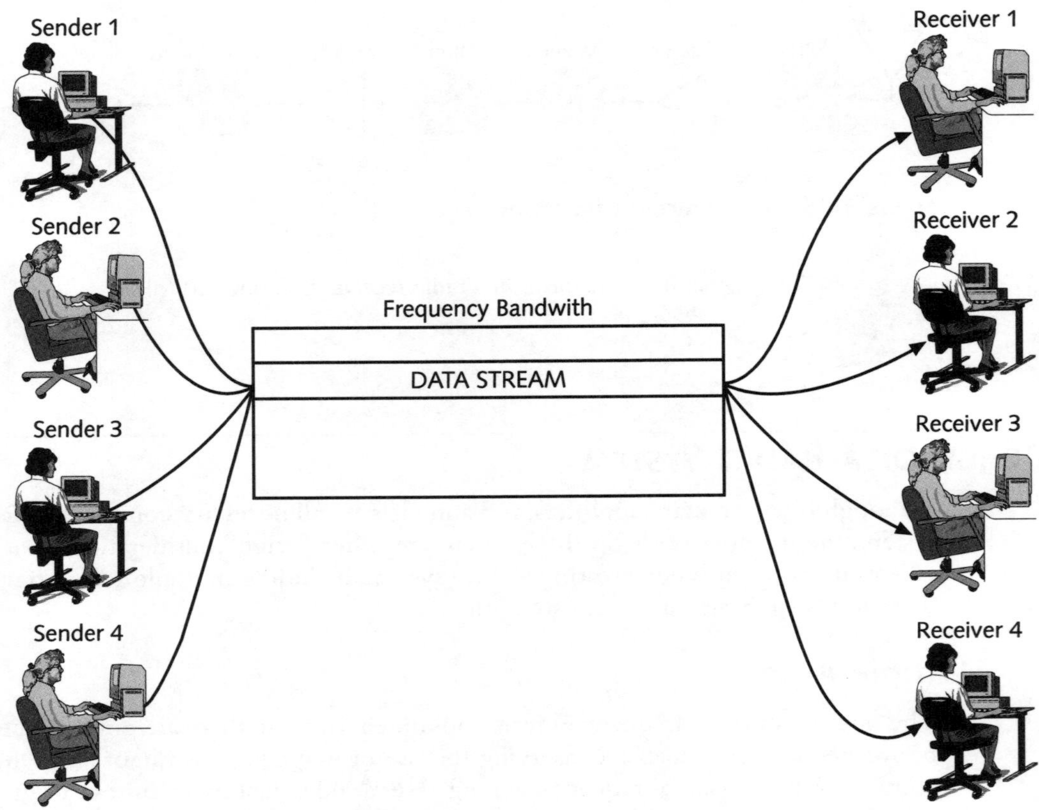

Figure 3-17 Multiple access

Frequency Division Multiple Access (FDMA)

Frequency Division Multiple Access (FDMA) divides the bandwidth of the frequency into several smaller frequencies. For example, a transmission band with a 50,000 Hz bandwidth can be divided into 1,000 channels, each with a bandwidth of 50 Hz. Each channel is dedicated to one specific user. This is illustrated in Figure 3-18. FDMA is most often used with analog transmissions.

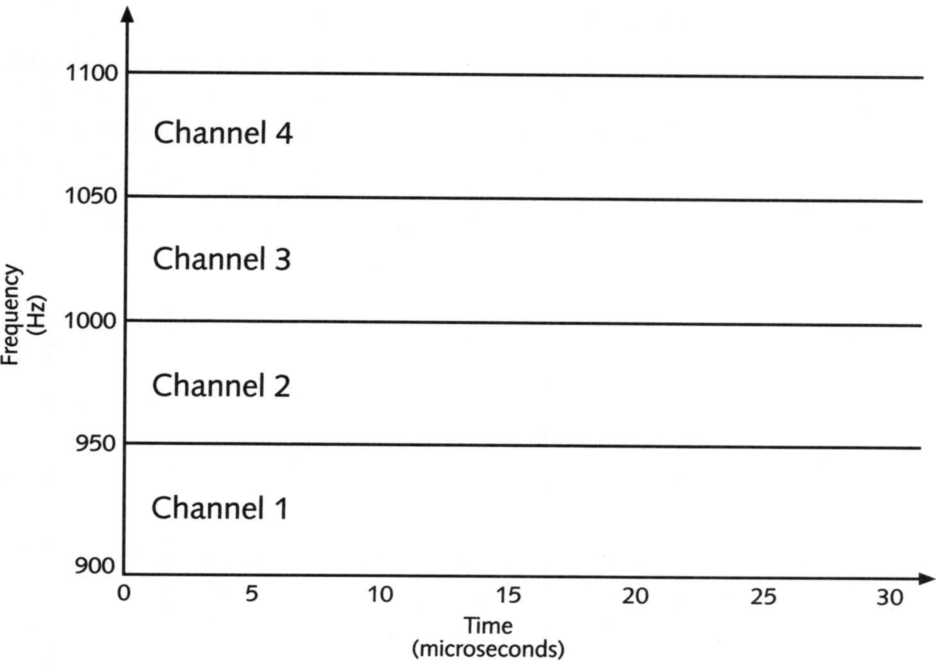

Figure 3-18 Frequency Division Multiple Access (FDMA)

Cable television is transmitted using FDMA over coaxial cable. Each analog television signal uses 6 MHz of the 500 MHz cable.

FDMA can be likened to a room full of 20 people with 10 one-on-one conversations taking place. In order for everyone to talk at the same time and be able to hear their partner speaking, one pair of individuals speaks at a regular volume, while the next pair speaks a little louder, and the next pair speaks louder still, until the final pair of conversationalists are screaming at each other at the top of their lungs. All of the conversations are going on simultaneously but at different levels of volume. This is similar to FDMA, where all of the transmissions are taking place at the same time but at different frequencies.

FDMA does, however, have some drawbacks. One is that when signals are sent at frequencies that are closely grouped, an errant signal may encroach on its neighbor's frequency. This phenomenon, known as **crosstalk**, causes interference on the other frequency and may disrupt the transmission.

Time Division Multiple Access (TDMA)

To overcome the problem of crosstalk, **Time Division Multiple Access (TDMA)** was developed. Whereas FDMA divides the bandwidth into several frequencies, TDMA divides the bandwidth into several time slots. Each user is assigned the entire frequency for the transmission for a fraction of time on a fixed, rotating basis. Because the duration of the transmissions is so short, the delays that occur while others use the frequency are not noticeable. Figure 3-19 illustrates TDMA. TDMA is most often used with digital transmissions.

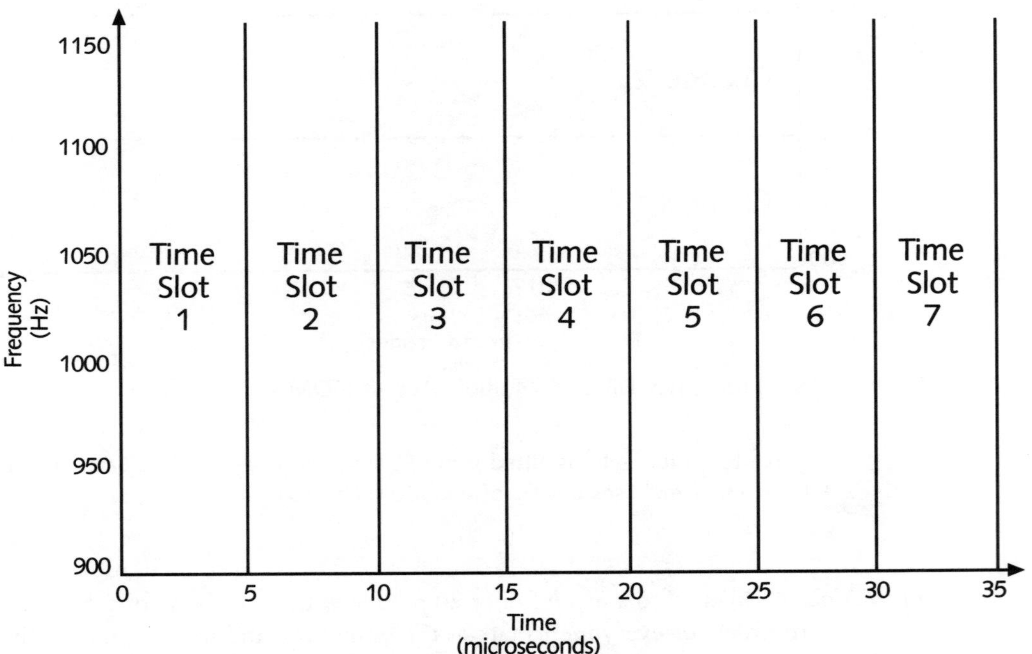

Figure 3-19 Time Division Multiple Access (TDMA)

If a user has no data to transmit during his or her assigned time slot with TDMA, the frequency remains idle.

Consider again the room of 20 people with 10 one-on-one conversations taking place. Instead of all the conversations taking place simultaneously and at different levels of volume (FDMA), this time the first pair speaks one sentence to each other at normal volume and then stops. Then the next pair speaks a sentence and stops. This continues until all 10 pairs of conversationalists have spoken one sentence, at which time the first pair will speak their second sentence and then wait. With TDMA, all of the transmissions are taking place at the same frequency but one at a time.

TDMA has several advantages over FDMA. TDMA uses the bandwidth more efficiently. Studies indicate that when using a 25 MHz bandwidth, TDMA can achieve over 20 times the capacity of FDMA. Also, TDMA allows both data and voice transmissions to be mixed using the same frequency.

Code Division Multiple Access (CDMA)

Code Division Multiple Access (CDMA) is unlike TDMA or FDMA. CDMA uses spread spectrum technology, which spreads the transmission over a larger range of frequency. CDMA also uses unique digital codes, rather than separate RF frequencies or channels, to differentiate between the different transmissions. A CDMA transmission is spread across the frequency and the digital codes are applied to the individual transmissions. When the signal is received, the codes are removed from the signal.

Think again about the room full of 20 people trying to have 10 simultaneous conversations. Suppose that each couple talks at the same time but they all use a different language. Because none of the listeners understand any language other than that of the individual with whom they are speaking, the other nine conversations don't bother them. CDMA is similar to this. With CDMA, each transmission has a unique code that separates it from all other transmissions. This is illustrated in Figure 3-20.

There are several advantages to CDMA. CDMA transmissions are much harder to eavesdrop on, since a listener would have difficulty picking out one conversation spread across the entire spectrum. Also, CDMA can carry up to three times the amount of data as TDMA.

Transmission Direction

The direction in which data travels on a wireless network is important. The flow must be controlled so that the sending and receiving devices know when data will arrive or when it needs to be transmitted. There are three types of data flow: simplex, half-duplex, and full-duplex.

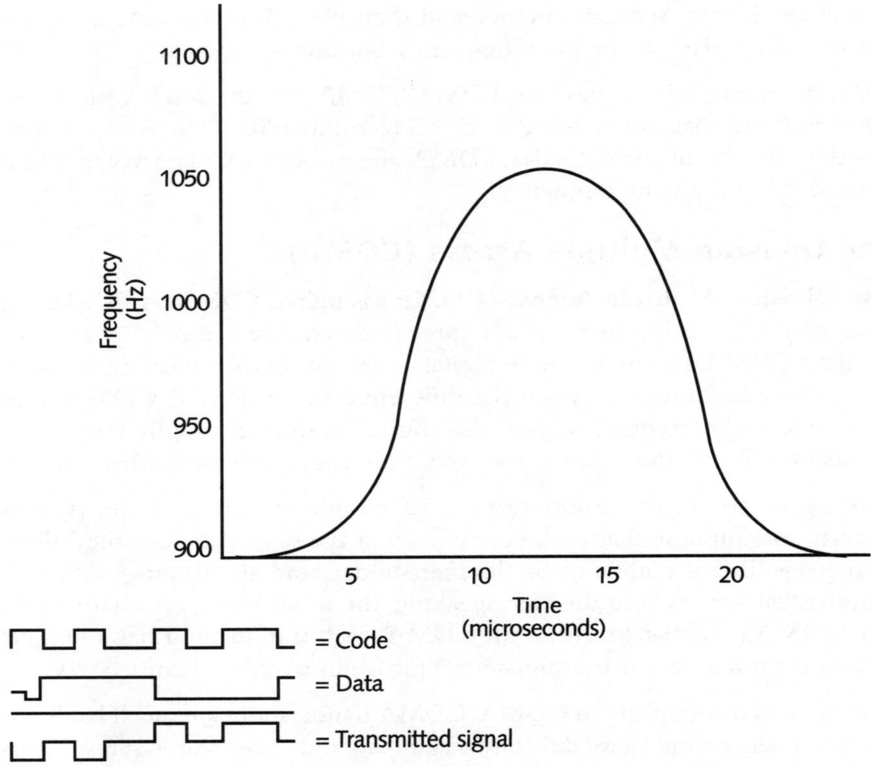

Figure 3-20 Code Division Multiple Access (CDMA)

Simplex transmission occurs in only one direction, from device 1 to device 2, as seen in Figure 3-21. A broadcast radio station is an example of simplex transmission: the signal goes from the radio transmitter to the user's radio, but the user has no means by which to send back information. Simplex is rarely used in wireless communication today except for broadcast radio and television. The reason is that the receiver is unable to give the sender any feedback regarding the transmission, such as if it was received correctly, or if it needs to be resent. Reliable transmission is almost impossible without this type of information.

Figure 3-21 Simplex transmission

Half-duplex transmission sends data in both directions, but only one way at a time, as seen in Figure 3-22. Half-duplex transmission is used in consumer devices such as citizens band (CB) radios or walkie-talkies. In order for User A to transmit a message to User B, he must hold down the "talk" button while speaking. While the button is being pressed, User B can only listen and not talk. User A must release the "talk" button before User B can press his "talk" button. Both parties can send and receive information, but only one at a time.

Figure 3-22 Half-duplex transmission

If a single antenna is used for wireless transmission and reception, a filter can be used to handle half-duplex transmissions. Because sending and receiving are conducted on separate frequencies, a transmission on the receive frequency will be filtered to the receiver, while the transmission on the send frequency will be passed on to the antenna. This is illustrated in Figure 3-23.

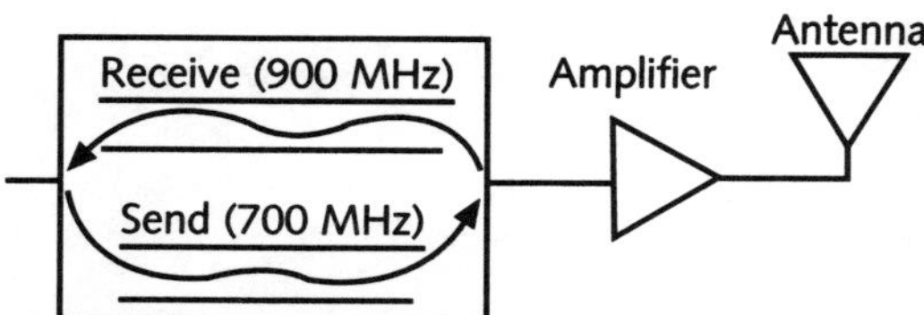

Figure 3-23 Single antenna for half-duplex transmission

Full-duplex transmissions enable data to flow in either direction simultaneously, as seen in Figure 3-24. A telephone system is an example of a type of full-duplex transmission. Most modern wireless systems like cellular telephones use full-duplex transmission.

Figure 3-24 Full-duplex transmission

Switching

The concept of **switching** is essential to all types of telecommunications, wireless as well as wired. Switching involves moving the signal from one wire or frequency to another. Consider for a moment the telephone in your home. You can use that one telephone to call a friend across the street, a classmate in another town, a store in a distant state—or anyone else around the world who also has a phone. How can one single telephone be used to call all other telephones on the earth? This is accomplished through a switch at the telephone company's central office. The signal from your phone goes out your telephone's wire and is then switched or moved to the wire of the telephone that belongs to your friend across the street. This is illustrated in Figure 3-25.

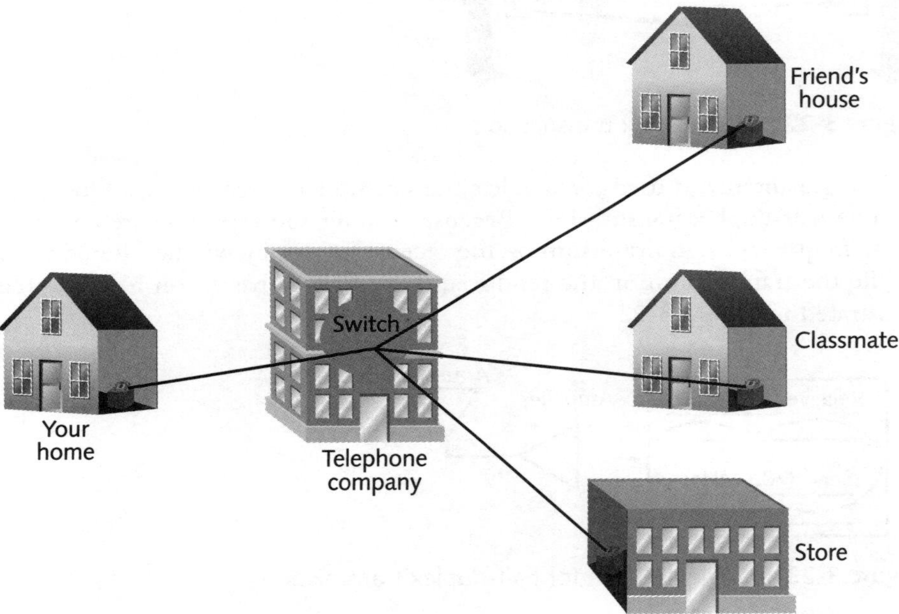

Figure 3-25 Telephone switch

The first telephone switches were not automatic. The switching was done manually on switchboards by switchboard operators. Today the telephone system is officially known as the Public Switched Telephone Network (PSTN).

Switching is also essential for modern local area network transmissions. Signals from the sending computer are sent down the wire to a switch that moves the signal from the sending computer's wire over to the wire of the receiving computer. Without a switch, each computer would have to be directly connected to all other computers in the network. This is seen in Figure 3-26.

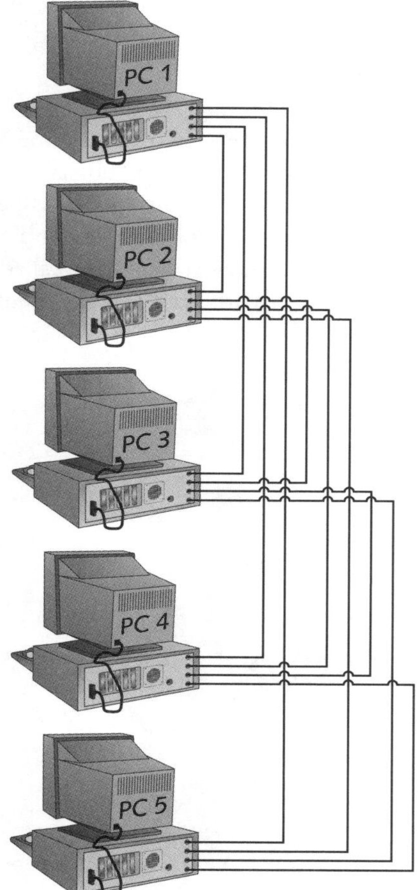

Figure 3-26 LAN without a switch

A wired computer network of 500 computers not using a switch would require 249,500 cables to connect all of the computers.

Although telephone systems and local area networks both use switching, the type of switching that they use is not identical. This is because of how the voice or data is transmitted. Telephone systems use a type of switching known as **circuit switching**. When a telephone call is made, a dedicated and direct physical connection is made between the caller and the recipient of the call through the switch. While the telephone conversation is taking place, the connection remains open between only these two users. No other calls can be made from that phone while the first conversation is going on, and anyone who calls that phone will receive a busy signal. This direct connection lasts until the end of the call, at which time the switch drops the connection.

Circuit switching is used for both wired and cellular wireless telephone systems.

Circuit switching is ideal for voice communications. However, circuit switching is not efficient for transmitting data. This is because data transmissions occur in "bursts" with periods of delay in between. The delay would result in time wasted while nothing was being transmitted. Instead of using circuit switching, data networks use **packet switching**. Packet switching requires that the data transmission be broken into smaller units called **packets**. Each packet is then sent independently through the network to reach the destination, as shown in Figure 3-27.

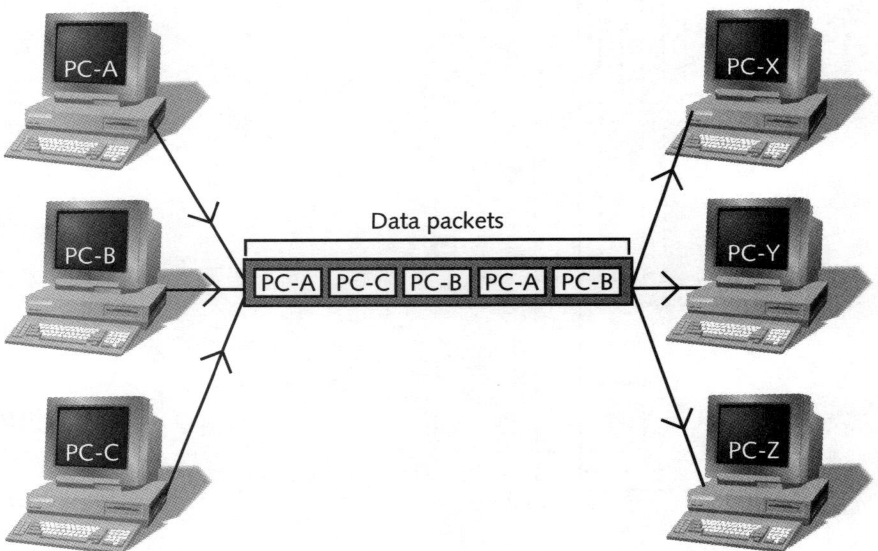

Figure 3-27 Packet switching

Packet switching has several advantages for data transmissions. First, it allows better utilization of the network. Circuit switching ties up the communications line until the transmission is complete, whereas packet switching allows multiple computers to share the same line or frequency. That's because packets from several different computers can be intermingled together while being sent. It is not necessary for the packets to arrive in the correct sequence; the receiving device accumulates packets and re-assembles them in the correct order based on the packet number. This is illustrated in Figure 3-27. A second advantage regards error correction. If there is a transmission error it will only affect one small packet. Only that packet and not the entire document would have to be re-sent.

Signal Strength

It is much more complicated to manage the strength of the signal in a wireless system than in a wired network. Because the signal is not confined to a pair of wires in an office building but may be transmitted in the open air space across town, many more types of interference can wreak havoc with a wireless signal. In addition, many types of objects, both stationary and moving, can impact the signal. The challenge is to design a radio system in which the signal strength is sufficient to reach its destination with the necessary signal.

Airlines require passengers to shut off all electronic devices such as cellular telephones and notebook computers prior to takeoff. This is a precaution to ensure that electrical interference from these devices will not disrupt the airplane's navigational or radio systems, although the possibility of this is only slight.

One factor that affects radio signal strength is **electromagnetic interference (EMI)**, also called **noise**. Consider again the room full of 20 people with 10 one-on-one conversations taking place. If everyone is talking freely then there is a great deal of "racket" or background noise with which to contend. With radio waves, background electromagnetic "noise" can impede a signal. Electromagnetic noise can come from a variety of man-made and natural sources, as seen in Figure 3-28.

The **signal-to-noise ratio (SNR)** refers to the measure of signal strength relative to the background noise. This is seen in Figure 3-29. When signal strength falls below the level of noise, interference can take place. However, when the strength of the signal is high, it is above the noise and has no interference. The amount by which the signal's maximum intensity exceeds its minimum detectable level (or noise) is called the **dynamic range**. Consider again the example of the room full of people trying to carry on a conversation. If someone moves closer to his or her partner so that they can be heard above the background noise, they are trying to achieve a higher SNR.

There are a variety of ways to attempt to reduce the interference of noise and create an acceptable SNR. Boosting the strength of the signal through the use of amplifiers is one common method. Another is through the use of filters. Also, using a technique such as frequency hopping spread spectrum can reduce the impact of noise on a signal.

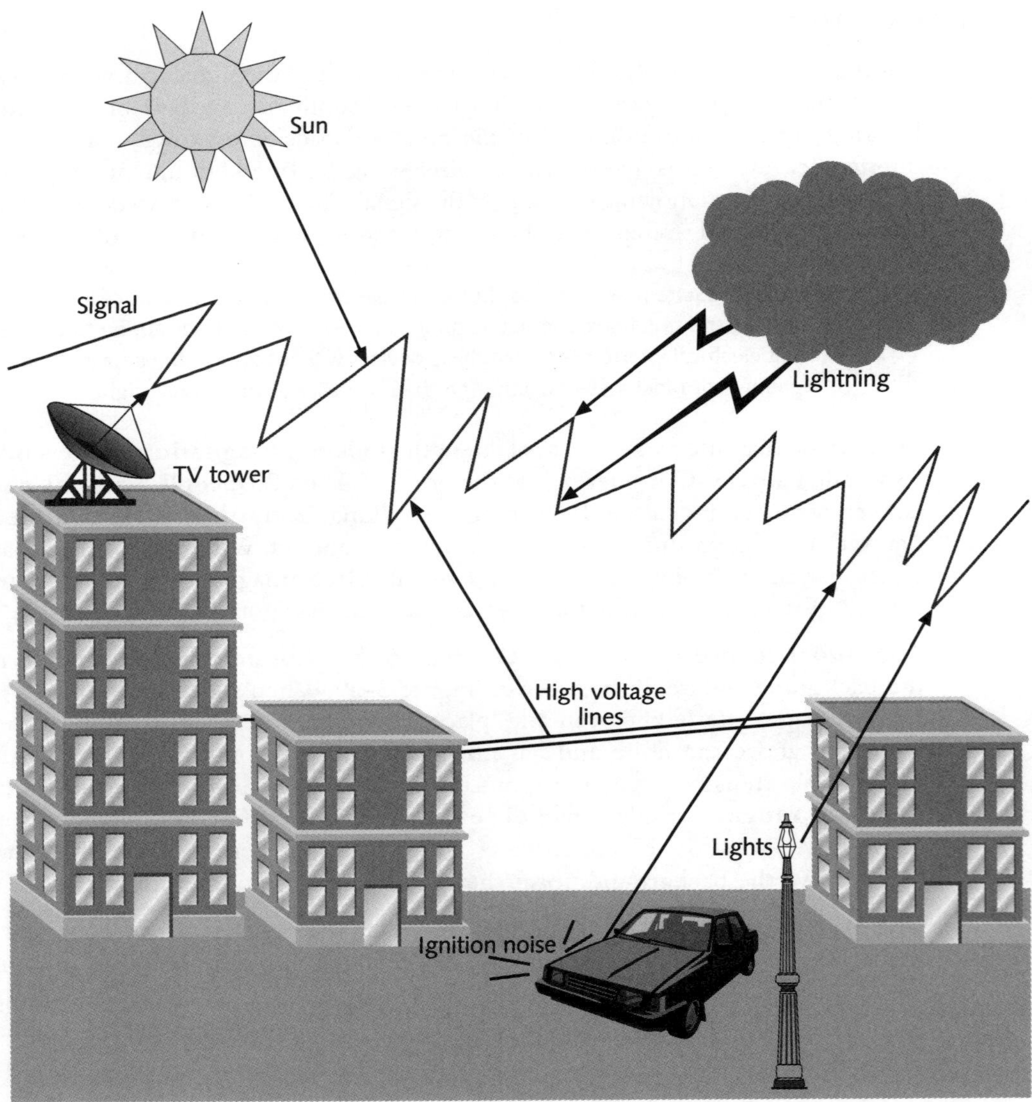

Figure 3-28 Sources of EMI or noise

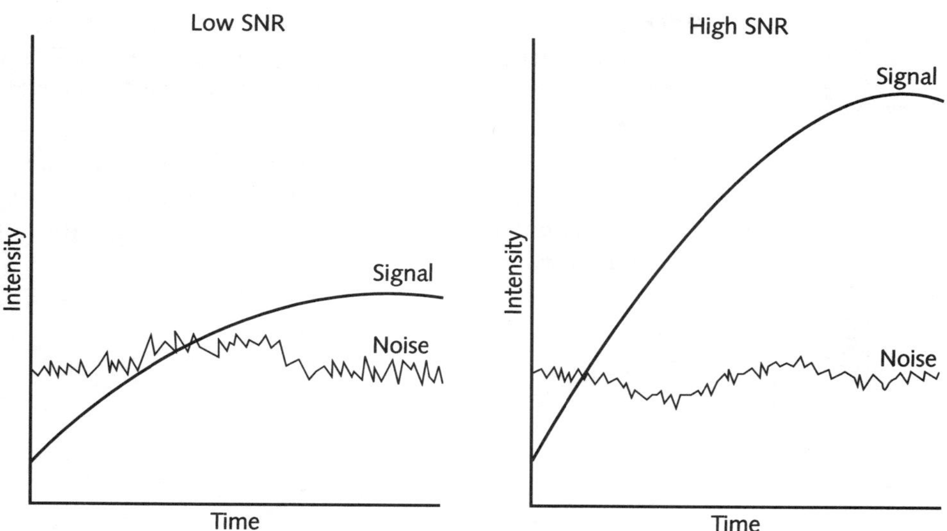

Figure 3-29 SNR

With a highly complex and expensive device, such as a radio telescope, the temperature of the circuits is lowered to –459 degrees Fahrenheit to minimize noise.

A loss of signal strength is known as **attenuation**. Attenuation can be caused by a variety of factors. Objects in the path of the signal generally cause the most attenuation. Man-made objects, such as walls and buildings, can decrease the strength of the signal. Table 3-2 shows examples of different building materials and their effect on radio transmissions. Amplifying a signal both before it is transmitted (to increase the power level) as well as after it is received helps to minimize attenuation.

Table 3-2 Materials and their effect on radio waves

Type of Material	Use in a Building	Impact on Radio Waves
Wood	Office partition	Low
Plaster	Inner walls	Low
Glass	Windows	Low
Bricks	Outer walls	Medium
Concrete	Floors and outer walls	High
Metal	Elevator shafts	Very high

Attenuation can also be caused by precipitation, such as rain or snow, at certain frequencies. Also, attenuation decreases as the altitude increases. This is because there is a decrease in air and water vapor density at higher altitudes.

As a radio signal is transmitted, the electromagnetic waves spread out. Some of these waves may reflect off of surfaces and slow it down. This results in the same signal being received not only from several different directions but also at different times, as seen in Figure 3-30. This is known as **multipath distortion**.

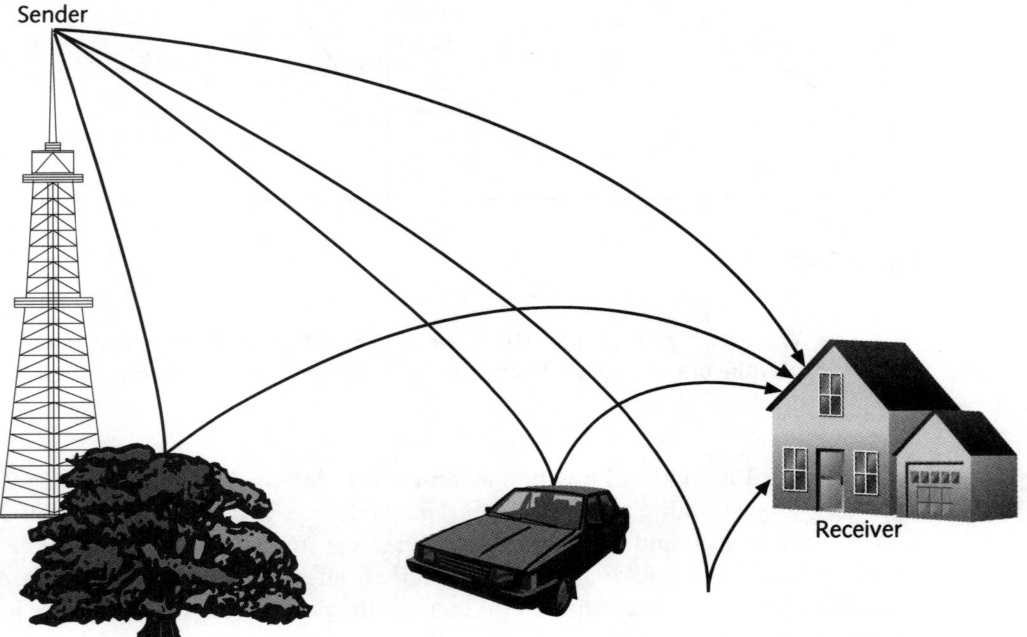

Figure 3-30 Multipath distortion

There are several steps that can be taken to minimize multipath distortion. These include increasing the size of the receiving antenna, inserting an amplifier in front of the receiver, or even transmitting the same signal on separate frequencies.

UNDERSTANDING STANDARDS

Standards for telecommunications have been in place almost since the beginning of the industry. They have played an important role in the rapid growth of communications as well as demonstrating the benefits of standards.

The Need for Standards

The role that standards play in a particular industry varies widely. Mention the word "standards" to someone who works in information technology (IT) and you may receive a strong negative response. This is because some in that industry believe that standards set for computer technologies stifle growth in this fast-paced field. They maintain that waiting for standards to catch up to the rapid changes in IT only slows everything down.

However, unlike IT, standards for telecommunications have been essential since the very beginning. This is because of the very nature of the industry. Telecommunications involves pieces of equipment interacting with other equipment. A lack of standards between devices would result in no communications being able to take place. Telecommunications experts rely totally on standards in order for the industry to function. Telecommunications would essentially be impossible without standards.

Advantages and Disadvantages of Standards

There are several advantages of standards. First, standards ensure that telecommunications devices from one vendor will interoperate with those from other vendors. Devices that are not based on standards may not be able to connect and communicate with similar devices from other vendors. Standards ensure that a device purchased from Vendor A can be seamlessly integrated into a communications network that contains devices from Vendor B.

A second benefit of standards is that it creates competition. If a vendor creates a new device on his own, it is called a **proprietary** device. The vendor owns the specifications and perhaps even a patent on the device. This makes it almost impossible for another manufacturer to produce a similar device. On the other hand, standards are open to everyone. Because they are widely available, any vendor who wants to enter that marketplace can do so. Thus standards can result in competition between vendors. And competition has several advantages.

Competition results in lower costs for consumers. A vendor who has created a proprietary device has no benefit in reducing his prices because he has no competition. Instead, because he has a captive market he may in fact regularly raise the prices at will. However, standards encourage competition between vendors. This is because vendors are all making the same product based on the same standards. In order to gain a larger portion of the market, vendors may reduce their prices below the competition's prices. Thus, the competition between vendors, due to standards, will usually result in lower costs to consumers.

Competition also results in lower costs for manufacturers as well. Because standards have already been established, manufacturers do not have to invest large amounts of capital in research and development. Instead, they can use the standards as a blueprint for their manufacturing. This reduces startup costs as well as the amount of time needed to bring a product to the market. Also, because standards increase the market for products that follow the standard, this encourages manufacturers to deploy mass production techniques and economies of scale in manufacturing and engineering. This keeps the production costs low that in turn are passed on to the consumer.

A third benefit is that standards help protect the investment in equipment. It is not uncommon for a proprietary vendor to phase out a product line of equipment. Businesses that purchased that line are left with two choices. They can continue to support this now-obsolete legacy system into the foreseeable future. However, the costs will dramatically escalate as replacement parts become more difficult to locate and support specialists who are more difficult to find. The second choice businesses have is to throw everything away and buy a new up-to-date system. Both choices are very expensive.

Standards, however, can help create a migration path. The body that is responsible for creating the initial standards will continue to incorporate new technologies into regularly revised standards. Generally these new standards will be backward compatible. This means that standards reduce the risk of "orphan" systems.

There are disadvantages to standards as well. International standards can be a threat to industries in large countries. This is because it opens their domestic markets to overseas competition. Manufacturers in foreign nations may have a lower overhead and be able to produce the device cheaper than manufacturers at home. Standards allow foreign manufacturers to produce and sell their products abroad, often threatening a domestic manufacturer's market share. However, this also means that standards can be a benefit to industries in smaller countries.

Another disadvantage to standards is that although they are intended to create unity, they can have the opposite effect. This is because of the way in which standards are adopted. Sometimes a specific nation will create a standard and offer it for consideration to other nations as a global standard. However, due to opposing political interests, another nation may reject that standard and attempt to create their own. Standardization is not always a technical matter but it is sometimes a political issue. This can result in each nation creating its own standards and decreasing the value of global communications.

Most experts agree that the advantages of standards far outweigh the disadvantages of standards, and are vital to industries such as telecommunications. A summary of the advantages and disadvantages can be seen in Table 3-3.

Table 3-3 Advantages and disadvantages of standards

Advantages	Disadvantages
Ensures that telecommunications devices from one vendor will interoperate with those from other vendors	Can threaten industries in large countries
Creates competition between vendors, which lowers costs for vendors and consumers	Due to political interests they can create national standards between countries
Helps protect the investment in equipment	

Types of Standards

There are two major types of standards in the telecommunications industry: de facto and de jure. A third emerging type of standard, by consortia, is increasingly influencing how standards are set.

De Facto

De facto standards are not really standards at all. Rather, they are common practices that the industry follows for various reasons. The reasons range from ease of use to tradition to what the majority of the users do. For the most part, de facto standards are established by success in the marketplace. For example, most industry experts would agree that Microsoft Windows has become the de facto standard operating system today for personal computers and network servers. This is because the overwhelming majority of users have elected to install and run Windows on their computers. There was no standards body that proclaimed Windows as the standard; the widespread use in the industry has created what amounts to be a standard.

The word *de facto* comes from Latin and means "from the fact."

De Jure

The second major type of standard is known as **de jure standards** (also called **official standards**). De jure standards are those that are controlled by an organization or body that has been entrusted with that task. The process for creating these standards can be very involved. Generally, the organization will develop subcommittees responsible for a specific technology. Within each subcommittee there are working groups, which are teams of industry experts who are given the task to create the initial draft. The draft will then be published, and requests for comments will be solicited from other organization members (these members may be developers, potential users, and other people having general interest in the field). The comments are then reviewed by the original committee and may be incorporated into the final draft. This is then reviewed by the entire organization before the final standards are officially published.

De facto standards sometimes become official standards by being approved by a committee. Ethernet is one example of a de facto standard that later became an official standard.

Consortia

One of the major complaints against de jure standards is the amount of time it takes for a standard to be completed. For example, the initial standard for wireless local area networks took seven years to complete. In the telecommunications and IT industries, this represents an extremely long period of time before products can be brought to the marketplace.

In reaction to this, consortia are often used today to create standards. **Consortia** are usually industry-sponsored organizations that have the goal of promoting a specific technology. Unlike de jure standards bodies, membership in consortia is not open to everyone. Instead, specific high-profile companies both create the consortia as well as serve on it. The goal of the consortia is to develop a standard that promotes their specific technology in a short period of time.

One of the most famous consortia is the World Wide Web Consortium (W3C), which is composed of industry giants such as Microsoft, Netscape, Sun, and IBM. The W3C is responsible for creating the standards that are widely used on the Internet today, including hypertext markup language (HTML), cascading style sheets (CSS), and the Document Object Model (DOM).

Telecommunications Standards Organizations

The need for standards in telecommunications is apparent. However, who sets these standards? It may be surprising to learn that several different national, multinational, and international standards organizations establish standards.

National

In the United States there are several standards organizations, each of which play a role in setting telecommunications standards. The **American National Standards Institute (ANSI)** functions largely as a clearinghouse for standards development in the U.S. Most ANSI standards are developed by one of its 271 affiliated organizations, which include the Water Quality Association and the Air Movement and Control Association.

One ANSI organization is known as the Turkey Roasters of Thanksgiving (TROT), which develops standards for turkey preparation.

Another of the ANSI affiliated organizations is the **Electronic Industries Association (EIA)**. The EIA is made up of industry vendors from four areas: electronic components, consumer electronics, electronic information, and telecommunications. Working with vendors, the EIA publishes "Recommended Standards" (RS) for the industry to follow. For example, the EIA developed and published a standard that defines how a computer's serial port, connector pin-outs, and electrical signaling should function.

A companion organization is known as the **Telecommunications Industries Association (TIA)**. The TIA is comprised of more than 1,100 members that manufacture or supply the products and services used in global communications. The function of the TIA is to advocate policy issues to legislative bodies and to establish standards in five areas: user premises equipment, network equipment, wireless communications, fiber optics, and satellite communications.

Two other organizations play a role in establishing national standards. The **Internet Engineering Task Force (IETF)** focuses on the lower levels of telecommunications technologies. The **Institute of Electrical and Electronics Engineers (IEEE)**, like the IETF, establishes standards for telecommunications as well. However, the IEEE also covers a wide range of IT standards. Some of its most well known standards are the IEEE 802.3, which is the standard for local area network Ethernet transmissions, and the IEEE 802.11b, which is the standard for WLAN transmissions.

Multinational

There are several standards organizations that span more than one nation. Many of these multinational standards organizations are found in Europe. The **European Telecommunications Standards Institute (ETSI)** is designed to develop telecommunications standards for use throughout Europe. Its membership is made up of European companies. The ETSI is currently working on standards for wireless digital cellular communications. The **European Committee for Electrotechnical Standardization/European Committee for Standardization (CEN/CENELEC)** is another multinational standards organization. Its role is to set standards regarding environmental and electromechanical issues.

International

Because telecommunications is truly global, there are also global organizations that set standards. The best known is the **International Telecommunications Union (ITU)**, which is an agency of the United Nations that is responsible for telecommunications. The ITU is composed of over 200 governments and private sector companies that coordinate global telecommunications networks and services. Unlike other bodies that set standards, the ITU is actually a treaty organization. The regulations set by the ITU are legally binding on the nations that have signed the treaty.

Two of the ITU's subsidiary organizations prepare recommendations on telecommunications standards. The ITU-T is responsible for establishing standards for telecommunications networks, while the ITU-R sets standards for radio-based communications, such as radio frequencies and standards for radio systems. Although these recommendations are not standards in themselves and are not binding to the nations that have signed other treaties, almost all of the nations elect to follow these recommendations and so they actually function as worldwide standards.

The ITU-T recently replaced a standards body known as the CCITT, whose origins date back to work on standards for telegraphs in the 1860s.

The **International Organization for Standardization (ISO)** is an organization based in Geneva, Switzerland. (Note that ISO is not an acronym; the word *iso* means "equal" in Greek.) Started in 1947, the ISO's goal is to promote international cooperation and standards in the areas of science, technology, and economics. Today, groups from over 100 countries belong to the ISO.

Several of the groups that belong to the ISO are actually national standards bodies. For example, the EIA plays a role in the ISO.

There are many national, multinational, and international telecommunications standards organizations that play a role in setting standards for wireless communications in the U.S. Table 3-4 summarizes those organizations.

Table 3-4 Telecommunications standards organizations

Organization Name	Jurisdiction
American National Standards Institute (ANSI)	National
Electronic Industries Association (EIA)	National
Telecommunications Industries Association (TIA)	National
Internet Engineering Task Force (IETF)	National
Institute of Electrical and Electronics Engineers (IEEE)	National
European Telecommunications Standards Institute (ETSI)	Multinational
European Committee for Electrotechnical Standardization/European Committee for Standardization (CEN/CENELEC)	Multinational
International Telecommunications Union (ITU)	International
International Organization for Standardization (ISO)	International

Regulatory Agencies

Although setting standards is important for telecommunications, enforcing telecommunications regulations is equally important. The marketplace itself enforces some standards. That is, a vendor who refuses to abide by standards for cellular telephone transmissions will find that nobody will buy his product. Telecommunications regulations, however, must be enforced by an outside regulatory agency, whose role is to ensure that all participants adhere to the prescribed standards. These regulations typically involve defining who can use a specific frequency when broadcasting a signal. Almost all nations have a national organization that functions as the regulatory agency to determine and enforce telecommunications policies.

In the United States, the Federal Communications Commission (FCC) serves as the primary regulatory agency for telecommunications. The FCC is an independent government agency that is directly responsible to Congress. The FCC was established by the Communications Act of 1934 and is charged with regulating interstate and international communications by radio, television, wire, satellite, and cable. The FCC's jurisdiction covers the 50 states, the District of Columbia, and U.S. territorial possessions.

In order to preserve its independence, the FCC is directed by five commissioners who are appointed by the President and confirmed by the Senate for 5-year terms. Only three commissioners may be members of the same political party, and none of them can have a financial interest in any FCC-related business.

The FCC's responsibilities are very broad. In addition to developing and implementing regulatory programs, they also process applications for licenses and other filings, analyze complaints, conduct investigations, and take part in congressional hearings. They also represent the U.S. in negotiations with foreign nations about telecommunications issues.

The FCC plays an important role in wireless communications. It regulates radio and television broadcast stations as well as cable and satellite stations. It also oversees cellular telephones, pagers, and two-way radios. The FCC regulates the use of radio frequencies to fulfill the communications needs of businesses, local and state governments, public safety service providers, aircraft and ship operators, and individuals.

Radio Frequency Spectrum

The **radio frequency spectrum** is the entire range of all radio frequencies that exist. This range extends from 10 KHz to over 30 GHz, as seen in Figure 3-31. The spectrum is divided into 450 different sections or **bands**. Table 3-5 lists the major bands, their corresponding frequencies, and some typical uses.

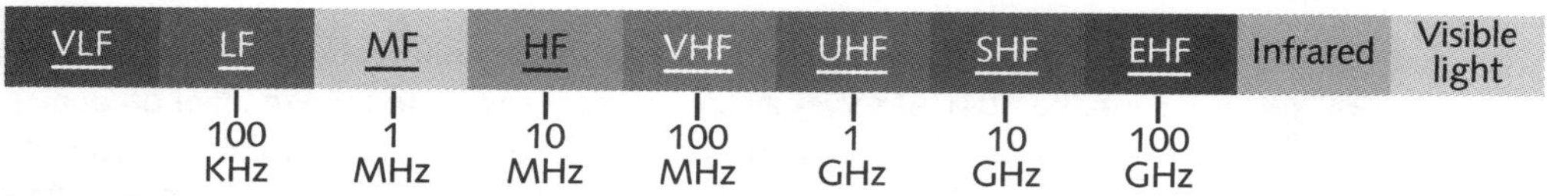

Figure 3-31 Radio frequency spectrum

Table 3-5 Radio frequency bands

Band	Frequency	Common Uses
Very Low Frequency (VLF)	10 KHz to 30 KHz	Maritime ship-to-shore
Low Frequency (LF)	30 KHz to 300 KHz	Cordless telephones
Medium Frequency (MF)	300 KHz to 3 MHz	AM radio
High Frequency (HF)	3 MHz to 30 MHz	Short wave radio, CB radio
Very High Frequency (VHF)	30 MHz to 144 MHz 144 MHz to 174 MHz 174 MHz to 328.6 MHz	TV stations 2-6, FM radio Taxi radios TV stations 7-13
Ultra High Frequency (UHF)	328.6 MHz to 806 MHz 806 MHz to 960 MHz 960 MHz to 2.3 GHz 2.3 GHz to 2.9 GHz	Public safety Cellular telephones Air traffic control radar WLANs (802.11b)
Super High Frequency (SHF)	2.9 GHz to 30 GHz	WLANs (802.11a)
Extremely High Frequency (EHF)	30 GHz and above	Radio astronomy

Radio frequencies of other common devices include:

- Garage door openers, alarm systems: 40 MHz
- Baby monitors: 49 MHz
- Radio-controlled airplanes: 72 MHz
- Radio-controlled cars: 75 MHz
- Wildlife tracking collars: 215 MHz–220 MHz
- Global positioning system (GPS): 1.227 GHz and 1.575 GHz

The U.S. is obligated to comply with the international spectrum allocations established by the ITU. However, the U.S. domestic spectrum uses may differ from the international allocations if these domestic uses do not conflict with international regulations or agreements.

Until 1993, the ITU held conferences at twenty-year intervals to review the international spectrum allocations. Since then, ITU conferences are convened every two to three years.

The Commerce Department's National Telecommunications and Information Administration (NTIA) serves as the principal adviser to the President on domestic and international communications and information issues. It also represents the views of the Executive Branch before the Congress, the Federal Communications Commission, foreign governments, and international organizations.

Although a license is normally required from the FCC to send and receive on a specific frequency, there is a notable exception. This is known as the **license exempt spectrum**, or **unregulated bands**. Unregulated bands are, in effect, radio spectrum that is available nationwide without charge to any users without a license. Devices that use these bands can be either fixed or mobile devices. The FCC says that it created the unregulated bands to "foster the development of a broad range of new devices, stimulate the growth of new industries, and promote the ability of U.S. manufacturers to compete globally by enabling them to develop unlicensed digital products for the world market."

There are some negative features of the unregulated bands. Because they are not regulated and licensed, devices from different vendors may attempt to use the same frequency. This conflict causes the signals to become intertwined between devices and prevents them from functioning properly. Thus the performance of devices using unregulated bands may be unpredictable.

The FCC does impose power limits on devices using the unregulated bands, which in effect reduces their range. This prevents manufacturers of devices such as long-range walkie-talkies from using these frequencies instead of the regulated frequencies intended for these products.

Table 3-6 outlines the unregulated bands. One unregulated band is the **Industrial, Scientific and Medical (ISM) band**, which was approved by the FCC in 1985. Devices such as WLANs that transmit at 11 Mbps use this band. Another unlicensed band is the **Unlicensed National Information Infrastructure (U-NII)**, approved in 1996. The U-NII band is intended for devices that will provide short-range, high-speed wireless digital communications. U-NII devices may provide a means for educational institutions, libraries, and health care providers to connect to basic and advanced telecommunications services. Educational institutions, for example, could form inexpensive wireless computer networks between classrooms. U-NII unlicensed wireless networks could help improve the quality and reduce the cost of medical care by allowing medical staff to obtain on-the-spot patient data, X-rays, and medical charts, and by giving health care workers in remote areas access to telecommunications services.

Table 3-6 Unregulated bands

Unlicensed Band	Frequency	Total Bandwidth	Common Uses
Industrial, Scientific and Medical (ISM)	902-928 MHz 2.4-2.4835 GHz 5.725-5.85 GHz	234.5 MHz	Cordless phones, WLANs, Wireless Public Branch Exchanges
Unlicensed Personal Communications Systems	1910-1930 MHz 2390-2400 MHz	30 MHz	WLANs, Wireless Public Branch Exchanges
Unlicensed National Information Infrastructure (U-NII)	5.15-5.25 GHz 5.25-5.35 GHz 5.725-5.825 GHz	300 MHz	WLANs, Wireless Public Branch Exchanges, campus applications, long outdoor links
Millimeter Wave	59-64 GHz	5 GHz	Home networking applications

Two recent developments may prove to have an impact on the crowded radio frequency spectrum. The first involves the direction of radio signals. Currently, when radio signals leave the sender's antenna they spread or radiate out (the word "radio" comes from the term "radiated energy") and can be picked up by multiple users. A new technique known as **adaptive array processing** replaces a traditional antenna with an array of antenna elements. These elements deliver RF signals to one specific user instead of sending signals out in a scattered pattern. Not only does this prevent eavesdropping by unapproved listeners, but it also allows more transmissions to take place in a given radio spectrum.

The second development is known as **ultra-wideband transmission (UWB)**. UWB does not use a traditional radio signal carrier sending signals in the regulated frequency spectrum. Instead, UWB uses low-power, precisely timed pulses of energy that operate in the same frequency spectrum as low-end noise, such as that emitted by computer chips, TV monitors, automobile ignitions, and fans. UWB is currently used in limited radar and position-location devices.

CHAPTER SUMMARY

- Several components are essential for communicating using radio frequencies (RF): filters, mixers, amplifiers, and antennas. These components are found on basically all radio systems.
- A filter is used to either accept or to block a radio frequency signal. With a low-pass filter, a maximum frequency threshold is set. All signals that are below that maximum threshold are allowed to pass through. Instead of setting a maximum frequency threshold, as with a low-pass filter, a high-pass filter sets a minimum frequency threshold. All signals that are above the minimum threshold are allowed to pass through, while those below the minimum threshold are turned away. A bandpass filter sets a passband, which is both a minimum and maximum threshold.
- The purpose of a mixer is to combine two inputs to create a single output. The single output is the highest sum and the lowest difference of the frequencies.
- An amplifier increases a signal's intensity or strength, while an antenna is used to convert an RF signal from the transmitter into an electromagnetic wave so that it can be sent through the air.
- Although filters, mixers, amplifiers, and antennas are all necessary components for a radio system, there are other design considerations that must be taken into account when creating a radio system. Because there are only a limited number of frequencies available, conserving the use of frequencies is important. One way to conserve is by sharing a frequency among several individual users.
- Frequency Division Multiple Access (FDMA) divides the bandwidth of the frequency into several smaller multiple frequencies. Time Division Multiple Access (TDMA) divides the bandwidth into several time slots. Each user is assigned the entire frequency for their transmission but only for a small fraction of time on a fixed, rotating basis. Code Division Multiple Access (CDMA) uses spread spectrum technology and unique digital codes, rather than separate RF frequencies or channels, to differentiate between the different transmissions.
- The direction in which data travels on a wireless network is important. There are three types of data flow. Simplex occurs in only one direction. Half-duplex transmission sends data in both directions, but only one way at a time, while full-duplex transmissions enable data to flow in either direction simultaneously.
- Switching involves switching or moving the signal from one wire or frequency to another. Telephone systems use a type of switching known as circuit switching. When a telephone call is made, a dedicated and direct physical connection is made between the caller and the recipient of the call through the switch. Instead of using circuit switching, data networks use packet switching. Packet switching requires that the data transmission be broken into smaller units called packets, and each packet is then sent independently through the network to reach the destination.

- In a wireless system, it is much more complicated to manage the strength of the signal than in a wired network. Electromagnetic interference (EMI), sometimes called noise, can come from a variety of man-made and natural sources. The signal-to-noise ratio (SNR) refers to the measure of signal strength relative to the background noise. A loss of signal strength is known as attenuation. Attenuation can be caused by a variety of factors, such as walls and buildings, that can decrease the strength of the signal. As a radio signal is transmitted the electromagnetic waves spread out. Some of these waves may reflect off of surfaces and slow it down. This results in the same signal being received not only from several different directions but also at different times. This is known as multipath distortion.
- Standards for telecommunications have been in place almost since the beginning of the industry. They have played an important role in the rapid growth of communications as well as demonstrating the benefits of standards. There are several advantages of standards including interoperability, lower costs, and a migration path. De facto standards are not really standards but are "common practices" that the industry follows. Official standards (also called de jure standards) are those that are controlled by an organization or body that has been entrusted with that task. Consortia are often used today to create standards. Consortia are usually industry-sponsored organizations that have the goal of promoting a specific technology. There are also standards organizations that span more than one nation. And because telecommunications is truly global, there are also global organizations that set standards. In the United States, the Federal Communications Commission (FCC) serves as the primary regulatory agency for telecommunications. The FCC is an independent government agency that is directly responsible to Congress.
- The radio frequency spectrum is the entire range of all radio frequencies that exist. This range extends from 10 KHz to over 30 GHz and is divided into 450 different bands. Although a license is normally required from the FCC to send and receive on a specific frequency, unregulated bands are available in the U.S. to any users without a license. Two unregulated bands are the Industrial, Scientific and Medical (ISM) band and the Unlicensed National Information Infrastructure (U-NII).
- Two recent developments may prove to have an impact on the crowded radio frequency spectrum. A new technique known as adaptive array processing replaces a traditional antenna with an array of antenna elements. These elements deliver RF signals to one specific user instead of sending signals out in a scattered pattern. Ultra-wideband transmission (UWB) does not use a traditional radio signal carrier sending signals in the regulated frequency spectrum. Instead, UWB uses low-power, precisely timed pulses of energy that operate in the same frequency spectrum as low-end noise such as that emitted by computer chips and TV monitors.

Key Terms

adaptive array processing — A radio transmission technique that replaces a traditional antenna with an array of antenna elements.

American National Standards Institute (ANSI) — A clearinghouse for standards development in the United States.

amplifier — A component that increases a signal's intensity.

attenuation — A loss of signal strength.

bandpass — A filter that passes all signals that are between the maximum and minimum threshold.

bands — Sections of the radio frequency spectrum.

circuit switching — A dedicated and direct physical connection is made between two transmitting devices.

Code Division Multiple Access (CDMA) — A technique that uses spread spectrum technology and unique digital codes to send and receive radio transmissions.

consortia — Industry-sponsored organizations that have the goal of promoting a specific technology.

crosstalk — Signals from close frequencies that may interfere with other signals.

de facto standards — Common practices that the industry follows for various reasons.

de jure standards — Standards are those that are controlled by an organization or body.

directional antenna — An antenna that sends the signal in one direction.

dynamic range — The amount by which a signal's maximum intensity exceeds its minimum detectable level.

electromagnetic interference (EMI) — Interference with a radio signal; also called noise.

Electronic Industries Association (EIA) — U.S. industry vendors from four areas: electronic components, consumer electronics, electronic information, and telecommunications.

European Committee for Electrotechnical Standardization/European Committee for Standardization (CEN/CENELEC) — A multinational standards organization whose role is to set standards regarding environmental and electromechanical issues.

European Telecommunications Standards Institute (ETSI) — A standards body that is designed to develop telecommunications standards for use throughout Europe.

filter — A component that is used to either accept or to block a radio frequency signal.

Frequency Division Multiple Access (FDMA) — A radio transmission technique that divides the bandwidth of the frequency into several smaller frequency bands.

full-duplex transmission — Transmissions that enable data to flow in either direction simultaneously.

gain — The measure of the directional intensity of an antenna pattern.

half-duplex transmission — Transmission that occurs in both directions but only one way at a time.

high-pass filter — A filter that passes all signals that are above a maximum threshold.

Industrial, Scientific and Medical (ISM) band — An unregulated radio frequency band approved by the FCC in 1985.

Institute of Electrical and Electronics Engineers (IEEE) — A standards body that establishes standards for telecommunications.

intermediate frequency (IF) — The output signal from the modulation process that is between 10 MHz and 100 MHz.

International Organization for Standardization (ISO) — An organization to promote international cooperation and standards in the areas of science, technology, and economics.

International Telecommunications Union (ITU) — An agency of the United Nations that sets international telecommunications standards and coordinates global telecommunications networks and services.

Internet Engineering Task Force (IETF) — A standards body that focuses on the lower levels of telecommunications technologies.

license exempt spectrum — Unregulated radio frequency bands that are available in the U.S. to any users without a license.

low-pass filter — A filter that passes all signals that are below a maximum threshold.

mixer — A component to combine two inputs to create a single output.

multipath distortion — The same signal being received not only from several different directions but also at different times.

noise — Interference with a signal.

official standards — See de jure standards.

omnidirectional antenna — An antenna that sends out the signal in a uniform pattern in all directions.

packet — A smaller segment of the transmitted signal.

packet switching — Data transmission that is broken into smaller units.

passband — A minimum and maximum threshold.

proprietary — A created device that is owned by a specific vendor.

radio frequency spectrum — The entire range of all radio frequencies that exist.

sidebands — The sum and the differences of the frequency carrier that serve as buffer space around the frequency of the transmitted signal.

signal-to-noise ratio (SNR) — The measure of signal strength relative to the background noise.

simplex transmission — Transmission that occurs in only one direction.

switching — Moving a signal from one wire or frequency to another.

Telecommunications Industries Association (TIA) — Over 1,100 members that manufacture or supply the products and services used in global communications.

Time Division Multiple Access (TDMA) — A transmission technique that divides the bandwidth into several time slots.

ultra-wideband transmission (UWB) — Low-power, precisely timed pulses of energy that operate in the same frequency spectrum as low-end noise, such as that emitted by computer chips and TV monitors.

Unlicensed National Information Infrastructure (U-NII) — An unregulated band approved by the FCC in 1996 to provide for short-range, high-speed wireless digital communications.

unregulated bands — See license exempt spectrum.

Review Questions

1. Each of the following is a type of filter except ________________.
   a. low-pass
   b. high-pass
   c. passband
   d. bandpass
2. The purpose of a(n) ________________ is to combine two inputs to create a single output.
   a. mixer
   b. codex
   c. filter
   d. amplifier
3. A(n) ________________ increases a signal's intensity or strength.
   a. transmitter
   b. demodulator
   c. amplifier
   d. antenna
4. The purpose of the ________________ is to send a magnetic signal into space.
   a. antenna
   b. modulator
   c. filter
   d. mixer
5. A(n) ________________ antenna sends out the signal in a uniform pattern in all directions.
   a. spray
   b. spectrum
   c. omnidirectional
   d. pen beam

6. A passband is both a minimum and maximum threshold. True or false?
7. The resulting output from the modulation process is known as the middle frequency (MF) signal. True or false?
8. The sum and the differences are known as the sidebands of the frequency carrier. True or false?
9. The gain of an antenna is the measure of how intense the direction of an antenna pattern is. True or false?
10. A directional antenna has a low gain. True or false?
11. The ________________ of an antenna depends upon the frequency of the RF signal and the gain.
12. ________________ divides the bandwidth of the frequency into several smaller multiple frequencies.
13. When signals are sent at frequencies that are closely grouped together, an errant signal may encroach on a close frequency causing ________________.
14. ________________ divides the bandwidth into several time slots.
15. A ________________ transmission uses spread spectrum technology and unique digital codes.
16. List and describe the three types of data flow.
17. List and discuss the advantages of standards.
18. What is switching? What type of switching is used with telephone transmissions, and what type is used for data transmissions?
19. Explain multipath distortion and how it can be minimized.
20. What does the Federal Communications Commission do?

Hands-on Projects

1. Draw and label a functional block diagram of a radio transmitter. The frequency of the transmission signal will be 36,000 Hz. Label the frequency of the signal as it moves from one component to the next.
2. Write a one-page paper on adaptive array processing systems. What are the technology barriers that it faces? In what applications will it be used? Who is spearheading its development? Use the Internet and other technology sources for your paper.
3. Ultra-wide transmissions (UWB) may dramatically change the way in which wireless voice and data are carried. Using the Internet and other appropriate sources, research UWB. Why is the military so interested in UWB? How is it being used today? What do its detractors claim that it will interfere with? What does the FCC think about UWB? Write a one-page paper on your findings.

4. Because telecommunications is truly global, the International Telecommunications Union (ITU) has become the predominant international agency that is responsible for telecommunications. Research the history of the ITU and its important sub-agencies. Who can join? How are its standards enforced? What are some of its most recent decisions? Write a one-page paper on your findings.
5. Objects in the path of a radio signal can cause a loss of signal strength or attenuation. Man-made objects, such as walls and buildings, can decrease the strength of the signal. Locate a notebook computer with a wireless local area network that transmits to an access point. Launch the utility that monitors the strength of the signal, and move away from the access point. Determine how far you can be from the access point before the signal is too weak to be useful. Record what objects in the path of the signal have the greatest impact. Write a paper on your findings.

Case Projects

The Baypoint Group (TBG), a company of 50 consultants who assist organizations and businesses with issues involving network planning and design, has again requested your services as a consultant. The Good Samaritan Center, which assists needy citizens in the area, needs to modernize their office facilities. As part of their community outreach program, TBG has asked you to donate your time to help the Good Samaritan Center.

The Good Samaritan Center wants to install a wireless network in its offices. One local vendor has been trying to sell them a proprietary system based on five-year old technology that does not follow any current standards. The price given for the product and its installation is low and is thereby attractive to the Center. However, they have asked TBG for their opinion. The Baypoint Group has asked you to become involved.

1. Create a PowerPoint slide presentation that outlines the different types of standards, the advantages and disadvantages of standards, and why they are needed. Include examples of products that did not follow standards and have vanished from the marketplace. Because the Good Samaritan Center is on the verge of buying the product, TBG has asked you to be very persuasive in your presentation. You are told that presenting the facts is not enough at this point; you must convince them why they should purchase a product that follows standards before you leave the room.
2. Your presentation casts a shadow of doubt over the vendor's proprietary product, but the Good Samaritan Center is still not completely convinced they should go with a standard product. TBG has just learned that the vendor's proprietary product uses a licensed frequency that will require the Center to secure a license from the FCC. TBG has asked you to prepare another presentation regarding the advantages of unregulated bands. Because an engineer who sits on the Board of the Good Samaritan Center will be there, this PowerPoint presentation should be detailed and technical in its scope.

OPTIONAL TEAM CASE PROJECT

A local engineering user's group has contacted The Baypoint Group requesting a speaker to discuss multiple access technologies (FDMA, TDMA, and CDMA). Form a team of two or three consultants and research these technologies in detail. Specifically, pay attention to how they are used as well as their strengths and weaknesses. Provide an opinion regarding which technology will become the dominant player in the future of wireless.

CHAPTER

4

INFRARED

After reading this chapter and completing the exercises you will be able to:

- Explain the differences between the OSI communications model and the IEEE 802 communications standards
- Tell how an infrared WLAN transmits data
- Describe the features of IrDA

Why consider infrared (IR) wireless technology when today the majority of wireless transmissions are based on radio frequency (RF) technology? The answer is that although more devices use radio frequency transmissions than infrared, infrared devices have not been squeezed out of the picture. Many cellular phones are equipped with infrared ports that allow them to transmit to a computer for dial-up networking connections. One of the most popular devices on the market today is the Personal Digital Assistant (PDA). These handheld devices from a variety of manufacturers use infrared ports for sending and receiving data.

An example of infrared technology use with PDAs can be seen in the U.S. military. Space on a Navy vessel is always limited, and most Navy destroyers only have a few desktop computers that over 300 crew members must share to read e-mail dispatches from family and friends. This problem has been solved with PDAs and infrared technology. Crew members on Navy destroyers can download e-mail messages and access the ship's Plan of the Day by pointing their PDA to one of 32 infrared ports in the ship's mess halls, passageways, and berthing areas. After downloading their e-mails they can read the messages and compose their replies at their leisure. Once the reply is ready, the crew member can point the PDA at an infrared port and send the message. This is just one demonstration that infrared wireless technology is alive and well.

This chapter will explore how infrared devices send and receive data and will look at two of the most common uses of infrared wireless technology, namely IrDA and wireless local area networks (WLANs). To understand how these wireless technologies function, we will first take a look at the most important wireless communications models and standards.

Communications Models and Standards

As you learned in Chapter 3, standards for telecommunications have been essential since the very beginning of the industry. Because telecommunications basically involves devices interacting with other devices over distance, a lack of standards for communication between devices results in no communications at all. Just as standards are essential to telecommunications, abstract models of communications have likewise proven to be very important in the development of telecommunications.

Communications Model: OSI

You will recall that the International Organization for Standardization (ISO) is an international organization whose goal is to promote international cooperation and standards in the areas of science, technology, and economics. In the mid-1970s the ISO began work on developing specifications for communications by computer-based networks. The goal of the ISO was not to create an official physical standard for all computer networks, but to create an abstract model of networking. Completed in 1983, these conceptual specifications became known as the **Open System Interconnect (OSI) model.**

Although the OSI model is most often associated with local area networks, it actually is used for all types of data communications.

The OSI model is intended to give a visual picture or concept of how telecommunications is accomplished. It breaks the many complex functions of data communications into seven basic layers (see Figure 4-1). Each layer performs a specific function in the operation of communications devices (see Table 4-1). Each specific function can involve different tasks using a variety of hardware or software. For example, one of the functions of Layer 2, the Data Link layer, is to detect and correct any transmission errors. To perform this function, many different tasks may take place using different hardware and software.

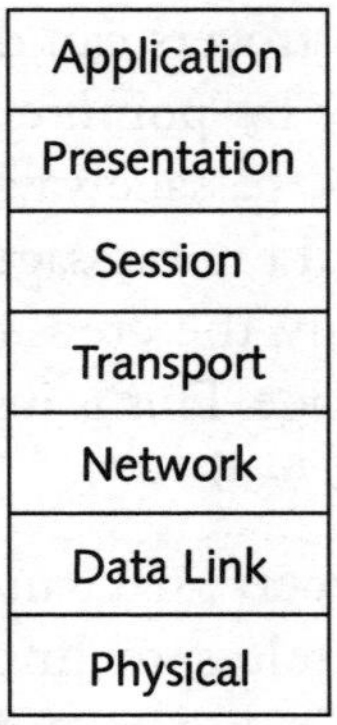

Application
Presentation
Session
Transport
Network
Data Link
Physical

Figure 4-1 OSI model

Table 4-1 OSI Layers and Functions

Layer	Function
Application (Layer 7)	Provides the user interface and allows communications services. These services may include such things as e-mail and transferring files.
Presentation (Layer 6)	Handles how the data is represented and formatted for the user.
Session (Layer 5)	Permits the devices to hold ongoing communications across the network. Handles session setup, data or message exchanges, and teardown when the session ends.
Transport (Layer 4)	Ensures that error-free data is given to the user.
Network (Layer 3)	Picks the route the transmissions takes and handles addressing for delivery.
Data Link (Layer 2)	Detects and corrects errors. If data is not received properly, the Data Link Layer would request it to be retransmitted.
Physical (Layer 1)	Sends signals or receives signals.

Although the OSI model is divided into seven layers, this does not mean that the layers function independently from one another. On the contrary, each layer cooperates with the layer immediately above it and below it by passing something to it or receiving something from it. When data is sent from a device, it flows down through the layers from Application to Physical, and when it is received, it flows up through the layers from Physical to Application, as seen in Figure 4-2. Consider again Layer 2, the Data Link layer. When a device is transmitting data, the Data Link layer receives data from the layer immediately above it, the Network layer. When the Data Link layer performs its function on that data, it then passes it on down to the Physical Layer (Layer 1). On the other hand, when a transmission is received, the Physical Layer passes it up to the Data Link layer, which then performs its function on the data. When completed, the Data Link layer passes it on to the next highest layer, the Network layer, where that layer performs its function on the data, and so on.

There are several important items to note about the OSI model:

- Each layer performs specific functions in terms of communications.
- To accomplish the function several tasks may be performed using different hardware and software.
- The flow between layers goes down when sending and up when receiving.

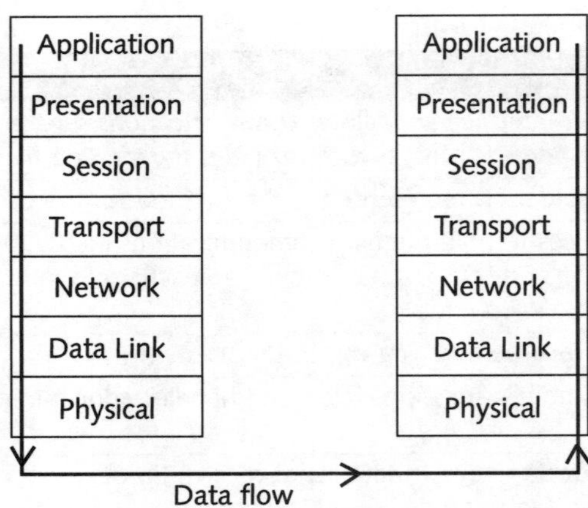

Figure 4-2 OSI data flow

It's important to remember that the OSI model is just that: an abstract model of how telecommunications is accomplished. It is not a picture of actual physical data communications, but a conceptual picture of how such communications work.

Communications Standards: IEEE 802

About the same time that the ISO was working on the OSI model, the Institute of Electrical and Electronics Engineers (IEEE) started **Project 802** to ensure interoperability among data network products. Although the primary focus of Project 802 was network standards, it also includes standards for such things as cable television communications.

Two of the most widely used Project 802 standards are the 802.3 (Ethernet) and 802.5 (Token Ring) networking standards. There is a difference between Project 802 and the OSI model in terms of how they are used. The OSI model is a *theoretical model* of how communications works. Project 802, on the other hand, sets *standards* for computer communications that are followed today. In short, the OSI model is theory while Project 802 sets standards for actual practice.

The IEEE's Project 802 used the OSI conceptual model as a framework for their specifications with some important differences. These are illustrated in Figure 4-3. Project 802 subdivides the OSI model Layer 2, Data Link, into two sublayers: the **Logical Link Control (LLC)** and **Media Access Control (MAC)** layers. For wireless networks, such as 802.11 WLANs, the IEEE also divides the Physical layer (known as the PHY) into two parts. The **Physical Medium Dependent (PMD) sublayer** includes the standards for the characteristics of the wireless medium (IR and RF) and defines the method for transmitting and receiving data through that medium. The second PHY sublayer is the **Physical Layer Convergence Procedure (PLCP) sublayer**. The PLCP performs two basic functions. First, when transmitting, it reformats the data received from the MAC layer into a packet (also known as a **frame**) that the PMD sublayer can transmit, as seen in Figure 4-4. Second, it "listens" to the medium to determine when the data can be sent.

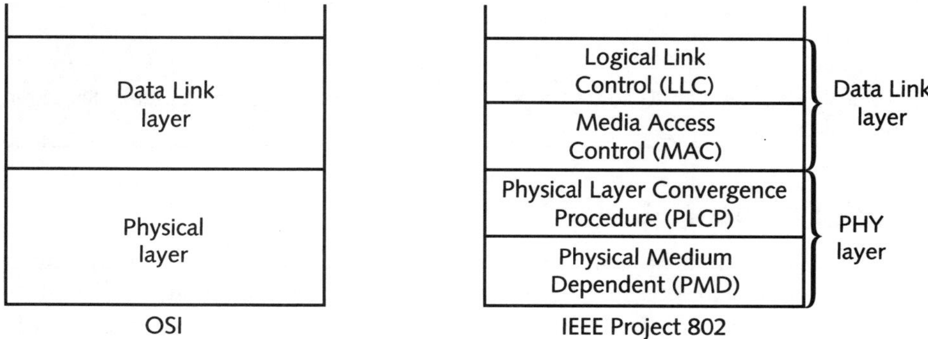

Figure 4-3 OSI model versus IEEE Project 802

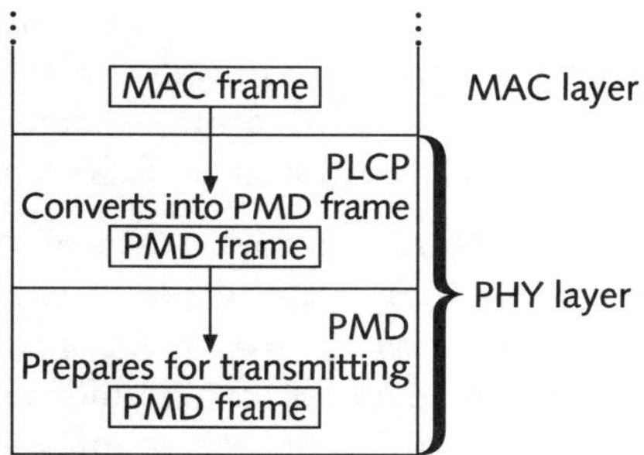

Figure 4-4 PLCP sublayer reformats MAC data

Table 4-2 summarizes the characteristics of the PMD sublayer and PLCP sublayer.

Table 4-2 Summary of PMD and PLCP sublayers

Function	Sublayer Performed
Standards for the characteristics of the wireless medium	Physical Medium Dependent (PMD)
Defines the method for transmitting and receiving data through the medium	Physical Medium Dependent (PMD)
Reformats data received from the MAC layer into a frame that the PMD sublayer can transmit	Physical Layer Convergence Procedure (PLCP)
Listens to the medium to determine when data can be sent	Physical Layer Convergence Procedure (PLCP)

Network Protocol Stacks

The dictionary defines protocol as, "The forms of ceremony and etiquette observed by diplomats and heads of state." In this sense, protocols are rules that a diplomat must observe while working in a different country. If a diplomat were to ignore protocols, he or she could offend the citizens of that host country. This might lead to a diplomatic incident or, even worse, a war.

Computer networks likewise have rules that all the network components must follow if the network is to work. A **network protocol** is the format and order of the messages exchanged between two or more communication devices based on standards. In other words, a network protocol is the communications rules that must be followed.

To help keep things simple, network engineers have organized these protocols into layers. These layers generally correspond to the layers in the OSI model. When a set of network protocols are taken together as a whole it is called a **network protocol stack**. There are a variety of network protocol stacks that are used for network communications. This is because different protocol stacks can accomplish different communications tasks. **Transmission Control Protocol/Internet Protocol (TCP/IP)** is the standard network protocol stack used on the Internet and has become the dominant protocol stack today. Older protocol stacks include **Internetwork Packet eXchange/Sequenced Packet eXchange (IPX/SPX)** found on Novell NetWare LANs and **AppleTalk**, used by Apple for its Macintosh computers.

Infrared WLANs

Infrared wireless local area networks date back almost 20 years. Since that time, a number of different IR WLANs have been developed and installed.

Characteristics

Infrared WLANs use the part of the electromagnetic spectrum just below visible light as the medium for transmitting. Because infrared light is near in wavelength to visible light, IR shares many of the same physical properties:

- Operates at high frequencies
- Travels in straight lines
- Does not penetrate physical objects such as walls and ceilings

Because of these properties, infrared transmissions have several advantages over RF. Infrared has an abundance of available bandwidth. The abundance of bandwidth also makes it possible for infrared to operate at high data rates. Infrared does not have to be regulated since the bandwidth is not scarce as with radio frequencies.

Another advantage of infrared is that it is more secure than radio frequency transmissions. Because IR does not penetrate through walls, the signal stays confined inside the room and eliminates unauthorized eavesdropping. Also, common sources of RF interference, such as microwave ovens and radio transmitters, cannot interfere with an IR signal. Finally, the components needed for infrared transmission are small and consume little power.

Although infrared signals cannot penetrate walls, they can pass through open doorways and reflect off walls and around corners, just like sunlight.

The wavelength of infrared light is lower in frequency than visible light but higher in frequency than radio waves. This high frequency means that IR cannot be modulated in the same way as radio frequencies.

Infrared wireless transmission can be either directed or diffused. A directed transmission requires that the emitter and detector be directly aimed at one another. The emitter sends a narrowly focused beam of infrared light to the detector that has a small receiving or viewing area. A diffused transmission relies on reflected light. Emitters on diffused infrared transmissions have a wide-focused beam that is pointed at the ceiling of a room and uses it as the reflection point. When the emitter transmits an infrared signal, the signal bounces off the ceiling and fills the room with the signal. The detectors are also pointed at the same reflection point and can detect the reflected signal.

Diffused infrared has several advantages over directed transmissions for a LAN. Since the deflected signal can follow many different paths to the detector, the receiving device with the detector can be positioned almost anywhere within the room. Also, one emitter can transmit simultaneously to multiple receivers. An object, such as a person moving in the room, does not cause a disruption in the signal because the signal can still bounce off of other objects to reach the receiver. However, because infrared energy is lost as it is dispersed throughout the room, the distance between devices and the data rates are significantly reduced. The highest data rate for a diffused infrared WLAN is about 4 Mbps, while the range between devices is typically 30 to 50 feet (9 to 15 meters).

IEEE 802.11 Infrared WLANs

The IEEE 802.11standards outline the specifications for infrared WLANs. The specification is based upon diffused transmissions. The PHY layer performs the functions of both reformatting the data received from the upper layers (PLCP) and transmitting the light impulses (PMD).

Diffused Infrared Physical Layer Convergence Procedure Standards

The diffused infrared Physical Layer Convergence Procedure (PLCP) reformats the data received from the MAC layer (when transmitting) into a frame that the Physical Medium Dependent (PMD) sublayer can transmit. An example of an infrared PLCP frame is illustrated in Figure 4-5.

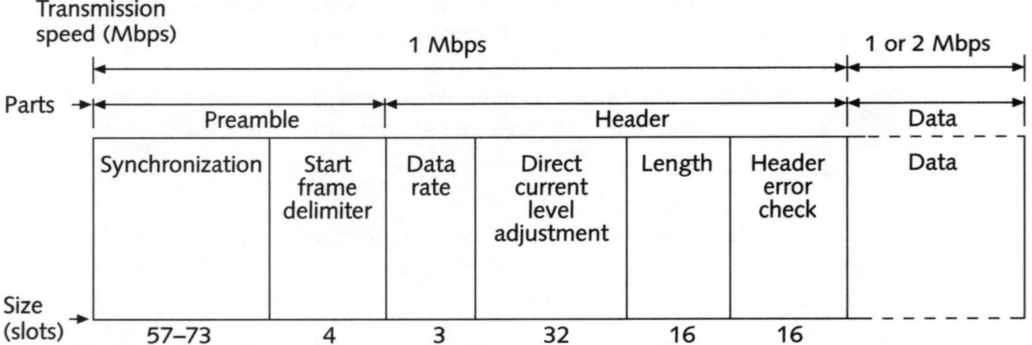

Figure 4-5 Infrared PLCP frame

The frame size is not measured in bits but in **time slots**. Infrared wireless systems send data by the intensity of the light wave instead of "on-off" signals of light. To transmit a 1 bit, an infrared emitter increases the intensity of the current and sends a pulse using infrared light. This pulse of infrared light is transmitted at a specific time slot. In the Synchronization field of an infrared PLCP frame the emitter may send between 57 and 73 pulses, each in its own time slot. The receiving device will then synchronize with the incoming signal. The Start Frame Delimiter is always the same bit pattern and defines the beginning of a frame. The Start Frame Delimiter for infrared is always 1001, where 1 represents a high-intensity pulse and 0 is a lower-intensity pulse.

The Data Rate value determines the speed of the transmission. The Direct Current Level Adjustment contains a pattern of infrared pulses that allows the receiving device to determine the signal level. Table 4-3 illustrates the possible values for these fields. The Length field indicates the time needed to transmit the entire frame. This is used by the receiving device to determine the end of the frame. The Header Error Check contains a value that the receiving device can use to determine if the data was received correctly. The Data field is the portion of the frame that contains the data and can be from 1 to 20,000 time slots.

Table 4-3 Infrared data rate and direct current level adjustment values

Transmission Speed (Mbps)	Data Rate Values	Direct Current Level Adjustment Values
1.0	000	00000000010000000000000001000000
2.0	001	00100010001000100010001000100010

There are two significant points regarding the transmission speed of the PLCP frame. First, the preamble and header of the PLCP frame are always transmitted at 1 Mbps. This allows for a slower sending device to talk to a faster receiving device because it is using the slowest speed. However, even if both devices are faster and can transmit at a faster rate, the two faster devices must still fall back to the 1 Mbps transmission rate for the preamble and header. Also, the current IEEE 802.11 standards specify that the data can be transmitted only at either 1 or 2 Mbps.

Diffused Infrared Physical Medium Dependent Standards

Once the PLCP has created the frame, it then passes it to the PMD sublayer. The PMD translates the binary 1s and 0s of the frame into light pulses that can be used for transmission. To transmit a 1 bit, the emitter increases the intensity of the current and sends a pulse using infrared light. The detector senses the higher intensity signal and produces a proportional electrical current.

The infrared PMD transmits the data using a series of light impulses. For transmissions at 1 Mbps, a **16-pulse position modulation (16-PPM)** is specified. 16-PPM translates four data bits into 16 light impulses, which are then transmitted to the receiving device. This is illustrated in Table 4-4. For transmissions at 2 Mbps, a **4-pulse position modulation (4-PPM)** is used instead, as seen in Table 4-5.

Table 4-4 16-PPM Values

Data Bit	16-PPM Value	Data Bit	16-PPM Value
0000	0000000000000001	1100	0000000100000000
0001	0000000000000010	1101	0000001000000000
0011	0000000000000100	1111	0000010000000000
0010	0000000000001000	1110	0000100000000000
0110	0000000000010000	1010	0001000000000000
0111	0000000000100000	1011	0010000000000000
0101	0000000001000000	1001	0100000000000000
0100	0000000010000000	1000	1000000000000000

Table 4-5 4-PPM Values

Data Bit	4-PPM Value
00	0001
01	0010
11	0100
10	1000

Each time slot is one 250 billionth of a second (**nanosecond** or **ns**), no matter which transmission speed is being used (1 Mbps or 2 Mbps). If each slot time is the same, how can the 4-PPM transmit at twice the speed? It is because four times the amount of data is contained in a 4-PPM transmission. Suppose that the data bits 1001 were to be transmitted. Using 16-PPM it would take 16 time slots (1000000000000000) to send the data bits 1001. However, using 4-PPM to transmit the same data bits of 1001, it would only take 8 time slots: 1000 to send the data bits 10, and 0010 to send the data bits 01. Thus 4-PPM can transmit at a maximum rate of 2 Mbps while 16-PPM can only transmit at 1 Mbps.

IrDA

The most common infrared connection today is based on a standard known as **IrDA**. IrDA is an acronym for the **I**nf**r**ared **D**ata **A**ssociation, which is a non-profit consortium with a membership of over 160 companies that represent computer and telecommunications hardware, software, components and adapters. The primary use for IrDA is to link notebook computers and Personal Digital Assistant (PDA) handheld devices with other devices. However, infrared ports conforming to the IrDA specifications are also found on desktop computers, printers, desktop adapters, cameras, phones, watches, pagers, storage devices, and kiosks.

The IrDA specifications include standards for both the physical devices and the network protocols they use to communicate with each other. The IrDA standards arose from the need to connect different computer and telecommunications devices together.

Some industry experts predict that IrDA infrared ports will soon be found on non-computer items such as copiers, fax machines, overhead projectors, bank ATMs, credit cards, game controls, and headsets.

Overview

The goal of the IrDA standards is to create a data interconnection based on infrared light. IrDA devices have a common set of characteristics:

- They are designed to provide "walk-up" connectivity. That is, there is a minimal amount of preconfiguration necessary for two IrDA devices to communicate.

- IrDA devices provide a point-to-point method of data transfer between only two devices at a time.
- Devices following the IrDA standards cover a broad range of computing and communicating devices.
- IrDA is inexpensively implemented because the infrared components are low in cost.

There are three versions of the IrDA specification. They are summarized in Table 4-6. However, unlike radio frequency (RF) devices that decrease the bandwidth as the distance between devices increases, IrDA devices do not vary the transmission speed. IrDA devices must be capable of maintaining a constant connection speed. If the distance between two IrDA devices is too great, a connection simply cannot be made.

Table 4-6 IrDA versions

IrDA Version	Speed
Serial Infrared (SIR)	9,600–115,200 bps
Fast Infrared (FIR)	4 Mbps
Very Fast Infrared (VFIR)	16 Mbps

In theory, an infrared port can transmit at 50 Mbps. This speed will not be available for several years due to current limitations of the technology.

Multiple Infrared Connections

Multiple simultaneous connections can be established over a single IrDA link. This feature allows several different programs to use a single infrared device simultaneously. For example, once two IrDA devices establish a connection users can simultaneously send and receive mail, update calendar and contact information, and print documents. Each activity can be controlled by a separate program on one computer that locates and connects to its corresponding program on the other computer. However, a single infrared device cannot link simultaneously with more than one other infrared device at a time.

IrDA devices communicate using infrared light emitting diodes (LEDs) to send and photodiodes to receive signals. Examples of these transceivers are seen in Figure 4-6. The transceivers are not flush with the edge of the device but instead are recessed into the device. They are then covered with a transparent window surrounded by opaque material, as seen in Figure 4-7.

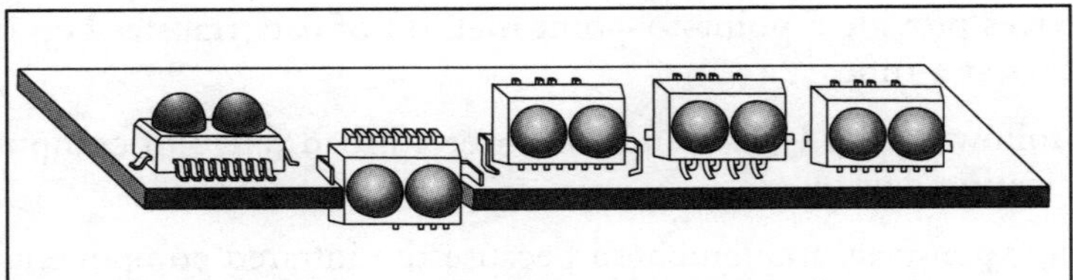

Figure 4-6 Infrared LEDs and photodiodes

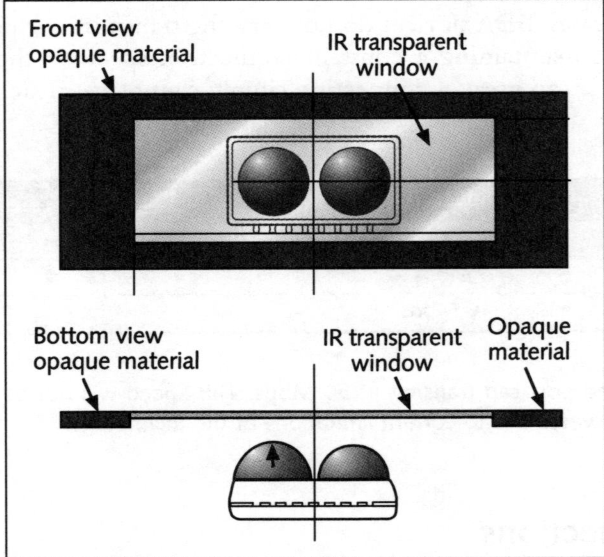

Figure 4-7 Diodes positioned in device

There are several design factors that can improve the performance of IrDA devices that are not readily apparent. The transparent window placed in front of the IR module should be flat instead of curved. This is because a curved window may alter the radiation pattern of the LED. Also, the recommended color of the window is violet. This color will allow for minimal loss of signal when transmitting. And, bright surrounding light (known as **ambient light**) can often interfere with the infrared signal. The performance of the transceivers when there is bright ambient light can be improved if the module is recessed into the device case by several millimeters. This creates an "overhang" over the photodiode that will minimize the amount of direct ambient light that the receiver sees. The transparent window will also help reflect ambient light away from the diodes.

IrDA Protocol Stack

The IrDA protocol stack is made up of several layers, as seen in Figure 4-8. Three of the layers are required: IrPHY, IrLAP, and IrLMP. The remaining layers are optional, depending upon how the device is being used. The functions of the layers are summarized below:

- *IrDA Physical Layer Protocol (IrPHY)*—This layer controls the hardware that sends and receives the LED pulses.
- *IrDA Link Access Protocol (IrLAP)*—IrLAP encapsulates the frames and describes how the devices establish a connection, close it, and how are they going to be internally numbered to ensure there is no internal conflicts between devices. IrLAP is similar to the IP protocol.
- *IrDA Link Management Protocol (IrLMP)*—The status of IrDA devices can change on a regular basis. For example, a user may turn on an IrDA PDA and place it within range of a notebook computer. Every IrDA device somehow must inform all other devices about itself. This is done through the IrLMP protocol. IrLMP's goal is to detect the presence of devices offering a service, to check the data flow, and then act as a multiplexer for the different configurations of the devices. Applications wanting to communicate with IrDA devices would use the IrLMP layer to ask if a specific IrDA device is within range and available.
- *IrDA Transport Protocols (Tiny TP)*—Tiny TP manages channels between devices, performs error corrections such as lost packets, divides data into packets, reassembles original data from packets, and defines a reliable way to create a channel. TinyTP is similar to the TCP protocol.
- *Other objects*—These are optional extensions to the protocol for specific types of devices. For example, these extensions can specify how mobile devices, like PDAs and cellular phones, transfer information (address books, calendars, dialing control, etc.) over specific networks. One object is known as IrWWW, which specifies how a wristwatch with an IrDA port can interface with other devices. Another object is IrTran-P (Infrared Transfer Picture) that is used by digital cameras that have an IrDA port. It specifies how to transfer pictures over that infrared interface. Infrared printing (IrLPT) and infrared networking (IrNet and IrComm) capabilities are also available.

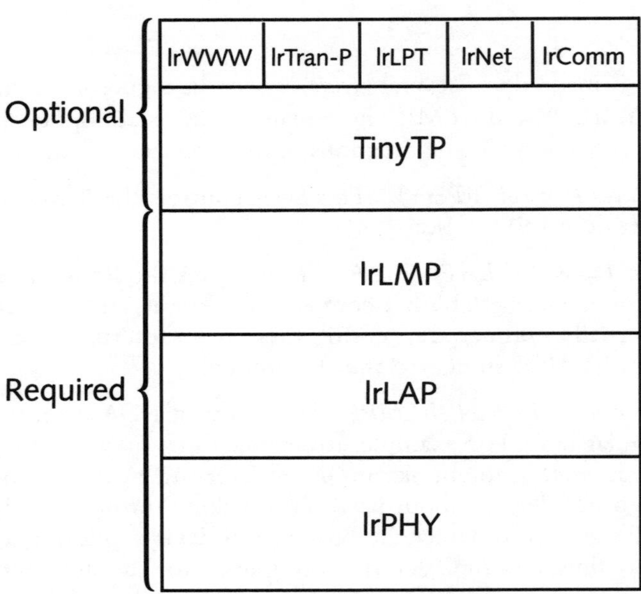

Figure 4-8 IrDA protocol stack

Microsoft Windows supports programs created by other software and equipment vendors. These vendors sell programs that use the Windows proprietary interface to provide infrared connections to modems, digital pagers, personal digital assistants, electronic cameras, organizers, cellular phones, and handheld computers.

IrDA Physical Layer Protocol (IrPHY)

The IrDA physical layer protocol controls the hardware that sends and receives the IR pulses. The function of the IrPHY varies depending on which standard, the Serial Infrared (version 1.0) or the Fast Infrared (version 1.1), is being used.

Serial Infrared (Version 1.0)

The functional block diagram of the SIR transmitter is illustrated in Figure 4-9. The SIR was designed to work like the standard serial port on a PC. As such, it uses the existing **UART (Universal Asynchronous Receiver/Transmitter)** chip found in the computer, which is also used for the serial port. The UART is a microchip that controls a computer's interface to its attached serial devices through a serial port or IrDA port. IrDA devices function like a serial port on a computer instead of a parallel port. With a serial port, bits are transmitted one after the other instead of all eight bits of a byte being transmitted simultaneously. This is seen in Figure 4-10.

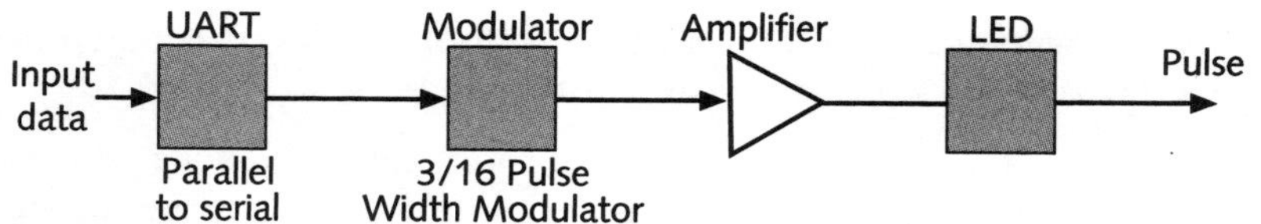

Figure 4-9 SIR transmitter block diagram

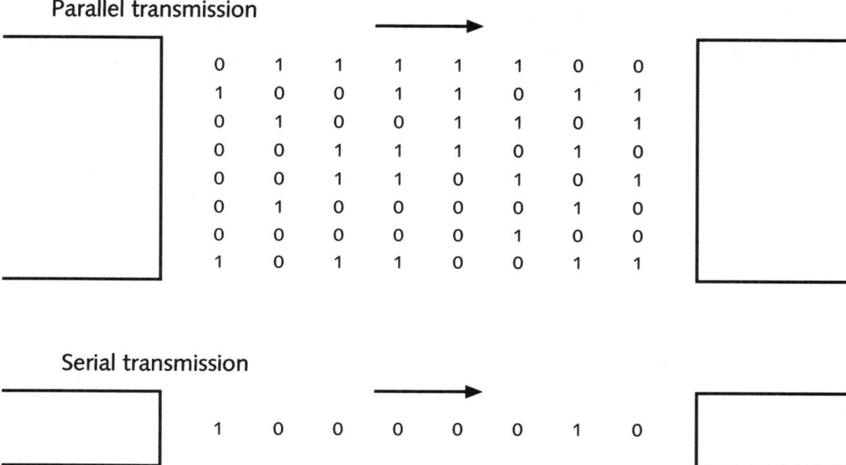

Figure 4-10 Parallel and serial transmission

A computer serial port is based on the Electronic Industries Association (EIA) recommended standard (RS), known as RS-232.

The functions of the UART are:

- It converts the bytes it receives from the computer's parallel circuits into a single serial bit stream for outbound transmission.
- On inbound transmission, it converts the serial bit stream into the parallel bytes.
- The UART can add an optional **parity bit** that checks for errors on outbound transmissions and checks the parity bit of incoming data.
- It can add and remove optional start and stop delineators that indicate when the transmitted byte starts and when it stops. These are known as **start** and **stop bits**. On outbound transmissions the UART adds these bits and strips them from inbound transmissions.

- UARTs provide some amount of buffering of data so that the computer and serial devices data streams remain coordinated.
- The UART may handle other kinds of interrupt and device management that require coordinating the computer's speed of that of the device connected through the serial or IR port.

The UART can be used for other tasks besides serial communications, like disk interrupts, interrupts from the keyboard and mouse (which are serial devices with special ports), screen refresh cycles, and other items that involve timing with a computer.

A conventional serial port using a UART chip uses the NRZ (non-return-to-zero) binary signaling technique. With NRZ the voltage signal remains high for the entire length of the bit period and there is no voltage for transmitting a 0 bit. The UART frame is illustrated in Figure 4-11 with a start and a stop bit.

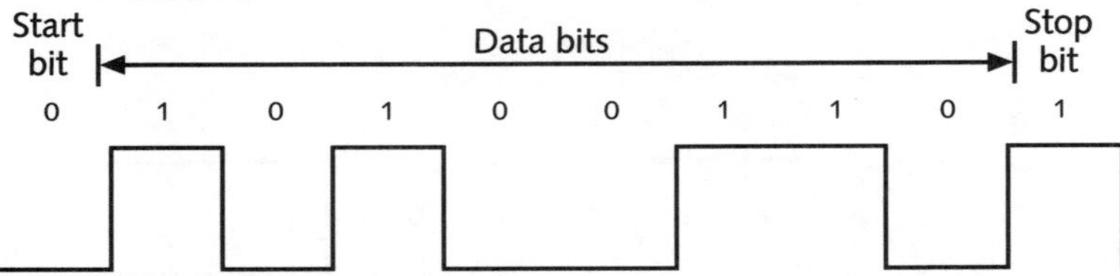

Figure 4-11 UART frame

Although NRZ is satisfactory for standard RS-232 serial ports, it cannot be used for infrared transmissions. With NRZ, the output is the same level for the entire bit period and can stay at one level for multiple bit periods, as illustrated in Figure 4-12. This is not optimal for an infrared system. A continuous string of the same bits could turn on the LED transmitter for a long period of time and would require a high level of power.

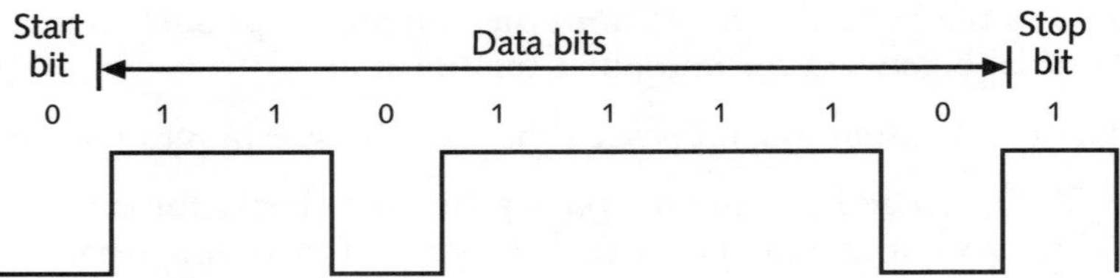

Figure 4-12 NRZ with same bit transmitted

IF NRZ was used in IR, the power in the LED would need to be limited, which would limit distance between devices.

Instead of using NRZ, IrDA uses a modified binary signaling technique known as **RZI (return to zero, inverted)**. The return-to-zero (RZ) technique calls for the voltage to increase to represent a 1 bit but for there to be no voltage for transmitting a 0 bit. RZI reverses ("inverts") this so that the voltage to represent a 0 bit instead of a 1 bit is increased.

IrDA requires the maximum pulse width to be 3/16 of the bit time. A 16x clock is available on UARTs. To transmit a 0 bit, the UART clock would wait for 7 clock cycles during the bit time and send an infrared pulse for 3 clock cycles, and then nothing for six clock cycles (7-3-6). When transmitting at 115,200 bps, this would mean the pulse would last 1.41 microseconds. Nothing would be sent to transmit a 1 bit during the 16 clock cycles of the bit time. This is illustrated in Figure 4-13.

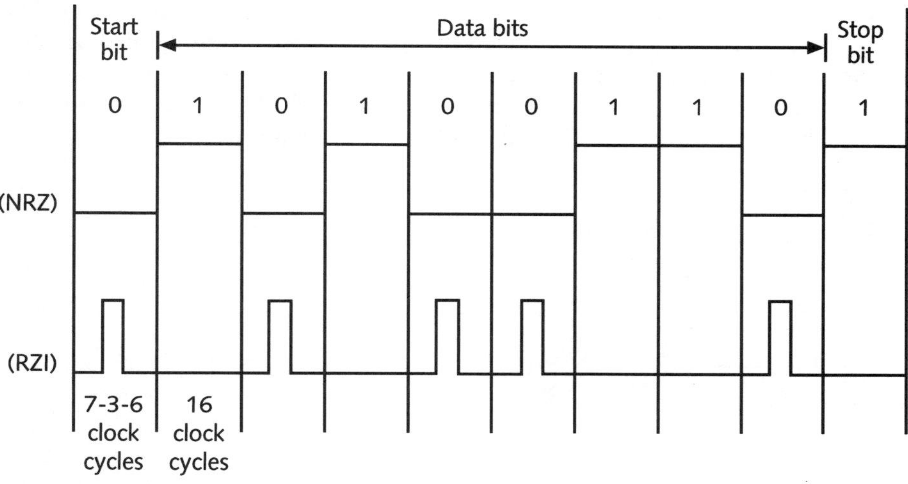

Figure 4-13 IrDA SIR transmission

Fast Infrared (Version 1.1)

The Fast Infrared version 1.1 of the IrDA specification extends the data rate to 4 Mbps while retaining backward compatibility with the slower SIR devices. This is possible because when two IrDA devices first communicate they both transmit at a transmission speed of only 9600 bps (at 9600 bps, a character arrives once every millisecond). They then exchange basic information, such as the higher transmission speeds that they can support. If both devices can accommodate the FIR higher speed, they will shift to that faster rate.

The functional block diagram of the FIR transmitter is illustrated in Figure 4-14. The block diagram for the FIR looks similar to the SIR block diagram except that the UART and 3/16 modulator are replaced with a device that is designed for 4 Mbps IrDA data communication. This device does the encoding and decoding of both the 3/16 and the 4 PPM modulation.

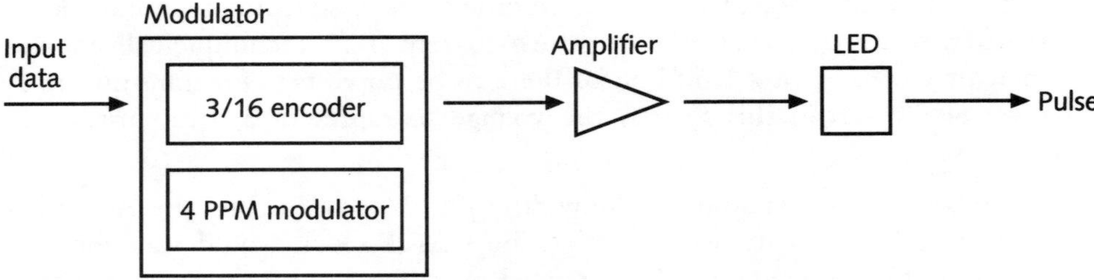

Figure 4-14 FIR transmitter block diagram

The FIR specification uses 4 PPM instead of the 3/16 modulation used for SIR. Information is conveyed by the position of a pulse within a time slot. Only two bits need to be transmitted using 4 PPM: 00, 01, 10, or 11. Depending on which two bits are to be transmitted, a single pulse is placed in either the first, second, third, and/or fourth part of the 500 ns time slot. The receiving device can determine the transmitted bits by the location of the pulse within the time slot. This is illustrated in Figure 4-15. While SIR sends 1 bit in 1 time slot, FIR can send 2 bits in 1 time slot.

Bit Pattern	Pulse Position
00	1000
01	0100
10	0010
11	0001

← 500 ns →

Figure 4-15 IrDA FIR transmission

Other Considerations

There are several other factors that must be considered when transmitting with infrared technology. These include latency, ambient light, and deflection angle.

Half-Duplex and Latency

IrDA devices cannot send and receive at the same time because the transmitter and receiver are not optically isolated. When the transmitter is sending IR light pulses it may even saturate its own receiver. Because a transmitted signal would interfere with an incoming signal, IrDA devices cannot send and receive simultaneously. Thus, communications between IrDA devices is always in half-duplex mode.

Half-duplex mode requires that there must be a time delay allowed from the time a device stops transmitting until it is ready to receive. This delay, from the time the transmitter stops sending light pulses to the time the receiver is guaranteed ready to receive data, is called **latency**. Latency is also known as receiver set-up time. The IrDA specification allows a period of 10 ms after completing the transmission for the receiver to regain its full sensitivity. However, shorter latency times may be negotiated between devices when they first link up.

Ambient Light

In order for IrDA devices to operate under a wide range of conditions, there are requirements for the amount of ambient light that should be rejected. IrDA specifies the test methods for measuring the data integrity of an IrDA connection under electromagnetic fields, sunlight, incandescent lighting, and fluorescent lighting. These specifications are given in terms of **lux.** Lux is a photometric measurement of light intensity. Maximum sunlight lux values at noon on a clear day in the tropics are generally considered to be 100,000 to 120,000 lux. An IrDA receiver must be able reject up to 10,000 lux of sunlight, 1000 lux of fluorescent light, and 1000 lux of incandescent light at a distance of 3 feet (1 meter). These values were chosen as typical of what may be encountered under normal use.

IrDA communications may still take place when conditions exceed these lux values but the devices would have to be closer to each other.

Deflection Angle

The angle at which the sending and receiving IrDA devices align or face each other is very important. When the infrared ports of two devices are exactly in line with each other, the **deflection angle** (or off-alignment angle) is zero. When the two devices have a deflection angle of no more than 15 degrees, the distance between devices can be up to 3 feet (1 meter). This is illustrated in Figure 4-16. However, if the deflection is between 15 and 30 degrees the devices must be moved closer together. A deflection angle of over 30 degrees will make infrared transmission impossible.

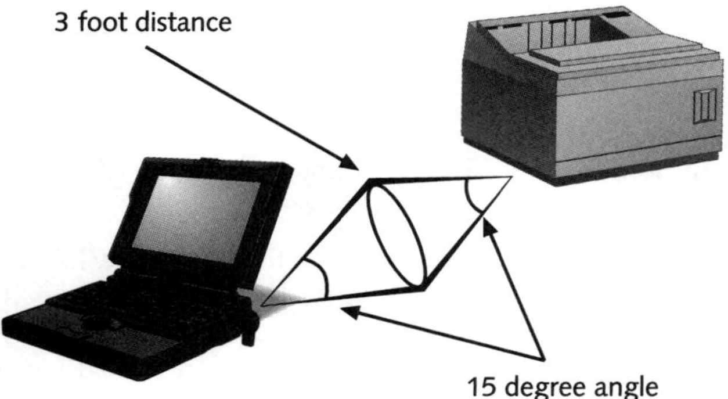

Figure 4-16 Deflection angle

CHAPTER SUMMARY

- In the mid-1970s the International Organization for Standardization (ISO) began work on developing specifications for communications by computer-based networks. The goal of the ISO was not to create an official physical standard for all computer networks, but to create an abstract model of networking. Completed in 1983, these conceptual specifications became known as the Open System Interconnect (OSI) model. The OSI model is intended to give a visual picture or concept of how telecommunications is done. It breaks the many complex functions of data communications into seven basic layers. Each layer does a specific function in the operation of communications devices and cooperates with the layer immediately above and below it by passing something to it or receiving something from it.

- About the same time that the ISO was working on the OSI model, the Institute of Electrical and Electronics Engineers (IEEE) started Project 802 to ensure interoperability among data network products. There is a difference between Project 802 and the OSI model in terms of how they are used. The OSI model is a theoretical model of how communications works. Project 802, on the other hand, sets standards for computer communications that are followed today. In short, the OSI model is theory while Project 802 sets standards for actual practice.

- Computer networks likewise have rules that all the network components must follow if the network is to work. A network protocol is the format and order of the messages exchanged between two or more communication devices based on standards. Network engineers have organized these protocols into layers. These layers generally correspond to the layers in the OSI model. When a set of network protocols are taken together as a whole it is called a network protocol stack.

- Infrared wireless local area networks date back almost 20 years. These wireless LANs can be either directed or diffused. A directed transmission requires that the emitter and detector be directly aimed at one another. A diffused transmission instead relies on reflected light. Diffused infrared has several advantages over directed transmissions for a LAN: the receiving device with the detector can be positioned almost anywhere within the room, one emitter can transmit simultaneously to multiple receivers, and a person moving in the room does not cause a disruption in the signal. Since infrared energy is lost as it is dispersed throughout the room, the distance between devices and the data rates are significantly reduced. The highest data rate for a diffused infrared WLAN is about 4 Mbps, while the range between devices is typically 30 to 50 feet (9 to 15 meters).

- The IEEE 802.11 standards outline the specifications for infrared WLANs. The specification is based on diffused transmissions. The PHY layer performs the functions of both reformatting the data received from the upper layers (PLCP) and transmitting the light impulses (PMD). The diffused infrared Physical Layer Convergence Procedure (PLCP) reformats the data received from the MAC layer (when transmitting) into a frame that the Physical Medium Dependent (PMD) sublayer can transmit. Once the PLCP has created the frame, it passes it to the

PMD sublayer. The PMD translates the binary 1s and 0s of the frame into light pulses that can be used for transmission. To transmit a 1 bit, the emitter increases the intensity of the current and sends a pulse using infrared light. The detector senses the higher intensity signal and produces a proportional electrical current.

- The most common infrared connection today is based on a standard known as IrDA. IrDA is an acronym for the Infrared Data Association. The primary use for IrDA is to link notebook computers and handheld devices with other devices such as printers, desktop adapters, cameras, phones, watches, pagers, storage devices, and kiosks.
- IrDA devices communicate using infrared light emitting diodes (LEDs) to send and photodiodes to receive signals. Unlike radio frequency devices that decrease the bandwidth as the distance between devices increases, IrDA devices do not vary the transmission speed. IrDA devices must be capable of maintaining a constant connection speed.
- The IrDA protocol stack is made up of several layers. Three of the layers are required: IrPHY, IrLAP, and IrLMP. The remaining layers are optional, depending on how the device is being used. The IrDA physical layer protocol controls the hardware that sends and receives the IR pulses. The function of the IrPHY varies depending on which standard, the Serial Infrared (SIR), version 1.0, or the Fast Infrared (FIR), version 1.1, is being used.
- IrDA devices cannot send and receive at the same time because the transmitter and receiver are not optically isolated. Communication between IrDA devices is always in half-duplex mode. Half-duplex mode requires that a time delay is allowed from the time a device stops transmitting until it is ready to receive. This delay, from the time the transmitter stops sending light pulses to the time the receiver is guaranteed ready to receive data, is called latency.
- Ambient light can impede an infrared transmission. IrDA specifies the test methods for measuring the data integrity of an IrDA connection under electromagnetic fields, sunlight, incandescent lighting, and fluorescent lighting.
- The angle at which the sending and receiving IrDA devices align or face each other is very important. When the infrared ports of two devices are exactly in line with each other the deflection angle (or off-alignment angle) is zero. When the two devices have a deflection angle of no more than 15 degrees, the distance between devices can be up to 3 feet (1 meter). If the deflection is between 15 and 30 degrees, the devices must be moved closer together.

Key Terms

16-pulse position modulation (16-PPM) — A modulation technique that translates four data bits into 16 light impulses.

4-pulse position modulation (4-PPM) — A modulation technique that translates two data bits into 4 light impulses.

ambient light — Bright surrounding light.

AppleTalk — A network protocol stack used by Apple for its Macintosh computers.

deflection angle — The off-alignment angle between two IrDA devices.

frame — Another name for a packet.

Internetwork Packet eXchange/Sequenced Packet eXchange (IPX/SPX) — A network protocol stack found on Novell NetWare LANs.

IrDA — An acronym for the **I**nfrared **D**ata **A**ssociation and also a standard for wireless infrared communications.

latency — A time delay from when a device stops transmitting until it is be ready to receive.

Logical Link Control (LLC) — One of the two sublayers of the IEEE Project 802 Data Link layer.

lux — A photometric measurement of light intensity.

Media Access Control (MAC) — One of the two sublayers of the IEEE Project 802 Data Link layer.

nanosecond (ns) — One billionth of a second.

network protocol — The format and order of the messages exchanged between two or more communication devices based on standards.

network protocol stack — A set of network protocols taken together as a whole.

Open System Interconnect (OSI) model — A seven-layer abstract model of networking developed by the ISO (International Organization for Standardization).

parity bit — An optional bit that is used for error checking.

Physical Layer Convergence Procedure (PLCP) sublayer — One of the two sublayers of the IEEE Project 802 PHY layer that reformats the data received from the MAC layer into a packet and determines when the data can be sent.

Physical Medium Dependent (PMD) sublayer — One of the two sublayers of the IEEE Project 802 PHY layer that includes standards for the characteristics of the wireless medium (IR and RF) and defines the method for transmitting and receiving data through that medium.

Project 802 — A set of specifications developed by the Institute of Electrical and Electronics Engineers (IEEE) to ensure interoperability among network devices.

RZI (return to zero, inverted) — A modified binary signaling technique in that the voltage to represent a 0 bit is increased.

start bit — An optional bit used as a delineator that indicates when the transmitted byte starts.

stop bit — An optional bit used as a delineator that indicates when the transmitted byte stops.

time slots — The measurement of a PLCP frame.

Transmission Control Protocol/Internet Protocol (TCP/IP) — The standard network protocol stack used on the Internet.

UART (Universal Asynchronous Receiver/Transmitter) — A microchip that controls a computer's interface to its attached serial devices through a serial port or IrDA port.

REVIEW QUESTIONS

1. The International Organization for Standardization created a conceptual model known as:
   a. ISO
   b. OSI
   c. IEEE
   d. 802
2. The model created by the ISO contains how many layers?
   a. 6
   b. 7
   c. 8
   d. 9
3. Each of the following is true about the model created by the ISO except:
   a. The model competes against the IEEE 802 standard.
   b. Each layer performs specific functions in terms of communications.
   c. To accomplish the function, several tasks may be performed using different hardware and software.
   d. The flow between layers goes down when sending and up when receiving.
4. The ________________ "listens" to the medium to determine when the data can be sent.
   a. Physical Layer Convergence Procedure (PLCP)
   b. IEEE 802.x
   c. Logical Link Control (LLC)
   d. Data Link layer
5. ________________ is the standard network protocol stack used on the Internet and has become the dominant protocol stack today.
   a. IPX/SPX
   b. AppleTalk
   c. TCP/IP
   d. GNU
6. Project 802 subdivides the OSI model Layer 2, Data Link, into two sublayers, the Logical Link Control (LLC) and Media Access Control (MAC) layers. True or false?
7. When a set of network protocols are taken together as a whole it is called a network protocol stack. True or false?
8. MacTalk is the network protocol stack used by Apple for its Macintosh computers. True or false?

9. Because infrared light is near in wavelength to visible light, IR shares many of the same physical properties. True or false?
10. Like RF, IR is regulated. True or false?
11. The ________________ sublayer includes the standards for the characteristics of the wireless medium (IR and RF) and defines the method for transmitting and receiving data through that medium.
12. A(n) ________________ is the format and order of the messages exchanged between two or more communication devices based on standards.
13. The highest data rate for a diffused infrared WLAN is about ______________ Mbps.
14. The IEEE 802.11 standards that outline the specifications for infrared WLANs are based on ________________ transmissions.
15. Infrared wireless systems send data by the ________________ of the light wave instead of "on-off" signals of light.
16. What is the difference between Project 802 and the OSI model?
17. How can the 4-PPM transmit at twice the speed of 16-PPM?
18. List and describe some of the characteristics of IrDA.
19. List some of the design factors that can improve the performance of the IrDA devices.
20. What is RZI? Why is it used with IR transmissions?

HANDS-ON PROJECTS

1. Set up two notebook computers for infrared transmission.
   a. Secure a notebook computer that has an IrDA port.
   b. Turn on the computer and press the necessary keys to enter the BIOS setup. For example, on a Dell Latitude press the **F2** key.
   c. Search for the page that contains the option to enable the IrDA port. For a Dell Latitude press **Alt** + **P** to move to the next page. Look for a value labeled "Infrared Data Port" or something similar.
   d. Enable the IrDA port. On some computers the options for the port are Disabled, COM1, or COM2. If there is already a standard serial port on this computer select COM2.
   e. Some computers also allow you to set the IrDA version. The choices may be Serial IR (or Slow IR), Fast IR, or Very Fast IR. Unless you are sure that other infrared devices you have support Fast IR, select Serial IR.
   f. Save this information and restart your computer. Windows XP should automatically identify this device. If it does not, click **Start** and then click **Control Panel**. Click **Add New Hardware**. Follow the Wizard instructions on the screen.

2. Transfer a file between a notebook computer and a PDA. In order to do this project you will need a notebook computer running Windows XP or 2000 and a PDA running Pocket PC 2002.

   a. Using one of the notebook computers that was set up in Project 1, open a text editor like Windows Notepad and create a document that contains your name and the current date and time. Save this as **Project 2 Your Name**.

   b. Align the IrDA port of the PDA so that they are approximately 6 inches apart and are directly aimed at each other. In Windows XP the IrDA icon will appear in the system tray and an icon entitled "Send Files to Another Computer" will appear on the desktop. This is seen in Figure 4-17. In Windows 2000 the same icon will appear in the system tray.

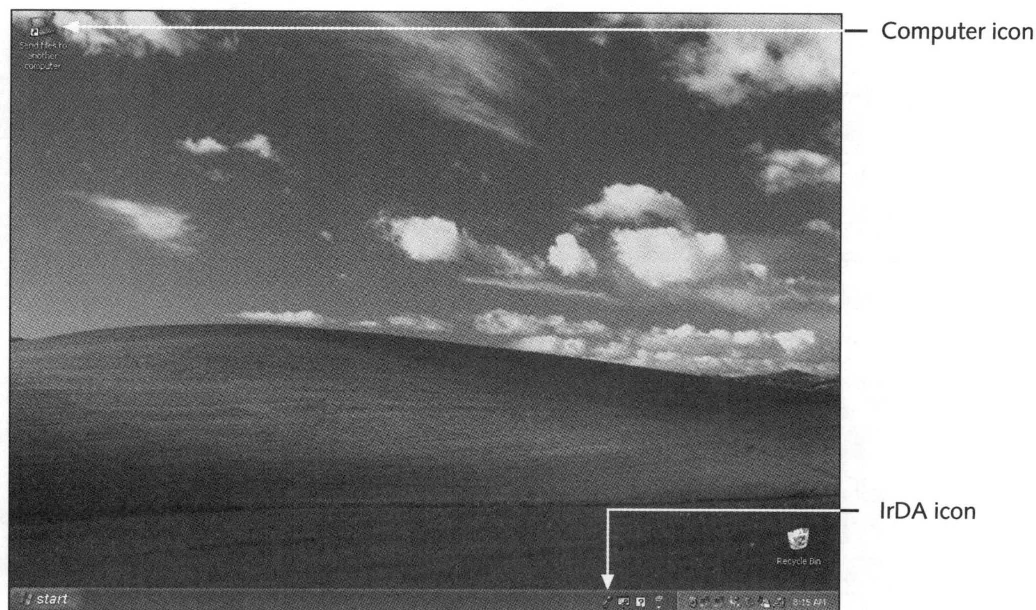

Figure 4-17 Windows XP IrDA icon and folder

   c. In Windows XP right click on the IrDA icon and then click on **Properties**. This will open the Wireless Link dialog box, as seen in Figure 4-18. Be sure that all of the options are checked on the **Infrared** tab. In Windows 2000 right click on the IrDA icon and then click on **Options**, as seen in Figure 4-19. Be sure that all of the options are checked in the **File Transfer** tab.

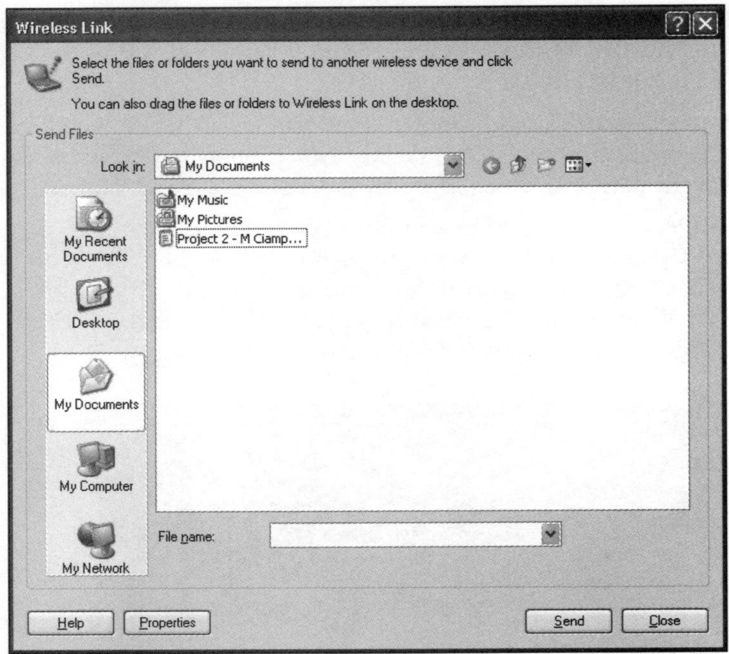

Figure 4-18 Windows XP Wireless Link dialog box

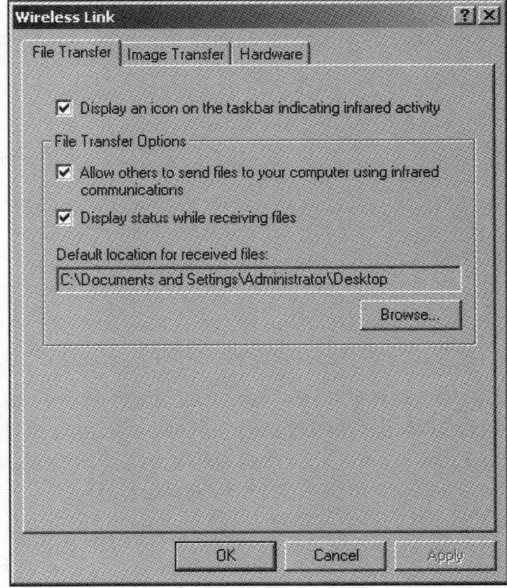

Figure 4-19 Windows 2000 Wireless Link dialog box

d. Double-click on the IrDA icon to open the Wireless Link Send Files dialog box. The Windows XP screen is seen in Figure 4-20. The Windows 2000 screen is seen in Figure 4-21. Locate the file **Project 2 Your Name** and click on it. Click the **Send** button.

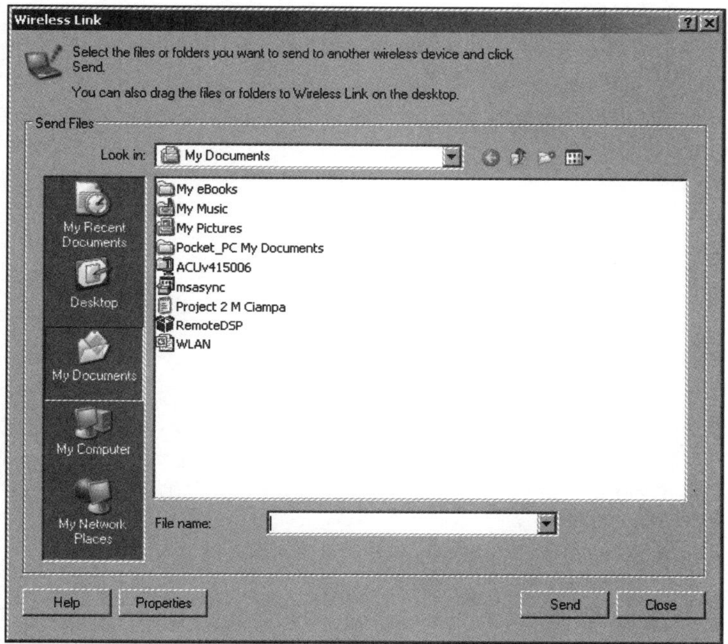

Figure 4-20 Windows XP Wireless Link Send Files dialog box

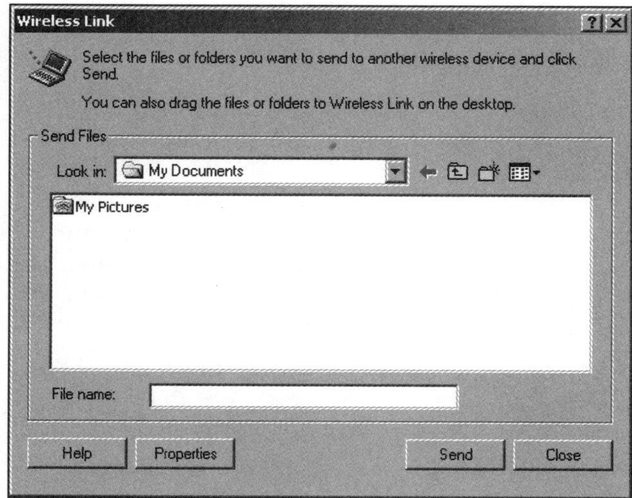

Figure 4-21 Windows 2000 Wireless Link Send Files dialog box

e. On the PDA device, tap on the **Start** icon to open the menu, as seen in Figure 4-22. Tap on the **File Manger** icon and locate the Temp folder. Tap on this folder to see the file that you just transferred over from the notebook.

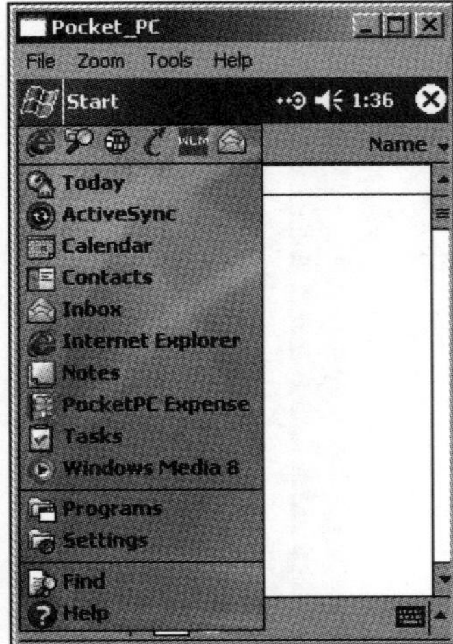

Figure 4-22 PDA start menu

3. Print a file using a PDA and a laser printer.

   a. Using a PDA, such as a Jornada 720 or similar device using Microsoft Pocket PC, open Microsoft Pocket Word by tapping on **Start** and tap on **Programs**. Select **Office** and then **Microsoft Pocket Word.** (*Note:* Not all PDAs support direct IrDA printing. Check your user's manual or the Web site of your PDA to determine its capabilities.)

   b. Create a new document that contains your name and today's date. Save this document as **Project 3 Your Name**.

   c. Tap on **File** and then **Print**.

   d. Select **PCL Laser** from the list of available printers.

   e. Select **IRDA** from the list of available ports.

   f. Align the IrDA port of the PDA with the IrDA port of the printer so that they are approximately 6 inches apart and directly aimed at each other. The laser printer does not need to be disconnected from a network port or a local computer in order for IrDA to function.

   g. Click **OK**. The document will print on the laser printer.

   h. Close Microsoft Pocket Word.

4. Transfer files between two notebook computers.
   a. Using a text editor like Windows Notepad, create a document on one computer that contains the current date and time. Save this file as **Project 4 Your Name A**. Create the same document on the second computer but name it **Project 4 Your Name B**.
   b. Move the notebook computers so their IrDA ports align and they are between 3 inches and 3 feet of each other. Within about 5 seconds the systems should establish a connection. When connection is established the infrared icon appears in the system tray on both notebooks.
   c. In Windows XP, right-click the IrDA icon and then click **Properties.** This will open the Wireless Link dialog box. Be sure that all of the options are checked on the **Infrared** tab. In Windows 2000 right-click the IrDA icon and then click **Options**. Be sure that all of the options are checked in the **File Transfer** tab.
   d. Double-click the IrDA icon to open the Wireless Link Send Files dialog box. The Windows XP screen is seen in Figure 4-23. The Windows 2000 screen is seen in Figure 4-24. Locate the file **Project 4 Your Name A** and click to select it. Click the **Send** button.

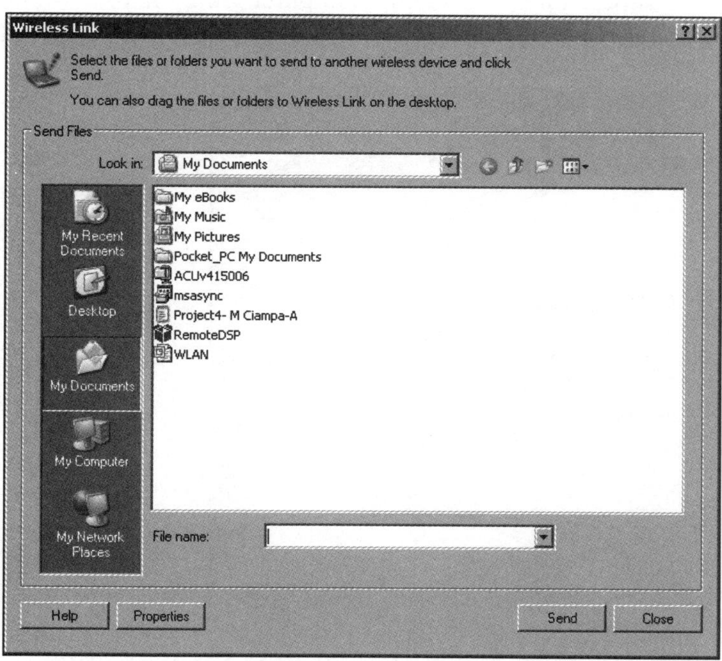

Figure 4-23 Windows XP Wireless Link Send Files dialog box

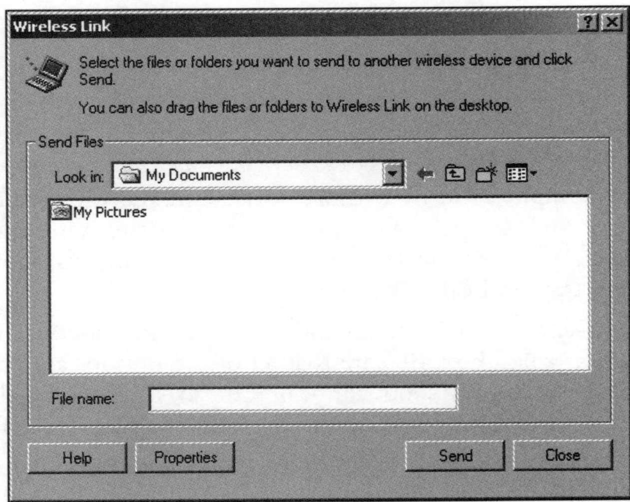

Figure 4-24 Windows 2000 Wireless Link Send Files dialog box

e. A message will appear on the receiving computer asking if you would like to accept the file, as seen in Figure 4-25. Click **Yes**.

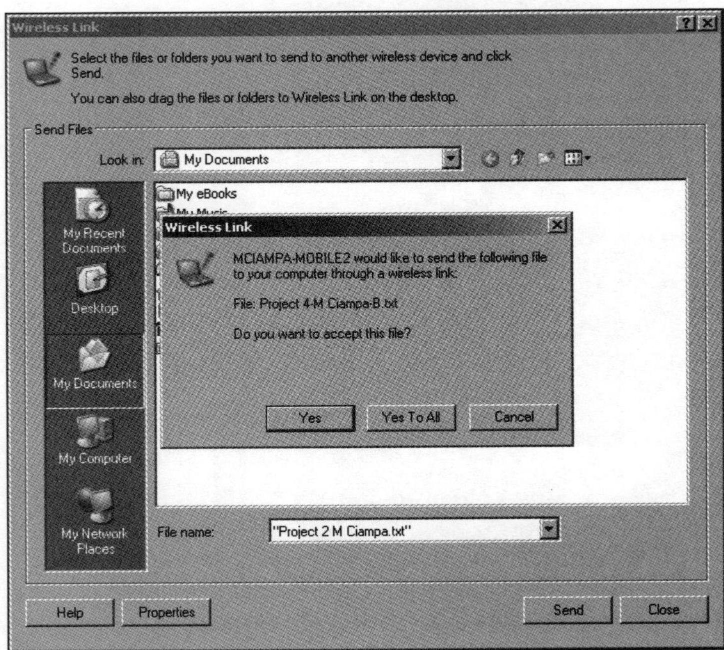

Figure 4-25 Receive file dialog box

f. Locate the file **Project 4 Your Name A** on the receiving computer (an icon for that file will be on the desktop) and open it.

g. Using the same procedure now transfer **Project 4 Your Name B** back to the other notebook.

5. Using two notebook computers or other devices with infrared ports, experiment regarding the angle, distance and ambient light between them. Use a variety of settings and conditions. What are the practical limits of infrared transmission? What guidelines would you establish for infrared use? What troubleshooting tips can you give? Write a one-page paper on your findings.
6. Windows XP allows you to set up an infrared network connection between two computers to access shared resources on one of the computers. When making this type of infrared network connection, you configure the portable computer as the guest and the desktop computer as the host. That is, when you create the network connections, specify the computer that has the information you want to access as the host computer, and the computer you are going to use to access the information as the guest computer. Use the Windows XP help file and information from Microsoft's Web site to write a one-page instruction sheet on how to set up and use this infrared network.
7. Very Fast IrDA (VFIR), which provides 16 Mbps half-duplex data transmission, is the most recent IrDA specification. Using the Internet, research VFIR. How is it different from SIR and FIR? What type of modulation scheme does it use? Which operating systems support it? How does it maintain compatibility with SIR and FIR? How will it be used? Write a one-page paper on your findings.

Case Projects

The Baypoint Group (TBG) has once again requested your services as a consultant. A regional restaurant chain, Thomas' Italian Grill, wants to speed up its service. The management of Thomas' Italian Grill has identified a bottleneck in their order process. Servers write down the customer's order and then must go to a central computer to enter the orders. On nights when the restaurant is very busy the servers may have to wait in line at the central computer to enter their orders.

TBG has proposed that servers be provided PDAs with IrDA ports. As the servers take the orders they will tap them into the PDA. Several infrared ports will be installed at different locations around the restaurant. Servers will only need to point their PDA devices at the IrDA port to transmit the customer's order into the computer system.

Because this is so new to Thomas' Italian Grill, they are reluctant to go along with the proposal. TBG has asked you to become involved.

1. Create a PowerPoint slide presentation that outlines how infrared technology works. Be sure to include information about IrDA standards, the advantages and disadvantages, and why IrDA would be the best solution for this project.

2. Your presentation convinced Thomas' Italian Grill management that PDAs using IrDA would be a good solution. They have now asked your opinion regarding the brand of PDA and operating system that would be best. Using the Internet, research different types of PDAs and their operating systems. Create a chart that shows the advantages and disadvantages of each type. Make a recommendation regarding which you feel would be the best for this application.

Optional Team Case Project

Thomas' Italian Grill uses a variety of lighting (incandescent lighting and fluorescent lighting) as well as large glass areas that let in sunlight during the daytime hours. TBG needs to make recommendations regarding what type of lighting should be installed around the fixed IrDA ports in the restaurant. They also need to know exactly how far back the servers can be to transmit the orders from the PDA to the fixed infrared port. Although the IrDA specifications state that 3 feet (1 meter) is the maximum, this distance can be lengthened or shortened by ambient light. Using two notebook computers or a PDA and a notebook computer, conduct several tests using different light and different distances between IrDA devices. Develop a table that indicates the maximum distance between IrDA devices under different lighting conditions.

CHAPTER

5

BLUETOOTH

After reading this chapter and completing the exercises you will be able to:

- Explain how Bluetooth is used
- Tell how Bluetooth works
- Describe several issues that Bluetooth faces

One of the most widely anticipated wireless technologies of the past ten years is a product known as Bluetooth. Despite its unusual name, Bluetooth holds great promise for sending and receiving radio frequency signals between PDAs, cell phones, and notebook computers. However, acceptance of Bluetooth has been much slower than was first predicted because of technology and economic considerations. Although most industry experts predict that Bluetooth will be a player in the wireless technology arena, its role as a major player is uncertain.

In this chapter we will look at Bluetooth and explore how it works. We will also discuss how Bluetooth fits into the global picture of the wireless world and what the future may hold for this wireless technology.

What Is Bluetooth?

Bluetooth is the name given to a wireless technology that uses short-range radio frequency (RF) transmissions. Originally designed in 1994 by Ericsson, a cellular telephone company, as a way to replace wires with radio-based technology, Bluetooth has moved beyond that original design. Bluetooth technology enables users to connect to a wide range of computing and telecommunications devices without the need to use cables. It provides for rapid "on the fly" connections between devices. In this section we will look at how Bluetooth is used and compare it with infrared. Also, we will explore the group responsible for maintaining the Bluetooth specifications.

How Bluetooth Is Used

Bluetooth is essentially a low-powered wireless data and voice transmission technology. It can be used any place where a small stream of data needs to flow. What makes Bluetooth so intriguing is that, unlike other "dumb" technologies such as IrDA that send and receive data only when the user initiates the process, Bluetooth can be "smart." It has the capability to recognize another Bluetooth device within its range and automatically synchronize with that device. This opens up a variety of applications for this technology. For example, a Bluetooth-enabled cellular telephone or pager could automatically switch to vibrate mode whenever the user passes through the doors of a movie theater. Or, a notebook computer and GPS (global positioning system) could automatically feed a display on a hand-held PDA that displays directions while traveling in a car. A user holding a cell phone could approach a vending machine that would automatically link up with a wireless payment system, allowing the user to tap a few keys on the phone and charge a vending machine purchase. These are not fanciful dreams but have actually been implemented using Bluetooth technology.

According to market research, Bluetooth-enabled devices will number over 1.4 billion by 2005. Of that number, 74% will be mobile telephones, 14% computing and peripheral devices, 8% accessories, cards and adapters, and 4% other devices.

Ericsson has recently introduced a Bluetooth Local Infotainment Point (BLIP), which serves as a central access point to which all Bluetooth devices could send their transmissions. The BLIP in turn would transmit the data to other Bluetooth devices.

One example of Bluetooth technology is a cellular telephone in a user's pocket that automatically dials an Internet Service Provider (ISP). Once that connection is made, the user's e-mail is downloaded to a notebook computer that is in a briefcase the user is carrying. An e-mail application on the notebook identifies an urgent message and sends it back to the cell phone where it is converted by the phone (using text-to-speech software) into audio and played for the user to hear. All of this takes places while the user is running through an airport. Bluetooth technology is at the heart of this scenario and demonstrates the capability of this wireless technology, as seen in Figure 5-1.

Figure 5-1 Bluetooth scenario

Researchers are working on a Bluetooth-enabled electrocardiogram (ECG) device that will send data directly to a technician's hand-held computer.

Bluetooth vs. IrDA

One of the best ways to understand the nature of Bluetooth is to compare it with infrared (IrDA) technology. Some consider Bluetooth to be in direct competition with IrDA. However, this is not completely accurate. There are situations and conditions where IrDA is better suited for transmitting data than Bluetooth, and vice versa. Each technology has its own pluses and minuses, and the places where IrDA falls short are the very ones in which Bluetooth excels, and vice versa. Each technology has its place, and although they can overlap, Bluetooth and IrDA actually complement one another more than they compete with each other.

Consider the example of electronically exchanging business cards. Li and Tracy meet face to face, in a large conference room where many other people are likewise carrying wireless devices and are also electronically exchanging cards. In this situation IrDA would be the technology of choice. IrDA is intended for a short-distance, narrow angle transmission. Li and Tracy are carrying on a conversation, meaning they are facing each other (narrow angle) and are face-to-face (short range). Li and Tracy could simply point their

PDA devices at each other and exchange business cards using IrDA technology. The limited range and narrow angle of IrDA also allows others in the room to electronically exchange cards without interfering with other transmissions. IrDA provides this simple form of security along with a natural ease of use. This is illustrated in Figure 5-2.

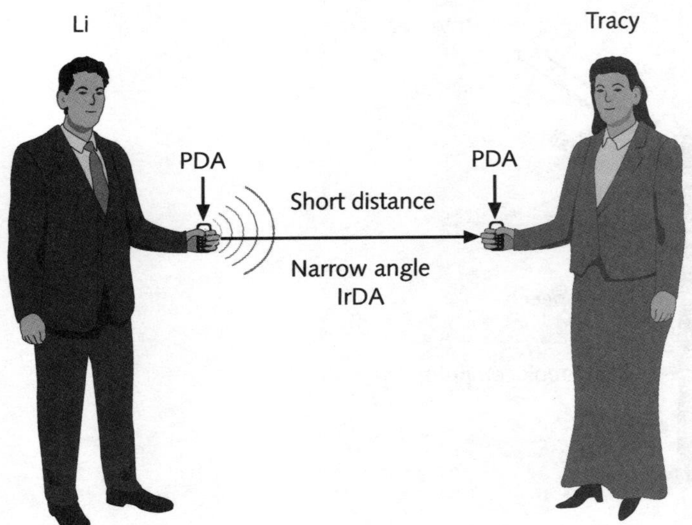

Figure 5-2 IrDA transmission

In this same situation Bluetooth would not be a viable wireless technology to use. Bluetooth radio frequency transmissions spread out over the entire room. Bluetooth does not allow the user to simply point at the intended recipient. Li's transmission would have difficulty just finding Tracy's PDA; instead, it would also see every other Bluetooth device in the room, as seen in Figure 5-3. This discovery operation of which devices are available could be time-consuming. Li would then have to choose Tracy's PDA based on a device address from a long list of devices that were discovered. Once Tracy's device was identified, Li and Tracy's devices would have to execute a security measure to ensure that nobody else in the room accidentally received the transmission.

In other data exchange situations Bluetooth is the better choice over IrDA. Because Bluetooth is based on RF instead of IR, Bluetooth devices can penetrate solid objects and can perform data exchanges while the user is mobile, something that is impossible with IrDA. For example, once Li receives Tracy's electronic business card on his PDA, that same device using Bluetooth can automatically synchronize with her notebook computer in her briefcase, updating the address book on the notebook. Because Bluetooth is omnidirectional, the synchronization starts whenever the PDA is brought into range of the notebook. And using Bluetooth for synchronization does not require that the PDA remain in a fixed location: if the PDA is carried in Li's pocket, the synchronization can occur while he moves around.

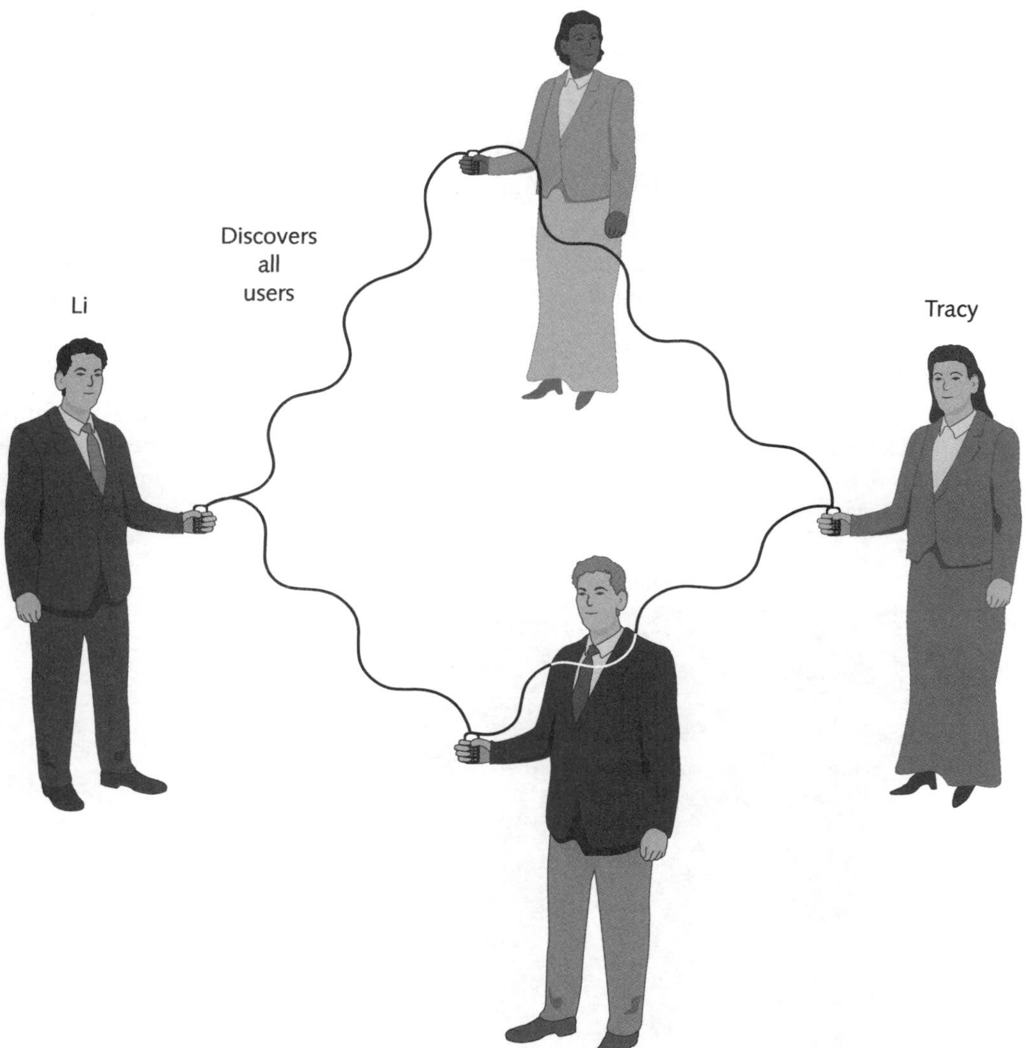

Figure 5-3 Bluetooth transmission

Bluetooth SIG

Bluetooth is supported by over 2,500 hardware and software vendors who make up the Bluetooth Special Interest Group (SIG). This consortium, which was originally comprised of only five companies, develops and promotes the Bluetooth global wireless technology. The goals of the SIG are to develop technical specifications that enable Bluetooth products to be used across different vendor devices (interoperability). The Bluetooth SIG also administers test facilities to ensure that different devices do conform to the standards.

The Bluetooth SIG has established 11 working subgroups, which include Audio/Visual, Car, Imaging, Local Positioning, and Printing. It also is currently working with the IEEE to make the Bluetooth technology an IEEE standard.

How Bluetooth Works

Bluetooth is considered to be a robust radio frequency technology. This section will explore the specifications of Bluetooth and how it functions by first looking at the overall Bluetooth protocol stack and then focus on the function of specific layers.

Protocol Stack

The Bluetooth protocol stack is seen in Figure 5-4. Generally speaking, the functions of the stack can be divided into two parts based on how they are implemented. The lower levels of the stack are accomplished through hardware, while the functions of the upper levels of the stack are achieved by software. These functions are discussed in the sections that follow.

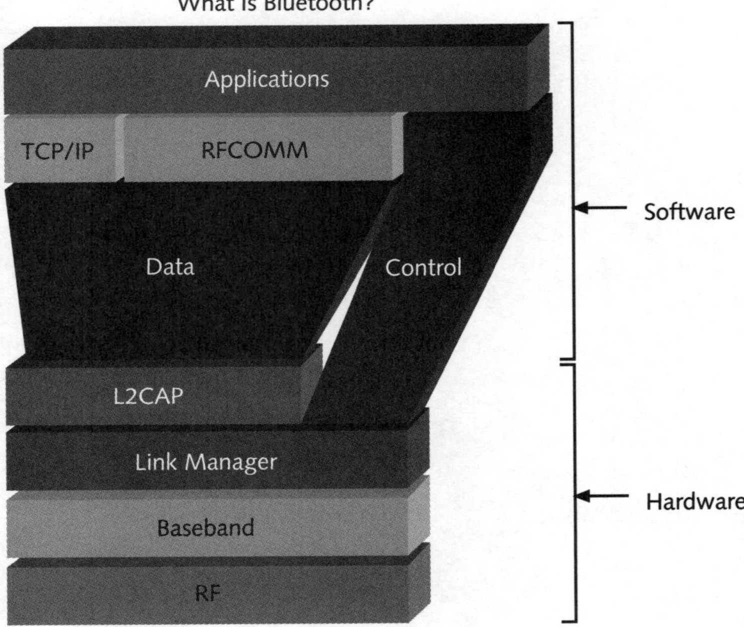

Figure 5-4 Bluetooth protocol stack

RF Layer

At the lowest level of the Bluetooth protocol stack is the RF layer. It defines how the basic hardware that controls the radio transmissions functions. At this level the data bits

(0 and 1) are converted into radio signals and transmitted, while at the same time the signals from other devices are received.

Radio Module

At the heart of Bluetooth is a single radio transmitter/receiver (transceiver). This single tiny chip is called a **Bluetooth radio module**. Figure 5-5 illustrates the relative size of a Bluetooth chip. It is the only hardware that is required for Bluetooth to function. The goal of the original Bluetooth design was that the transceiver have the following characteristics:

- The basic functions must be performed by a single chip
- The technology should be as generic or "mainstream" as possible
- It should be low-cost
- There should be a minimum of supporting off-chip components

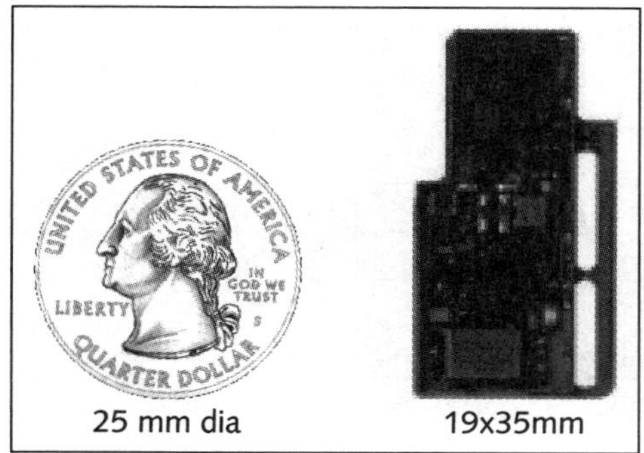

Figure 5-5 Bluetooth transceiver

The Bluetooth designers were able to achieve these goals. A functional block diagram of the transceiver they created is shown in Figure 5-6. The transceiver can interface with the host device through a variety of connections. A **UART (Universal Asynchronous Receiver/Transmitter)** serial port connection is the most common. Another option is through a USB connection. **Universal Serial Bus (USB)** is a serial interface that operates at a maximum speed of 12 Mbps. A third option is **Peripheral Component Interface (PCI)**. PCI is the standard 32-bit PC bus architecture found on almost all computers today.

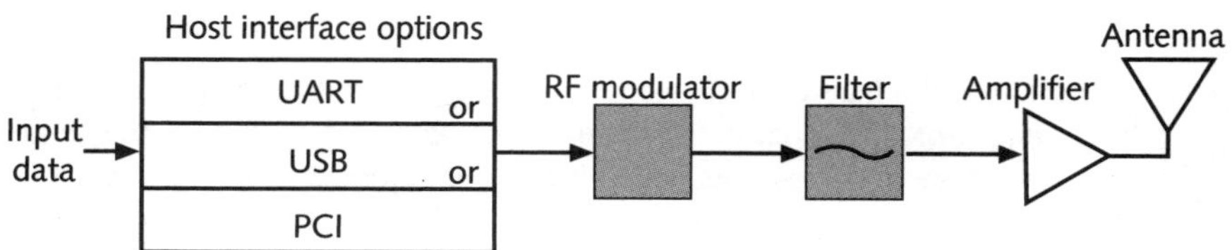

Figure 5-6 Functional block diagram of a Bluetooth transceiver

The impact of having Bluetooth hardware contained on a single chip is significant. Instead of requiring expensive external devices, such as PC Cards, to add Bluetooth functionality to a device, the functionality can be built into the product itself by adding a single Bluetooth chip in the manufacturing process. Because devices with a Bluetooth chip have a Bluetooth transceiver built in, they are ready to send and receive Bluetooth transmissions the moment the box is opened.

Bluetooth can transmit at a speed of 1 Mbps under the current Bluetooth specification (version 1.1). The next generation of Bluetooth devices should be able to send and receive at 2 Mbps. Table 5-1 compares Bluetooth speed with other internal and external computer connections.

Table 5-1 Connection speeds

Connection Name	Speed	Common Uses
Serial (RS232c)	115 Kbps	External modems
Parallel (IEEE 1284)	500 Kbps–2 Mbps	Printers
Bluetooth (1.1)	1 Mbps	Cell phones, PDAs
Small Computer System Interface (SCSI-2)	5 Mbps–10 Mbps	External scanners
Universal Serial Bus (USB)	12 Mbps	Digital cameras
IrDA (VFIR)	16 Mbps	Notebooks
FireWire (IEEE 1394)	50 Mbps	Digital video
Ultra ATA/100	100 Mbps	Internal hard drives
Peripheral Component Interface (PCI)	132 Mbps (33 MHz)	Internal expansion cards
Ultra-3 SCSI	160 Mbps	Internal hard drives
Fibre Channel (ISO 1496-1)	1 Gbps	Server farms

Bluetooth has three power classes for transmitting. These are summarized in Table 5-2. The level of power that sends the radio signal is measured in **milliwatts** (mW or thousandths of a watt). A **watt** is a single unit of electrical power. In contrast, home electrical power is measured in **kilowatts** (kW or thousands of watts). Today almost all Bluetooth devices are based on Power Class 2. This means that the distance between Bluetooth devices is a maximum of 33 feet (10 meters). However, because Bluetooth is based on RF transmission, objects such as walls and interference from other sources can affect the range of transmission.

An option to the Bluetooth RF standard allows a radio transceiver to measure the strength of the signal that is being received and determine if the sender should increase or decrease its power level. This adjusted power level must not exceed the amount specified in the power class.

Table 5-2 Power classes

Name	Power Level	Distance
Power Class 1	100 mW	330 feet (100 meters)
Power Class 2	2.5 mW	33 feet (10 meters)
Power Class 3	1 mW	3 inches (10 centimeters)

A recent test of a Power Class 2 device in a completely unobstructed environment achieved a range of almost 330 feet (100 meters).

Because Bluetooth devices are mobile and require battery power, conserving power is essential. The power consumption of devices using Bluetooth varies depending upon what is being transmitted. For Bluetooth devices, power consumption is measured in **milliamps** (mA or thousandths of an amp). An **ampere** or amp is a measure of the number of electrons that move through a conductor. When voice transmissions are being sent and received, only 10 milliamps of power is used. At that rate a typical battery would not have to be recharged for 75 hours. When data transmissions are occurring, only 6 milliamps are consumed and a battery would last 120 hours before it had to be recharged. When a Bluetooth is in a standby mode waiting for a transmission, it only requires .3 milliamps of power, which means the battery would hold a charge for 3 months.

Although amps and watts are sometimes confusing, think of watts as the measure of the power needed to push the radio signal out while amps is the measure of power that is used to make that push.

Modulation Technique

The Bluetooth specifications at the RF Layer include the modulation technique to be used. Bluetooth uses a variation of the frequency shift keying (FSK), which is a binary modulation technique that changes the frequency of the carrier signal. (You learned about FSK in Chapter 2.) With FSK the number of "waves" needed to send a 1 data bit are more than the number to send a 0 data bit. The variation of FSK that Bluetooth uses is known as **two-level Gaussian frequency shift keying (2-GFSK)**. 2-GFSK uses two different frequencies to indicate whether a 1 or a 0 is being transmitted in addition to varying the number of "waves." The amount that the frequency varies, called the **modulation index**, is between 280 KHz and 350 KHz. To represent a 0 the frequency would be decreased, while to represent a 1 the frequency would be increased.

For example, suppose Bluetooth is transmitting at 2.402 GHz (equivalent to a frequency of 2,402,000,000 Hz) and the modulation index is 280 KHz. The center of that frequency would be 2,402,500,000 Hz (normally a transmission would take place as close to the center of the frequency as possible to minimize any interference from adjacent frequencies). A 1 would be transmitted at 2,402,780,000 Hz, and a 0 would be transmitted at 2,402,220,000 Hz:

Center of frequency	2,402,500,000
Modulation index	+ 280,000
Transmission frequency for a 1	2,402,780,000
Center of frequency	2,402,500,000
Modulation index	– 280,000
Transmission frequency for a 0	2,402,220,000

The sine wave of this 2-GFSK is illustrated in Figure 5-7.

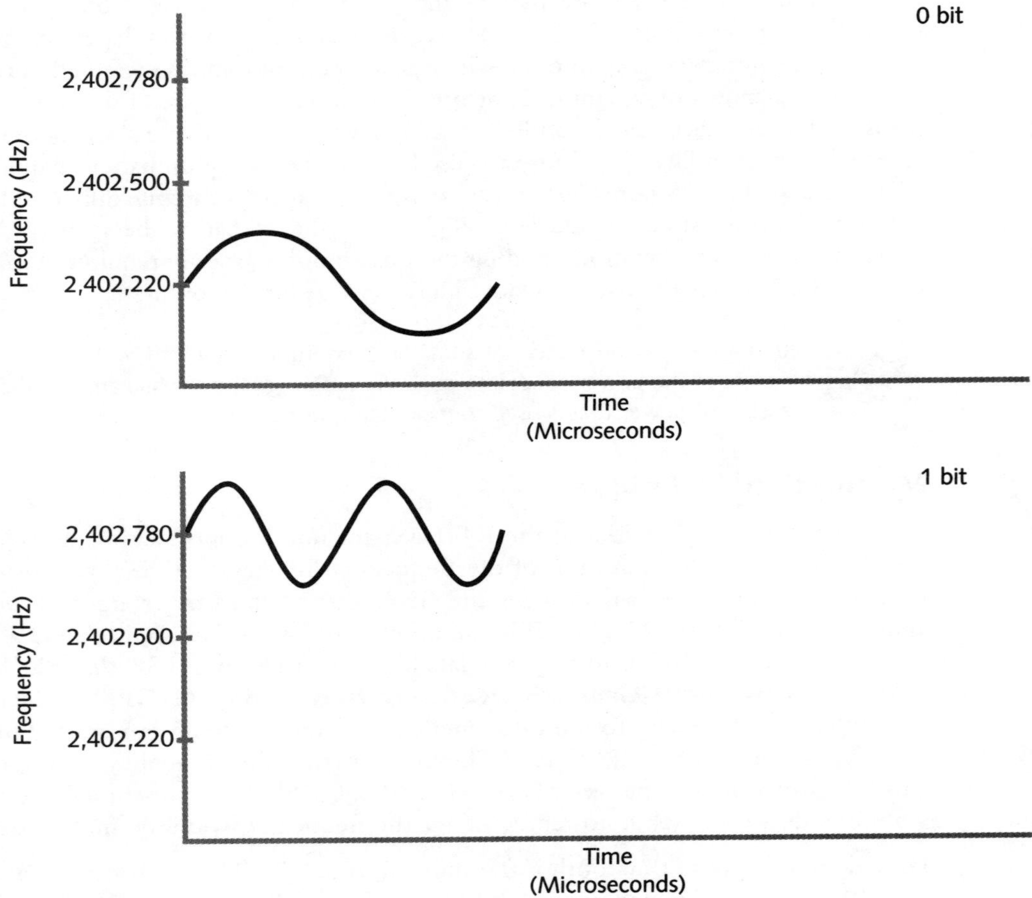

Figure 5-7 2-GFSK

Baseband Layer

The Baseband layer lies on top of the RF layer in the Bluetooth stack. This layer manages physical channels and links, handles packets, and does paging and inquiry to access and inquire about Bluetooth devices in the area.

Radio Frequency

The part of the spectrum in which Bluetooth operates is the 2.4 GHz Industrial, Scientific, and Medical (ISM) band. Bluetooth divides this 2.4 GHz frequency into 79 different frequencies (called **channels**) spaced 1 MHz apart. Bluetooth uses the frequency hopping spread spectrum (FHSS) technique to send a transmission. This means that the radio frequency "hops" or changes rapidly through the 79 different frequencies during transmission. This is illustrated in Figure 5-8. In just one second of Bluetooth transmission the frequency will change 1,600 times, or once every 625 microseconds.

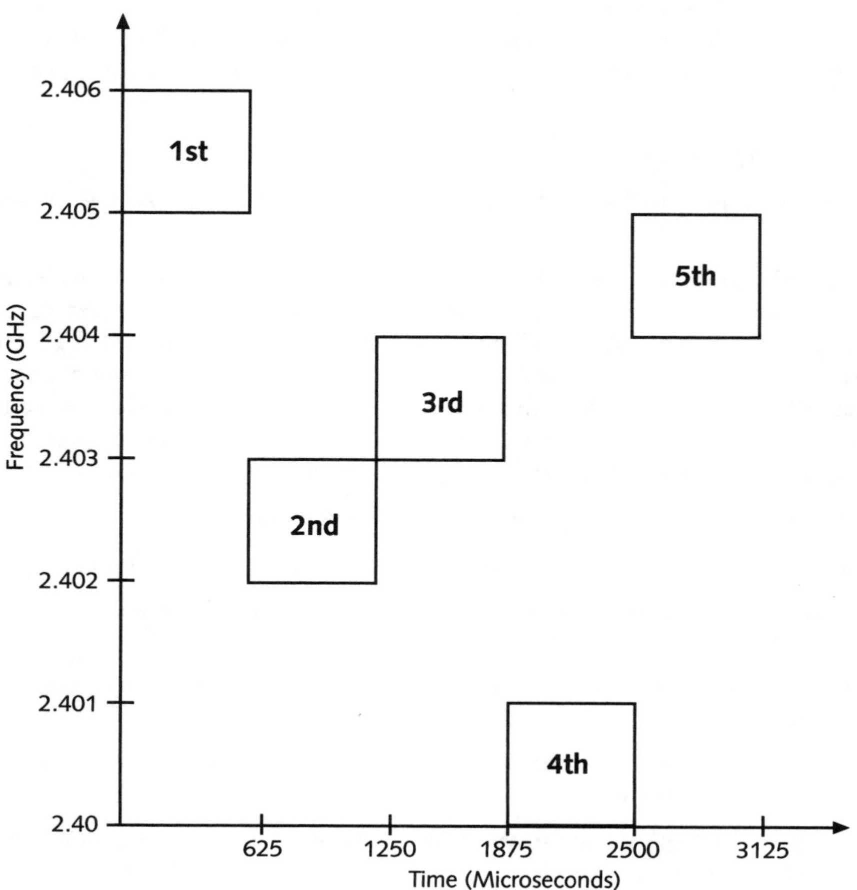

Figure 5-8 Bluetooth FHSS

Unfortunately, not all nations had the 2.4 GHz frequency available for Bluetooth use. France, Japan, Spain, and other countries allocated this frequency for other noncommercial purposes, such as for military communications. To accommodate these countries, Bluetooth version 1.0b defined a second hop count that avoided select areas of the 2.4 GHz spectrum with which there were conflicts and divided the frequency into 23 channels. This made Bluetooth devices that used the 79 channels incompatible with those that used 23 channels. However, the Bluetooth SIG negotiated with these countries to free up this spectrum for Bluetooth. All of the countries eventually agreed to the change so that devices conforming to the current 1.1 version of Bluetooth all use the 79 channels and are completely compatible with each other.

Even though the spectrum conflict with some nations was resolved, another frequency spectrum conflict still exists. Bluetooth uses the same frequency as IEEE 802.11b WLANs. Devices that use Bluetooth could interfere with 802.11b WLANs and vice versa. Several solutions are available to avoid this conflict. Special software can be added to the 802.11b WLAN that manages the traffic flow by telling the 802.11b network to be quiet when Bluetooth communications are detected. Also, the IEEE committee is currently working on a standard that allows both Bluetooth and 802.11b devices to function better in shared space.

Network Topology

There are two types of Bluetooth network topologies. These are known as piconet and scatternet.

When two Bluetooth devices come within range of each other, they automatically connect with one another. One device is the **master**, which controls all of the wireless traffic. The other device is known as a **slave**, which takes commands from the master. A Bluetooth network that contains one master and at least one slave that use the same channel forms a **piconet**. Bluetooth slave devices that are connected to the piconet and are sending transmissions are known as **active slaves**; devices that are connected but are not actively participating are called **parked slaves**. Examples of piconets are illustrated in Figure 5-9.

Devices in a piconet can be in one of five different modes:

- Standby—A device in **standby mode** is waiting to join a piconet.
- Inquire—In **inquire mode**, a Bluetooth device is looking for other devices with which to connect.
- Page—**Page mode** is when a master device is asking to connect to a specific slave.
- Connected—When a device is either an active slave or a master it is in **connected mode**.
- Park/Hold—A device in **park/hold mode** is part of the piconet but is in a low-power state.

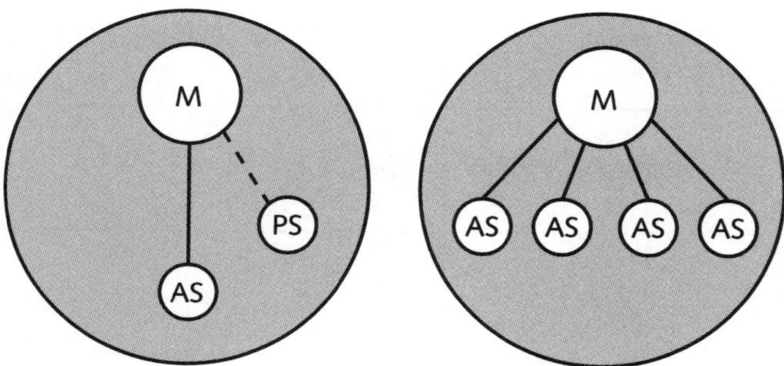

M = Master
AS = Active slave
PS = Parked slave

Figure 5-9 Piconets

Each Bluetooth device is preconfigured with addresses that are needed when participating in the piconet. Three of the significant addresses are summarized in Table 5-3.

Table 5-3 Piconet radio module addresses

Name	Description
Bluetooth device address	Unique 48-bit number
Active member address	3-bit number valid only as long as device is an active slave
Parked member address	8-bit number valid only as long as device is a parked slave

All devices in a piconet must change frequencies both at the same time and in the same sequence in order for communication to take place. The timing (called the phase) in the hopping sequence is determined by the clock of the Bluetooth master. Each active slave is synchronized with the master's clock. All 79 channels on which Bluetooth transmits are divided into time slots of 625 microseconds. The hopping sequence—that is, which slot will be used next—is unique for each piconet and is determined by the Bluetooth device address of the master. This is illustrated in Figure 5-10.

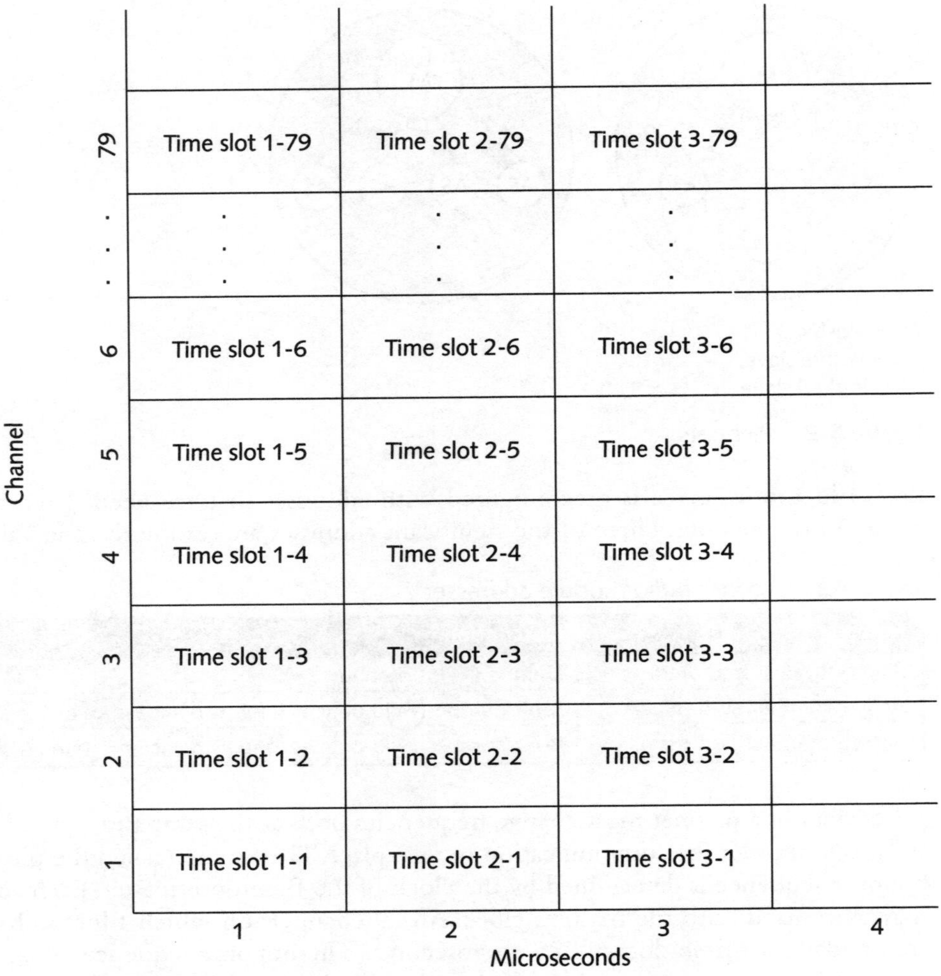

Channel	1	2	3	4
79	Time slot 1-79	Time slot 2-79	Time slot 3-79	
. . .	. . .	. . .	. . .	
6	Time slot 1-6	Time slot 2-6	Time slot 3-6	
5	Time slot 1-5	Time slot 2-5	Time slot 3-5	
4	Time slot 1-4	Time slot 2-4	Time slot 3-4	
3	Time slot 1-3	Time slot 2-3	Time slot 3-3	
2	Time slot 1-2	Time slot 2-2	Time slot 3-2	
1	Time slot 1-1	Time slot 2-1	Time slot 3-1	

Microseconds

Figure 5-10 Time slots

In a piconet, the master and slave alternatively transmit. The master starts its transmission in even-numbered time slots only, and the slave starts its transmission in odd-numbered time slots only.

A connection between Bluetooth devices is normally a two-step process. The first step is known as the inquiry procedure. The **inquiry procedure** enables a device to discover which devices are in range and determine the addresses and clocks for the devices. When a Bluetooth device enters into the range of other devices, it first attempts to find what other devices are in the area. In Figure 5-11, Device A, with its own clock and device ID, moves into the area where other Bluetooth devices exist. Device A wants to find the other Bluetooth devices in the area, so it goes into inquire mode and sends out a transmission. Devices B, C, D and E receive that transmission.

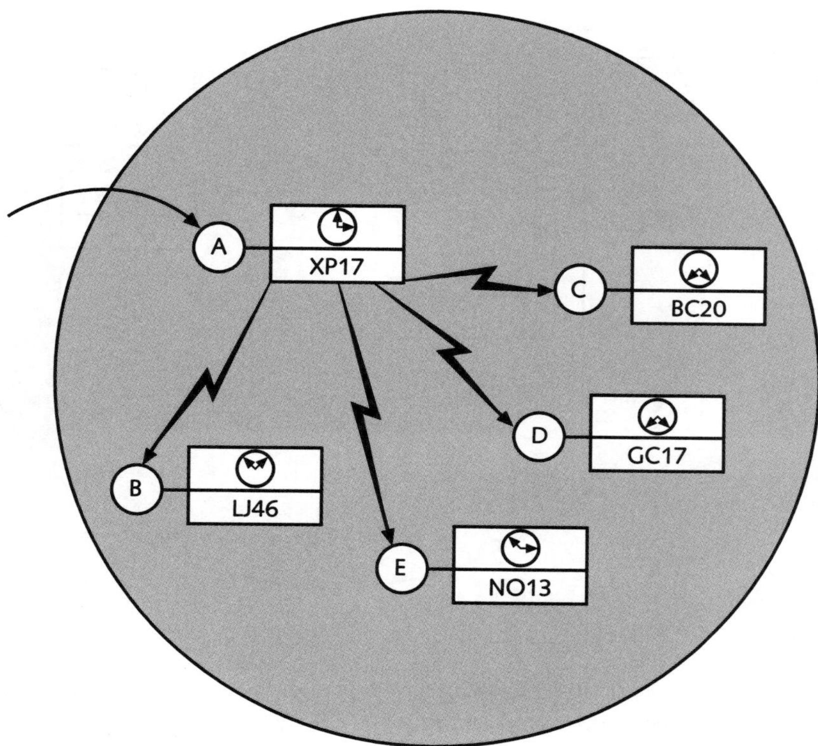

Figure 5-11 Device A inquiry

When Device B receives the inquiry, it responds by sending back its own device ID and clock. Device A now knows the clock and device ID of Device B. Device A sends a confirmation back to Device B. This is illustrated in Figure 5-12.

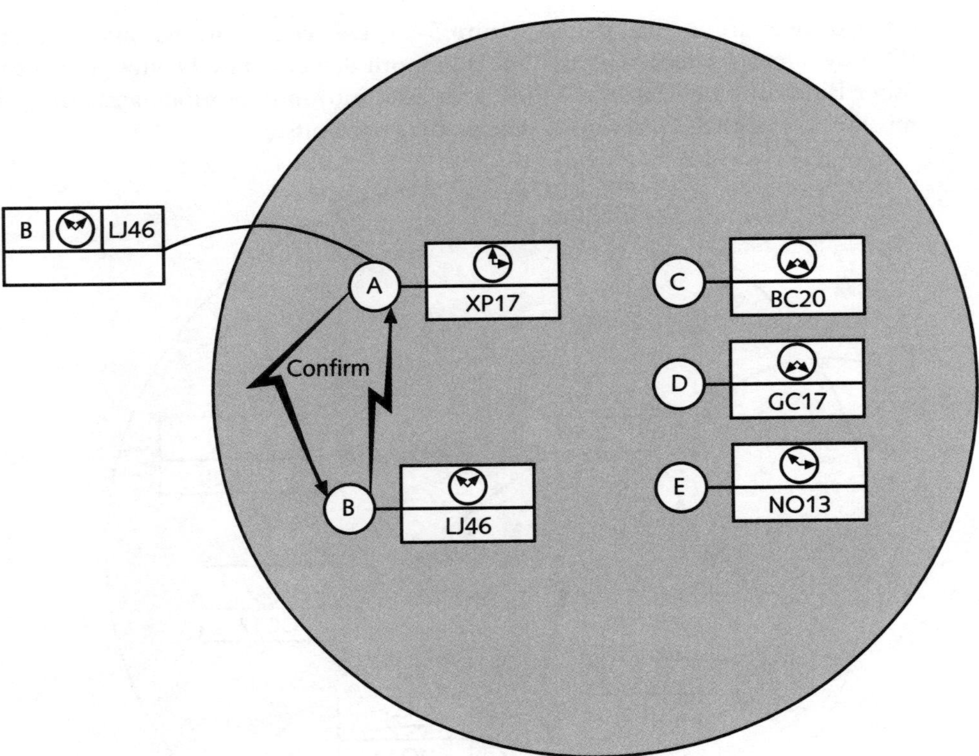

Figure 5-12 Device B response

However, when Devices C and D attempt to respond, they simultaneously transmit and the data becomes corrupted, as seen in Figure 5-13. Because Device A does not respond with a confirmation to Devices C and D, they both know that the transmission was not received. Each device now waits a random number of time slots before it starts to listen again. Device C may wait 7 slots and Device D may wait 24 slots. Device A sends out another inquiry. Because Device C had a shorter time to wait, it "awakens" first, receives the inquiry, and sends its response of its device ID and clock, as seen in Figure 5-14. After Device A sends back a confirmation to Device C it again sends out an inquiry. This time Device D awakens, sends its response, and receives confirmation. Device E does the same. Now Device A knows the device ID and clock of all other Bluetooth devices in the area.

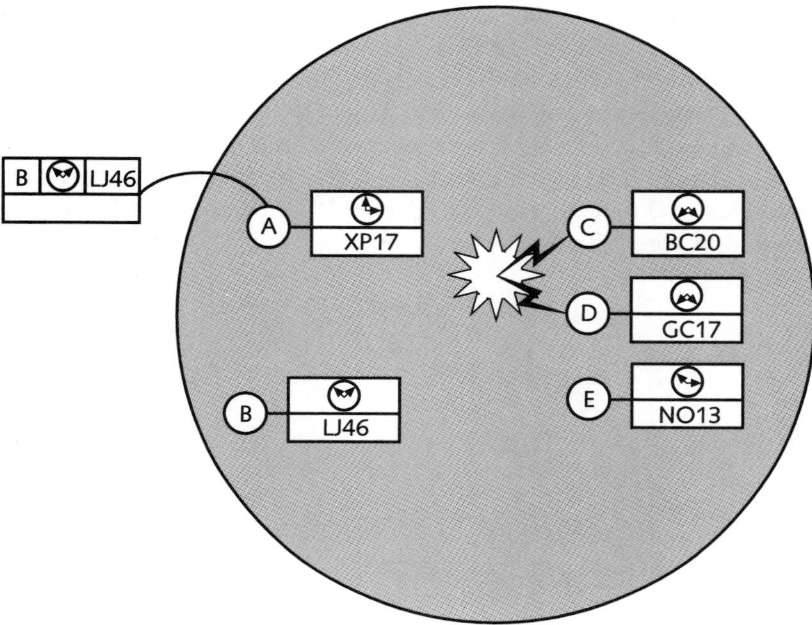

Figure 5-13 Collision

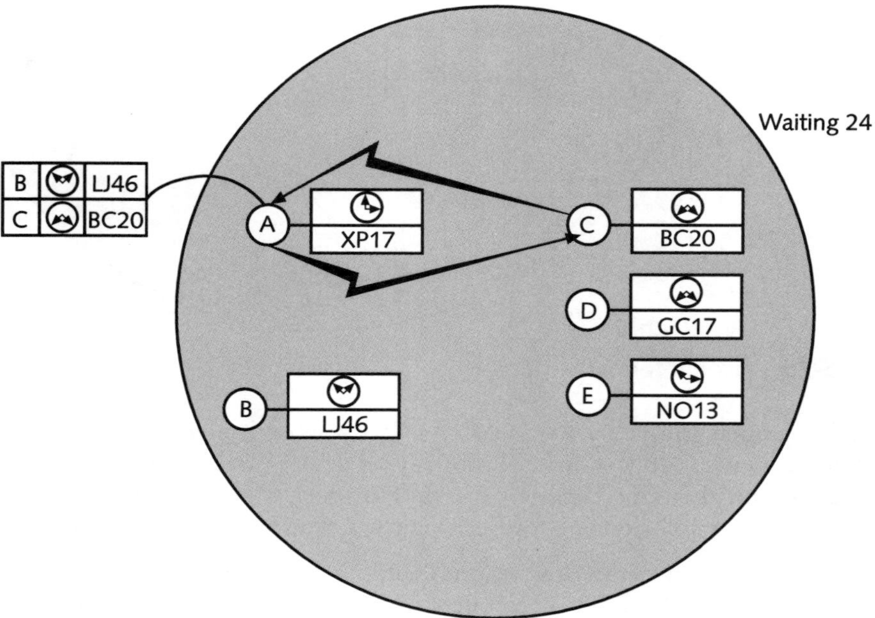

Figure 5-14 Device C response

The step after the inquiry procedure is known as the **paging procedure**, when an actual connection can be established. A unit that establishes a connection will carry out a paging procedure and will automatically be the master of the connection. The procedure occurs as follows. Device A switches to page mode and pages Device B with B's device ID. Device B responds back to Device A. Device A now sends to B its (Device A's) device ID and clock. This is the information that Device B needs to synchronize with Device A. Device A now connects with Device B to form a piconet. Device A is the master and Device B is the slave. This is illustrated in Figure 5-15.

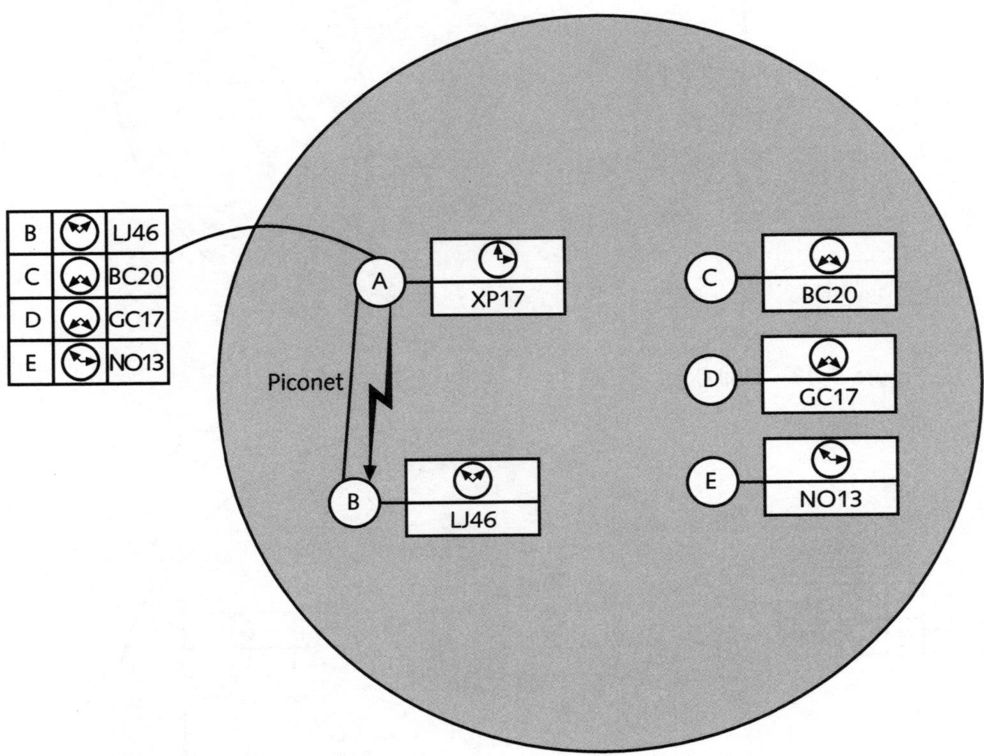

Figure 5-15 Piconet formed

Multiple piconets can cover the same area. Because each piconet has a different master and hop sequence, the risk for collisions (two devices attempting to send at the same microsecond on the same channel) is slim. However, if many more piconets are added, the probability of collisions increases, which will impact the speed of the network.

If multiple piconets cover the same area, a Bluetooth device can be a member in two or more overlaying piconets. A group of piconets in which connections exist between different piconets is called a **scatternet**. A scatternet is illustrated in Figure 5-16. In order to communicate in its respective piconets, the device must use the master device address and clock for each piconet.

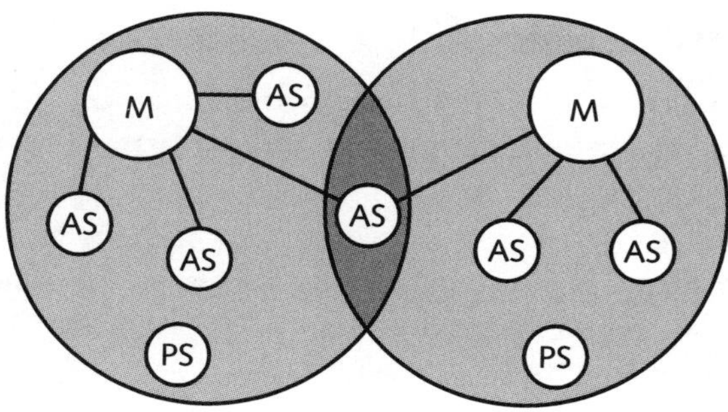

M = Master
AS = Active slave
PS = Parked slave

Figure 5-16 Scatternet

A Bluetooth device can be a slave in several piconets but can be a master in only one piconet.

A master and slave can switch roles in a piconet.

Bluetooth Frames

The packet or frame of a Bluetooth transmission is illustrated in Figure 5-17. Each frame consists of three parts:

- Access code (72 bits)—The access code contains data used for timing synchronization, paging, and inquiry.
- Header (54 bits)—The header contains information for packet acknowledgment, packet numbering, the slave address, the type of payload, and error checking.
- Payload (0–2745 bits)—The payload field can contain data, voice, or both.

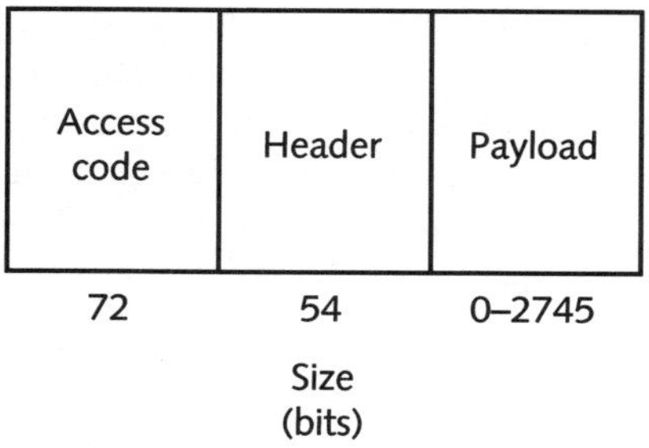

Access code	Header	Payload
72	54	0–2745

Size (bits)

Figure 5-17 Bluetooth frame

Link Manager Protocol (LMP) Layer

The duties of the Link Manger Protocol (LMP) layer in the Bluetooth stack can be divided into two broad categories: managing the piconet and performing security.

Piconet Management

Managing the piconet involves such actions as regulating the steps for attaching and detaching slaves from the master as well as overseeing the master-slave switch. These are all handled by the LMP layer of the Bluetooth protocol stack.

Another function of this layer involves establishing the links between Bluetooth devices. There are two types of physical links between devices. The first is **synchronous connection-oriented (SCO) link**. The SCO link is a symmetric point-to-point link between a master and a single slave in the piconet. This link functions like a circuit-switched link by using reserved slots at regular intervals. The master can support up to three simultaneous SCO links while slaves can support two or three SCO links. The SCO link mainly carries voice transmission at a speed of 64 Kbps.

The second type of link is an **asynchronous connection-less (ACL) link**. This is a packet-switched link that is used for data transmissions. The ACL link is from one master to all the slaves participating on the piconet. It is sometimes called a point-to-multipoint link. Only a single ACL link can exist. In the slots times not reserved for the SCO links the master can establish an ACL link to any slave. A slave already engaged in an SCO link can also have an ACL link.

If an error occurs on an ACL packet, that packet is retransmitted. An SCO packet is never retransmitted.

There are three kinds of error correction schemes used in the Bluetooth protocol. In **1/3 rate Forward Error Correction (FEC)** every bit is repeated three times for redundancy. The **2/3 rate FEC** scheme uses a mathematical formula to add extra error correction bits to the data sent. These extra bits are examined by the receiving device to determine if an error took place in the transmission. For example, if 10 bits of data were to be sent they would be expanded into 15 bits, which includes the error correction data. The third scheme is known as **automatic retransmission query (ARQ)**. In the ARQ scheme, certain data fields of a packet are continuously retransmitted until an acknowledgment is received or a timeout value is exceeded. Bluetooth uses a fast acknowledgment procedure to indicate that the data was received. However, if the recipient does not acknowledge receipt of the packet and the timeout value is exceeded, Bluetooth retransmits the packet (if it is an ACL packet).

You will recall that because Bluetooth devices are mobile and require battery power, so conserving power is essential. Even though the power consumption of devices using Bluetooth is measured in milliamps (thousandths of an amp), it still is important to conserve power whenever possible.

Once a Bluetooth device is connected to a piconet, it can be in one of four connection modes: Active, Hold, Sniff, or Park. Devices synchronized to a piconet can enter into one of the power-saving modes (Hold, Sniff, or Park) in which device activity is lowered:

- *Active mode.* In **Active mode**, the Bluetooth unit actively participates on the channel. The master schedules the transmission based on traffic demands to and from the different slaves. In addition, it supports regular transmissions to keep slaves synchronized to the channel. Active slaves listen in the master-to-slave slots for packets.
- *Sniff mode.* In **Sniff mode**, a slave device listens to the piconet master at a reduced rate so that it uses less power. The interval is programmable and depends on the application. It is the least power efficient of the power-saving modes.
- *Hold mode.* The master unit can put slave units into **Hold mode**, where only the slave's internal timer is running. Slave units can also demand to be put into Hold mode. Data transfer restarts instantly whenever the slave moves from Hold mode back to Active mode.
- *Park mode.* **Park mode** is the most efficient of the power-saving modes. In Park mode, a device is still synchronized to the piconet but it does not participate in the traffic. Bluetooth devices that are in this mode have given up their Active Member Address. These slaves occasionally listen to the traffic of their master in order to resynchronize and check on broadcast messages.

Security

Security for Bluetooth transmission, as with all wireless communications, can be an area of concern. Bluetooth provides security at the LMP layer and also provides encryption services. Security in a Bluetooth piconet is based on identifying the device itself and not who is using the device. There are three levels of Bluetooth security:

- Level 1—No security. At this level a Bluetooth device will not initiate any security steps.
- Level 2—Service-level security. At Level 2 security is established after a connection is made. This is done at the higher levels of the protocol stack.
- Level 3—Link-level security. Link-level security is performed before a connection is made and is done at the lower levels of the protocol stack.

The two major areas in which Bluetooth provides security features are authentication and encryption. **Authentication** is verifying that the device asking to join the piconet should be allowed to join. The Bluetooth authentication scheme is a **challenge-response strategy**, where a process is used to check if the other device knows a shared identical secret key. If both devices have the same response, then the new device is authenticated and allowed to join the piconet.

The Authentication scheme works as follows and is illustrated in Figure 5-18:

1. Master A generates a random number and sends it to Slave B.

2. Both Master A and Slave B take the same random number and use their Bluetooth device address and a private link key to generate a response number.
3. Slave B sends its response number back to Master A, which then verifies that the responses match. If they do, then Slave B is considered authenticated.

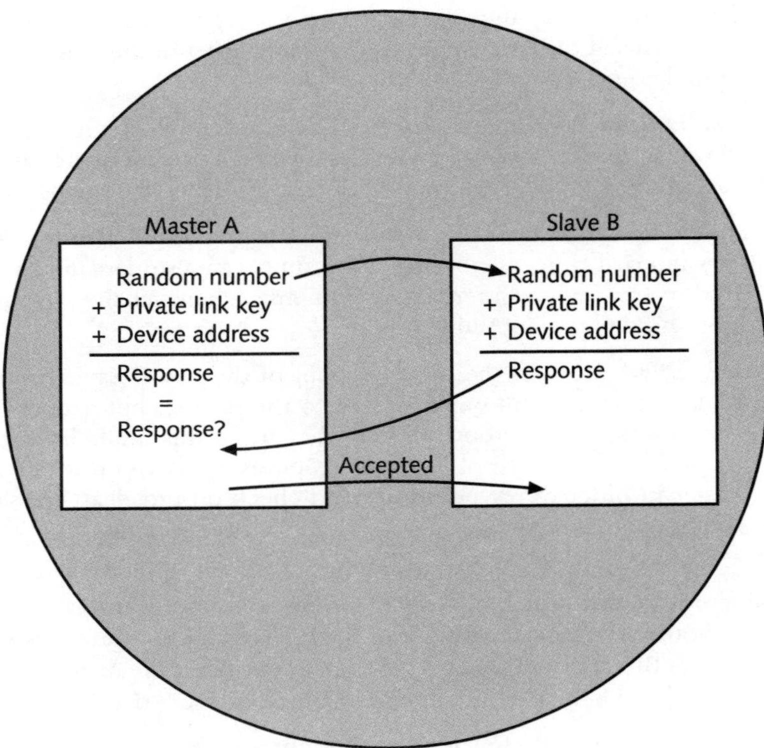

Figure 5-18 Authentication

If the authentication fails, there is a waiting time before the slave can make another attempt at authentication. This waiting time can increase depending on the number of previous authentication attempts.

In previous versions of the Bluetooth standard, authentication was a problem. This is because it was assumed that a master device would be the one that has completed its calculation of the response number before the slave device could return its calculation. However, if a faster slave device could calculate its response number and return it before the master was completed, then both devices would think they were the master and no link could be established. This problem was rectified in Bluetooth version 1.1 by requiring that each device first confirm its role as either master or slave before the response number was generated.

The second area of security is encryption. **Encryption** is the process of encoding communications and ensures that the transmissions cannot be easily intercepted and decoded. There are three encryption modes:

- Encryption Mode 1—Nothing is encrypted.
- Encryption Mode 2—Traffic from the master to one slave is encrypted, but traffic from the master to multiple slaves is not encrypted.
- Encryption Mode 3—All traffic is encrypted.

Figure 5-19 illustrates how Bluetooth encryption is performed:

1. Master A sends a message to Slave B that it wants to use encryption mode 1, 2, or 3. Slave B responds back with a "yes" or "no" to use encryption.
2. If the answer is "yes," the next step is to negotiate the size of the key to use for encryption. The encryption key size can be from 8 to 128 bits. Either device (master or slave) can propose a key size or reject the other's key size suggestion.
3. Once the encryption key size is agreed on, encrypted transmissions may begin.

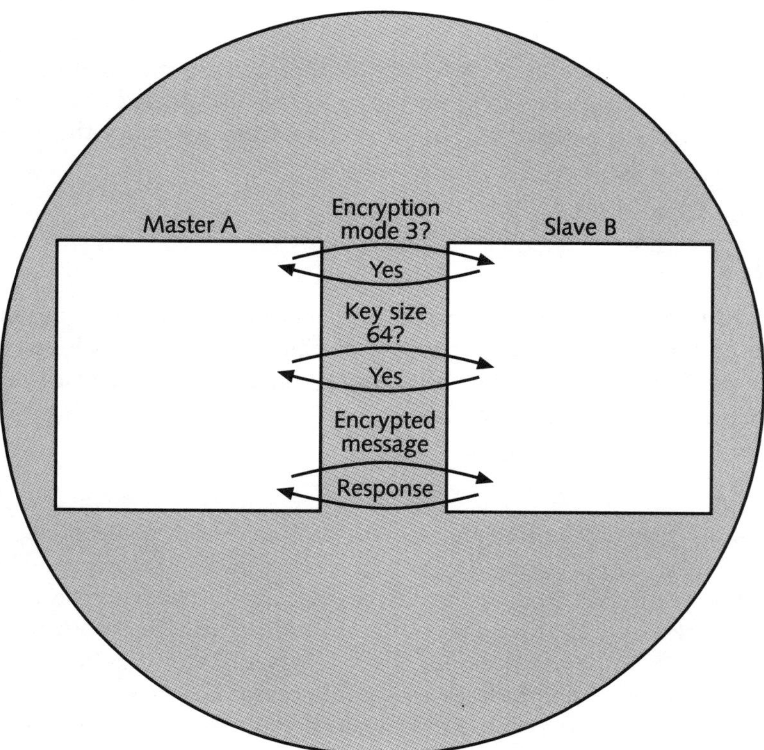

Figure 5-19 Encryption

Every application defines a minimum acceptable encryption key size. If this minimum key size requirement is not met during the encryption key size negotiation, then encryption cannot be used. The purpose of this requirement is to prevent a rogue device from forcing a lower encryption setting than should be used.

The authentication key and the encryption key are two different keys. The reason for separating them is to allow the use of a shorter encryption key without weakening the strength of the authentication key.

Other Layers and Functions

Some of the remaining layers and parts of the Bluetooth protocol stack play less significant roles than other parts. In Figure 5-4, the L2CAP is the logical link control layer that is responsible for segmenting and reassembling data packets. These data packets are then sent through standard data protocols such as TCP/IP for transmission. The RFCOMM data protocol stands for Radio Frequency Virtual Communications Port Emulation. This data protocol provides serial port emulation for Bluetooth data. It "packages" the data so that it appears as if it were sent through the computer's standard serial port.

Just as data is sent by one Bluetooth device to another, control information is also transmitted, such as sending a message for a device to switch from master to slave. This control information comes through the LMP layer but then by-passes the L2CAP layer, which is only used for transmitted data streams.

BLUETOOTH ISSUES

As exciting as Bluetooth is, there are several challenges that face this technology before it will become as pervasive as its designers hoped. These challenges include cost, limited support, shortcomings in the protocol itself, positioning in the marketplace, and conflicts with other devices on the radio spectrum.

Cost

One of the factors that has limited the growth of Bluetooth has been the cost of the radio module. These chips originally cost in excess of $75. However, the cost has decreased to around $15. Yet even at this lower cost many industry experts believe that the price must be reduced to around $5 per chip in order for Bluetooth to reach competitive advantage. There are two reasons for this way of thinking. First, adding a $15 chip to a $2,500 notebook computer is irrelevant because the cost can easily be absorbed in the total cost. However, adding a $15 chip to a PDA that costs $150 will certainly mean that the price of the PDA would have increase to cover the cost of the Bluetooth chip. Until the price is reduced to the point where it does not have a significant impact on the total cost of the device, Bluetooth's market penetration will be limited.

Another reason why the cost of a Bluetooth chip needs to be reduced can be seen by looking at the technology it is replacing. Using a chip that costs $15 to replace a cable that costs only $7 does not make sense economically. Unless the Bluetooth chip cost is equal to or even less than the technology that it is replacing, it will be difficult to justify.

Limited Support

Many industry experts see Bluetooth as caught in the "chicken-or-the-egg" scenario. Bluetooth is not fully supported by the hardware and software vendors because of its low market penetration. These vendors do not want to spend the time and money to produce Bluetooth products or support the technology if there are few Bluetooth users. However, as long as vendors do not support Bluetooth, then users will be reluctant to purchase this technology.

Several vendors are attempting to "straddle the fence" with Bluetooth support, but they only end up confusing users. For example, Microsoft provides Bluetooth support in their version of Pocket PC 2002, which runs on hand-held devices. However, Microsoft decided not to support Bluetooth in Windows XP. What's especially puzzling is that these versions of software were released to the public within weeks of each other. Until the industry embraces Bluetooth and provides sufficient support, many experts are unsure how deeply Bluetooth will penetrate the market.

Protocol Limitations

One of the major limitations of the Bluetooth protocol is its lack of hand-offs between piconets. Unlike a cell phone that easily switches from one cell to the next as the user drives down the road, when a Bluetooth device moves from one piconet area to the next there is no transparent hand-off. Instead, the connection is broken and must be restored with the new master.

Other limitations of the Bluetooth protocol are that it authenticates devices instead of users, making security less than optimal. Also, although Bluetooth devices can discover other Bluetooth devices in the area, at present they can not determine how the functions of other devices can be used in a cooperative setting. These are concerns that Bluetooth needs to address.

Market Position

Where does Bluetooth fit in the wireless world? At the present time, Bluetooth's position in the market is being squeezed from both the top and the bottom. From the top side, IEEE 802.11x WLANs are becoming the preferred technology for connecting wireless devices to form a network. This technology is mature, robust, flexible, and very popular. From the bottom, cell phones and other devices now have integrated capabilities that reduce dependence upon Bluetooth. The trend today is for fewer devices instead of more devices that connect together. Bluetooth is feeling the squeeze from both ends.

Spectrum Conflict

As noted previously, because Bluetooth uses the ISM 2.4 GHz band for its transmissions, it can conflict with other technologies that use the same spectrum. One of the major conflicts comes with IEEE 802.11b WLANs. Using Bluetooth and 802.11b devices in close proximity to each other may cause the WLAN to drop the connection if it detects that another device is sharing its frequency. There are solutions to this problem. Moving the Bluetooth device away from the 802.11b device is the most obvious fix. Also, several vendors have demonstrated products that let Bluetooth and 802.11b WLANs share the spectrum by first checking to see if the airwaves are clear for transmission. And, because the new 802.11a WLAN standard uses a different frequency, moving to that standard will eliminate the conflict altogether.

Chapter Summary

- Bluetooth is a wireless technology that uses short-range radio frequency (RF) transmissions. Bluetooth technology enables users to connect to a wide range of computing and telecommunications devices without the need to use cables. Although Bluetooth can replace the wired connections, such as between a keyboard and a computer, it can also do much more than that. This technology can also be used for devices to create a small network.

- Bluetooth is supported by over 2,500 hardware and software vendors who make up the Bluetooth Special Interest Group (SIG). This consortium develops and promotes the Bluetooth global wireless technology. The goals of the SIG are to develop technical specifications that enable Bluetooth products to be used interoperably across different vendor devices. The Bluetooth SIG also administers test facilities to ensure that different devices do conform to the standards.

- The Bluetooth protocol stack functions can be divided into two parts based on how they are implemented: the lower levels of the stack are accomplished through hardware, while the functions of the upper levels of the stack are achieved by software. At the lowest level of the Bluetooth protocol stack is the RF layer. It defines how the basic hardware that controls the radio transmissions functions. At the heart of Bluetooth is a single radio transmitter/receiver (transceiver) that performs all of the necessary functions. This tiny single chip adds Bluetooth functionality to a device by adding one chip to the manufacturing process. Because devices have an embedded Bluetooth transceiver, they are immediately ready to send and receive transmissions. Bluetooth can transmit at a speed of 1 Mbps and has three different power classes for transmitting.

- Bluetooth uses the binary modulation technique known as a two-level Gaussian frequency shift keying (2-GFSK). 2-GFSK uses two different frequencies to indicate whether a 1 or a 0 is being transmitted in addition to varying the number of "waves." The amount that the frequency varies is called the modulation index.
- The part of the spectrum at which Bluetooth operates is the 2.4 GHz Industrial, Scientific, and Medical (ISM) band. Bluetooth divides this 2.4 GHz frequency into 79 different frequencies (called channels) spaced 1 MHz apart. Bluetooth uses the frequency hopping spread spectrum (FHSS) technique to send a transmission. When two Bluetooth devices come within range of each other, they automatically connect with one another. One device is the master, which controls all of the wireless traffic. The other device is known as a slave that takes commands from the master. A Bluetooth network that contains one master and at least one slave and that use the same channel forms a piconet. All devices in a piconet must change frequencies both at the same time and in the same sequence in order for communications to take place. If multiple piconets cover the same area, a Bluetooth device can be a member in two or more overlaying piconets. A group of piconets in which connections exist between different piconets is called a scatternet.
- There are three kinds of error correction schemes used in the Bluetooth protocol. The 1/3 rate Forward Error Correction (FEC) repeats every bit three times for redundancy. The 2/3 rate FEC uses a mathematical formula to add extra error correction bits to the data sent. The automatic retransmission query (ARQ) continuously retransmits fields until an acknowledgement is received or timeout value is exceeded.
- Once a Bluetooth device is connected to a piconet, it can be in one of four connection modes: Active, Hold, Sniff, or Park. Devices synchronized to a piconet can enter into one of the power-saving modes (Hold, Sniff, or Park) in which device activity is lowered.
- The two major areas in which Bluetooth provides security features are authentication and encryption. Authentication is verifying that the device asking to join the piconet should be allowed to join. The Bluetooth authentication scheme is a challenge-response strategy, where a process is used to check if the other device knows a shared identical secret key. Encryption ensures that the transmissions cannot be intercepted and decoded.
- There are several challenges that face Bluetooth technology before it will become as pervasive as was hoped when it was first designed. These challenges include cost, limited support, shortcomings in the protocol itself, positioning in the marketplace, and conflicts with other devices on the radio spectrum.

KEY TERMS

1/3 rate Forward Error Correction (FEC) — An error correction scheme that repeats each bit three times for redundancy.

2/3 rate Forward Error Correction (FEC) — An error correction scheme that uses a mathematical formula to add extra error correction bits to the data sent.

active mode — A state in which the Bluetooth device actively participates on the channel.

active slaves — Slave devices that are connected to the piconet and are sending transmissions.

ampere — Measure of the number of electrons that move through a conductor.

asynchronous connection-less (ACL) link — A packet-switched link that is used for data transmissions.

authentication — The process of verifying that the device asking to join the piconet should be allowed to join.

automatic retransmission query (ARQ) — An error correction scheme that continuously retransmits until an acknowledgement is received or timeout value is exceeded.

Bluetooth radio module — A single radio transmitter/receiver (transceiver) that performs all of the necessary transmission functions.

challenge-response strategy — A process used to check if the other device knows a shared identical secret key.

channels — Another name for frequencies.

connected mode — A state when a device is either an active slave or a master.

encryption — The process of encoding communications and ensures that the transmissions cannot be easily intercepted and decoded.

hold mode — A state in which the Bluetooth device can put slave units into hold mode where only the slave's internal timer is running.

inquire mode — A state when a device is looking for other devices with which to connect.

inquiry procedure — A process that enables a device to discover which devices are in range and determine the addresses and clocks for the devices.

kilowatts (kW) — Thousands of watts.

master — A device on a Bluetooth piconet that controls all of the wireless traffic.

milliamps (mA) — Thousandths of an amp.

milliwatt (mW) — One thousandths of a watt.

modulation index — The amount that the frequency varies.

page mode — A state when a master device is asking to connect to a specific slave.

paging procedure — A process that enables a device to make an actual connection to a piconet.

park mode — A state in which the Bluetooth device is still synchronized to the piconet but it does not participate in the traffic.

park/hold mode — A state when a device is in part of the piconet but is in a low-power mode.

parked slaves — Slave devices that are connected to the piconet but are not actively participating.

Peripheral Component Interface (PCI) — The standard 32-bit PC bus architecture.

piconet — A Bluetooth network that contains one master and at least one slave that use the same channel.

scatternet — A group of piconets in which connections exist between different piconets.

slave — A device on a Bluetooth piconet that takes commands from the master.

sniff mode — A state in which the Bluetooth device listens to the piconet master at a reduced rate so that it uses less power.

standby mode — A state when a device waiting to join a piconet.

synchronous connection-oriented (SCO) link — A symmetric point-to-point link between a master and a single slave in the piconet that functions like a circuit-switched link by using reserved slots at regular intervals.

two-level Gaussian frequency shift keying (2-GFSK) — A binary signaling technique that uses two different frequencies to indicate whether a 1 or a 0 is being transmitted in addition to varying the number of waves.

Universal Asynchronous Receiver/Transmitter (UART) — A microchip that controls a computer's interface to its attached serial devices through a serial port or IrDA port.

Universal Serial Bus (USB) — A low-speed serial interface that operates at a maximum speed of 12 Mbps.

watt — A single unit of electrical power.

Review Questions

1. Each of the following is an example of a Bluetooth communication except ____________.
   a. cell phone to PDA
   b. notebook computer to PDA cradle
   c. hard drive to memory
   d. notebook computer to GPS
2. Which of the following is not an advantage of infrared over Bluetooth?
   a. Narrow angle
   b. Master controls slave
   c. Short range
   d. Low power

3. The organization that develops and promotes Bluetooth is known as ________________.
   a. Bluetooth SIG
   b. IEEE Bluetooth Group
   c. Ericsson Bluetooth TIA
   d. Bluetooth Standards Organization
4. The lower levels of the stack are accomplished through ________________.
   a. software
   b. hardware
   c. IR
   d. Data Link layer
5. At the lowest level of the Bluetooth protocol stack is the ________________ Layer.
   a. RF
   b. LMP
   c. TCP/IP
   d. IR
6. At the heart of Bluetooth is a single radio transmitter/receiver (transceiver) that performs all of the necessary functions. True or false?
7. Bluetooth can transmit at a speed of 10 Mbps under the current Bluetooth specification (version 1.1). True or false?
8. Bluetooth has seven different power classes for transmitting. True or false?
9. Objects such as walls and interference from other sources do not affect the range of Bluetooth transmissions. True or false?
10. Bluetooth devices are usually not mobile, so conserving this power is not necessary. True or false?
11. For Bluetooth devices the power consumption is measured in ________________ (mA or thousandths of an amp).
12. The Gaussian frequency shift keying (2-GFSK) uses ________________ different frequencies to indicate whether a 1 or a 0 is being transmitted.
13. The amount that the frequency varies is called ________________ and is between 280 KHz and 350 KHz.
14. The ________________ Layer lies on top of the Bluetooth radio layer in the Bluetooth stack.
15. Bluetooth divides the 2.4 GHz frequency into 79 different frequencies called ________________ that are spaced 1 MHz apart.
16. Describe the problem with the 2.4 GHz frequency in foreign nations and what the Bluetooth SIG did about it.

17. What is the problem with Bluetooth and IEEE 802.11b WLANs using the same frequency? What can be done about it?
18. What is the difference between a piconet and a scatternet?
19. What is the difference between the paging procedure and the inquiry process?
20. List and describe the three types of error correction used with Bluetooth.

HANDS-ON PROJECTS

Different Bluetooth products have different software and procedures. These project instructions and illustrations are for devices that use Xircom BlueView and Intellisync software. If necessary, adjust the specific steps to fit the software for your Bluetooth device(s).

Transfer Files Between Bluetooth Devices

1. Install a Bluetooth card in a notebook computer.
   a. Insert the Bluetooth card into the Type II slot of a notebook computer. If the computer is running Windows 2000 or Windows XP, it will automatically discover that new hardware has been installed and the "Found Card" information box will appear.
   b. When using Windows 2000 the "Found New Hardware Wizard" dialog box will appear, as seen in Figure 5-20. Click **Next**.

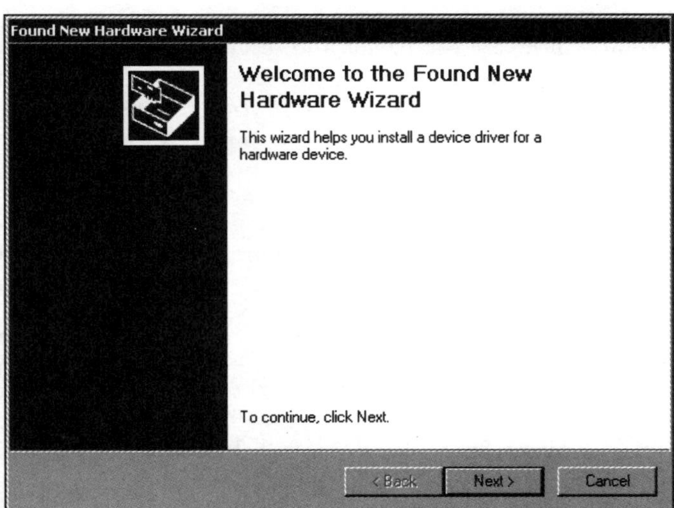

Figure 5-20 Found New Hardware Wizard dialog box

   c. The next Found New Hardware Wizard dialog box appears. Be sure that **Search for a suitable driver for my device** is selected. Click **Next**.

d. Windows 2000 will then look for the driver files for the Bluetooth device. A dialog box illustrated in Figure 5-21 asks where to look for these files. Check the box **CD-ROM drive** and insert the CD-ROM that came with the device into the CD-ROM drive. Click **Next**.

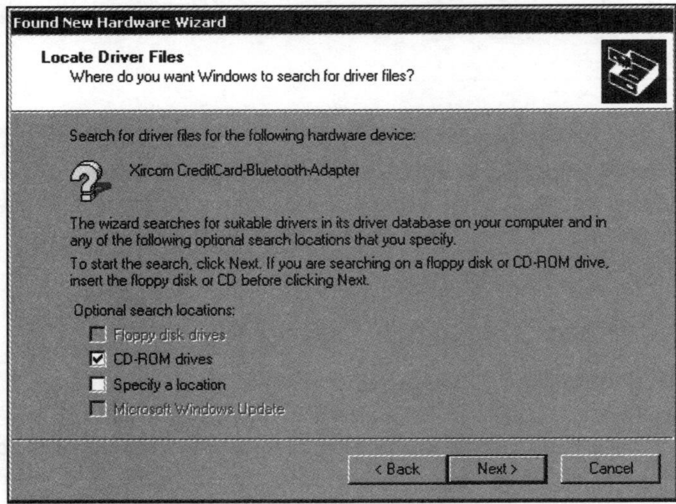

Figure 5-21 Locate Driver Files dialog box

e. Windows 2000 will locate the appropriate files on the CD-ROM drive and display that information, as seen in Figure 5-22. Click **Next** to install the driver. Windows 2000 will locate the driver and install it. Depending upon the vendor, you may receive a message stating that the driver software is not accompanied by a certificate from Microsoft. If you are satisfied with the software follow the instructions on the screen to complete the installation. Click **Finish** when the driver is installed.

f. There may be additional vendor software to install. Follow the installation instructions on the screen or check the documentation that came with your Bluetooth card.

g. If you are using Windows XP, the Welcome to the Found New Hardware Wizard will appear after installing the card, as seen in Figure 5-23. There are two options for locating the driver. If you click the "Install the software automatically (Recommended)" radio button, Windows XP will search its own internal list of drivers for this hardware. Since Windows XP does not natively support Bluetooth it will then try to search the Internet for the correct driver. If you click the "Install from a list or a specific location (Advanced)" Windows XP will look for the driver on the installation CD-ROM. Click **Install from a list or a specific location (Advanced)** and then click **Next**.

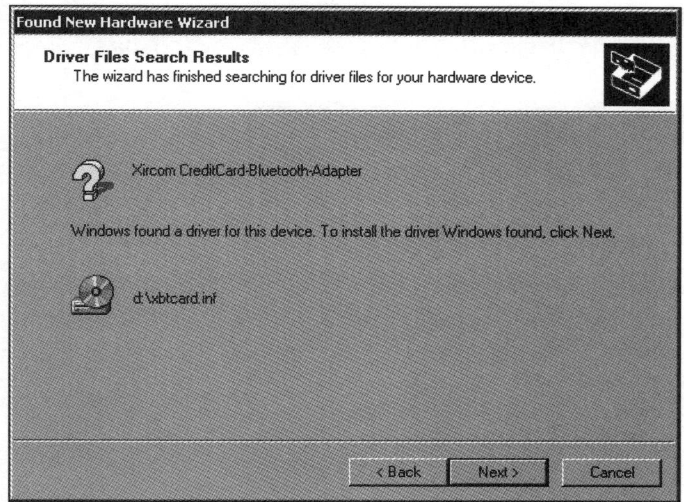

Figure 5-22 Driver Files Search Results dialog box

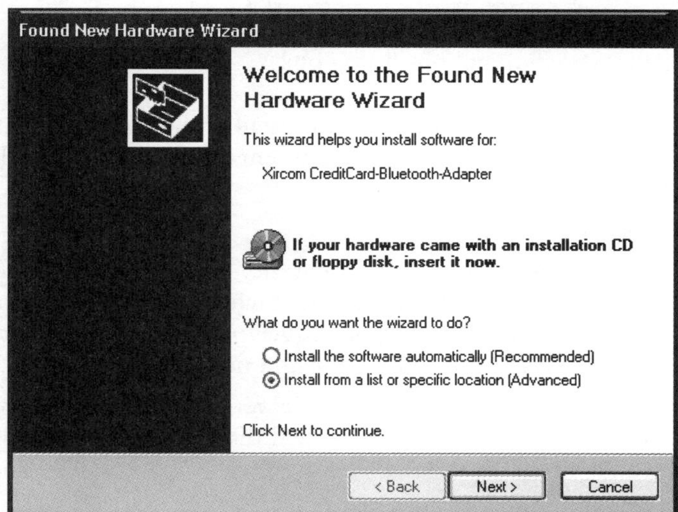

Figure 5-23 Welcome to the Found New Hardware Wizard dialog box

h. Windows XP will then ask for your search and installation options. Click the button **Search removable media (floppy, CD-ROM, …)** and insert the CD-ROM that came with the device into the CD-ROM drive. Click **Next**. Windows XP will locate the driver and install it. Depending upon the vendor, you may receive a message stating that the driver software is not verified for compatibility by Microsoft. If you are satisfied with the software, follow the instructions on the screen to complete the installation by clicking on **Continue Anyway**. Click **Finish** when the driver is installed.

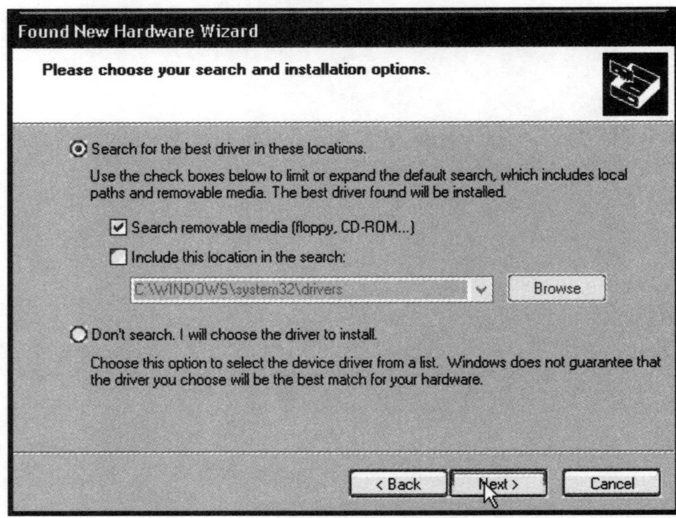

Figure 5-24 Search and installation options dialog box

i. There may be additional vendor software to install. Follow the installation instructions on the screen or check the documentation that came with your Bluetooth card.

2. Locate another Bluetooth device.

   a. Position two Bluetooth devices in close proximity to each other. Generally the devices must be within 33 feet (10 meters) of each other. Select one of the devices to be the master who is trying to actively join the piconet and the other device to be the slave who will accept the new device.

   b. On both the master and slave, start the specific vendor Bluetooth software by clicking on an icon in the system tray. This will display a screen like that shown in Figure 5-25.

   c. By default, Bluetooth devices cannot be seen by other devices. Make sure that the Bluetooth radio is on by clicking the **Radio on** box. In the left pane of the master, click on **New Devices in Range**. Click on the **Refresh** button. A screen will appear searching for other devices in the area, as seen in Figure 5-26.

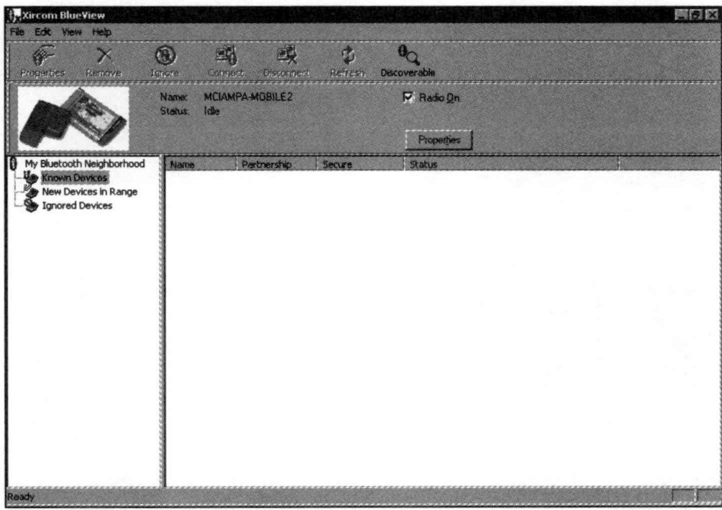

Figure 5-25 Xircom Blue View screen

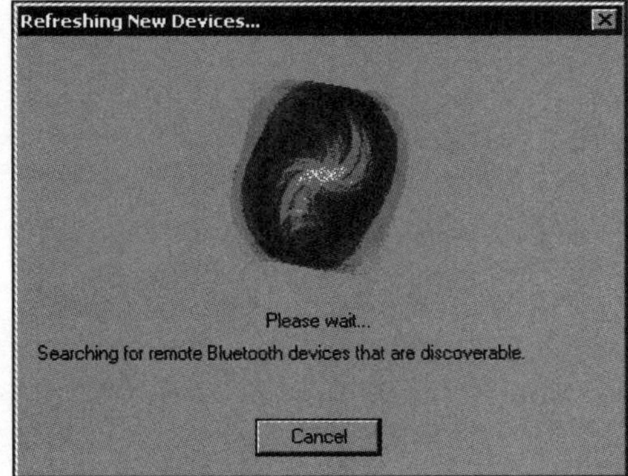

Figure 5-26 Refreshing New Devices screen

d. Move to the slave and click the **Discoverable** button. This will display the screen as seen in Figure 5-27. On the master, click **OK** to continue the search.

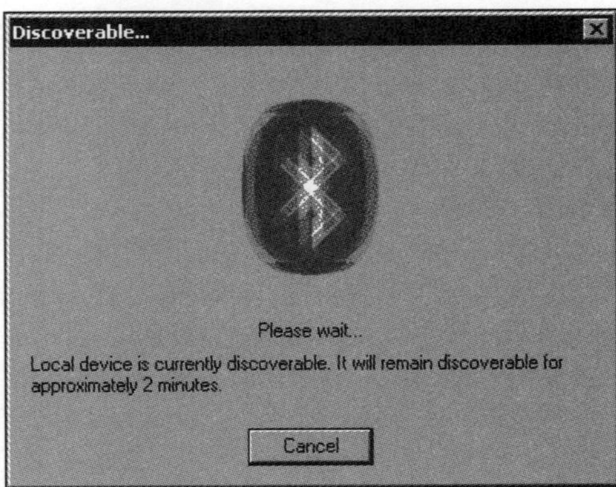

Figure 5-27 Discoverable screen

e. After several seconds the slave device will be located and displayed on the master's screen, as seen in Figure 5-28. If it does not appear, click the **Refresh** button.

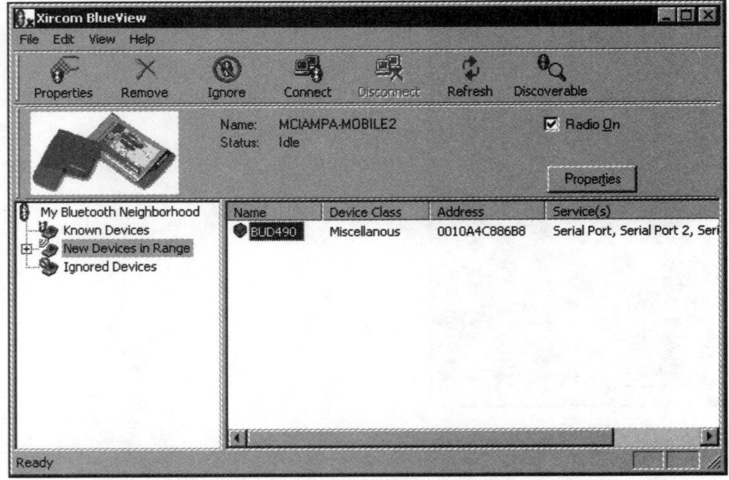

Figure 5-28 Slave device displayed on master

f. Keep the BlueView screen open for each device for the next project.

3. Transfer files.

   a. After the slave has been located a connection between it and the master must be made. Click the **Connect** button on the master to display the Connect to remote Bluetooth device dialog box, as seen in Figure 5-29. Click the **One time** radio button and then click **OK**.

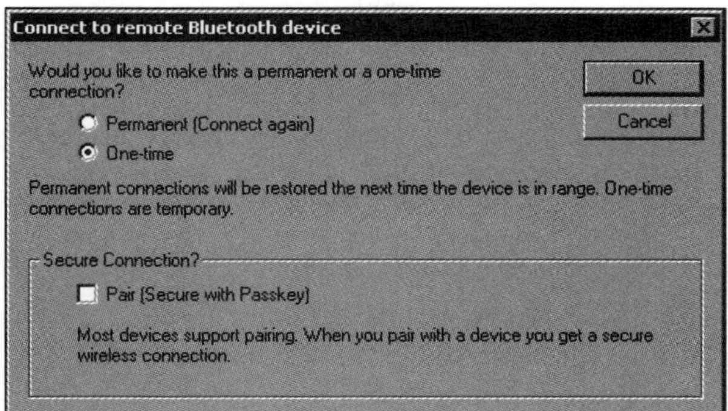

Figure 5-29 Connect to remote Bluetooth device dialog box

b. The **Select Device Service?** dialog box will display. Click on **Intellisync**, as seen in Figure 5-30.

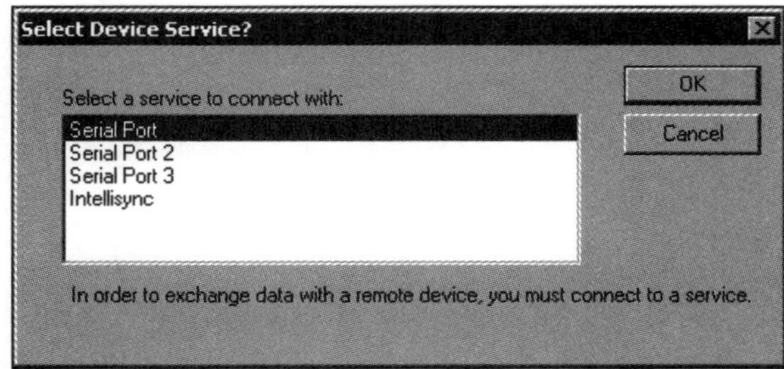

Figure 5-30 Select Device Service? dialog box

c. The BlueView screen will now display information about the connection to the slave device, as seen in Figure 5-31.

d. On the master, launch the Intellisync program by clicking **Start**, then **Programs**, click on **Intellisync** and finally click on **Intellisync agent**. This will bring up the "Getting Started Intellisync" screen. Click **OK** to display the Intellisync agent screen, as seen in Figure 5-32. Click the first icon (wrench and screwdriver) to launch the Connection Setup Manager. Click **Close** if the information screen appears, and then click on the Remote Connections tab.

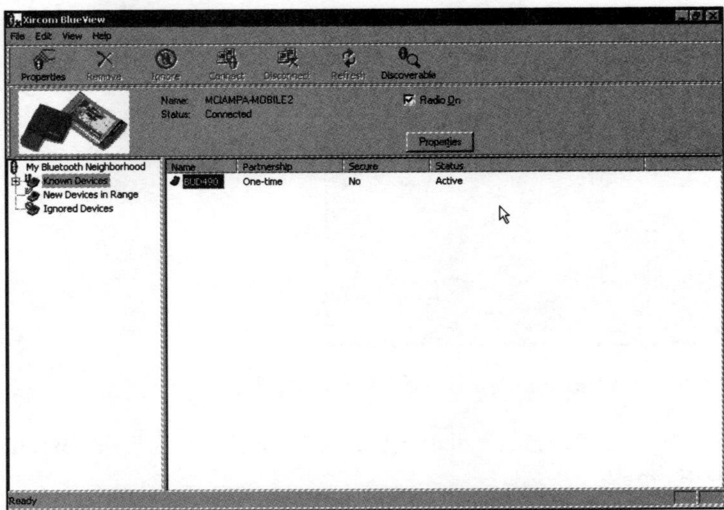

Figure 5-31 Connection information about slave

Figure 5-32 Intellisync agent toolbar

e. On the slave computer, launch the Intellisync program by clicking **Start**, then **Programs**, click **Intellisync**, and finally click **Intellisync agent**. This will bring up the "Getting Started Intellisync" screen. Click **OK** to display the Intellisync agent screen. Click the first icon (wrench and screwdriver) to launch the Connection Setup Manager. Click **Close** if the information screen appears, and then click on the Remote Connections tab. A connection will be established between the two computers. On the master it will appear in the Connection Setup Manager window, as seen in Figure 5-33. Do not close the Connection Setup Manager dialog box on either master or slave computer or the connection will be lost.

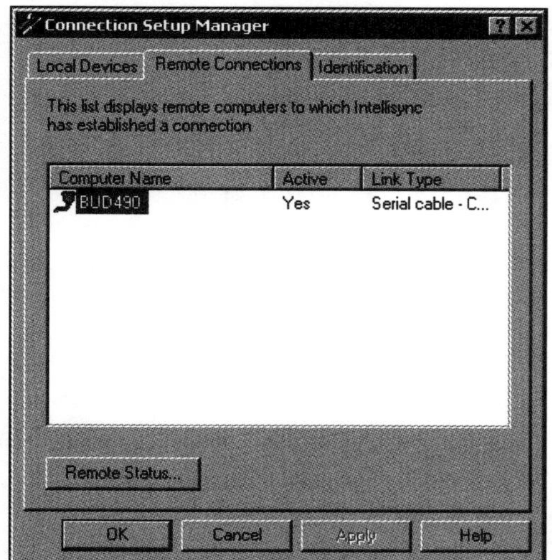

Figure 5-33 Connection with slave

f. Create a document on the master computer and insert your name and the current date. Save this file as **Project 3-Your Name-Master**. Click the second icon (document, arrow, and file folder) on the Intellisync agent screen to launch the Getting Started – File Transfer screen. Click **Close** if the information screen appears. This will display the File Transfer screen, as seen in Figure 5-34. In the left pane, find the name of the master computer and then locate your document so that it appears in the right pane, as seen in Figure 5-35.

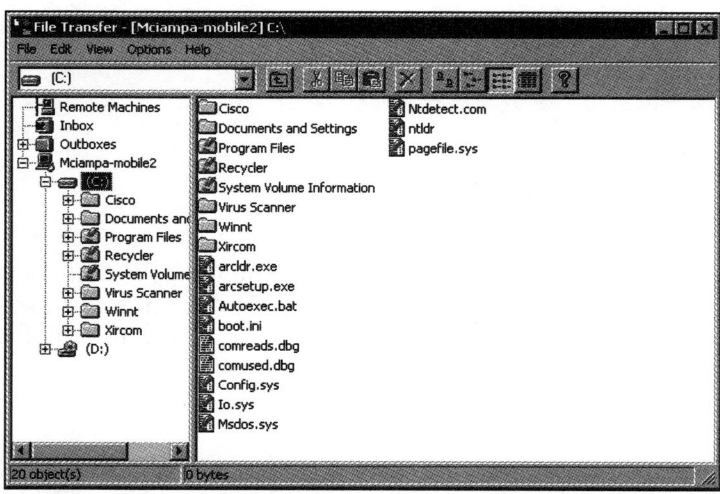

Figure 5-34 File Transfer screen

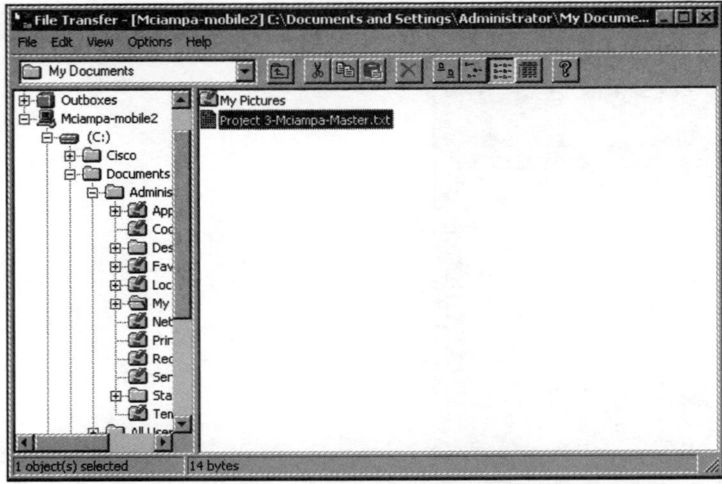

Figure 5-35 Document to transfer

g. Right-click the document, click **Express**, and then click on the name of the slave computer.

h. Go to the slave computer. Click the second (file transfer) icon on the Intellisync agent screen to launch the Getting Started – File Transfer screen. Click **Close** if the information screen appears. This will display the File Transfer screen. An information screen will appear on the master asking if you want to transfer the files, as seen in Figure 5-36. Click **Yes**. Close the First Connected dialog box.

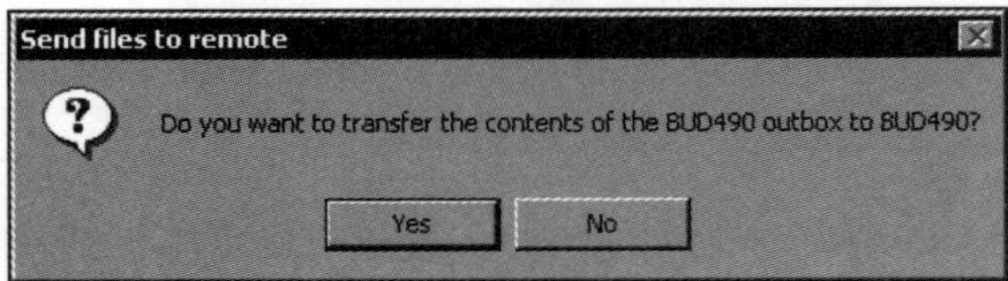

Figure 5-36 Send files to remote dialog box

i. On the slave computer, click the inbox icon in the left pane. The transferred file will appear in the right pane. Double-click **My Computer** and locate the file that was transferred. Double-click the file to open it. Close the file when you are finished viewing it.

j. Close all open windows.

Experiment with Bluetooth Communications

What are the factors that impact Bluetooth communications? Using two Bluetooth devices, experiment regarding the maximum distance you can achieve between devices, what obstacles such as walls and doors have the greatest impact, and RF interference from other devices. Write a paper summarizing your findings.

Research Bluetooth

The industry is currently divided regarding the future of Bluetooth. Using the Internet and other sources, acquire data that shows Bluetooth market share as compared to infrared and other wireless technologies. Explore the major computer vendors' Bluetooth offerings at the present and also what support they plan for the future. In your opinion, where should Bluetooth be positioned in today's market? What types of future investments would help Bluetooth? Write a one-page paper on your findings.

Case Project

The Baypoint Group (TBG) has hired you once again as a consultant. The county's economic industrial board is holding a series of Tuesday luncheon workshops that explore a variety of technology issues for its members, which include several information technology (IT) vice presidents and directors from large area businesses. One of the topics that was proposed for a luncheon workshop was Bluetooth.

TBG would like for you to attend the luncheon and make a presentation. Be sure to cover the history of Bluetooth, how it is being used today, and what future uses may be in store for this wireless technology, along with some of its technical features. Create a PowerPoint presentation of at least 15 slides.

Optional Team Case Project

Your presentation at the Tuesday luncheon was a big success and has generated a great deal of interest among the attendees. You have been asked to return in several weeks to hold a roundtable discussion regarding the viability of Bluetooth and what might happen to it in the future. Create two groups, one of which takes the position that Bluetooth will be a tremendous success in the marketplace, and one which takes the position that Bluetooth will fail and will disappear completely in the next three years. Research your positions and hold a mock discussion where each group presents its findings.

CHAPTER

6

LOW-SPEED WIRELESS LOCAL AREA NETWORKS

After reading this chapter and completing the exercises you will be able to:

- Give examples of how WLANs are used today
- List the components and modes of a WLAN
- Tell the advantages and disadvantages of HomeRF
- Explain the background of IEEE 802.11 WLANs
- Describe how an IEEE 802.11b network functions

Without question, the wireless technology that attracts the most attention today is radio frequency (RF) wireless local area networks (WLANs). Since the standard was approved in the late 1990s, the interest in and growth of WLANs have surpassed all projections. Sales of WLAN equipment doubled in the first two years these devices were available, taking in an estimated $1.1 billion. By the year 2004, the value of WLAN installations is expected to top $34 billion on sales of 12 million units per year. When you consider that WLAN devices were almost nonexistent until the year 2000, that growth is nothing short of astonishing. WLANs have taken the computing world by storm.

One of the most attractive features of WLANs is the broad range of uses for the technology. Historically, a new technology is projected to fit a specific niche in the marketplace and might later expand into new areas. WLANs have turned that model upside down. From the very beginning, WLAN devices have found uses in the office and the classroom, their anticipated niche. But almost as soon as they were available, users were finding a wide range of new uses for WLANs that WLAN designers had not dreamed of. Coffee houses set up WLANs for their customers. Airlines installed WLANs to provide Internet access to passengers during flights. Stadiums created wireless networks to allow fans to access statistics and view instant replays from their seats. Individuals have installed wireless technology to create pockets of free wireless Internet access around the world. And the list of uses grows daily.

This chapter is the first of two chapters that look at this exciting new technology. We will begin by looking at ways in which WLANs are used. Then, we'll focus on low-speed (less than 15 Mbps) WLANs and see how they function. In the next chapter we will explore the newer high-speed WLANs.

WLAN Applications

WLAN applications can be found everywhere that users need mobility without being confined to a specific location. WLANs are an ideal application for colleges and schools. Students do not have to go to a specific computer lab or the library to get to the computer network; instead, they can access the school network from almost any location on campus through the wireless network. As they move to different classrooms in different buildings, they remain connected to the network. Teachers can also take advantage of WLAN technology by creating classroom presentations on the notebook computer in their office and then carry that computer with them right into the classroom. They do not have to plug and unplug cables to attach to the campus network. Instead, their notebook automatically makes the wireless connection as soon as they walk into the room. Teachers can also send handouts directly to students sitting in the classroom who have brought their own wireless devices with them to class.

WLANs have changed the way businesses function as well. Instead of having meetings in conference rooms where employees are away from the data that they need to help make decisions, wireless technologies allow them to bring their wireless notebook computers to that conference room and remain connected to the network. They can access their data to make immediate decisions wherever the need arises.

Warehouse management was one of the first uses of WLAN technology and may still be one of the largest. Forklift trucks in the warehouse are outfitted with a wireless computer device, and employees are also given portable wireless devices. All of these devices can be connected to the WLAN system. Warehouse management system (WMS) software can manage all of the activities from receiving through shipping. And since this network is tied into the front office computer system, managers can have statistics that are current at any given moment.

United Parcel Service (UPS) is investing $100 million in a WLAN network that will be installed throughout its worldwide distribution hubs. The system will replace terminals used by package sorters with combined WLAN and Bluetooth ring scanners and hip-mounted devices. A package sorter employee will wear a cordless ring scanner to capture data from packages. The ring scanner uses Bluetooth technology to send the package data to the terminal worn on the hip. The hip terminal receives data from the scanner and then retransmits the information via a WLAN to the worldwide UPS network. It is estimated that the new system will pay for itself in 16 months.

Airports are likewise turning to wireless technologies. WLANs are being installed to support aircraft maintenance and baggage handling and to keep crewmembers informed of last-minute changes. Many large airport terminals transmit wireless signals that waiting passengers can pick up on their wireless notebook computers or PDAs while waiting for their flights. For a nominal fee, waiting passengers can surf the Internet or read e-mail. Some airplanes have wireless capabilities for passengers on flights. Like their earth-bound counterparts, these passengers can access the Internet or view their corporate data from their seat at 30,000 feet.

These are not the only applications for WLANs. Some of the more interesting uses include:

- Hotels are providing lobby and meeting room WLAN access. Hotel guests can meet a hotel clerk anywhere in the lobby or at an entrance and check in via a PDA connected to a WLAN. Once the reservation is confirmed, the clerk can even generate a room-key card on the spot.
- Coffeehouses and cafes are installing WLANs. The goal is to encourage coffee drinkers to surf while they sip their lattes, hoping that they will stay longer and order more beverages. Several coffeehouses are stocking WLAN equipment to loan or even sell to users.
- Shopping malls are providing WLAN coverage to their tenants, who pay a monthly fee for the service. These stores can then access the Internet or their headquarters to share data.
- The Alaska Department of Transportation and Public Facilities is using a WLAN as a ship-to-shore wireless communications system for its fleet of ferries. As soon a ship comes into the range of a WLAN system in port, the network starts transferring e-mail, crew schedules, supply orders for the ships and their onboard snack bars, and other types of administrative data. The WLAN system has been tested to a range of 3.5 miles.
- Free wireless networks are springing up in cities all over the U.S. and even around the world. Users with WLAN devices can roam into one of these areas of coverage and have free access to the Internet and e-mail. In some cities the area of coverage extends for several miles.
- Bands performing on the road include WLANs with their instruments and sound, lighting, and stage equipment. The WLANs, which can be quickly set up and taken down, help to manage accounting and production tasks.
- The Caribbean island of Anguilla has installed a WLAN system that covers the entire 16-mile long island. Because hurricanes frequently strike the island and knock down transmission lines and poles, switching to a wireless system minimizes that risk.

How WLANs Operate

Although there are a variety of radio frequency WLANs on the market, there are similarities among the different products. All radio frequency WLANs use similar parts or components and operate in a similar way.

Components

The list of components needed for a WLAN is surprisingly short. Only wireless network interface cards and access points are needed for communication to take place.

Wireless Network Interface Card

Recall that the hardware that allows a computer to be connected to a wired network is called a **network interface card (NIC)**, also called a **network adapter**. A NIC is the device that connects the computer to the network so that it can send and receive data. One end (or edge) of the NIC is connected to the computer while the other end has a port for a cable connection, as seen in Figure 6-1. The cable connects the NIC to the network, thus establishing the link between the computer and the network.

Figure 6-1 NIC

A wireless NIC performs the same functions as a wired NIC with one major exception: there is no port for a wire connection to the network. In its place is an antenna to send and receive RF signals. Specifically, when wireless NICs transmit, they:

1. Change the computer's internal data from parallel to serial transmission.
2. Divide the data into packets (smaller blocks of data) and attach the sending and receiving computer's address.
3. Determine when to send the packet.
4. Transmit the packet.

A wireless NIC is most often a separate card that is inserted into one of the computer's expansion slots. For desktop computers, wireless NICs are available for a Peripheral Component Interface (PCI) expansion slot, as seen in Figure 6-2. Some wireless NIC cards even have retractable antennas that can slide into the card when not in use, as seen in Figure 6-3. There are also external devices that function like a wireless NIC that connect to the computer's serial port or the Universal Serial Bus (USB) connection.

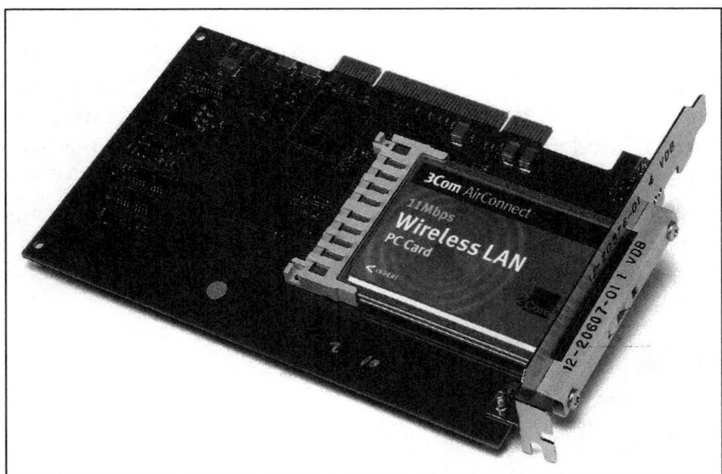

Figure 6-2 PCI wireless NIC

A few WLAN vendors offer wireless NICs that insert into an Industry Standard Architecture (ISA) expansion slot. The ISA expansion slot connects to the ISA bus in the computer that sends 16 bits at 10 MHz, or a total of 5 million bytes per second. This is much slower than a PCI bus in a computer that can transmit 32 bits at 33 MHz (132 million bytes per second).

Figure 6-3 PC Card wireless NIC with retractable antenna

For notebook computers, wireless NICs are available in two different formats. The first is for the standard PC Card Type II slot, as seen in Figure 6-4. The newer format is known as the **Mini PCI**. A Mini PCI is a small card that is functionally equivalent to a standard PCI expansion card. It was specifically developed for integrating communications peripherals such as modems and NICs onto a notebook computer. Some vendors have enhanced the Mini PCI slot by embedding an antenna in the case of the notebook that surrounds the screen. When a wireless NIC Mini PCI card is used, it automatically activates the antenna to improve the reception of the RF signal.

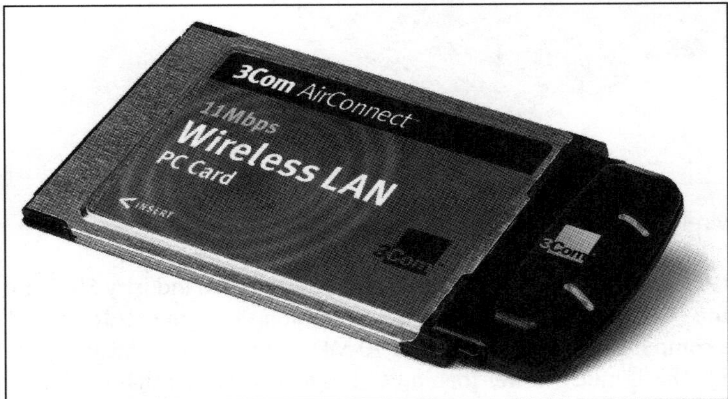

Figure 6-4 PC Card wireless NIC

Prior to Mini PCI cards, notebook vendors often integrated modem chips on the motherboard itself as a way of saving the PC Card slots for other devices. However, because modems had to be certified in each international market in which the computer was sold, this often led to significant delays before they could be imported.

For smaller devices like PDAs, there are also two options for wireless NICs, depending on the manufacturer. Some PDAs will accept a standard Type II PC Card wireless NIC like those that can be used in a notebook computer. However, sometimes an external attachment known as a **sled** must be purchased and connected to the PDA. The sled contains a Type II PC Card slot for a wireless NIC or other device. The second option is a **compact flash (CF) card**, as seen in Figure 6-5. CF cards consist of a small circuit board that contains flash memory chips and a dedicated controller chip. **Flash memory** is a type of solid-state technology in which there are no moving parts. There are two advantages of CF wireless NICs over Type II PC Cards: they are smaller and they consume less power.

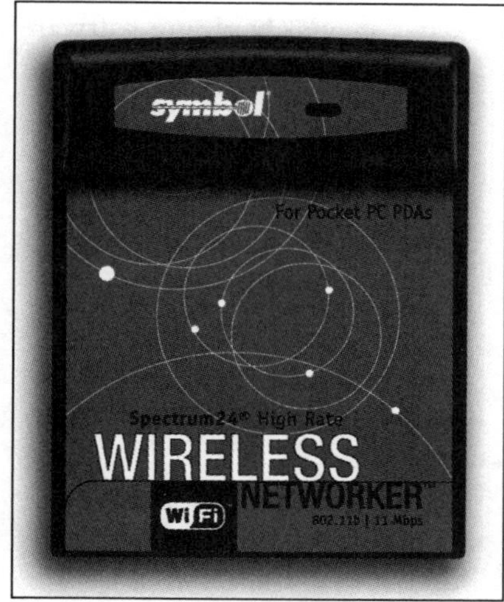

Figure 6-5 CF Card wireless NIC

Due to the tremendous popularity of WLANs, separate wireless NICs may soon be a thing of the past. Some vendors have already announced plans to integrate the components of a wireless NIC directly onto a single chip that could be included on the motherboard, thus eliminating the need for a separate card altogether. Yet not all vendors agree with this solution. Some notebook manufacturers want to keep RF signals from entering the notebook to reduce the likelihood of interference with the notebook's audio system. Instead of integrating the components of a wireless NIC on the motherboard of the computer, they integrate the wireless NIC into the top of the notebook behind the LCD display, thus keeping the RF waves away from the motherboard.

The software that interfaces between the wireless NIC and the computer can either be part of the operating system itself or a separate program that is loaded onto the computer. Beginning with Microsoft Windows XP, all Microsoft desktop operating systems will recognize a wireless NIC without the need for any external software drivers; previous versions of the Windows operating system require these external drivers. Incorporating them into the operating system eases installation and also provides additional features such as the ability to connect automatically to different WLANs as the user roams, instead of manually configuring the settings. Some wireless NIC vendors include software drivers for other operating systems such as DOS, Windows 3.x, and Linux. Operating systems for PDAs are expected in the future to include the wireless NIC interface. Microsoft Pocket PC 2002 does not recognize a wireless NIC card and requires external drivers to be installed.

Access Point

An **access point (AP)**, seen in Figure 6-6, is a device that consists of three major parts. First, it contains an antenna and a radio transmitter/receiver to send and receive signals. Second, it has an RJ-45 wired network interface that allows it to connect by cable to a standard wired network. Finally, an access point has special bridging software installed.

Figure 6-6 Access point

It is possible to use a standard PC as an access point. Installing a wireless NIC (which functions at the transmitter/receiver), a standard NIC (which serves as the wired network interface), and special AP control software will allow a PC to serve as an AP.

An access point has two basic functions. First, the access point acts as the base station for the wireless network. All of the devices that have a wireless NIC transmit to the AP, which in turn redirects the signal to the other wireless devices. The second function of an AP is to act as a bridge between the wireless and wired networks. The AP can be connected to the standard network by a cable, allowing the wireless devices to access the data network through it, as seen in Figure 6-7.

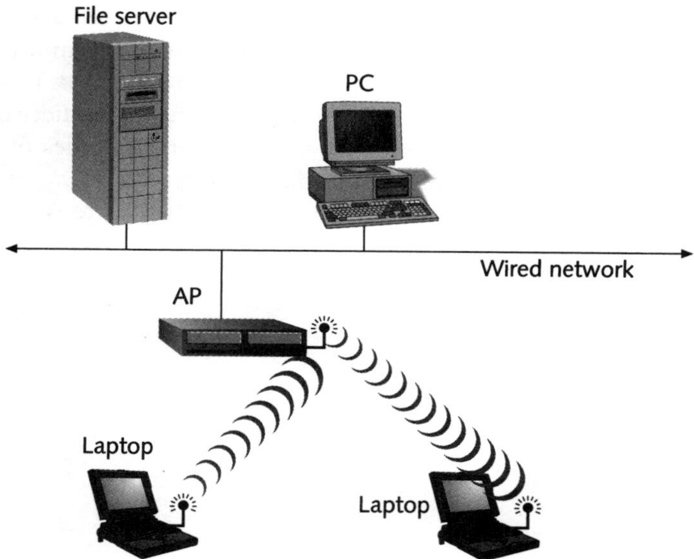

Figure 6-7 Access point as a bridge

The range of an access point acting as the base station is approximately 375 feet (115 meters) in a typical office environment. The number of users that a single access point can support varies, but is generally over 100. However, because the RF is shared among users, most vendors recommend one access point for each 50 users if they are performing basic e-mail, light Web surfing, and occasional transferring of medium-sized files. On the other hand, if the users are using constant network access and transferring large files, the ratio may be more like 20 users per AP.

Access points are typically mounted on a ceiling or a similar area high off the ground to reduce interference from surrounding objects. However, electrical power outlets are generally not found in these locations. A recent innovation known as **power over Ethernet** has solved this problem. Instead of receiving power directly from an AC outlet, DC power is delivered to the AP through the unused wires in a standard unshielded twisted pair (UTP) Ethernet cable that connects the AP to the wired network. This eliminates the need for expensive electrical wiring to be installed in the ceiling and makes the mounting of APs more flexible.

Modes

There are two modes in which data can be sent and received in an RF WLAN: ad hoc mode and infrastructure mode.

Ad Hoc Mode

The first mode that can be used by wireless clients in a WLAN is usually called the **ad hoc mode** or **peer-to-peer mode**, although its formal name is the **Independent Basic Service Set (IBSS)** mode. In ad hoc mode, wireless clients communicate directly among themselves without using an access point, as seen in Figure 6-8. This mode is useful for a quick and easy setup of a wireless network anywhere that a network infrastructure does not already exist or is not permanently required. Examples of locations that use ad hoc mode WLANs are hotel rooms or convention centers. The drawback is that the wireless clients can only communicate among themselves; there is no access to a wired network.

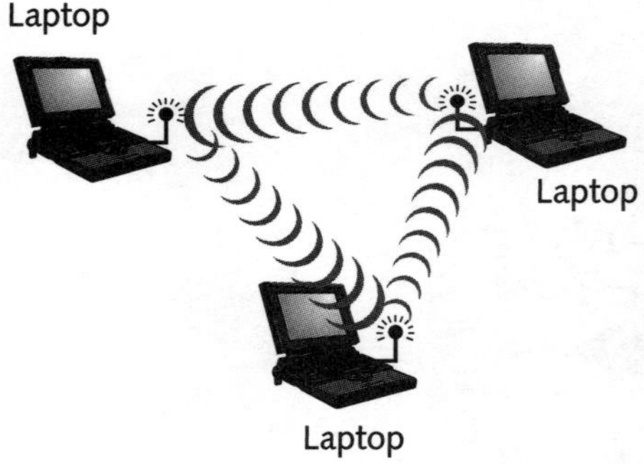

Figure 6-8 Ad hoc mode

Infrastructure Mode

The second wireless network mode that can be created is the **infrastructure mode**, also known as the **Basic Service Set (BSS)**. Infrastructure mode consists of wireless clients and an access point. If more users need to be added to the WLAN, or the range of coverage area needs to be increased, more access points can be added. This creates an **Extended Service Set (ESS)**. An ESS is simply two or more BSS wireless networks, as seen in Figure 6-9.

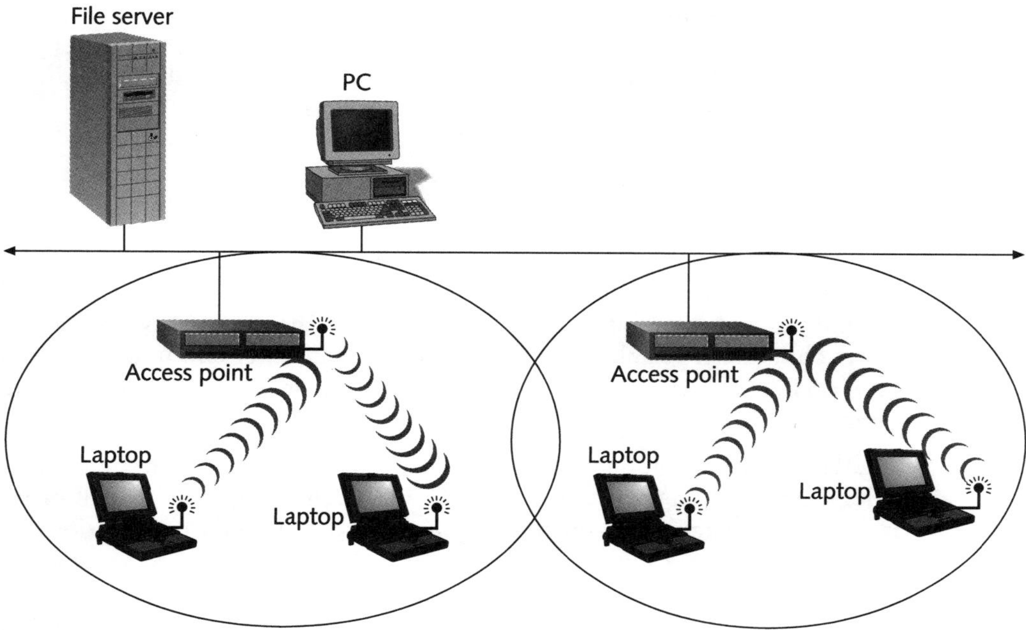

Figure 6-9 Extended Service Set (ESS)

When multiple access points are used they create areas of coverage, much like cells in a cellular telephone system. These cells overlap to facilitate roaming. When a mobile user carrying a wireless notebook computer enters into the range of more than one AP, his wireless device will choose an access point to associate with, usually based on signal strength. Once that device is accepted by the AP, the client device "tunes" to the radio frequencies at which the AP is set.

On a regular basis, wireless clients will survey all the radio frequencies to determine if a different access point can provide better service. If it finds one (perhaps because the user has moved again), then it associates with the new AP, tuning to the radio frequency to which it is set. This is called a handoff. To the user it is seamless because the wireless device never has an interruption of service.

Some APs allow you to specify which access point you want to connect with.

A drawback of ESS WLANs is that all wireless clients and access points must be part of the same network in order for users to be able to freely roam between each AP. However, it can sometimes be difficult to manage one large network. Network managers like to subdivide a network into smaller units known as **subnets** because subnets are easier to manage than the entire network. Yet if an ESS were divided into subnets, a mobile user could not freely roam between APs but would have to reconnect each time he or she moved between subnets. Software is now available that essentially "tricks" the wireless network into thinking that the subnets are one network. If that software is not used then care must be taken in designing the wireless network.

HomeRF

HomeRF, also known as Shared Wireless Access Protocol (SWAP), is an open industry specification that defines how wireless devices that conform to this specification can communicate and share information in and around the home. It is designed as a way to connect computers, peripherals, cordless phones, and other consumer electronic devices together. HomeRF is wireless home networking that combines wireless data, cordless telephony, and streaming media.

HomeRF-compliant products operate in the license-free 2.4 GHz frequency band and use frequency-hopping spread spectrum (FHSS) technology. One benefit of HomeRF is that it provides **quality-of-service (QoS)**. Audio and video transmissions, unlike data transmissions, are time sensitive and need to arrive in a prescribed sequence. If they do not, the video is "jerky" or there is silence in the audio. Transmissions that are sent across a network from User A as packets are mixed together with packets sent from User B. QoS allows for transmissions that are time sensitive, like audio and video, to be prioritized and arrive in the correct sequence, even if it means "bumping" standard data transmissions so that they arrive later. HomeRF supports prioritized streaming media sessions.

HomeRF version 1.0 products were introduced in 2000. The transmission speed was 1.6 Mbps. Nearly all of the early products were computer related and supported data applications. HomeRF version 2.0 was released in 2001 and has a transmission speed of 10 Mbps. Advantages of the new version include support for more phone lines (up from 4 to 8), new features designed for digital music and standard definition TV, and even roaming.

The future is very bright for wireless networking in the home. By 2004 it is estimated that over 30 million American homes will have multiple computers and 58 percent of these homes will network those computers together. However, the future for HomeRF is cloudy. With the rapid development of IEEE 802.11 products, the price has quickly dropped to the consumer level and 802.11 devices are rapidly being installed in homes. One of the fastest growing home consumer products is a device known as a **wireless gateway**. This device follows the 802.11 standard and combines a wireless access point, a **Network Address Translator (NAT)** router that hides the internal network addresses from the outside world for security, a **firewall** that prevents unauthorized access to the network, connections for DSL and cable modems, and other features. With 802.11 wireless gateways and wireless products penetrating the home market so quickly, it appears that HomeRF has a very shaky future.

IEEE 802.11

In 1990 the IEEE formed a committee to develop a standard for WLANs operating at 1 and 2 Mbps. Several different proposals were initially recommended before a draft was developed. This draft went through seven different revisions that took almost seven years to complete. On June 26, 1997 the IEEE approved the final draft.

The **802.11 standard** defines a local area network that provides cable-free data access for clients that are either mobile or in a fixed location at a rate of either 1 or 2 Mbps. The 802.11 standard also specifies that the features of a WLAN be transparent to the upper levels of the 802.11 standard. That is, the functions of the PHY and MAC layers provide full implementation of all of the WLAN features so that no modifications are needed at any other layers. This is illustrated in Figure 6-10. Because all of the WLAN features are isolated in the PHY and MAC layers, any network operating system or LAN application will run on a WLAN without any modification necessary. In order to accomplish this, some features that are usually associated with higher layers are now performed at the MAC layer.

The slow bandwidth of only 2 Mbps for the 802.11 standard is not sufficient for most network applications. As a result, the IEEE body revisited the 802.11 standard shortly after it was released to determine what changes could be made to increase the speed.

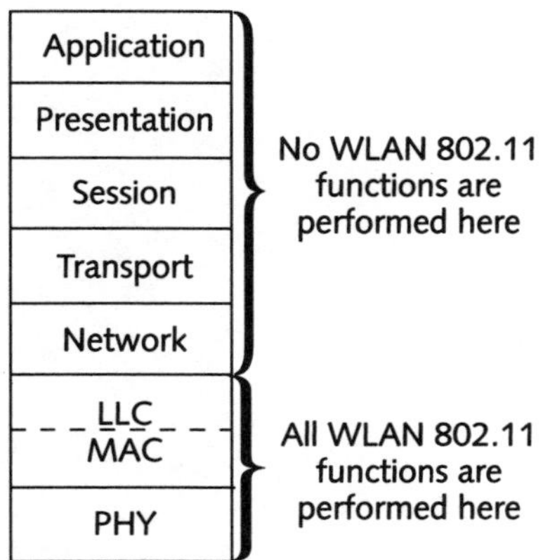

Figure 6-10 WLAN features in PHY and MAC layers

IEEE 802.11b

In September 1999, a new 802.11b High Rate was amended to the 802.11 standard. The **802.11b standard** added two higher speeds, 5.5 Mbps and 11 Mbps, to the original 1 or 2 Mbps 802.11 standard. With the faster data rates, 802.11b, also known as **Wi-Fi**, quickly became the standard for WLANs. (IEEE also released the 802.11a standard in 1999, a standard for even higher speed WLANs that you will learn about in Chapter 7.)

The Wireless Ethernet Compatibility Alliance (WECA) owns the trademark to Wi-Fi and claims that it should be the official name of this technology, much like Ethernet is the name of IEEE 802.3. However, most industry professionals believe that IEEE 802.11b is the name that will be used for this technology.

Physical Layer

Recall that the basic purpose of the IEEE PHY layer is to send the signal to the network and receive the signal from the network. The 802.11b PHY layer is divided into two parts, as seen in Figure 6-11. The Physical Medium Dependent (PMD) sublayer includes the standards for both the characteristics of the wireless medium (such as DSSS or FHSS) and defines the method for transmitting and receiving data through that medium. The second sublayer of the PHY layer is the Physical Layer Convergence Procedure (PLCP). The PLCP performs two basic functions: it reformats the data received from the MAC layer (when transmitting) into a frame that the PMD sublayer can transmit, as seen in Figure 6-12, and it "listens" to the medium to determine when the data can be sent.

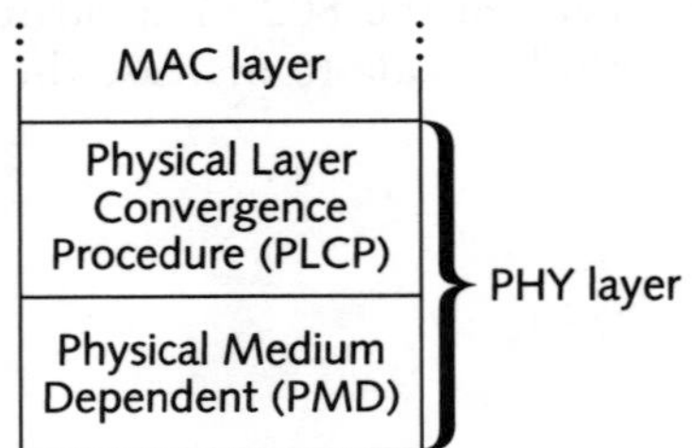

Figure 6-11 PHY sublayers

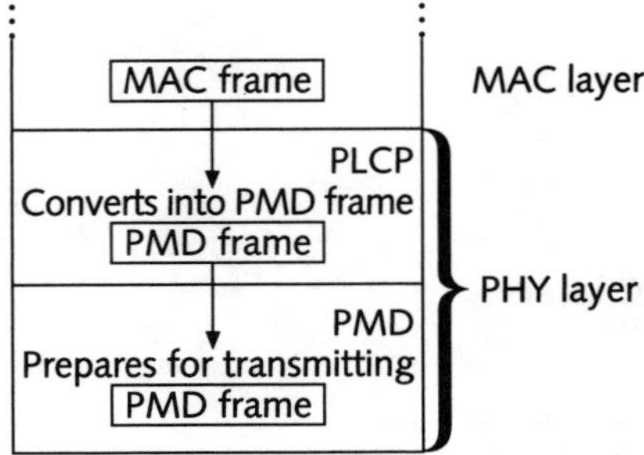

Figure 6-12 PLCP sublayer reformats MAC data

The 802.11b standard made changes only to the PHY layer of the original 802.11 standard.

Physical Layer Convergence Procedure Standards

The Physical Layer Convergence Procedure (PLCP) standards for 802.11b are based on direct sequence spread spectrum (DSSS). The PLCP must reformat the data received from the MAC layer (when transmitting) into a frame that the PMD sublayer can transmit. An example of a PLCP frame is illustrated in Figure 6-13.

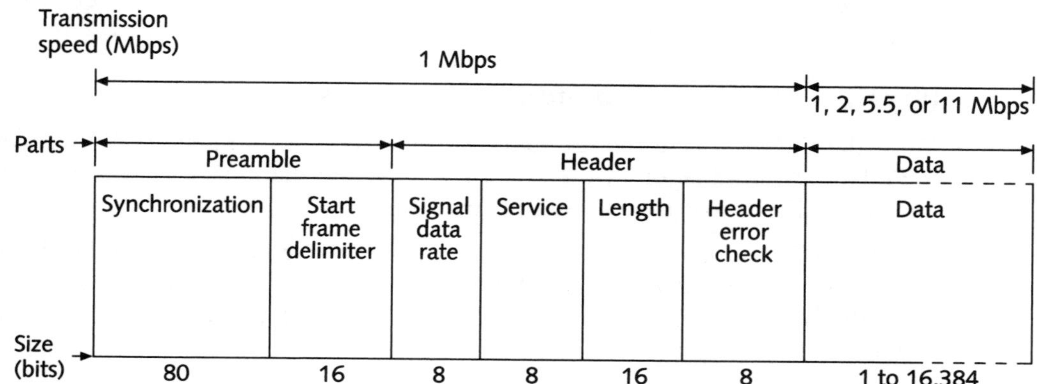

Figure 6-13 PLCP frame

The frame is made up of three parts, which are the preamble, the header, and the data. The preamble allows the receiving device to prepare for the rest of the frame. The header provides information about the frame itself. The data portion of the PLCP frame is the information that is to actually be transmitted. The size of the data portion can be from 1 to 16,384 bits. A description of the fields is as follows:

- *Synchronization*—Consists of alternating 0's and 1's to alert the receiver that a message may be on its way so that the receiving device will then synchronize with the incoming signal.
- *Start Frame Delimiter*—Always the same bit pattern (1111001110100000) and it defines the beginning of a frame.
- *Signal Data Rate*—Tells how the signal is being sent.
- *Length*—Indicates how long the frame is.
- *Header Error Check*—Contains a value that the receiving device can use to determine if the data was received correctly.
- *Data*—Can be from 1 to 16,384 bits.

The PLCP frame preamble and header are always transmitted at 1 Mbps. This allows for a slower sending device (like an 802.11 device) to talk to a faster receiving device (like an 802.11b device) because it is using the slowest speed. Another advantage of the slower PLCP preamble and header transmission speed is that a slower signal can cover a larger area than a faster signal can. The disadvantage of using the lowest common denominator speed is that two faster devices must still fall back to the 1 Mbps transmission rate for the preamble and header. However, the data can be sent at the faster rate once the connection is established.

Physical Medium Dependent Standards

Once the PLCP has created the frame, it then passes it on to the PMD sublayer of the PHY layer. Again, the job of the PMD is to translate the binary 1's and 0's of the frame into radio signals that can be used for transmission.

The 802.11b standard uses the Industrial, Scientific, and Medical (ISM) band for its transmissions. The 802.11b standard specifies 14 frequencies that can be used, beginning at 2.412 GHz and incrementing by .005 GHz (except for Channel 14). These are listed in Table 6-1.

Table 6-1 802.11b ISM channels

Channel Number	Frequency (GHz)
1	2.412
2	2.417
3	2.422
4	2.427
5	2.432
6	2.437
7	2.442
8	2.447
9	2.452
10	2.457
11	2.462
12	2.467
13	2.472
14	2.484

The United States and Canada use channels 1–11; channels 12–14 are used in Europe, France, and Japan.

The PMD can transmit the data at 11, 5.5, 2, or 1 Mbps. For transmissions at 1 Mbps, a two-level differential binary phase shift key (PSK) is specified. The phase change for PSK bit 0 is 0 degrees while the phase change for bit 1 is 180 degrees. For transmissions at 2, 5.5, and 11 Mbps, a four-level phase change is used. Instead of having only two variations in phases for 0 and 1, the four-level phase change has four variations in phases for the bits 00, 01, 10, and 11.

You will recall that DSSS uses an expanded redundant code, called the Barker code, to transmit each data bit. The Barker code is used when 802.11b is transmitting at 1 Mbps or 2 Mbps. However, to transmit at rates above 2 Mbps the **Complementary Code Keying (CCK)** code is used instead. This code consists of a set of 64 8-bit code words. As a set, these code words have unique mathematical properties that allow them to be correctly distinguished from one another by a receiver. The 5.5 Mbps rate uses CCK to encode 4 bits per carrier, while the 11 Mbps rate encodes 8 bits per carrier.

Medium Access Control Layer

The 802.11b Data Link layer consists of two sublayers: Logical Link Control (LLC) and Media Access Control (MAC). The 802.11b standard specifies no changes to the LLC sublayer (the LLC remains the same as for wired networks). All of the changes for 802.11b WLANs are confined to the MAC layer.

On a WLAN all of the devices share the same RF spectrum. In order for this sharing to occur there must be a coordination that takes place between the devices. The standard coordination protocol for 802.11b WLANs is known as distributed coordination function. There is also an optional function known as point coordination function.

Distributed Coordination Function

Because the RF spectrum is shared, there must be rules for cooperation among the devices that are sharing it to ensure that the network can effectively function. The different ways of sharing are called **channel access methods**. One type of channel access method is known as **contention**. The "philosophy" of contention is that computers contend or compete with each other to use the network. With contention any computer can attempt to transmit a message anytime it wants to. However, if two computers start sending messages at the same time, a **collision** results and all the messages can become scrambled, as seen in Figure 6-14. One way to prevent network collisions is to first listen to make sure no other device is transmitting.

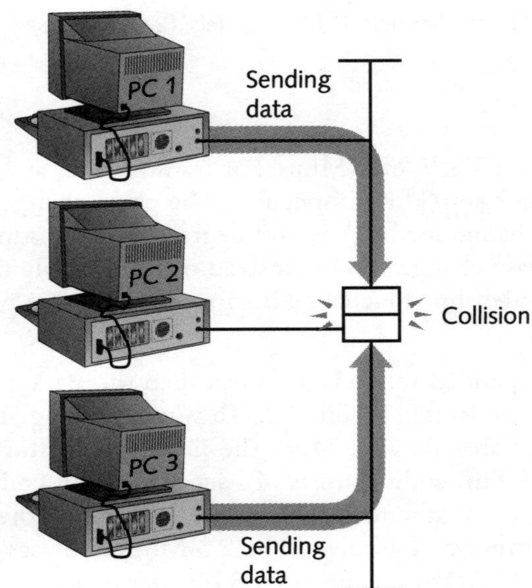

Figure 6-14 Collision

The IEEE 802.3 Ethernet standard specifies contention with "listening" as its channel access method. It is called **Carrier Sense Multiple Access with Collision Detection (CSMA/CD)**. CSMA/CD specifies that before a computer starts to send a message it should first listen on the cable (called **carrier sense**) to see if any other computer is transmitting. If it hears traffic, it should wait until that traffic is finished. If it hears no traffic, then the computer can send its message. However, what if two computers simultaneously listen and hear nothing on the cable and then both start to send at exactly the same time? A collision would still result. CSMA/CD also specifies that each computer must continue to listen while sending their message. If they hear a collision, each computer stops sending data and instead a "jam" signal is broadcast over the network. This tells all other computers to not send any messages temporarily. The two sending computers then pause a random amount of time (called a **backoff interval**) before attempting to resend, as seen in Figure 6-15.

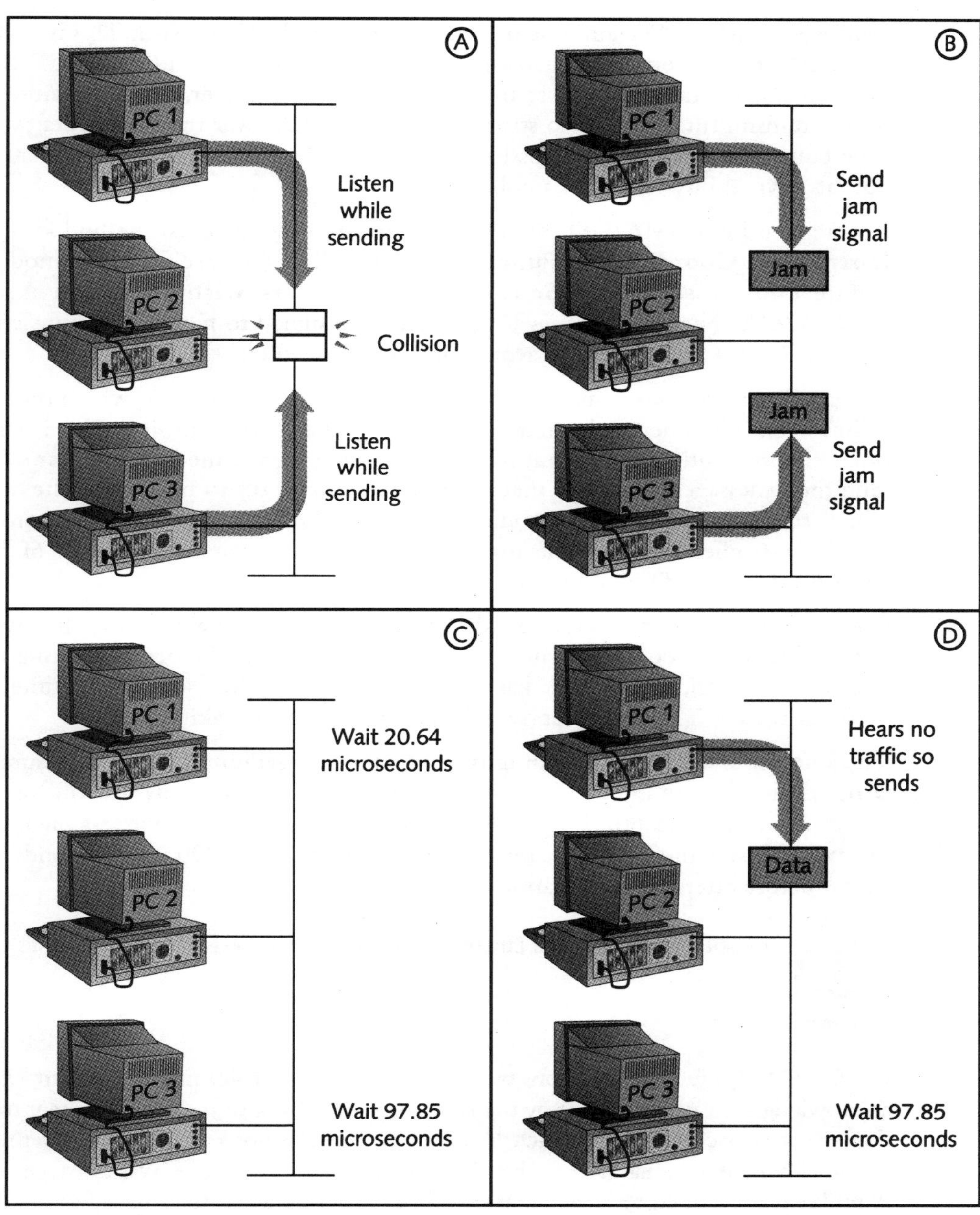

Figure 6-15 CSMA/CD

However, CSMA/CD cannot be used in a wireless 802.11b network. This is because collision detection is very difficult with wireless transmissions. With CSMA/CD the clients must be able to transmit and listen at the same time. However, in RF systems the signal from a transmitting client is so strong that it will overpower that same client's ability to simultaneously receive a transmission. In short, while it is transmitting, a client "drowns out" its own ability to detect a collision.

Instead of using CSMA/CD, the 802.11b standard uses an access method known as the **Distributed Coordination Function (DCF)**. The DCF specifies that a modified procedure known as **Carrier Sense Multiple Access with Collision Avoidance (CSMA/CA)** be used. Whereas CSMA/CD is designed to handle collisions when they occur, CSMA/CA attempts to avoid collisions altogether.

When using a contention-based channel access method, the time at which the most collisions occur is immediately after a client completes its transmission. This is because all other clients wanting to transmit have been waiting for the medium to clear so they can send their messages. Once the medium is clear they all try to transmit at the same time, which results in more collisions and delays. CSMA/CD handles the collisions by having the two clients responsible for the collision wait a random amount of time (the backoff interval) before attempting to resend.

CSMA/CA handles the situation differently. Instead of making just the two clients responsible for the collision wait a random amount of time before attempting to resend after the collision, CSMA/CA has *all* clients wait a random amount of time after the medium is clear. This significantly reduces collisions from taking place.

The amount of time that a client must wait after the medium is clear is measured in **slot time**. Each client must wait a random amount of slot times as its backoff interval. The slot time for a DSSS 802.11b WLAN is 20 microseconds. If a wireless client's backoff interval is 3 slot times, then it must wait 60 microseconds (20 microseconds × 3 slot times) before attempting to transmit.

The slot time for an 802.3 Ethernet 10 Mbps transmission is 51.2 microseconds.

CSMA/CA also reduces collisions by using explicit **packet acknowledgment (ACK)**. An acknowledgment packet is sent by the receiving client back to the sending client to confirm that the data packet arrived intact. If the ACK frame is not received back by the sending client, either the original data packet was not received or the ACK was not received intact. A problem is assumed to have occurred and the data packet is transmitted again after waiting another random amount of time. This explicit ACK mechanism handles interference and other radio-related problems. CSMA/CA and ACK is illustrated in Figure 6-16.

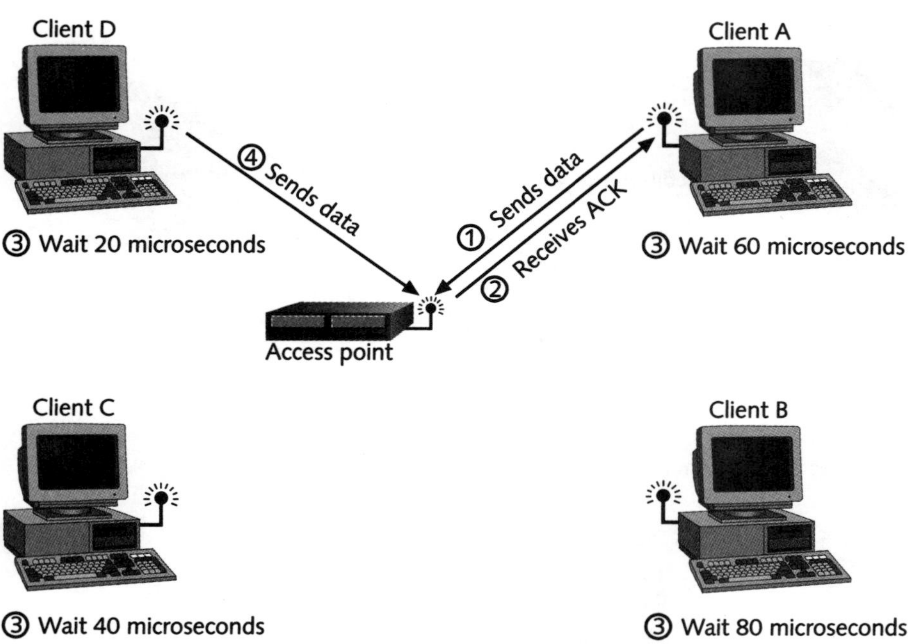

Figure 6-16 CSMA/CA

Although CSMA/CA will dramatically reduce the potential for collisions, it will not eliminate them altogether. The 802.11b standard provides two options that may be used to reduce collisions. The first is known as **virtual carrier sensing** or the **Request to Send/Clear to Send (RTS/CTS)** protocol. RTS/CTS is illustrated in Figure 6-17. A request-to-send (RTS) frame is transmitted by the wireless client, Client B, to the access point. This frame contains a duration field that defines the length of time needed for both the transmission and the returning ACK frame. The access point alerts all wireless clients that Client B needs to reserve the medium for a specific period of time. The access point then responds back to the client with a clear-to-send (CTS) frame that also tells all clients that the medium is now being reserved and they should suspend any transmissions. Once the client receives the CTS frame it can then proceed with transmitting its message.

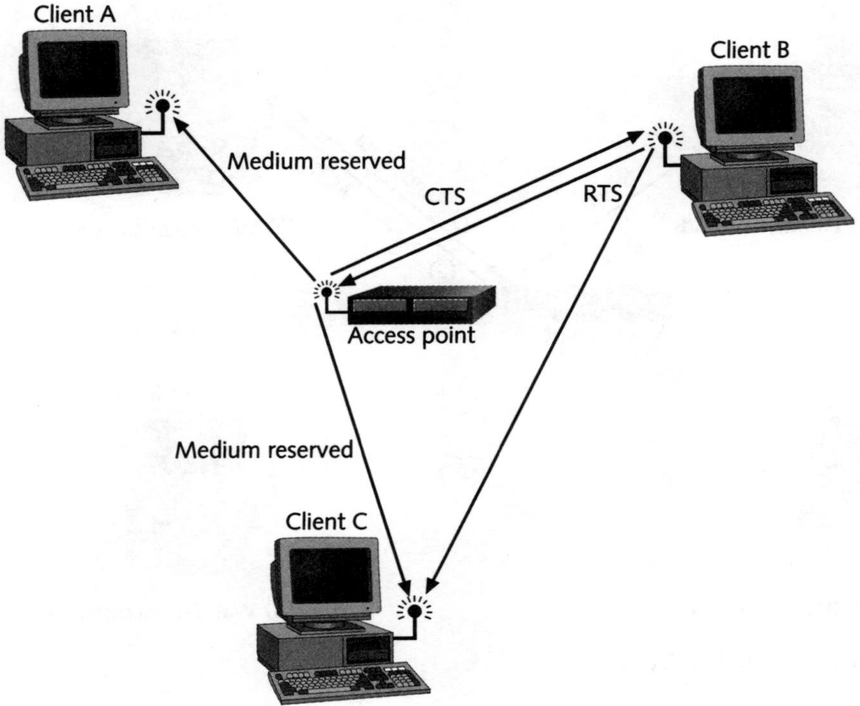

Figure 6-17 RTS/CTS

The RTS/CTS protocol imposes additional overhead and is not used unless there is poor network performance due to excessive collisions.

The second option to reduce collisions is **fragmentation**. Fragmentation involves dividing the data to be transmitted from one large frame into several smaller ones. Sending many smaller frames instead of one large frame reduces the amount of time that the wireless medium is being used and likewise reduces the probability of collisions.

If the length of a data frame to be transmitted exceeds a specific value, the MAC layer will divide or fragment that frame into several smaller frames. Each fragmented frame is given a fragment number (the first fragmented frame is 0, the next frame is 1, etc.). The frames are then transmitted to the receiving client. The receiving client receives the frame, sends back an ACK, and then is ready to receive the next fragment (a client can support receiving fragmented frames from up to three different senders). Upon receiving all of the fragments they are reassembled, based on their fragment numbers, back into the one original frame.

Fragmentation can reduce the probability of collisions and is an alternative to RTS/CTS. However, fragmentation does have additional overhead associated with it for sending a separate ACK from the receiving client for each fragmented frame received. Fragmentation does not always have to be used separately from RTS/CTS. The 802.11b standard permits both to be used simultaneously.

Point Coordination Function

The channel access method known as contention, in which any computer can attempt to transmit a message at any time, is the basis for CSMA/CA. Another type of channel access method is **polling**. With this method each computer is polled or asked in sequence if it wants to transmit. If the answer is yes, then it is given permission to transmit while all other devices must wait. If the answer is no, then the next device in sequence is polled. It is a very orderly way of allowing each device to send a message when it becomes its turn, as seen in Figure 6-18. Polling effectively prevents collisions because every device must wait until it receives permission before it can transmit.

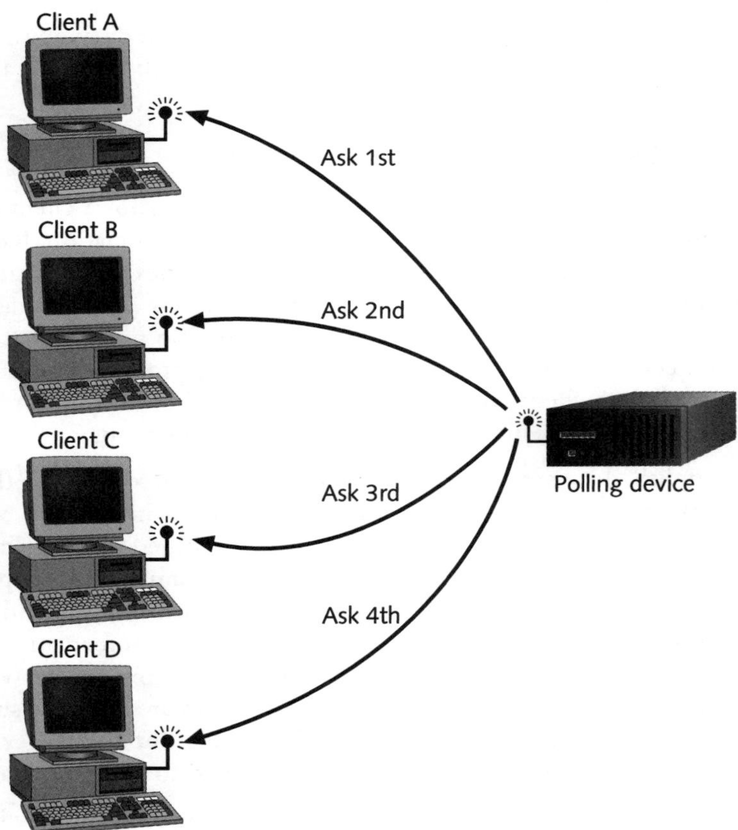

Figure 6-18 Polling

The 802.11b standard provides for an optional polling function known as **Point Coordination Function (PCF)**. With PCF the access point serves as the polling device or point coordinator. It queries each client in an orderly fashion to determine if the client needs to transmit.

When using PCF, the point coordinator first listens for wireless traffic. If it hears no traffic, then it sends out a frame to all clients known as a **beacon frame**. One field of this frame contains a value that indicates the length of time that PCF (polling) will be used instead of DCF (contention). After the clients receive this beacon frame they must stop any transmissions for that length of time. The point coordinator then sends out another frame to a specific client, granting it permission to transmit one frame to any destination. If it has nothing to send, then that client returns a **null data frame** back to the point coordinator.

PCF is most often used in WLANs that transmit time-sensitive frames. These types of transmissions, like audio or video, depend heavily upon each frame arriving in an orderly sequence very quickly one after the other. Delays in transmission can result in a video that "freezes" on the screen or a conversation that has gaps of dead space. Data transmissions, on the other hand, are not as sensitive to time. DCF cannot distinguish between voice, video, and data frames. Using PCF or a combination of DCF and PCF allows for the smooth transmission of time-sensitive frames.

Association and Reassociation

The MAC layer of the 802.11b standard provides the functionality for a client to join a WLAN and stay connected. This is known as association and reassociation. Recall that there are two different modes in RF WLANs. Ad hoc mode defines wireless clients that communicate directly among themselves without using an access point. Infrastructure mode consists of wireless clients and at least one access point. No matter what mode is being used, it is still necessary for a client first to go through a process of communicating with the other wireless clients or the access point in order that it can become accepted as part of the network. This process is known as **association**.

Association is accomplished by **scanning**. The client wanting to connect to the wireless network must scan the airwaves for information that it needs in order to begin the association process. There are two types of scanning. The first is called **passive scanning**. Passive scanning involves a client listening to each available channel for a set period of time (usually 10 seconds). The client is listening for a beacon frame transmitted from all available access points. The beacon frame contains the necessary information for the client to begin a dialog with one access point regarding connecting to the WLAN. It includes the time of the transmission, how often beacon frames are sent, the supported transmission rates of the network, and the access point's **Service Set Identifier (SSID)** number. The SSID is a unique identifier that has been assigned to an access point.

The second type of scanning is **active scanning**. Active scanning involves the client first sending out a special frame on each available channel, called a **probe** frame. It then waits for an answer from all available access points, known as a **probe response** frame. Like the beacon frame, the probe response frame has the needed information for the client to begin a dialog with the access point.

Once the client has the information from the access point by either active or passive scanning, it then begins to negotiate with one access point. The client sends an **associate request frame** to the access point that includes the client's own capabilities and supported rates. The access point will then send back an **associate response frame**. This contains a status code and client ID number for that client. At this point the client now becomes part of the network and can began transmitting.

If there are multiple access points, the client wanting to make an association may have many different access points from which to choose. The choice can be based on several criteria. A client can be preconfigured to connect only to a specific access point. In this case the client already contains the SSID of the access point with which it needs to connect. As it receives beacon frames or probe response frames from the different access points, it compares their SSID with the SSID with which it needs to connect. The client will reject all access points until it finds a match, at which time it will then send an associate request frame to that access point. If a client has not been preconfigured to connect with a specific access point, it will connect with the access point from which it has received the strongest radio signal.

Once a client connects with a specific access point it does not mean that it must remain associated only with that access point. Rather, a client may drop the connection with one access point and reestablish the connection with another. This is known as **reassociation**. There are several reasons why reassociation is necessary. A mobile client may roam beyond the coverage of one access point but into the coverage area of another access point. The mobile client must then sever its association with the original access point and reassociate itself with the new access point. Another reason why reassociation is necessary is that the signal that a client receives from an access point may become weak. This can be due to interference from another object that moves into the transmission path of the signal. The client would then begin the reassociate process to find an access point with a stronger signal.

When a client determines that the link to its current access point is poor, it begins scanning to find another access point. The client sends a **reassociation request frame** to the new access point. If the new access point accepts the reassociation request, it will send back a **reassociation response frame** to indicate its acceptance. The new access point will then send a **disassociation frame** to the old access point. This is to terminate the old access point's association with the client. This process is illustrated in Figure 6-19.

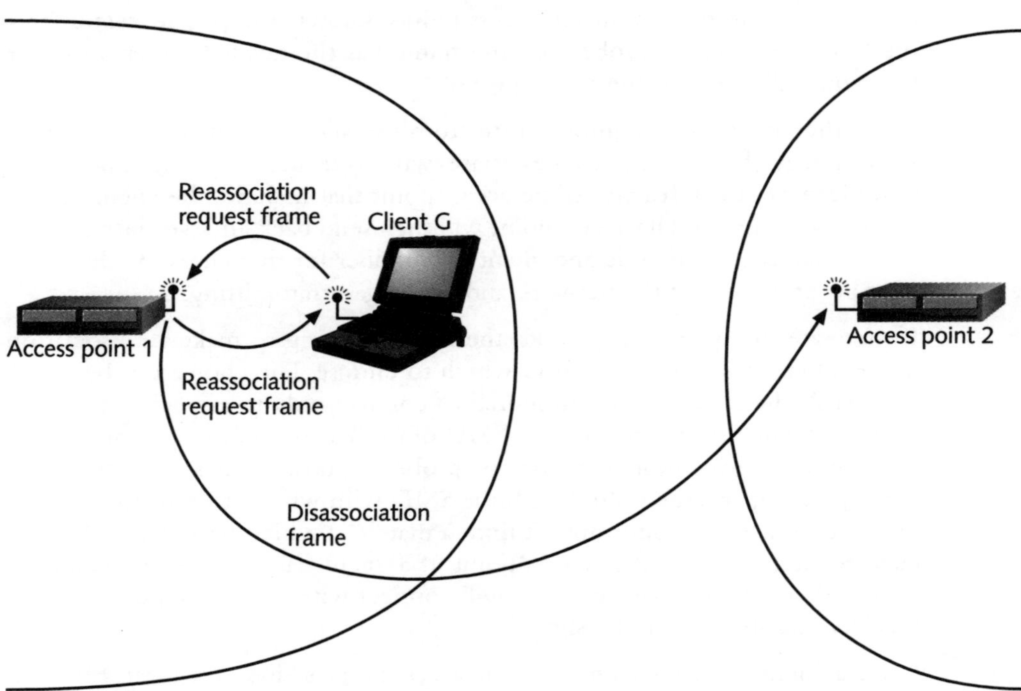

Figure 6-19 Reassociation process

Power Management

Most clients in a WLAN are portable notebook computers or PDAs, giving the users the freedom to roam without being tethered to the network by wires. These mobile devices depend upon batteries as their primary power source. To conserve battery power they can go into **sleep mode** after a period of time, when particular functions (hard drive, display screen, etc.) are temporarily powered down by the computer.

However, when that device is part of a WLAN it must continue to remain awake in order to receive network transmissions. Missing transmissions because it is in sleep mode may cause the device to lose the network connection altogether. This is because the original IEEE 802 standard assumed that computers were always ready to receive a network message. The dilemma is, how can the laptop power down into sleep mode during idle periods to preserve battery life yet continue to be active to hear network transmissions?

The answer to the dilemma is known as power management, as defined by the 802.11b standard. **Power management** allows the mobile client to be off as much as possible to conserve battery life but still not miss out on data transmissions. Power management is transparent to all protocols and applications so that it will not interfere with normal network functions. The 802.11b power management function can only be used in infrastructure mode.

The key to power management is synchronization. Every client on a WLAN has its own local timer. The AP sends out at regular intervals a beacon signal that contains a timestamp to all clients. When the clients receive this frame from the access point, they calibrate their local timers to be in synch with the access point.

When a mobile 802.11b client goes into sleep mode the access point (AP) is informed. The AP keeps a record of those clients that are awake and those that are sleeping. As the AP receives transmissions it first checks its records to determine if that client is in sleep mode. If it is sleeping, the AP temporarily stores those frames (called **buffering**).

At predetermined set times, the AP will send out a beacon frame to all clients. This frame contains a list, known as the **traffic indication map (TIM)**, of the clients that have buffered frames waiting at the AP. At that same set time all clients that have been sleeping will switch from sleep mode into an active listening mode (this is possible because a client's local timer does not sleep). If a client learns that it has buffered frames waiting, that client can send a request to the access point to have those frames forwarded to it. If it has no buffered frames it can return back to sleep mode. This is illustrated in Figure 6-20.

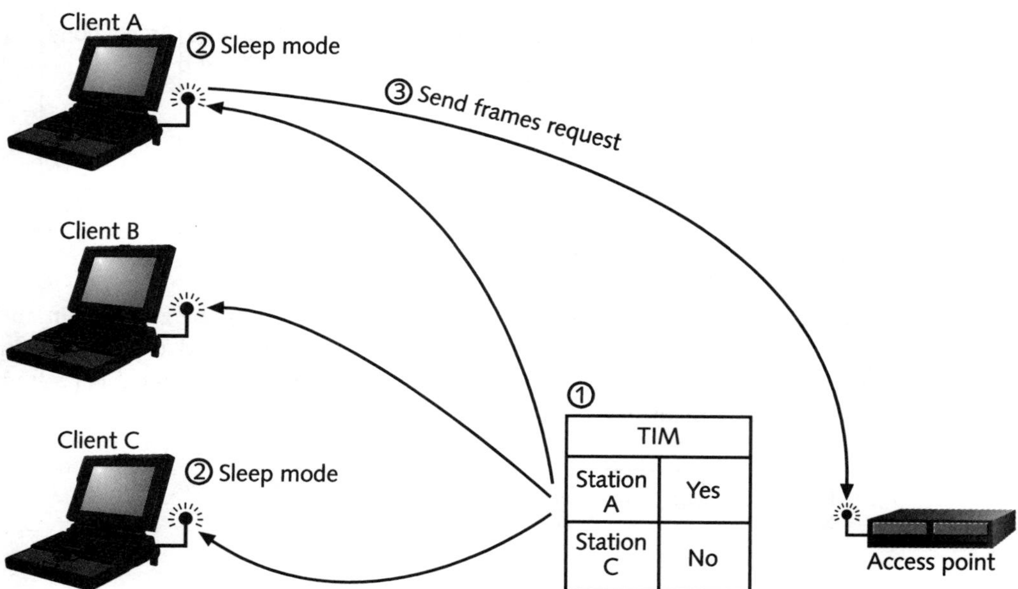

Figure 6-20 Power management

The amount of sleep time for a mobile client is generally set to 100 milliseconds.

MAC Frame Formats

The 802.11b standard specifies three different types of MAC frame formats. The first are known as **management frames**. These are used to set up the initial communications between a client and the access point. The reassociation request frame, the reassociation response frame, and the disassociation frame are all types of management frames. The format of a management frame is illustrated in Figure 6-21. The Frame Control field contains information such as the current version number of the standard and if any encryption is being used. The Duration field contains the number of microseconds needed to transmit. This value will be different depending upon if the mode being used is point coordination function or distributed coordination function. Sequence Control is the sequence number for the packet and packet fragment number.

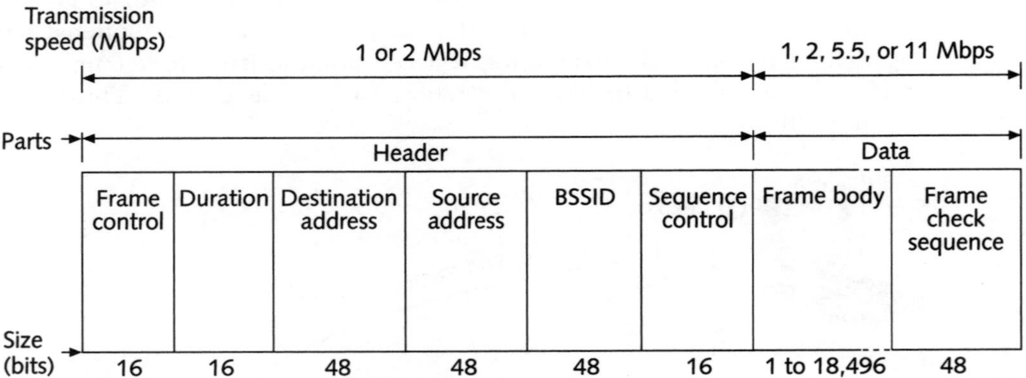

Figure 6-21 Structure of a management frame

Control frames are the second type of MAC frames. After the association and authentication between the clients and the access points are established, the control frames provide assistance in delivering the frames that contain the data. A typical RTS frame, which is a control frame, is illustrated in Figure 6-22.

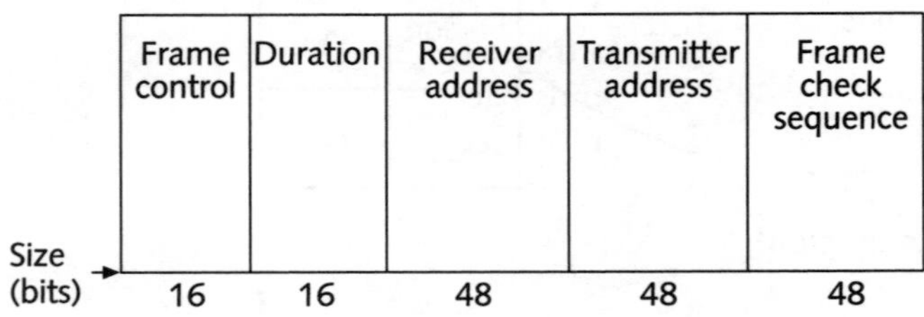

Figure 6-22 RTS frame

The final type of MAC frames are **data frames**, which carry the information to be transmitted to the destination client. The format of a data frame is illustrated in Figure 6-23.

The fields Address 1 through Address 4 contain the address of the SSID, the destination address, the source address, the transmitter address or the receiver address. Their contents vary depending upon the mode of transmission.

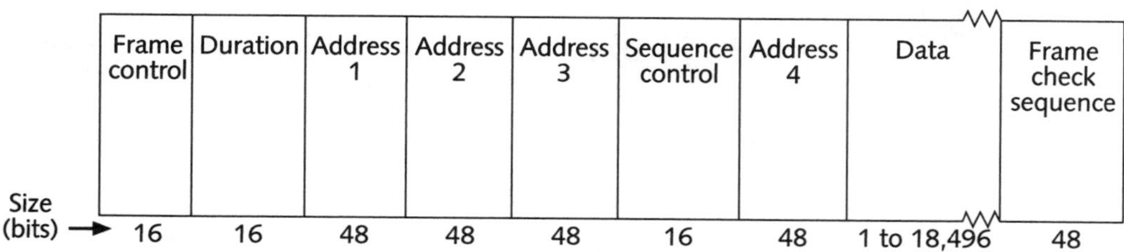

Figure 6-23 Data frame

The 802.11b standard also defines three different **interframe spaces (IFS)**, or time gaps. These are standard spacing intervals between the transmissions of the data frames. Instead of being just "dead space," these time gaps are used for special types of transmissions. The **Short IFS (SIFS)** is used for immediate response actions such as ACK. The **Point Coordination Function IFS (PIFS)** is the interval that clients use when polling nodes that have a specific time requirement. The **Distributed Coordination Function IFS (DIFS)** is the standard interval between the transmission of data frames.

The times of these space intervals, measured in microseconds, are seen in Table 6-2.

Table 6-2 Interframe spaces

Interframe Space	DSSS
SIFS	10
PIFS	30
DIFS	50

Figure 6-24 illustrates a transmission by Client A using DSSS with a backoff interval of 3. Client A starts listening (carrier sensing) before transmitting. At the completion of the DIFS space (50 microseconds) if there is no traffic Client A starts transmitting. When the transmission is over, the receiving client sends back an ACK in the SIFS gap acknowledging that the transmission was successful. Once received, the process starts all over again with Client A carrier sensing at the next DIFS. This time, if no traffic is detected, Client A starts its backoff interval of 60 microseconds (20 microseconds × 3). At the end of each slot time interval (20 microseconds) Client A again listens for traffic. If at the end of its backoff interval Client A still detects no traffic then it transmits its second frame. Once the ACK packet is received, then the process resumes again.

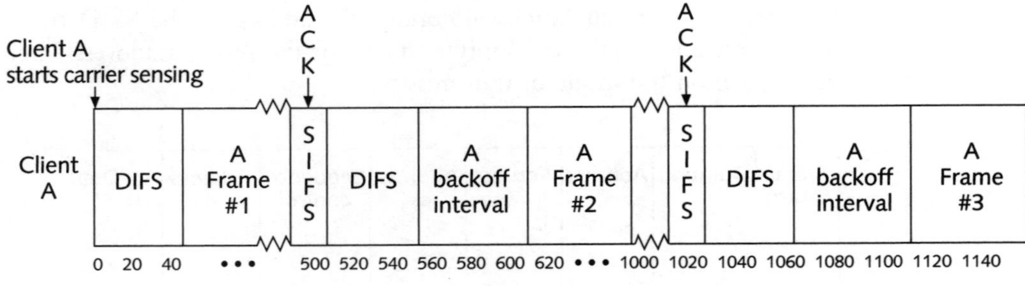

Figure 6-24 CSMA/CA with one client transmitting

When two clients need to transmit, it becomes more complicated, as seen in Figure 6-25. Client A is using DSSS with a backoff interval of 3 while Client B has a backoff interval of only 2. Client A begins carrier sensing and then transmitting its first frame. Client B then begins carrier sensing while Client A's first frame is being sent. Because it detects traffic, Client B waits. Once Client A has received its ACK, both Clients begin carrier sensing during the second DIF. At the end of the second DIF, Clients A and B begin their backoff interval. Because Client B's interval is only 2 (20 microseconds × 2), it will finish its backoff interval before Client A (20 microseconds × 3). Client B then begins transmitting its first packet.

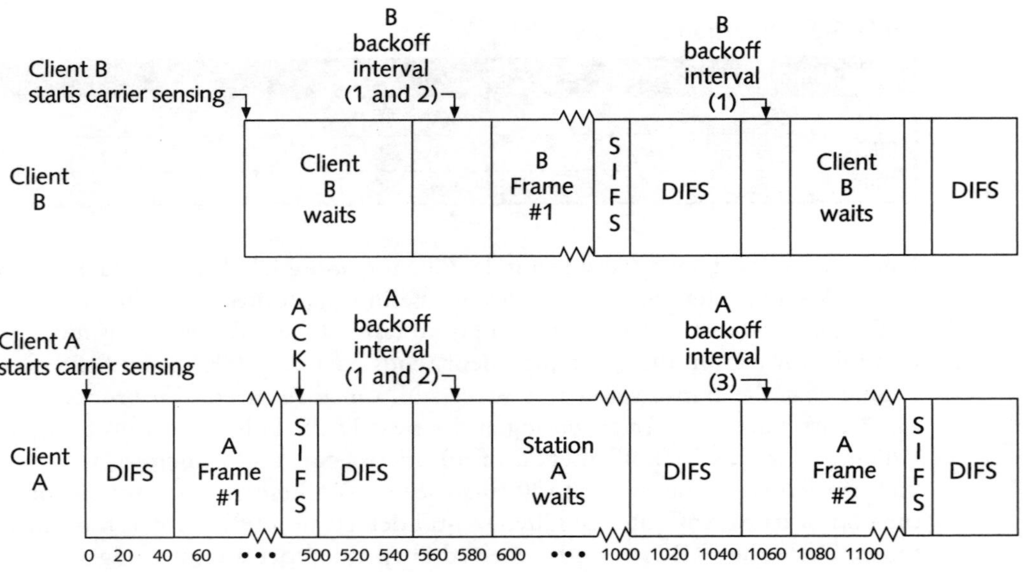

Figure 6-25 CSMA/CA with two clients transmitting

Because each client continues to carrier sense at the end of each of its time slots, Client A detects that Client B is now transmitting. Client A "remembers" that it has already counted off two of its slot times. Client A must now wait until B's transmission and acknowledgement is complete and the next DIF begins. After the DIF gap time, Client A and B both begin their backoff interval. However, this time Client A only has to wait one slot time. This is because Client A already waited for two of its slot times previously. If a client is "bumped" by another client from transmitting, it only has to wait the remaining number of time slots and not start all over again. This increases the probability that those clients that are waiting will transmit sooner than a new client will.

CHAPTER SUMMARY

- The wireless technology that attracts the most attention today is radio frequency (RF) wireless local area networks (WLANs). One of the unique features of WLANs is their broad range of usage. From coffeehouses setting up WLANs for their customers, to airlines installing WLANs to provide Internet access to passengers during flights, to stadiums creating these wireless networks to allow fans to access statistics and view instant replays from their seats, WLANs have taken the computing world by storm.
- A wireless NIC performs the same functions as a wired NIC except there is no port for a wire connection to the network. In its place is an antenna to send and receive RF signals. Wireless NICs are most often a separate card that is inserted into one of the computer's expansion slots. For desktop computers, wireless NICs are available for the Peripheral Component Interface (PCI) expansion slot. For notebook computers, wireless NICs are available as PC Card Type II devices and mini PCI. Smaller devices like a PDA will accept wireless NICs as a standard Type II PC Card or a Compact Flash (CF) Card.
- An access point (AP) is a device that consists of three major parts: it contains an antenna and a radio transmitter/receiver to send and receive signals, it has an RJ-45 wired network interface that allows it to connect by cable to a standard wired network, and it has special bridging software installed. An access point has two basic functions. First, the access point acts as the base station for the wireless network. All of the devices that have a wireless NIC transmit to the AP, which will in turn redirect the signal to the other wireless devices. The second function of an AP is to act as a bridge between the wireless and wired networks.
- There are two different modes in which data can be sent and received in an RF WLAN. The first mode that can be used by wireless clients in a WLAN is usually called the ad hoc or peer-to-peer mode. In ad hoc mode, the wireless clients communicate directly between themselves without using an access point. The second mode that can be created is the infrastructure mode, also known as the Basic Service Set (BSS). Infrastructure mode consists of wireless clients and an access point. If more users need to be added to the WLAN or the range of coverage area needs to be increased, more access points can be added. This creates an Extended Service Set (ESS), which is two or more BSS wireless networks.

- HomeRF, also known as Shared Wireless Access Protocol (SWAP), is an open industry specification that defines how wireless devices that conform to this specification can share and communicate in and around the home. It is designed as a way to connect together computers, peripherals, cordless phones, and other consumer electronic devices. HomeRF version 1.0 products were first introduced in 2000. The transmission speed was 1.6 Mbps. Version 2.0 was released in 2001 and has a transmission speed of 10 Mbps.

- The IEEE 802.11 standard defines a local area network that provides cable-free data access for clients that are either mobile or in a fixed location at a rate up to 2 Mbps. The 802.11 standard also specifies that the features of a WLAN be transparent to the upper levels of the 802.11 standard. However, the slow bandwidth of only 2 Mbps for the 802.11 standard was not sufficient for most network applications.

- The IEEE 802.11b standard added two higher speeds, 5.5 Mbps and 11 Mbps, to the original 802.11 standard. With the faster data rates the 802.11b quickly became the standard for WLANs. The Physical Layer Convergence Procedure Standards (PLCP) for 802.11b are based on direct sequence spread spectrum (DSSS). The PLCP must reformat the data received from the MAC layer (when transmitting) into a frame that the PMD sublayer can transmit. The frame is made up of three parts, which are the preamble, the header, and the data. The 802.11b standard uses the Industrial, Scientific and Medical (ISM) band for its transmissions. The PMD can transmit the data at 11, 5.5, 2, or 1 Mbps.

- The 802.11b standard uses an access method known as the Distributed Coordination Function (DCF). The DCF specifies that a modified procedure known as Carrier Sense Multiple Access with Collision Avoidance (CSMA/CA) be used. CSMA/CA attempts to avoid collisions. Instead of making just the two clients responsible for the collision wait a random amount of time before attempting to resend after the collision, CSMA/CA has *all* clients wait a random amount of time after the medium is clear. CSMA/CA also reduces collisions by using explicit packet acknowledgment (ACK). Although CSMA/CA will dramatically reduce the potential for collisions, it will not eliminate them altogether. The 802.11b standard provides two options that may be used to reduce collisions. The first is known as Request to Send/Request to Clear (RTS/CTS) protocol. RTS/CTS reserves the medium for a single client to transmit. The second option to reduce collisions is fragmentation. Fragmentation involves dividing the data to be transmitted from one large frame into several smaller ones.

- The 802.11b standard provides for an optional polling function known as Point Coordination Function (PCF). With PCF, the access point serves as the polling device and queries each client in an orderly fashion to determine if the client needs to transmit. The MAC layer of the 802.11b standard provides the functionality for a client to join a WLAN and stay connected. This is known as association and reassociation. Association is the process of communicating with the other wireless clients or the access point in order that it can become accepted as part of the network. Association is accomplished by scanning. There are two types of scanning: passive scanning and active scanning. A client may drop the connection with one access point and reestablish the connection with another. This is known as reassociation. Most clients in a WLAN are portable notebook computers or PDAs, giving the users the freedom to roam without being tethered to the network by wires. These mobile devices depend upon batteries as their primary power source. To conserve battery power they can go into sleep mode after a period of time. Power management as defined by the 802.11b standard allows the mobile client to be off as much as possible to conserve battery life but still not miss out on data transmissions.

- The 802.11b standard specifies three different types of MAC frame formats. The first are known as management frames that are used to set up the initial communications between a client and the access point. Control frames are the second type of MAC frames and they provide assistance in delivering the frames that contain the data. Data frames carry the information to be transmitted. The 802.11b standard also defines three different interframe spaces (IFS) or time gaps, which are standard spacing intervals between the transmissions of the data frames. Instead of being just "dead space," these time gaps are used for special types of transmissions.

Key Terms

802.11 standard — An IEEE standard released in 1990 that defines wireless local area networks at a rate of either 1 Mpbs or 2 Mpbs. All WLAN features are contained in the PHY and MAC layers.

802.11b standard — A 1999 addition to the IEEE 802.11 standard for WLANs that added two higher speeds, 5.5 Mbps and 11 Mbps. Also known as Wi-Fi.

access point (AP) — A device connected to the wired local area network that receives signals and transmits signals back to wireless clients.

active scanning — The process of sending frames to gather information.

ad hoc mode — A WLAN mode in which wireless clients communicate directly among themselves without using an access point.

associate request frame — A frame sent by a client to an access point that contains the client's capabilities and supported rates.

associate response frame — A frame returned to a client from the access point that contains a status code and client ID number.

association — The process of communicating with other wireless clients or the access point so that the client can become accepted as part of the network.

backoff interval — A random amount of time that two computers wait before attempting to resend.

Basic Service Set (BSS) — A WLAN mode that consists of wireless clients and one access point.

beacon frame — A frame sent from the access point to all stations.

buffering — The process that the access point uses to temporarily store frames for clients that are in sleep mode.

carrier sense — The process of listening before sending in order to detect other traffic.

Carrier Sense Multiple Access with Collision Avoidance (CSMA/CA) — The IEEE 802.11 standard procedure used by WLANs to avoid packet collisions.

Carrier Sense Multiple Access with Collision Detection (CSMA/CD) — The IEEE 802.3 Ethernet standard that specifies contention with a backoff interval if a collision occurs.

channel access methods — The different ways of sharing in a network environment.

collision — A conflict between packets sent by two computers that transmit packets at the same time.

compact flash (CF) card — An expansion card that is used with PDA devices.

Complementary Code Keying (CCK) — A code of a set of 64 8-bit code words used for transmitting at speeds above 2 Mbps.

contention — One type of channel access method in which computers compete with each other for the use of the network.

control frames — MAC frames that assist in delivering the frames that contain data.

data frames — MAC frames that carry the information to be transmitted to the destination clients.

disassociation frame — A frame sent by the new access point to the old access point to terminate the old access point's association with the client.

Distributed Coordination Function (DCF) — The default access method for WLANs.

Distributed Coordination Function IFS (DIFS) — The standard interval between the transmission of data frames.

Extended Service Set (ESS) — A WLAN mode that consists of wireless clients and multiple access points.

firewall — A device that prevents unauthorized access of a network.

flash memory — Solid-state technology memory that contains no moving parts.

fragmentation — The division of data to be transmitted from one large frame into several smaller frames.

Independent Basic Service Set (IBSS) — A WLAN mode in which wireless clients communicate directly among themselves without using an access point.

infrastructure mode — A WLAN mode that consists of wireless clients and one access point.

interframe spaces (IFS) — Time gaps used for special types of transmissions.

management frames — MAC frames that are used to set up the initial communications between a client and the access point.

Mini PCI — A small card that is functionally equivalent to a standard PCI expansion card used for integrating communications peripherals onto a notebook computer.

network adapter — A hardware device that connects a computer to the network.

Network Address Translator (NAT) — A router that hides the internal network addresses from the outside world for security.

network interface card (NIC) — A hardware device that connects a computer to the network.

null data frame — The response that a client sends back to the access point to indicate that the client has no transmissions to make.

packet acknowledgment (ACK) — A procedure for reducing collisions by requiring the receiving station to send an explicit packet back to the sending station.

passive scanning — The process of listening to each available channel for a set period of time.

peer-to-peer mode — A WLAN mode in which wireless clients communicate directly among themselves without using an access point.

Point Coordination Function IFS (PIFS) — A time gap interval that clients use when polling nodes that have a specific time requirement.

Point Coordination Function (PCF) — The 802.11 optional polling function.

polling — A channel access method in which each computer is asked in sequence whether it wants to transmit.

power management — An 802.11 standard that allows the mobile client to be off as much as possible to conserve battery life but still not miss out on data transmissions.

power over Ethernet — A technology that provides power over an Ethernet cable.

probe — A frame sent by a client when performing active scanning.

probe response — A frame sent by an access point when responding to a client's active scanning probe.

quality-of-service (QoS) — A technology that allows transmissions to be prioritized.

reassociation — The process of a client dropping the connection with one access point and reestablishing the connection with another.

reassociation request frame — A frame sent from a client to a new access point asking whether it can associate with the access point.

reassociation response frame — A frame sent by an access point to a station indicating that it will accept its reassociation with that access point.

Request to Send/Clear to Send (RTS/CTS) — An 802.11 option that allows a station to reserve the network for transmissions.

scanning — The process that a client uses to examine the airwaves for information that it needs in order to begin the association process.

Service Set Identifier (SSID) — A unique identifier assigned to an access point.

Short IFS (SIFS) — A time gap used for immediate response actions such as ACK.

sled — An external attachment known for a PDA that permits external cards to attach to the device.

sleep mode — A power-conserving mode used by notebook computers.

slot time — The amount of time that a station must wait after the medium is clear.

subnets — A smaller unit of a network.

traffic indication map (TIM) — A list of the stations that have buffered frames waiting at the access point.

virtual carrier sensing — An 802.11 option that allows a station to reserve the network for transmissions.

Wi-Fi — Another name for the IEEE 802.11b standard.

wireless gateway — A combination of several technologies that permits a home user to have wireless capabilities.

Review Questions

1. A wireless NIC performs the same functions as a wired NIC except that ________________.
   a. it does not transmit the packet
   b. it uses an antenna instead of a wired connection
   c. it contains special memory
   d. it does not use parallel transmission
2. Wireless NICs are available in each of the following formats except ________________.
   a. PCI card
   b. PC Card Type I
   c. CF card
   d. Mini PCI
3. Some vendors have already announced plans to integrate the components of a wireless NIC directly onto the notebook's ________________.
   a. motherboard
   b. floppy drive
   c. hard drive
   d. CD-ROM drive
4. Which of the following is not a function of an access point?
   a. Sends and receives signals
   b. Connects to the wired network
   c. Serves as a router
   d. Has special bridging software

5. The range of an access point acting as the base station is approximately ________________.
   a. 37.5 feet
   b. 375 feet
   c. 3,750 feet
   d. 37,500 feet
6. Power over Ethernet delivers power to an access point through the unused wires in a standard unshielded twisted pair (UTP) Ethernet cable. True or False?
7. In ad hoc mode, the wireless clients communicate directly with the access point. True or false?
8. An Extended Service Set (ESS) is two or more BSS wireless networks. True or false?
9. On a regular basis wireless clients will survey all the radio frequencies to determine if a different access point can provide better service. True or false?
10. Network managers like to subdivide networks into smaller units known as supernets because subnets make it easier to manage the entire network. True or false?
11. ________________, also known as Shared Wireless Access Protocol (SWAP), is an open industry specification that defines how wireless devices that conform to this specification can share and communicate in and around the home.
12. The IEEE ________________ standard defines a local area network that provides cable-free data access for clients that are either mobile or in a fixed location at a rate up to 2 Mbps.
13. Because all of the IEEE WLAN features are isolated in the PHY and ________________ layers, any network operating system or LAN application will run on a WLAN without any modification necessary.
14. The Physical Layer Convergence Procedure Standards (PLCP) for 802.11b are based on ________________ ________________ spread spectrum (DSSS).
15. The frame is made up of three parts, which are the preamble, the header, and the ________________.
16. The PLCP frame preamble and header are always transmitted at 1 Mbps. What are the advantages and disadvantages of this?
17. Tell how Carrier Sense Multiple Access with Collision Avoidance (CSMA/CA) is different from Carrier Sense Multiple Access with Collision Detection (CSMA/CD) works.
18. Explain how packet acknowledgment works.
19. What is RTS/CTS? What are its advantages and how does it work?
20. What is polling? How does it differ from contention?

HANDS-ON PROJECTS

Install and Configure a Cisco Aironet 340 Wireless NIC on a Notebook Computer

A. Install the Cisco Aironet 340 wireless NIC and driver software

1. Turn on the notebook computer. Log onto the system as a user with administrative privileges. The utilities do not install or operate correctly for users not logged in with administrative rights.
2. Hold the PC card with the Cisco logo facing up and insert it into the PC card slot, applying just enough pressure to make sure it is fully seated.
3. For Windows 2000 computers, the system detects the inserted card and opens the Found New Hardware window. Click **Next**. If a Digital Signature Not Found window appears, click **Yes**. Put the Cisco Aironet 340 Series Client Adapters CD into the CD-ROM drive. If the Insert Disk window appears, click **OK**.
4. Click **Search for a suitable driver for my device (recommended)** and then click **Next**.
5. Select **CD-ROM drives**. Click **Next**.
6. When the client adapter driver is displayed, click **Next** to copy the required files. If a Digital Signature Not Found window appears, click **Yes**.
7. When you receive a message indicating that Windows has finished the installation, click **Finish**.
8. For Windows XP computers, the system detects the inserted card and automatically loads the correct drivers.

B. Configure the wireless NIC for Windows 2000

9. Double-click **My Computer**, double-click **Control Panel**, and then click **System**.
10. In the System Properties window, click the **Hardware** tab.
11. Click **Device Manager**. In the Device Manager window, double-click **Network Adapters**.
12. Select the Cisco Systems wireless LAN adapter, as seen in Figure 6-26. Right-click it and then click **Properties**. In the Properties window, click the **Advanced** tab.

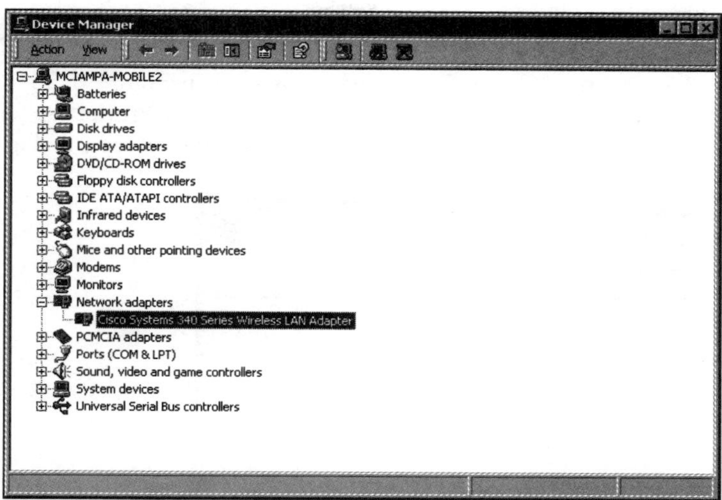

Figure 6-26 Cisco Systems wireless LAN adapter

13. In the Advanced window, select Client Name, and enter your computer's unique client name in the Value dialog box.
14. Select SSID, and enter the wireless network's case-sensitive SSID in the Value dialog box, as seen in Figure 6-27. See your network system administrator for this information. Click **OK**. If you are prompted to restart your computer, click **Yes**.

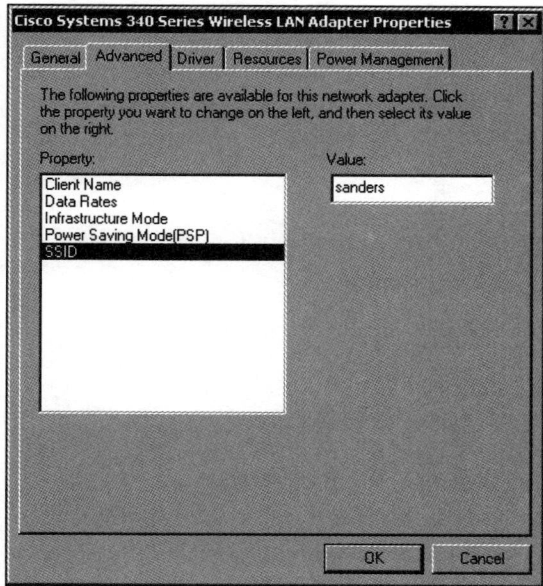

Figure 6-27 SSID

15. If you are not connected to a DHCP server you will need to set the IP addresses. Double-click **My Computer**, **Control Panel**, **Network and Dial-up Connections**. Select **Local Area Connection**, as seen in Figure 6-28. Right click it and then click **Properties**. In the Local Area Connection Properties window, click **Internet Protocol (TCP/IP)** and then **Properties**, as seen in Figure 6-29.

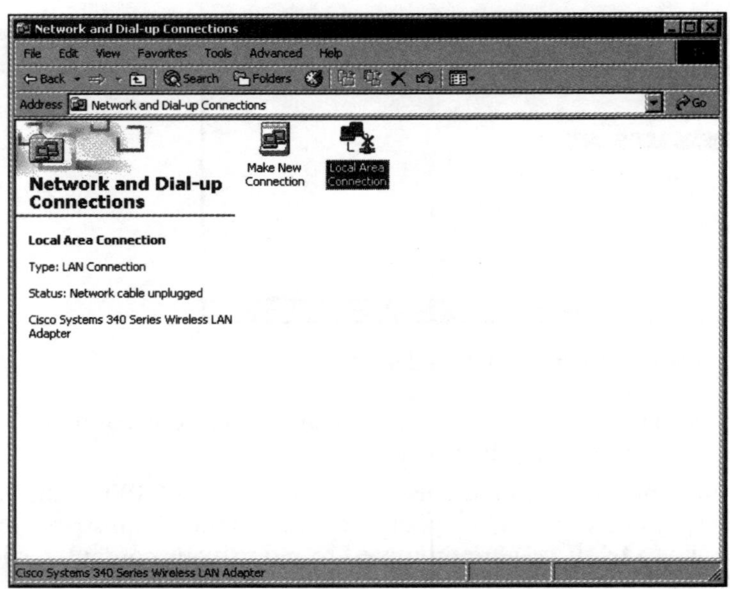

Figure 6-28 Local area network connection

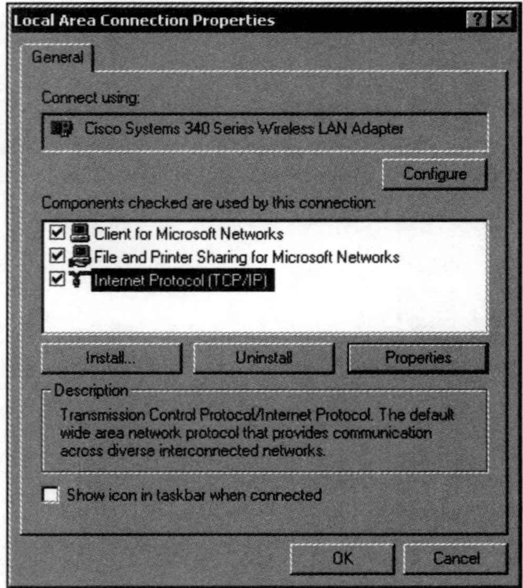

Figure 6-29 Internet protocol (TCP/IP)

16. Click **Use the following IP address** and enter the IP address, subnet mask, default gateway, and DNS server address for your computer, which can be obtained from your network system administrator. Click **OK**.
17. In the Local Area Connection Properties window, click **OK**. If you are prompted to restart your computer, click **Yes**.

C. Configure the wireless NIC for Windows XP

18. Click **Start**, click **Control Panel**, and then double-click **Network Connections**. Right-click the **Wireless Network Connection**, and then click **Properties**. Click the Wireless Networks tab to display Figure 6-30.

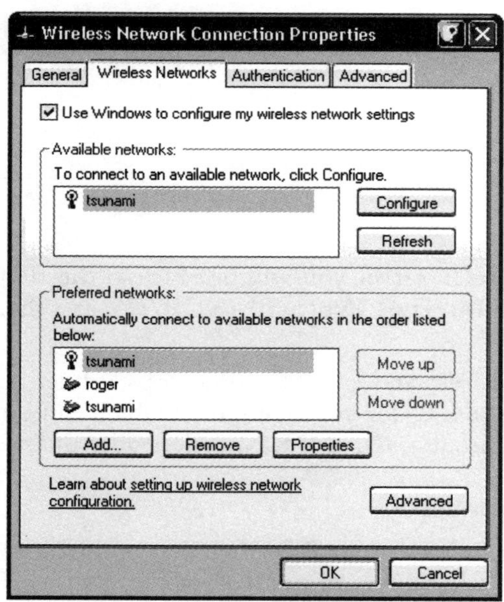

Figure 6-30 Wireless networks

19. Under Preferred Networks, click **Add**.
20. Select **Network Name (SSID)** and enter the wireless network's case-sensitive SSID in the Value dialog box, as seen in Figure 6-31. See your network system administrator for this information. Click **OK**.

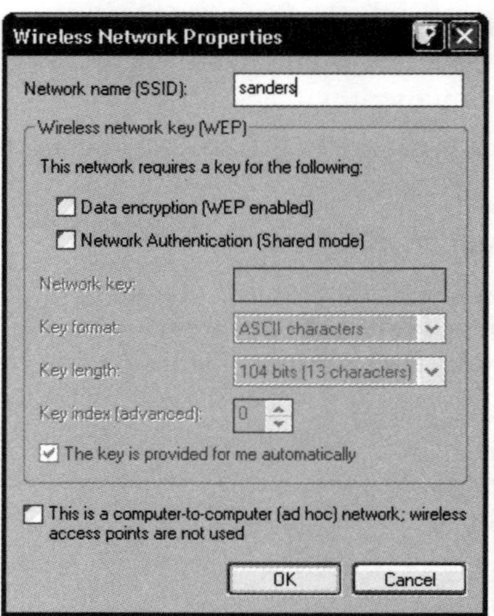

Figure 6-31 Network name (SSID)

21. If you are not connected to a DHCP server you will need to set the IP addresses. Click the **General** tab and click **Internet Protocol (TCP/IP)** and then **Properties**.
22. Click **Use the following IP address** and enter the IP address, subnet mask, default gateway and DNS server address for your computer, which can be obtained from your network system administrator. Click **OK**, and close all windows.

D. Install Cisco utilities on Windows 2000

23. The Aironet Client Utility (ACU), Link Status Meter (LSM), and Client Encryption Manager (CEM) are additional utilities that can be used with the Cisco Aironet system. Click **Start** and then **Run** and enter the following path (where D is the letter of your CD-ROM drive): **D:\Utils\setup.exe**. At the Welcome screen, click **Next**. In the Choose Location dialog box, click **Next**.
24. In the Authentication Method screen, select the server-based authentication method preferred for wireless network access in your location. Select **None** unless you are using server-based authentication. Check with your network system administrator. Click **Next**.
25. In the Select Components screen, check all three client utilities, as seen in Figure 6-32. Click **Next**.

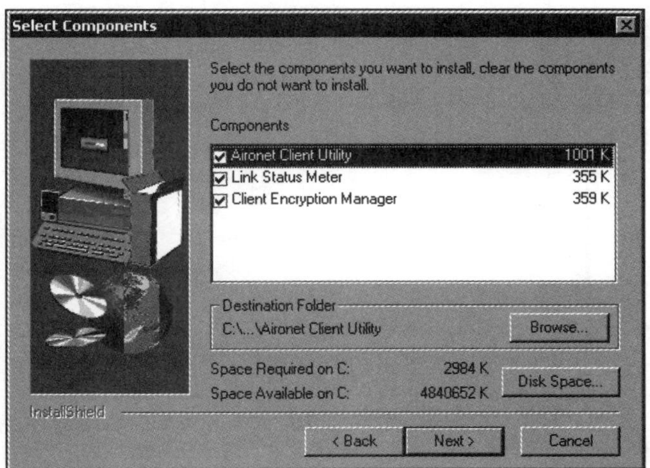

Figure 6-32 Select components

26. In the Select Program Folder screen, click **Next** to allow icons for the client utilities to be placed in the Cisco Systems, Inc. folder. On the Desktop Icons screen, click the box if you want the icons to be placed on the desktop. Click **Next**.

For Windows XP systems, these utilities are not needed because the functions they provide are performed by the operating system.

Install and Configure a Cisco Aironet 340 Wireless NIC on a Handheld Device using Pocket PC 2002

1. Use a serial or USB cable to connect the handheld device to a computer running Active Sync and for which a partnership already exists.
2. Locate the latest version of the drivers for the version of the software you are using on Cisco's Web site (*www.cisco.com*). Download the file onto the computer running Active Sync and double-click it. Follow the instructions on the screen to install the software onto the hand-held device.
3. Disconnect the hand-held device from the computer. Insert the Cisco wireless NIC card and restart the device.
4. Tap **Start** and then **Programs**. Open the Cisco folder and tap **Aironet Client Utility**. Enter the SSID of the access point that you want to attach to, as seen in Figure 6-33. Tap **OK**.

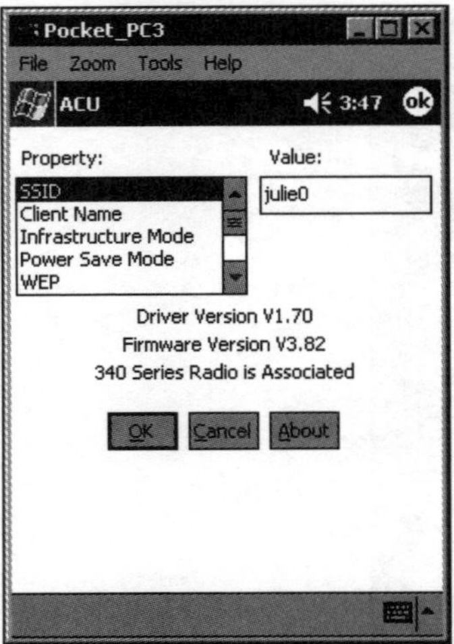

Figure 6-33 SSID

5. Tap **Start** and then **Settings**. Tap the **Connections** tab, and then tap **Network Adapters**, as seen in Figure 6-34. Tap the Cisco Wireless Lan Adapter and tap **Properties**.

Figure 6-34 Network adapters

6. If the network is using DHCP, tap the button User server-assigned IP address. If it is not using DHCP, tap the button Use specific IP address and enter the IP address, subnet mask, and default gateway, as seen in Figure 6-35. Tap **OK** when finished.

Figure 6-35 IP address

6

Set Up an Ad-hoc Network between a Windows 2000 Computer and a Windows XP Computer

If you have two Windows 2000 or XP computers then apply the respective instructions to each computer.

1. For the Windows 2000 computer, click **Start**, **Programs**, click **Cisco Systems, Inc.**, then click **Aironet Client Utility (ACU)** to start the ACU program, as seen in Figure 6-36.
2. Click **Commands** and then **Edit Properties** to display the 340 Series Properties page. Make the following changes, as seen in Figure 6-37:
   a. Current Profile: select **Use Home Networking Configuration**.
   b. Network Type: select **Ad Hoc**.
3. Click the **Home Networking** tab. Under **Home Radio Network Name**, enter **sanders-ah** or an ad hoc name obtained from your network system administrator. Click **OK** and then close the ACU program.
4. For Windows XP computers click **Start** and then **Control Panel** and then click **Network Connections**. Right-click the **Wireless Network Connection** and then click **Properties**. Click the **Wireless Networks** tab.

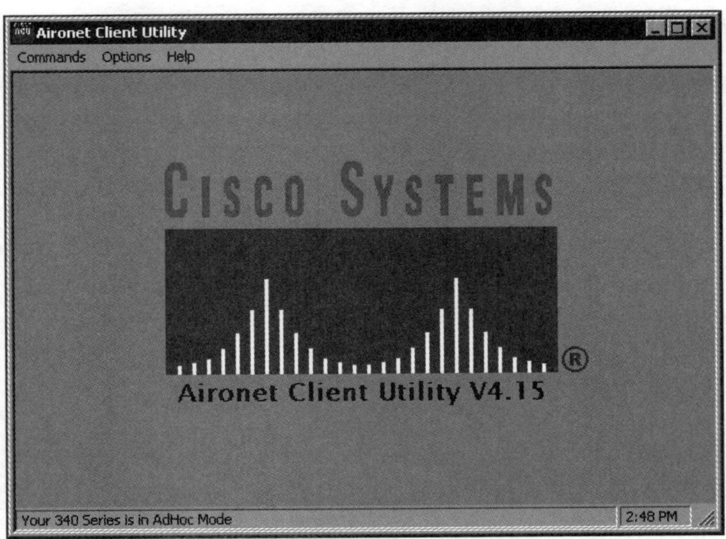

Figure 6-36 Aironet client utility

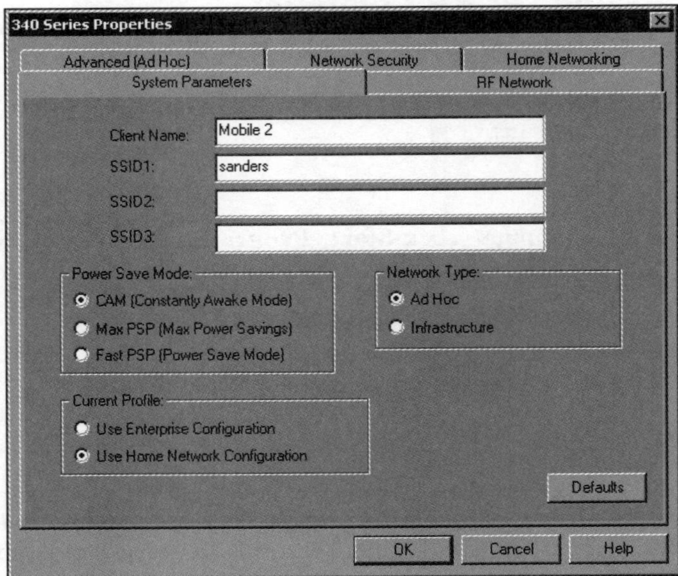

Figure 6-37 System parameters

5. Under Preferred Networks click **Advanced** to display the Advanced window, as seen in Figure 6-38. Click **Computer-to-computer (ad hoc) networks only**. Click **Close**.

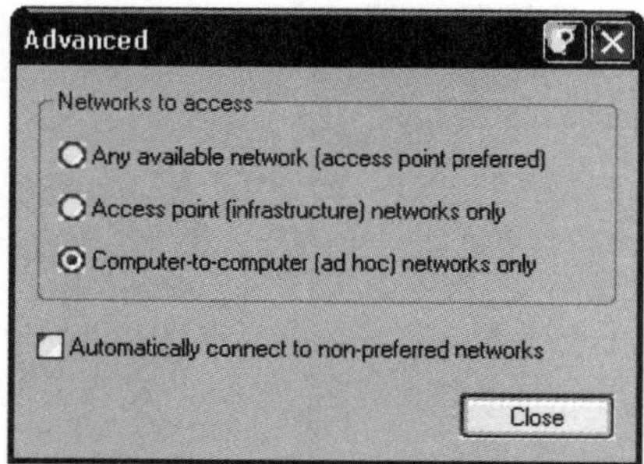

Figure 6-38 Networks to access

6. Click **Refresh**. The sanders-ah icon should appear in the list of available networks. Click **Configure**, and then click **OK**.
7. Click **Start** and then **My Computer**. Select a folder to be shared across the wireless network. Right-click that folder to bring up the folder's properties window, as seen in Figure 6-39.

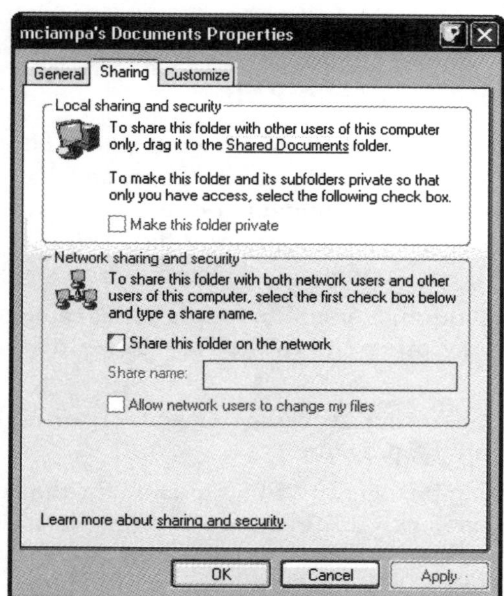

Figure 6-39 Document properties

8. Click the **Sharing** tab, and then click **Share this folder on the network**. Click **Apply** and then **OK**.
9. On the Windows 2000 computer double click **My Network Places** to open the windows as seen in Figure 6-40.
10. Double-click **Computers Near Me**. Double-click the computer name of the Windows XP computer. You may be asked to enter a username and password. The shared folders will appear.

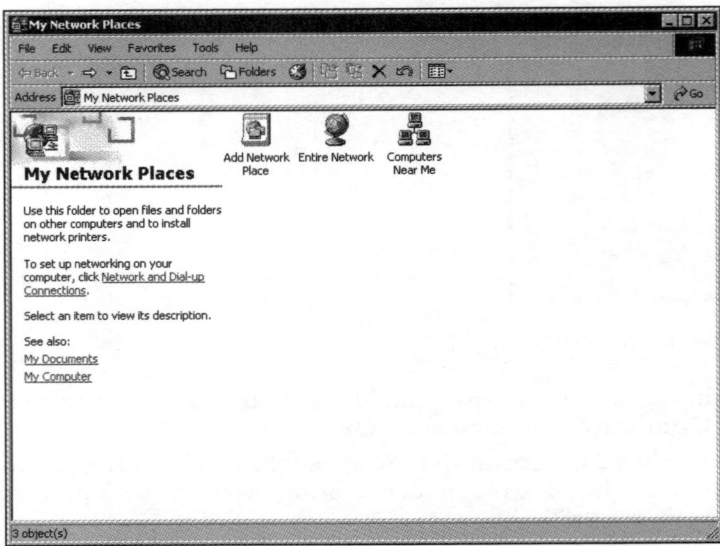

Figure 6-40 My Network Places

Configure a Cisco Aironet 340 Access Point

Cisco provides a number of different ways to configure an access point. These include using a utility known as IPSU (IP Set Up), available from Cisco, and Reverse ARP (Reverse Address Resolution Protocol), which is configured into the AP. However, network configurations settings sometimes make these options difficult to use. The most reliable is to connect a cable to the AP and configure it directly:

1. Attach one end of 9-pin, straight-through, male-to-female serial cable to the serial port on the computer and the other end to the RS-232 on the back of the access point.
2. Click **Start** and **Programs**, and then click **Accessories** and **Communications**. Click **Hyperterminal** to bring up the program.
3. The Connection Description dialog box appears. Enter a name for the connection, such as Access Point, and then click OK. When the Connect To dialog box appears, change the Connect Using line to the communication port that the serial cable is attached (such as, Direct to Com1). This is illustrated in Figure 6-41.
4. The Communications Properties window will appear. Configure the settings as follows:
   - Bits Per Second: **9600**
   - Data Bits: **8**
   - Parity: **None**
   - Stop Bits: **1**

- Flow Control: **Xon/Xoff**

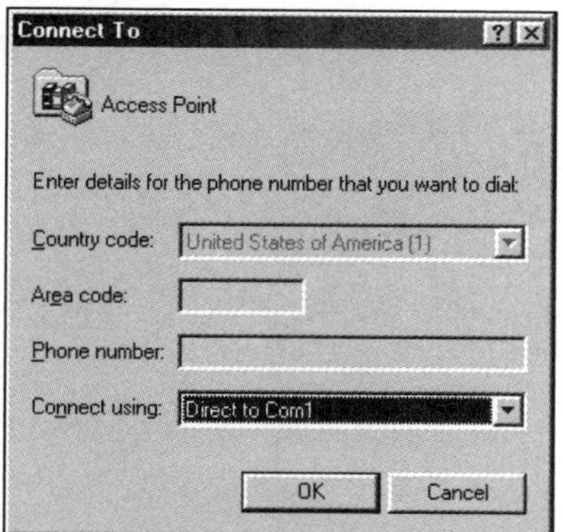

Figure 6-41 Connect To dialog box

5. The Express Setup screen appears in the HyperTerminal window. If text does not appear immediately, press the equals sign (=) or Enter. This displays the default settings of the access point, as seen in Figure 6-42.

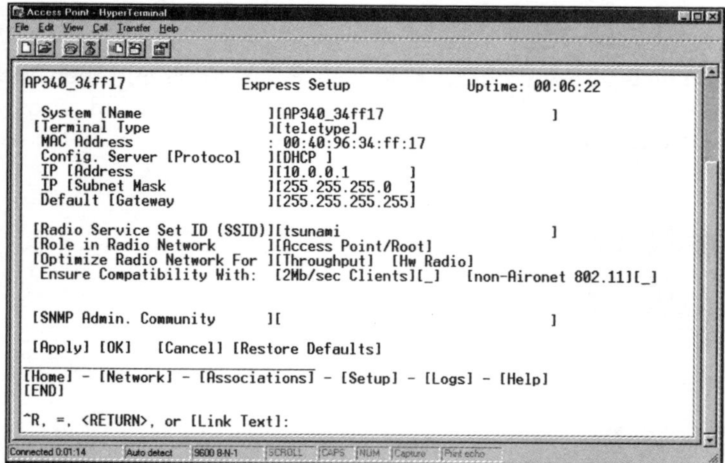

Figure 6-42 AP default settings

6. If you are not using DHCP, type **ad** (for address) and press **Enter**. Then type in the IP number that is to be assigned to the access point and press **Enter**. If you are using DHCP, record the IP address assigned to the AP.
7. Type **g** (gateway) and press **Enter**. Type in the default gateway address and press **Enter**.
8. Type **ra** (radio service set ID) and enter the SSID for this access point and then press **Enter**.

9. Type **ap** (apply) and press **Enter**. Exit the terminal emulator program.
10. Using a Web browser on the notebook, enter the IP address to display the Summary Status Page, as seen in Figure 6-43.

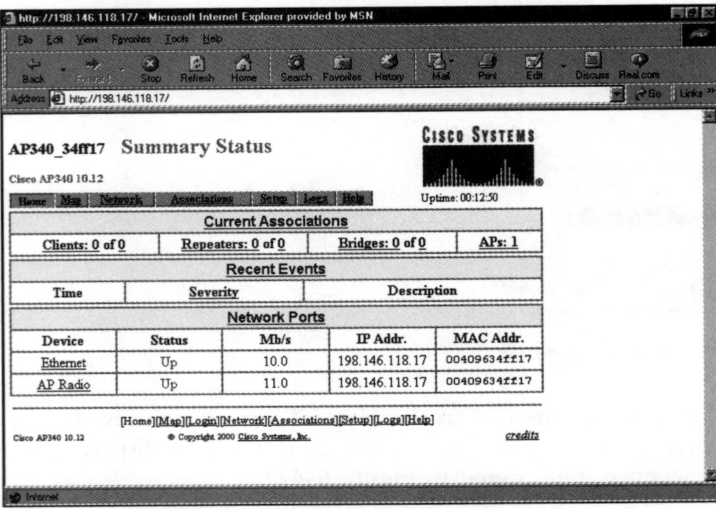

Figure 6-43 Summary Status page

11. This can also be viewed from a hand-held device. Tap **Start** and then **Internet Explorer**. If the address bar does not appear on the browser window, tap **View**, and then tap **Address Bar**. Enter the IP address of the AP to view the settings, as seen in Figure 6-44.

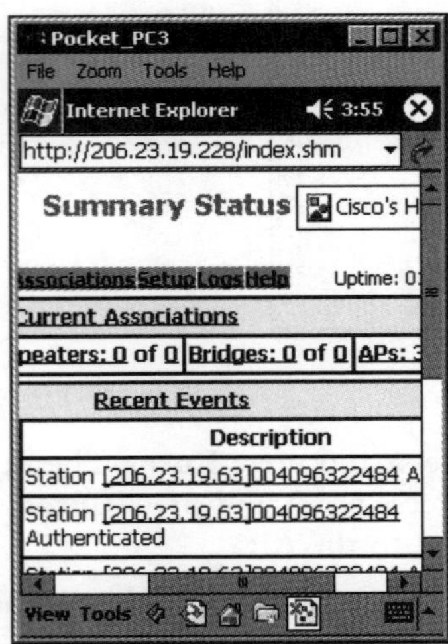

Figure 6-44 Summary Status page from hand-held device

Case Project

The Baypoint Group (TBG) wants to hire you again as a consultant. The Academic Computing department of the local community college is interested in setting up a WLAN for its students and faculty. Students will be able to carry notebooks and PDAs into classes and remain connected to the network as well as check their e-mail between classes in the courtyard. Faculty can carry their computers with them into classrooms and always be connected no matter where they are located.

However, there is a small group of faculty on campus who are opposed to spending any more money on technology this fiscal year. The Academic Computing department has agreed to hire an independent outside consultant, TBG, to discuss the pros and cons of WLANs with these faculty members.

TBG has asked you to develop a presentation about WLANs for next week's faculty meeting. The presentation should cover what a WLAN is and how it could benefit the students and faculty at the college. You will only have about 15 minutes, so the presentation must be no more than 12-15 PowerPoint slides. Because there will be a large audience of faculty, it should not be technically oriented.

Optional Team Case Project

Although the faculty members were generally impressed by your presentation, a few who have HomeRF units at home are arguing that this technology should be used instead of IEEE 802.11b because it is much cheaper. You've been asked by TBG to return to the campus and moderate a forum between the Academic Computing group and these faculty members. To help you prepare for the discussion, divide into two groups with one group taking HomeRF and the other IEEE 802.11b technology. Create an argument why your technology is best and should be used at the college.

CHAPTER

7

HIGH-SPEED WLANS AND WLAN SECURITY

After reading this chapter and completing the exercises, you will be able to:

- Tell how IEEE 802.11a networks function, and how they differ from IEEE 802.11b networks
- List the advantages and disadvantages of an IEEE 802.11g network
- Describe HiperLAN/2 networks
- Compare low-speed and high-speed WLANs
- Explain basic and enhanced WLAN security features

Faster has been the key word for microcomputers and local area networks (LANs) ever since they first appeared over 20 years ago. The first IBM PC, introduced in 1981, ran at 4.77 MHz and could be connected to a 10 Mbps network. Although it was lightning fast for its time, almost immediately the quest began for even faster computers and networks to be able to handle more tasks. Even with today's computers at speeds of over 2 GHz and LANs communicating at 1,000 Mbps, the need for faster computers and networks continues to drive the industry. As users access huge databases, process vast amounts of information, and require immediate downloads of high-quality graphic images over the Internet, ever-faster speeds are demanded by users.

The same is true of wireless local area networks (WLANS). The original IEEE standard established in 1997 was for WLANs operating at 1 and 2 Mbps. Today WLANs operating at over 100 Mbps are becoming commonplace, and research continues for even faster speeds for WLANs.

In this chapter we will look at higher speed WLANs, namely those with speeds of over 15 Mbps. These networks include IEEE 802.11a, 802.11g, and HiperLAN/2. We will compare these high-speed WLANs to the lower-speed WLANs you've learned about in earlier chapters, and we will explore a primary concern for WLANs of all speeds—security. Because network transmissions are broadcast over radio frequencies, anyone within range of those transmissions could possibly receive the signals. This chapter investigates ways that wireless networks can be made secure to prevent unauthorized access.

IEEE 802.11a

Recall from Chapter 6 that the slow bandwidth of 1 or 2 Mbps for the original 802.11 standard was not sufficient for most network applications, and that in 1999 the IEEE approved the 802.11b standard that added two higher speeds, 5.5 Mbps and 11 Mbps. At that time, IEEE also issued the **IEEE 802.11a** standard with even higher speeds. 802.11a, also called **Wi-Fi5** by the WECA, has a maximum rated standard speed of 54 Mbps and also supports 108, 48, 36, 24, 18, 12, 9, and 6 Mbps transmissions. 802.11a WLANs are very attractive to users because the speed of transmission is a significant increase over 802.11b systems. This can be seen in the sales projections for faster 802.11a WLANs that are significantly greater than for slower 802.11b networks. It is estimated that from 2001 to 2005 the 802.11b market will have a compound growth rate of 82%, while at the same time 802.11a systems will grow at a rate of 375%.

Although the 802.11a and 802.11b specifications were published at the same time by IEEE, 802.11b products started to appear almost immediately, while 802.11a products did not arrive until late 2001. 802.11a products came to the market later because of technical issues along with the high cost of implementing them. Devices based on the 802.11a standard cannot use a complementary metal oxide semiconductor (CMOS) as the semiconductor like that used in 802.11b WLANs. Instead, they must use a compound such as gallium arsenide (GaAs) or silicon germanium (SiGe). These semiconductors are more expensive and require more capital investment and time to develop the manufacturing process.

The 802.11a standard maintains the same medium access control (MAC) layer functions as 802.11b WLANs. The differences are confined to the physical layer. 802.11a achieves its increase in speed and flexibility over 802.11b through a higher frequency, more transmission channels, its multiplexing technique, and a more efficient error-correction scheme. These factors are detailed in the sections that follow.

U-NII Frequency Band

Recall that the 802.11b standard uses one part of the unlicensed Industrial, Scientific, and Medical (ISM) band for its transmissions and specifies 14 frequencies that can be used, beginning at 2.412 GHz and increasing by increments of .005 GHz. IEEE 802.11a uses another unlicensed band, the Unlicensed National Information Infrastructure (U-NII). The U-NII band is intended for devices that will provide short-range, high-speed wireless digital communications. A comparison of ISM and U-NII can be seen in Table 7-1.

Table 7-1 ISM vs. U-NII

Unlicensed Band	Frequency	WLAN	Total Bandwidth
Industrial, Scientific, and Medical (ISM)	902-928 MHz 2.4-2.4835 GHz	802.11b	234.5 MHz
Unlicensed National Information Infrastructure (U-NII)	5.15-5.25 GHz 5.25-5.35 GHz 5.725-5.825 GHz	802.11a	300 MHz

The U.S. Federal Communications Commission (FCC) has segmented the 300 MHz of U-NII spectrum into three bands. Each band has a maximum power limit. These bands and their maximum power outputs are seen in Table 7-2:

Table 7-2 U-NII spectrum

U-NII Band	Frequency (GHz)	Maximum Power Output (mW)
U-NII Low Band	5.15-5.25	40
U-NII Middle Band	5.25-5.35	200
U-NII High Band	5.725-5.825	800

Although 802.11b wireless NICs can legally radiate as much as 1 watt in the ISM band, most only use 30 mW in order to conserve battery life and minimize the level of heat generated.

The U-NII High Band is more commonly used for building-to-building wireless transmissions.

Outside the United States, however, the 5 GHz bands are allocated to users and technologies other than WLANs, and the bands have different power limitations. For example, the High Band is available in the U.S., but not in Europe or Japan where it has already been reserved for outdoor applications (although the 5.470-5.725 band is available in Europe for WLANs, it cannot be used in the U.S.). In addition, the maximum power output for the Low Band is 200 mW in Europe and Japan compared to only 40 mW in the U.S. This is not a problem for WLANs contained within a single country, but it is for multinational companies and individuals who travel internationally and are required to maintain different networks in different countries. Although there are several efforts underway to unify the 5 GHz bands globally, due to the various agencies and groups with technologies operating in the bands already, it is estimated that the unification would not occur until 2003 at the earliest. And there is no guarantee that such unification will ever take place.

Although other devices such as 2.4 GHz cordless phones, microwave ovens, and Bluetooth devices may cause interference problems with 802.11b networks in the 2.4 GHz ISM band, these devices do not interfere with 802.11a transmissions. This is because 802.11a operates in the 5 GHz frequency range and is not subject to interference from 2.4 GHz devices or networks. Although there is nothing prohibiting a cordless phone vendor from offering 5 GHz products, it is doubtful that will happen because 5 GHz cordless phones would have a reduced range outdoors compared to 2.4 GHz phones.

802.11a devices are able to transmit at faster rates because of the higher frequencies and increased power at which they operate. And although it is segmented, the total bandwidth available for IEEE 802.11a WLANs using U-NII is almost four times that available for 802.11b networks using the ISM band. The ISM band offers only 83 MHz of spectrum in the 2.4 GHz range while the U-NII band offers 300 MHz.

Channel Allocation

A second reason for the faster speed of an 802.11a WLAN is increased channel allocation. Recall that with 802.11b the available frequency spectrum (2.412 to 2.484 GHz) is divided into 11 channels in the U.S. The center point of each channel (2.412, 2.417, 2.422, etc.) is where the transmission actually occurs. Because there must be a 25 MHz passband, only three non-overlapping channels are available for simultaneous operation. This is illustrated in Figure 7-1.

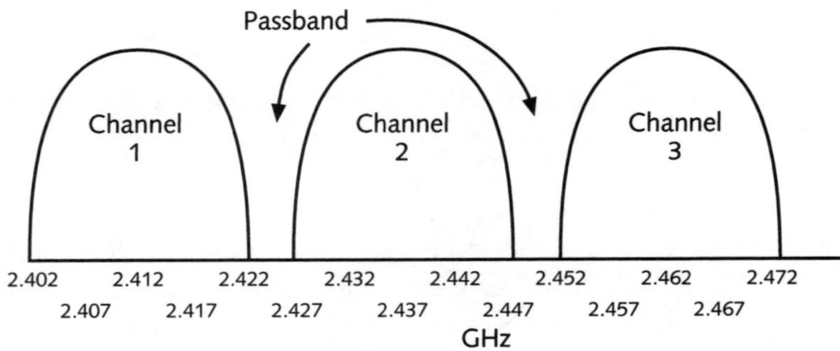

Figure 7-1 802.11b channels

In 802.11a, however, eight frequency channels can overlap and operate simultaneously in the Low Band (5.15 to 5.25 GHz) and Middle Band (5.25 to 5.35 GHz). Within each frequency channel there is a channel 20 MHz wide that supports 52 carrier signals, with each signal 300 KHz wide. The center points for the eight channels are 5.18, 5.20, 5.22, 5.24, 5.26, 5.28, 5.30, and 5.32 GHz. This is illustrated in Figure 7-2.

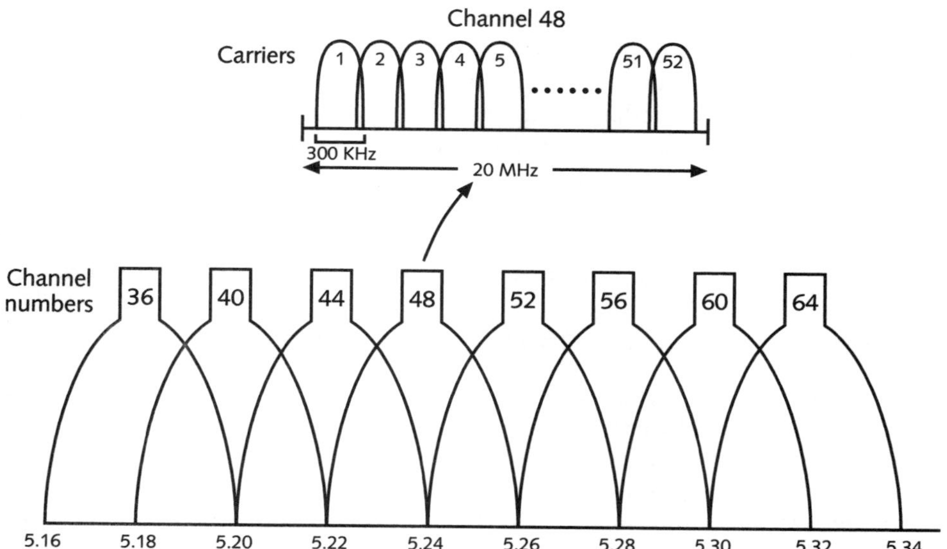

Figure 7-2 802.11a channels

With an 802.11b WLAN, there are only three available channels (or networks) per AP coverage area. With an 802.11a WLAN, there can be up to eight networks per AP. Because there are an increased number of available channels, more users can access more bandwidth when the WLAN is managed correctly. This is illustrated in Figure 7-3.

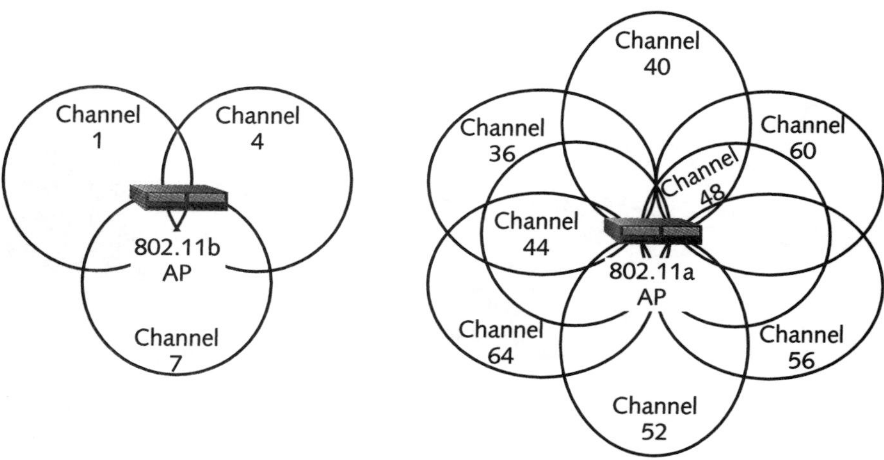

Figure 7-3 802.11b vs. 802.11a channel coverage

There are additional advantages of having more channels. When multiple APs are used, more users can be supported by assigning specific channels to users associated with specific APs. Also, if a neighbor is using an 802.11a WLAN within range of the network, it can cause interference and bandwidth contention. With more available channels there is the ability to set the AP to use a specific channel and eliminate the interference. In addition, vendors are working on developing load-balancing technologies to automatically spread the load so one channel doesn't get overcrowded when others are available. Although 802.11 WLANS do not support quality of service (QoS), an **IEEE 802.11e Task Group** is currently working on a standard that would prioritize transmissions across an 802.11 network using QoS.

Orthogonal Frequency Division Multiplexing

Recall from Chapter 3 that as a radio signal is transmitted the electromagnetic waves spread out. Some of these waves may reflect off of surfaces. This causes the waves to be delayed in reaching their destination, as seen in Figure 7-4. This is known as multipath distortion. The receiving device gets the signal from several different directions and at different delayed times (called reflections). Even though the receiving device may have already received the signal, it must still wait until all reflections are received before it can do anything.

Figure 7-4 Multipath distortion

Consider for a moment the analogy of a school crossing guard at a local elementary school. The crossing guard stops all automobile traffic while children cross the street. Even though one student may sprint across the street and arrive well ahead of all other children, nevertheless all traffic is held up by the crossing guard until the slowest child drags across the street.

This is similar to the problem that 802.11b WLANs face. With multipath distortion, the radio frequency (RF) signals bounce off walls and furniture and are delayed reaching the receiver. The receiving device must wait until all reflections are received before it can transmit. If it does not, then some of the delayed signal may spread into its next transmission. Increasing the speed of the WLAN only causes longer delays in waiting for reflections. Because a device must wait to transmit until it receives the last reflection, this in effect puts a ceiling limit on the overall speed of the WLAN. With current technology this ceiling is between 10 and 20 Mbps.

A baseband processor, or equalizer, is required in 802.11b systems to "unravel" the delayed radio frequency signals as they are received.

The 802.11a standard solves this problem through a new multiplexing technique called **Orthogonal Frequency Division Multiplexing (OFDM)**. Although OFDM was modified specifically for indoor wireless use, its history dates back to the mid-1960s and is used today in European digital TV and audio transmissions. OFDM is not a modulation technique but instead is a multiplexing technique. Its primary role is to split a high-speed digital signal into several slower signals running in parallel.

OFDM is also the technology used for consumer-based Digital Subscriber Line (DSL) service, which provides home Internet access over standard telephone lines at speeds of 1.5 Mbps. DSL is a replacement to analog dial-up modems and is a direct competitor to cable modems with several advantages: DSL has a faster upload speed than cable modems, the bandwidth is not shared among other users, and the telephone line can still be used to make calls while surfing the Internet.

Instead of sending one long stream of data across a single channel, OFDM sends the transmission in parallel across several lower-speed channels. The sending device breaks the transmission down into pieces and then sends it over the channels in parallel. The receiving device combines the signals received from the individual channels to re-create the transmission. By using parallel transmission channels, OFDM can combine several lower-speed channels to send data at a higher speed. This is illustrated in Figure 7-5.

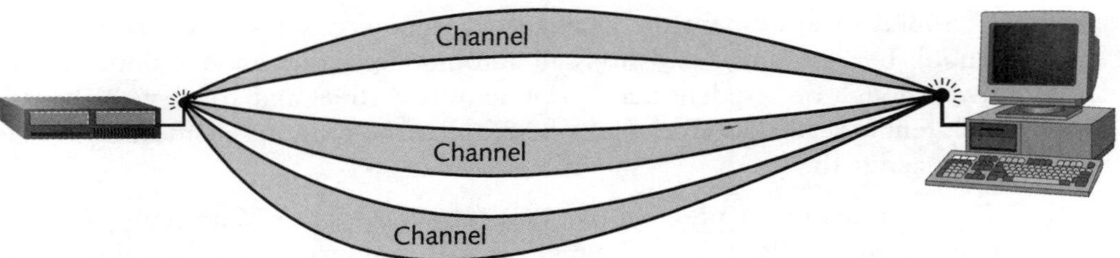

Figure 7-5 Multiple channels

Although it may seem contradictory, OFDM breaks the 802.11b ceiling limit by sending the data more slowly. OFDM avoids problems caused by multipath distortion by sending the message slowly enough that any delayed copies (reflections) are late by a much smaller amount of time than 802.11b transmissions. This means that the network does not have to wait long for the reflections. And because the transmissions are sent in parallel, the total throughput is actually increased. That is, in a given unit of time the total amount of data sent in parallel is greater and time spent waiting for reflections is less with OFDM than with a single channel transmission. This amounts to a higher throughput and a faster WLAN.

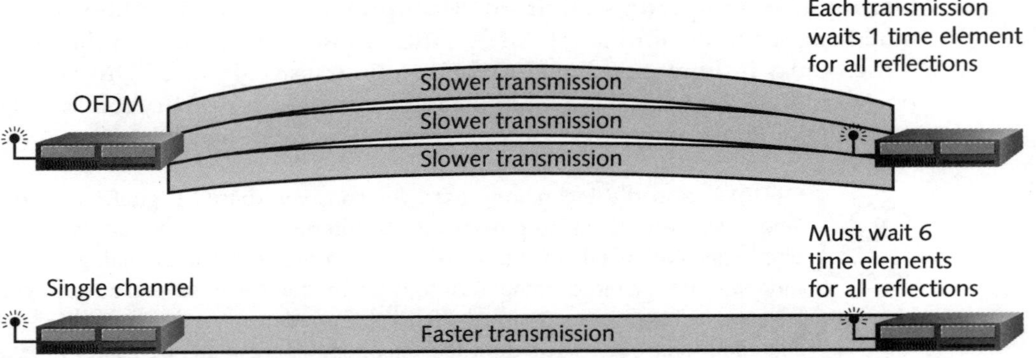

Figure 7-6 OFDM vs. single channel

Consider for a moment a single-lane toll road that handles automobile traffic and has one toll booth. This road backs up every morning and afternoon during rush hour. The best solution to this bottleneck is not to raise the speed limit for cars going through the toll booth. Although that would slightly increase the number of cars getting through, the traffic flow would still be limited by all of the cars waiting at a single toll booth. The best solution is to add multiple toll booths on parallel lanes for the drivers to use. And, if a person was stationed in the road before cars got to the booths in order to direct the cars to an empty toll booth, that would speed the process even more. This in effect is OFDM: multiple transmission paths with traffic directed to the appropriate lane.

The 802.11a standard specifies eight frequency channels that can overlap and operate simultaneously in the Low Band and Middle Band. Within each frequency channel there is a channel 20 MHz wide. This channel is divided into 52 **subchannels**. Each subchannel's signal is 300 KHz wide. OFDM uses 48 of these subchannels for data, while the remaining four are used for error correction.

The modulation techniques used to encode the data vary depending upon the speed:

- *6 Mbps*—When transmitting at this speed phase shift keying (PSK) is used (see Chapter 2 for a review on PSK). The change in the starting point of the cycle will vary depending on if a 0 or a 1 bit is being transmitted, as seen in Figure 7-7. PSK can encode 125 Kbps of data per each of the 48 subchannels, resulting in a 6,000 Kbps (125 Kbps × 48), or 6 Mbps, data rate.

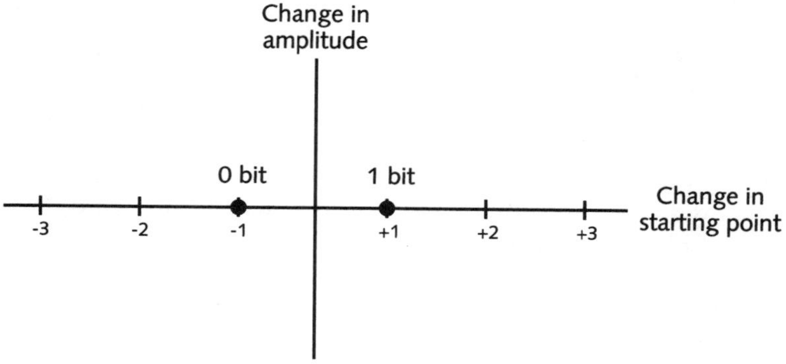

Figure 7-7 Phase shift keying (PSK)

- *12 Mbps*—Whereas PSK only has a change in starting point, **quadrature phase shift keying (QPSK)** also has a change in amplitude, similar to quadrature amplitude modulation (see Chapter 2 for a review). This is illustrated in Figure 7-8. QPSK can double the amount of data encoded over PSK to 250 Kbps per channel, which produces a 12 Mbps (250 Kbps × 48) data rate.

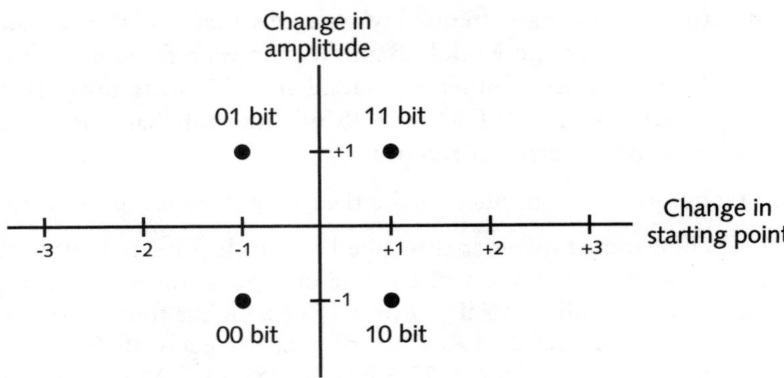

Figure 7-8 Quadrature phase shift keying (QPSK)

- *24 Mbps*—Transmitting at 24 Mbps requires a **16-level quadrature amplitude modulation (16-QAM)** technique. 16-QAM has 16 different signals that can be sent, as seen in Figure 7-9. Whereas QPSK requires two signals to send 4 bits, 16-QAM can transmit the same in only one signal. For example, to transmit the bits 1110, QPSK would send 11 and then 10 by modifying the phase and amplitude. 16-QAM would only send one signal (1110). 16-QAM can encode 500 Kbps per subchannel.

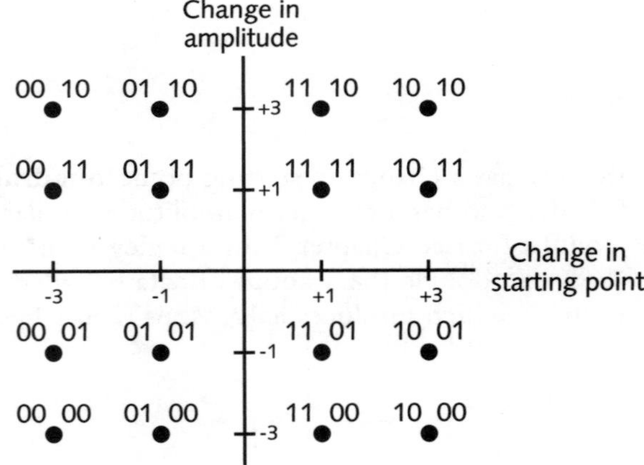

Figure 7-9 16-level quadrature amplitude modulation (16-QAM)

- *54 Mbps*—Data rates of 54 Mbps are achieved by using **64-level quadrature amplitude modulation (64-QAM)**. 64-QAM, illustrated in Figure 7-10, can transmit 1.125 Mbps over each of the 48 subchannels.

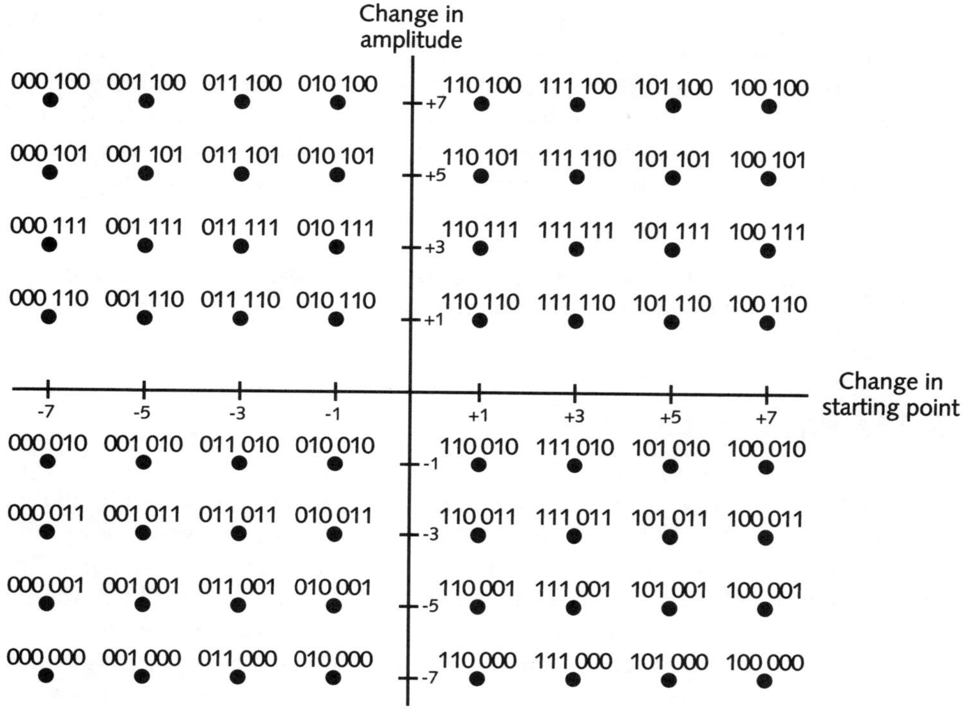

Figure 7-10 64-level quadrature amplitude modulation (64-QAM)

Although 54 Mbps is the "official" top speed of 802.11a, the IEEE specification also allows for higher speeds as well. These higher speeds are known as **turbo mode** or **2X mode**. 2X mode can be developed by each vendor and is not specified in the IEEE standard. Developers cannot further increase the complexity of the modulation on the subcarriers beyond the maximum 54 Mbps rate because of the amount of noise allowed. Instead, vendors can do such things as combine two frequency channels resulting in 96 subchannels for speeds up to 108 Mbps. Other 2X mode techniques include increasing and reallocating the individual carriers and using different coding rate schemes.

It is important to remember that 2X mode is proprietary. One vendor's AP running at 2X mode is not guaranteed to support wireless NIC from another vendor.

Error Correction

IEEE 802.11a also handles errors differently than 802.11b. The number of errors is significantly reduced due to the nature of 802.11a transmissions. Because transmissions are sent over parallel subchannels, radio interference from an outside source is minimized.

Instead of the interference impacting the entire data stream, it will generally affect only one subchannel. Error correction in 802.11a is also enhanced. **Forward Error Correction (FEC)** transmits a secondary copy along with the primary information. Of the 52 subchannels, 48 are used for standard transmissions and 4 are used for FEC transmissions. If part of the primary transmission is lost, the secondary copy can be used to recover (through sophisticated algorithms) the lost data. This eliminates the need to retransmit if an error occurs, which saves time.

Because of its high speed, 802.11a can accommodate the FEC overhead with a negligible impact on performance.

802.11a Physical Layer

The 802.11a standard made changes only to the physical layer (PHY layer) of the original 802.11 and 802.11b standards; the MAC layer remains the same. Recall that the basic purpose of the IEEE PHY layer is to send the signal to the network and receive the signal from the network. The 802.11a PHY layer is divided into two parts. The Physical Medium Dependent (PMD) sublayer makes up the standards for both the characteristics of the wireless medium (such as OFDM) and defines the method for transmitting and receiving data through that medium. The Physical Layer Convergence Procedure (PLCP) reformats the data received from the MAC layer (when transmitting) into a frame that the PMD sublayer can transmit and "listens" to the medium to determine when the data can be sent.

The PLCP for 802.11a is based on OFDM instead of direct sequence spread spectrum (DSSS). The PLCP must reformat the data received from the MAC layer (when transmitting) into a frame that the PMD sublayer can transmit. An example of a PLCP frame is illustrated in Figure 7-11.

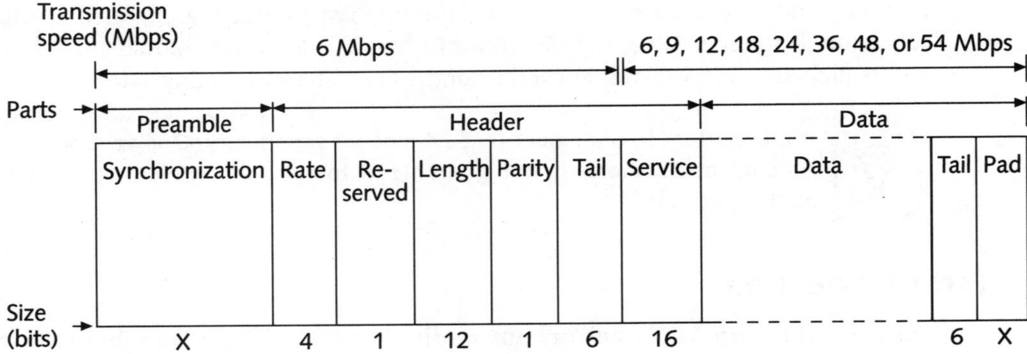

Figure 7-11 802.11a PLCP frame

The frame is made up of three parts: the preamble, the header, and the data. The preamble allows the receiving device to prepare for the rest of the frame. The header provides information about the frame itself. The data portion of the PLCP frame is the information that is to actually be transmitted. A description of the fields shown in Figure 7-11 is as follows:

- *Synchronization*—The Synchronization field consists of 10 repetitions of a short training sequence signal and two repetitions of a long training sequence signal. The purpose of these signals is to establish timing and frequency with the receiver. The Synchronization field is transmitted in 16 microseconds.
- *Rate*—The Rate field, which is 4 bits in length, specifies the transmission rate of the Data field. The rate field values are seen in Table 7-3.
- *Length*—This field contains the value that indicates the length of the Data field, from 1 to 4095.
- *Parity*—Parity is used for error checking.
- *Tail*—This field indicates the end of the Header. All 6 bits are set to zero.
- *Service*—The Service field is used to synchronize again with the receiver. The first 6 bits are set to zero while the remaining 9 bits are reserved for future use and are also set to zero. Although the Service field is part of the Header, it is transmitted at the same rate as the Data field.
- *Data*—The actual data to be transmitted is contained in this field. The length of the Data field is from 1 to 4095 bits.
- *Pad*—The IEEE standard specifies that the number of bits in the Data field must be a multiple of 48, 96, 192, or 288. If necessary, the length of the Data field may need to be "padded" with extra bits, which are found in this field.

7

Table 7-3 802.11a rate field values

Data Rate (Mbps)	Rate Field Contents
6	1101
9	1111
12	0101
18	0111
24	1001
36	1011
48	0001
54	0011

802.11a WLANs are rapidly being deployed in areas that demand higher transmission speeds. The disadvantage to 802.11a networks is that they have a shorter range of coverage. An 802.11a WLAN has a range of approximately 225 feet, compared to 375 feet for an 802.11b WLAN. Of course, this depends upon a number of factors such as walls and other obstacles that can affect the RF transmission.

IEEE 802.11G

The tremendous success of the IEEE 802.11b standard shortly after its release prompted the IEEE to re-examine the 802.11b and 802.11a standards in order to determine if a third intermediate standard could be developed. This "best of both worlds" approach would preserve the stable and widely accepted features of 802.11b but increase the data transfer rates to those similar to 802.11a. The IEEE formed an initial body called a task group to explore this possibility. By late 2001 a draft standard was proposed known as **IEEE 802.11g**.

The IEEE 802.11g draft was a compromise on input from several different chip manufacturers who had a major stake in the outcome. Although most major commercial wireless networking product vendors will build and sell products based upon whatever standard is approved, the same is not true for the chip manufacturers. These businesses must make huge monetary investments in designing, sampling, and manufacturing the silicon chips used in the wireless network products. They must then try to sell their chips to product vendors that design and build commercial products based on the chip sets.

The 802.11g draft specifies that it operates entirely in the 2.4 GHz ISM frequency and not the U-NII band used by 802.11a. The draft outlines two mandatory modes along with two optional modes. The first mandatory mode is the same CCK (Complementary Code Keying) mode used by 802.11b at 11 Mbps. The second mandatory mode uses the same OFDM (Orthogonal Frequency Division Multiplexing) mode used by 802.11a but in the 2.4 GHz frequency at 54 Mbps. However, the number of channels available is still only three with 802.11g compared with eight channels for 802.11a. The two optional modes can transmit at 22 Mbps but use different methods. One method is known as **PBCC-22 (Packet Binary Convolutional Coding)**, which can transmit between 6 and 54 Mbps. The second optional mode is a combination known as **CCK-OFDM**. CCK-OFDM has a maximum speed of 33 Mbps.

Although it appears that the 802.11g draft with these four modes will be ratified and become a standard, it is difficult to predict when products based on this standard will appear. Most industry experts believe that it may be at least 2003 before IEEE 802.11g products arrive on the shelves.

HIPERLAN/2

HiperLAN/2 is a proposed high-speed WLAN that is similar to the IEEE 802.11a standard. HiperLAN/2 was standardized by the ETSI, the European Telecommunications Standards Institute, an organization formed to develop telecommunications standards for use throughout Europe. Close cooperation between ETSI and IEEE has ensured that there are similarities between HiperLAN/2 and 802.11a, although the two standards remain very different in their implementation. Products based on HiperLAN/2 may start to appear on the market as early as 2003.

The protocol stack for the HiperLAN/2 is seen in Figure 7-12. There are three basic layers to the stack: Physical layer, Data Link layer, and Convergence layer.

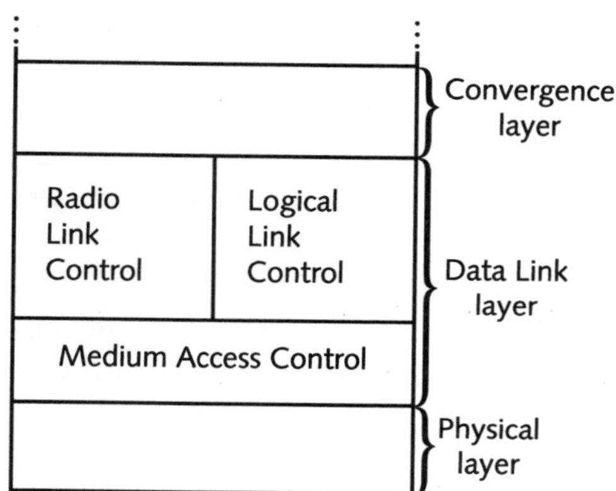

Figure 7-12 HiperLAN/2 protocol stack

Physical Layer

The PHY layers of IEEE 802.11a and HiperLAN/2 are almost identical. Both operate in the 5 GHz band, use OFDM, can transmit up to 54 Mbps, and will connect seamlessly to wired Ethernet networks. However, beyond the PHY layer IEEE 802.11a and HiperLAN/2 are very different.

Data Link Layer

The Medium Access Control (MAC) sublayer of the Data Link layer is used for access to the RF medium. Whereas IEEE 802.11 networks use CSMA/CA, HiperLAN/2 uses an entirely different approach. Control of the RF medium is centralized at the access point (AP), which informs the clients, known as mobile terminals (MTs), when they are allowed to send data. Channel allocation is based upon dynamic time-division multiple access (TDMA). (See Chapter 3 for a review of TDMA.) TDMA divides the bandwidth into several time slots. Each user is assigned the entire frequency for their transmission but only for a small fraction of time on a fixed rotating basis. Because the transmissions occur so quickly, the delay that occurs while others use the frequency is not noticeable. HiperLAN/2 time slots are allocated dynamically depending on the need of the MT and the condition of the network. This is also known as Quality of Service (QoS).

The Radio Link Control (RLC) sublayer has three primary functions:

- *Connection setup procedure and connection monitoring*—The HiperLAN/2 network supports authentication and encryption. Both the AP and the MT can authenticate each other to ensure authorized access to the network (MT) or that the network operator (AP) is valid. Encryption can be used on established connections to protect against eavesdropping. In HiperLAN/2, each communicating node is given a HiperLAN ID (HID) and a Node ID (NID). The combination of these two IDs uniquely identifies any client and restricts the way in which it can connect to other HiperLAN/2 clients.
- *Radio resource handling, channel monitoring, and channel selection*—The HiperLAN/2 APs have built-in support for automatic transmission frequency allocation within the coverage area. This is known as **Dynamic Frequency Selection (DFS)**. An appropriate radio channel is selected based on what radio channels are already in use by other APs in order to minimize interference.
- *Association procedure and reassociation procedure*—HiperLAN/2 automatically performs standardized handoff to the nearest AP by MTs that are roaming.

The Logical Link Control sublayer is also part of the Data Link layer. Its function is to perform error checking.

Convergence Layer

Whereas IEEE 802.11 networks can connect only to wired Ethernet networks, HiperLAN/2 offers high-speed wireless connectivity with up to 54 Mbps and seamless connectivity with other types of communications systems. HiperLAN/2 can connect with cellular telephone systems and **Asynchronous Transfer Mode (ATM)**, which is wide-area network technology that uses fiber-topic media to transmit at 622 Mbps. HiperLAN/2 allows users to communicate over a high-speed external serial bus that can transmit at 400 Mbps known as **IEEE 1394**, also called **FireWire**.

Summary: High- and Low-Speed WLANs

With all of the different types of WLANs available—HomeRF/SWAP, IEEE 802.11, 802.11b, 802.11a, 802.11g, and HiperLAN/2—it is only natural to compare these technologies, to see how each one stacks up. However, in doing a comparison of WLANs, it is important to remember that they should not all be considered as *competing* technologies, in that one will be the winner and the rest losers. Instead, many of these should be considered as *complementary* technologies, with each WLAN having its place in the market due to its strengths and weaknesses.

HomeRF is a wireless standard for home networks. HomeRF is intended to combine wireless data, cordless telephony, and streaming media by connecting computers, peripherals, cordless phones, and other consumer electronic devices together. Two of the strengths of HomeRF are its support of QoS and its increased transmission speed from 1.6 Mbps to 10 Mbps with version 2.0. Although the future is very bright for wireless networking in the home, with the rapid development and competitive prices of IEEE 802.11b products. These devices are being installed in homes instead of HomeRF systems. Most industry experts agree that 802.11b will be the choice of consumers for wireless networking in the home.

The *IEEE 802.11* standard approved in 1997 defines a LAN that provides cable-free data access for clients that are either mobile or in a fixed location at a rate of 1 or 2 Mbps. This slow transmission speed is insufficient for today's networking applications. Products based on the 802.11 are rapidly giving way to faster WLANs and soon will no longer be found in the marketplace.

Currently *IEEE 802.11b (Wi-Fi)* is the most popular choice for business wireless networking. Operating in the 2.4 GHz ISM frequency range, 802.11b has a maximum data rate of 11 Mbps and can use three simultaneous channels. 802.11b has a great advantage in that it is accepted worldwide. Yet one of the more significant disadvantages of 802.11b is that the ISM band is crowded and subject to interference from other networking technologies, cordless phones, and Bluetooth. Another drawback is that there are no means to prioritize transmissions (QoS). In spite of these limitations, IEEE 802.11b is the current leader in business WLANs and is rapidly gaining share in home applications as well.

IEEE 802.11a products, which started to ship in late 2001, are much faster than 802.11b. The 802.11a has a 54 Mbps standard data rate but it can be increased to 108 Mbps in non-standard 2X mode. 802.11a, also known as Wi-Fi5, operates in the 5GHz U-NII frequency range and allows eight simultaneous channels of transmission. Another advantage to 802.11a is that it is not subject to interference from Bluetooth or other 2.4 GHz frequency devices. However, this also means that 802.11a is not compatible with 802.11b networks. Another disadvantage of 802.11a networks is that the area of service is smaller than with an 802.11b network due to the increased power requirements. For an organization wanting to replace an existing 802.11b network with an 802.11a network, the process is not as easy as simply replacing APs. Instead, more 802.11a APs are needed to cover the same area. In addition, the frequency spectrum for 802.11a is not available worldwide. And like 802.11b, 802.11a does not support QoS.

The advantages of *IEEE 802.11g* are that it maintains compatibility with 802.11b networks and offers faster data rates. The number of channels available, however, is not increased because channels are related to the amount of frequency spectrum. The 802.11g has only three channels compared with eight for 802.11a. Another disadvantage of 802.11g is that it is using the already-crowded 2.4 GHz ISM frequency, which will get even more crowded. The IEEE 802.11g draft may not be approved until sometime in 2002. This means that products based on this standard will not start to be seen until

2003 or beyond. By that time, 802.11b and 802.11a products may be so firmly entrenched that there will be little market space for 802.11g.

HiperLAN/2 has several advantages over 802.11a: dynamic time-division multiple access (TDMA), time slots are allocated dynamically depending on the need of the mobile terminal (MT) and the condition of the network, both the AP and the MT can authenticate each other, it uses Dynamic Frequency Selection (DFS), and it has high-speed wireless connectivity with other types of communications systems. HiperLAN/2 is already popular in Europe. However, HiperLAN/2 also faces some serious challenges. Because it is still a draft proposal, no HiperLAN/2 products are expected to be available until 2002 or later. Also, the spectrum used by HiperLAN/2 is not available worldwide. With the head start already established by 802.11b and 802.11a, will there be a market for HiperLAN/2? We'll have to wait and see.

In summary, HomeRF and 802.11 networks may soon be obsolete. HiperLAN/2 may become the standard in Europe, yet it is probably entering the race too late to catch up in the U.S. 802.11g may likewise have difficulty competing with 802.11b and 802.11a, but it has a better chance of being successful in the U.S. 802.11b networks will be used in environments that require moderate transmission speeds, while 802.11a networks will be deployed where higher speeds are important. Table 7-4 compares IEEE and HiperLAN/2 wireless networks.

Table 7-4 WLAN comparison

WLAN	802.11	802.11b	802.11g	802.11a	HiperLAN/2
Spectrum	2.4 GHz	2.4 GHz	2.4 GHz	5 GHz	5 GHz
Standard maximum speed	2 Mbps	11 Mbps	54 Mbps	54 Mbps	54 Mbps
Optional maximum speed				108 Mbps	
Medium access control	CSMA/CA	CSMA/CA	CSMA/CA, OFDM	OFDM	TDMA
Frequency selection	FHSS or DSSS	DSSS	DSSS, single carrier	Single carrier	Dynamic Frequency Selection
QoS	No	No	No	No	Yes
Radio link quality control	No	No	No	No	Yes

802.11 Security

No discussion of WLANs of any speed can be complete without looking at the topic of security. A WLAN's greatest strength—allowing users to roam freely without being connected to the network by wires—is also its Achilles heel. Just as a roaming user can receive radio frequency signals anywhere in the building, an unauthorized user sitting in the parking lot outside the building could also receive those same RF signals. Broadcasting network traffic over the airwaves has created an entirely new set of issues for keeping the network secure. These issues have been heightened by studies that reveal that some of the security provisions in IEEE WLANs are flawed. This section will look at the basic security in IEEE WLANs (802.11b, 802.11a, and 802.11g), types of network attacks that may occur, and what can be done to make a WLAN more secure.

Basic Security

The IEEE standard provides basic security in two areas: authenticating users and keeping transmissions private.

Authentication

Authentication is a process that verifies that the user has permission to access the network. Although authentication is important with wired local area networks, it is critical with WLANs because of the open nature of a wireless network. With a traditional wired LAN, an intruder must first gain access to a building and then locate an unattended computer on the network in order to attempt to break into the network. However, with a wireless network, anyone within range of the network could attempt to break into the WLAN over radio waves.

IEEE WLANs provide a basic means of authenticating potential users. Each WLAN client can be given the Service Set Identifier (SSID) of the network. This value is transmitted to the access point when the client is negotiating with it for permission to connect to the network. Only those clients that know the SSID are then authenticated as valid users and are allowed to connect to the network.

SSIDs provide only a rudimentary level of security because they apply only to devices, not individual users, and because SSIDs themselves are not well secured.

A wireless client can be given an SSID in one of two ways. First, the SSID can be manually entered into the wireless device. Yet once it is entered, anyone who has access to that wireless device can see the SSID and freely distribute it. The second way is even less secure. Access points (APs) can freely advertise the SSID to any mobile device that comes into the range of the AP. The default setting on most APs is to freely broadcast SSIDs.

IEEE WLAN authentication is in addition to the authentication tools that are used by the particular network operating system, such as Microsoft Windows or Linux. These network operating systems use standard security measures such as login names and passwords.

Privacy

Privacy is different from authentication. Authentication ensures that the user (or device) has permission to be part of the network. Privacy, on the other hand, makes certain that transmissions themselves are not read by unauthorized persons. The IEEE standard provides an optional **Wired Equivalent Privacy (WEP)** specification for data encryption between wireless devices to prevent eavesdropping.

Data encryption requires the use of mathematical keys to both encrypt and decrypt messages. These keys have a numerical value that is used by an algorithm to scramble information and make it readable only to users who have the corresponding decryption key. There are two types of keys. **Public key** cryptography uses matched public and private keys for encryption and decryption. One key is used to encrypt the message and a different key is used to decrypt it. The public key does not have to be kept secret; it can be openly distributed without damaging the private key. **Shared key** cryptography uses the same key to encrypt and decrypt the message. The key must be kept secret or the confidentiality will be compromised. IEEE uses shared key cryptography, which again may compromise privacy if the key is not kept secure.

The AP and each client can have up to four shared keys. Each key must be manually entered and must correspond to the same key position in each of the other devices. In Figure 7-13, the AP and Client 1 each have four keys defined. The AP can encrypt a message with Key-A and send it to Client 1. Because Client 1's Key-A is the same as the AP's Key-A, Client 1 can decipher the message received. However, the AP cannot send a message to Client 2 using Key-D because it is different than the AP's Key-D.

The strength of encryption rests not only on keeping the keys secret but also on the length of the key itself. The longer the key, the stronger the encryption because a longer key is more difficult to break. With faster and more powerful computers it is easier to break keys and decrypt sensitive messages than just a few years ago. Keys that are 56 bits in length have been broken in just a few hours. The IEEE WEP standard specifies data encryption using only a 40-bit shared key.

The IEEE standard also allows proprietary privacy extensions by WLAN vendors. Several vendors offer their own 128-bit encryption mechanism.

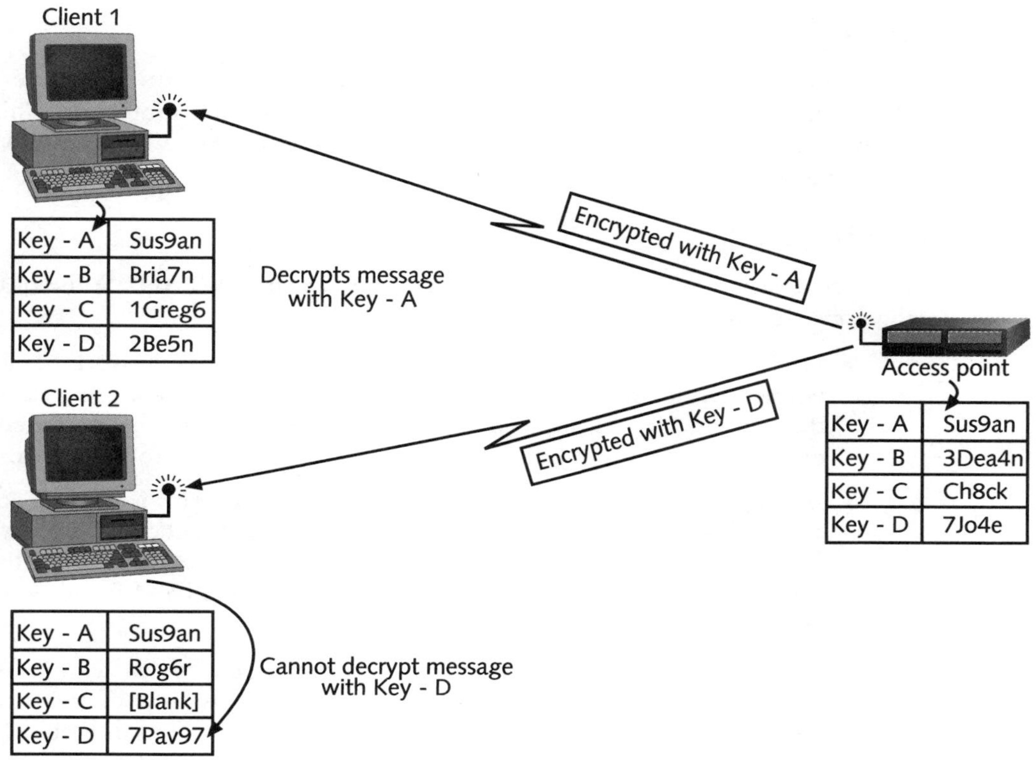

Figure 7-13 WEP

Concerns have been raised over WEP privacy on a WLAN. In late 2000, it was revealed that the "initialization vector" used to encrypt transmissions with WEP is reused about once every five hours. In theory, a person who could capture these packets over the airwaves could see the pattern in reuse and be able to break the WEP encryption. In 2001, researchers at various universities around the country went beyond the theory and outlined how one could actually collect the necessary data for breaking WEP encryption. They showed that by using a series of mathematical computations, skilled hackers could uncover the plain text of certain encrypted messages and then use those packets to intercept and decrypt messages encrypted with the same key. By late 2001, researchers were able to recover the 128-bit WEP key used in a WLAN transmission in less than two hours.

Due to these problems with IEEE WEP—that it is a shared key cryptography, the key length is only 40 characters, and that the initialization vector can easily be broken—many industry experts have serious doubts about using WEP. Some have even stated that IEEE WLANs should be treated as insecure.

Enhanced Security

Because of the limitations of IEEE WLAN security, enhanced security measures are considered important for wireless transmissions that require such protection. This section will explore the types of attacks that may be generated against WLANs and what steps can be taken to prevent them.

WLAN Attacks

There are a variety of attacks that can be generated against WLANs. Some of the more dangerous are summarized below:

- *Hardware theft*—Hardware theft is a threat to a wireless network because a wireless device may contain information to assist someone in breaking into the network. For example, if the SSID or WEP keys can be recovered from a device, then they can be used to attempt to gain access to the network.
- *Access point impersonation*—A drawback to IEEE WLANs is that clients authenticate themselves to APs, but APs do not authenticate themselves to clients. A "rogue" AP can be set up and force clients to associate with it. Information from the wireless clients can be obtained and form the basis for other types of security attacks.
- *Passive monitoring*—Data transmissions can be monitored to acquire information such as the addresses of APs and wireless clients, time of association and disassociation with the network, etc. Over time a profile can be built based on statistical analysis that may provide assistance to unauthorized users trying to break into the network. In other cases it is possible to determine the contents of the transmission itself.
- *Denial of service*—Because the messages to associate or disassociate from the WLAN are not encrypted, these can be intercepted and data can be gleaned from them. An unauthorized user can use this information to flood the network with transmissions and deny others access to the AP.

Additional Security Procedures

In order to increase the security of IEEE 802 WLANs, an IEEE task group is working on a draft known as **IEEE 802.1x**. This will allow WLANs to centralize the authentication of wireless clients. The 802.1x draft uses a protocol known as **Extensible Authentication Protocol (EAP)**. EAP allows a client to negotiate authentication protocols with a separate authentication server. 802.1x also makes use of **Remote Authentication Dial-In User Service (RADIUS)**. The 802.1x draft proposes that authentication would be performed as follows and illustrated in Figure 7-14:

1. A user on a wireless device connects to the access point and enters a username and password.
2. The AP requests authentication of that user by sending the information to a RADIUS server on the wired network.
3. The RADIUS server reviews the request and can accept, reject, or further challenge the request. If it accepts the request, the RADIUS server sends the security keys and other data for that wireless client to the AP so that it can establish a secure connection with the client.

The 802.1x standard will apply to all IEEE 802 local area networks, including Ethernet (802.3) and Token Ring (802.5) as well as wireless networks (802.11).

7

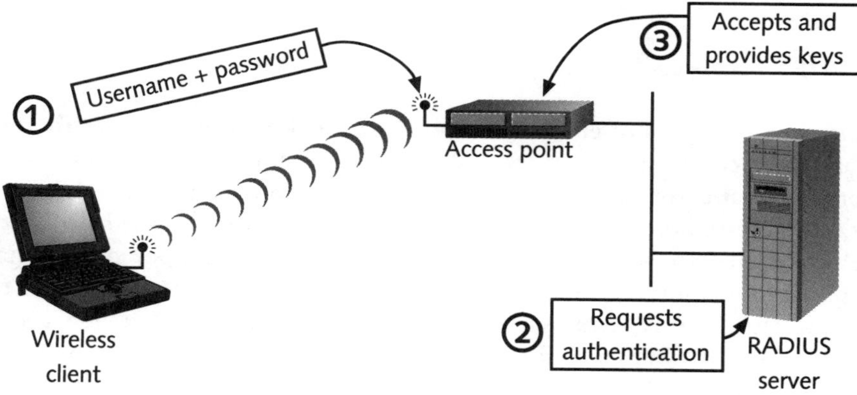

Figure 7-14 802.1x security

There are other steps that can be taken with WLANs to help make the network secure. When authenticating users, most APs allow a list of approved users to be entered into the AP. These users are designated by their **MAC address**, which is a unique 48-bit number that is burned into the network interface card when it is manufactured. A list of approved MAC addresses can be entered into the **access control list**. Only those clients on the access control list can be provided admittance. This is illustrated in Figure 7-15.

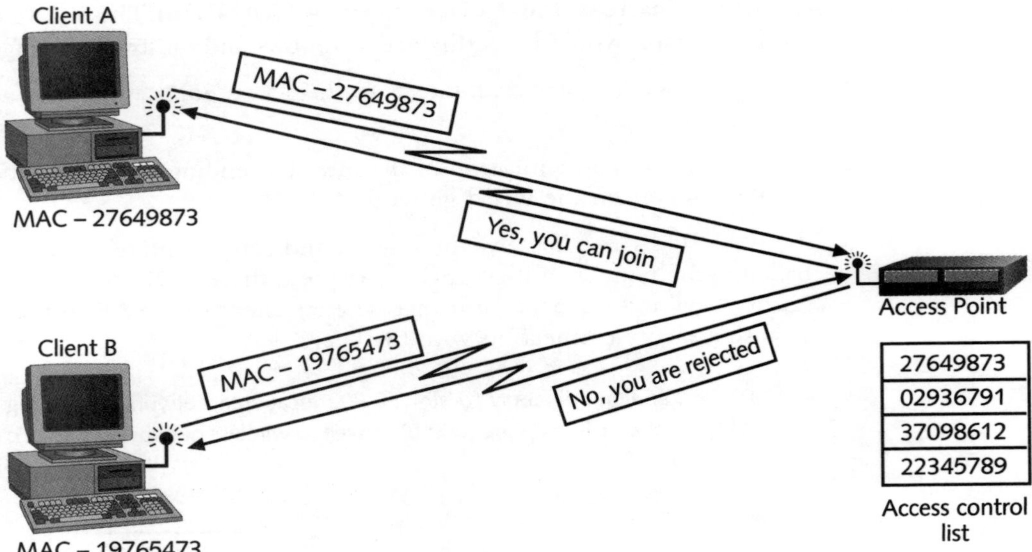

Figure 7-15 Access control list

In addition, other types of encryption can enhance WEP. **Digital certificates** are data files that are used for secure, encrypted online communication. They act as electronic passports. Digital certificates are issued by a trusted third party that validates the identity of a certificate holder and "signs" the certificate to attest that it hasn't been forged. Digital certificates can be used with WLANs. A **digital wrapper** is a program that is "wrapped" around another program or file. The wrapper acts as a gatekeeper to encrypt and secure the data. WLAN systems from some vendors can provide a unique and dynamic WEP that is different for each user and for each session that the user logs into the WLAN. These keys are stored on a special server. In addition, the initialization vector can be changed for each packet being transmitted.

If WLAN data requires a higher level of security, most industry experts suggest the follow solutions:

- Use a **Virtual Private Network (VPN)**. A VPN is a secure, encrypted connection between two points. VPNs transfer information by encrypting and encapsulating traffic in IP packets before sending them (called tunneling).
- Reduce the amount of transmission power used in a WLAN. This will decrease the distance that the radio waves can travel, thus limiting the range in which hackers can pick up the signals.

- Do not leave WLAN security settings on the default settings. Instead, customize them for each environment.
- If a WLAN is available in a public area of a building, keep its traffic separate from that on the wired network.
- Use 128-bit WEP keys, which are much harder to break than 40-bit keys.

Chapter Summary

- The slow bandwidth of 1 or 2 Mbps for the 802.11 standard released in 1990 was not sufficient for most network applications. In 1999, IEEE approved two new standards, 802.11b and 802.11a.
- Operating in the 2.4 GHz ISM frequency range, 802.11b has a maximum data rate of 11 Mbps, and has been widely accepted. However, the ISM band is crowded and subject to interference from other networking technologies, cordless phones, and Bluetooth. Another drawback is that there are no means to prioritize transmissions (QoS).
- The 802.11a standard has a maximum rated speed of 54 Mbps and also supports 48, 36, 24, 18, 12, 9, and 6 Mbps. 802.11a achieves its increase in speed and flexibility over 802.11b through a higher frequency, more transmission channels, and a new multiplexing technique.
- IEEE 802.11a networks use the Unlicensed National Information Infrastructure (U-NII) band, intended for devices that will provide short-range, high-speed wireless digital communications. Outside the U.S., however, the 5 GHz bands are allocated to users and technologies other than WLANs and the bands have different power limitations. The total bandwidth available for IEEE 802.11a WLANs using U-NII is almost four times that available for 802.11b networks using the ISM band.
- In 802.11a, eight frequency channels can overlap and operate simultaneously. Within each frequency channel there is a channel 20 MHz wide that supports 52 carrier signals, with each signal 300 KHz wide. Because there is an increased number of available channels, more users can access more bandwidth in an 802.11a WLAN when managed correctly.
- IEEE 802.11b WLANs face a problem with multipath distortion as the radio frequency (RF) signals bounce off walls and furniture and are delayed reaching the receiver. The receiving device must wait until all reflections are received before it can transmit. This puts a ceiling limit on the overall speed of the WLAN. The 802.11a standard solves this problem through a new multiplexing technique called Orthogonal Frequency Division Multiplexing (OFDM). OFDM sends transmissions in parallel across several channels instead of one long stream of data sent across a single channel. OFDM avoids problems caused by multipath distortion by sending the message slowly enough so that any delayed copies (reflections) are late by only a small fraction of time. And because the transmissions are sent in parallel, the total throughout is acually increased.

- The 802.11a standard specifies eight frequency channels that can overlap and operate simultaneously in the Low Band and Middle Band. Within each frequency channel there is a channel 20 MHz wide. This channel is divided into 52 subchannels. Each subchannel's signal is 300 KHz wide. OFDM uses 48 of these subchannels for data, while the remaining four are used for error correction. The modulation techniques used to actually encode the data vary depending upon the speed.
- IEEE 802.11a standard handles errors differently than 802.11b. The number of errors is significantly reduced due to the nature of 802.11a transmissions. Because transmissions are sent over parallel subchannels, radio interference from an outside source is minimized. Error correction is also enhanced. Forward Error Correction (FEC) transmits a secondary copy along with the primary information. If part of the primary transmission is lost, the secondary copy can be used to recover (through sophisticated algorithms) the lost data. This eliminates the need to retransmit if an error occurs, which saves time.
- The 802.11a standard made changes only to the physical layer (PHY layer) of the original 802.11 and 802.11b standard; the MAC layer remains the same. The 802.11a PHY layer is divided into two parts. The Physical Medium Dependent (PMD) sublayer makes up the standards for both the characteristics of the wireless medium (such as OFDM) and defines the method for transmitting and receiving data through that medium. The Physical Layer Convergence Procedure (PLCP) reformats the data received from the MAC layer (when transmitting) into a frame that the PMD sublayer can transmit and "listens" to the medium to determine when the data can be sent.
- IEEE developed the 802.11g standard to preserve the stable and widely accepted features of 802.11b but increase the data transfer rates to those similar to 802.11a. The 802.11g draft specifies that it operates entirely in the 2.4 GHz ISM frequency and not the U-NII band used by 802.11a.
- HiperLAN/2 is a high-speed WLAN specification that is similar to the IEEE 802.11a standard. HiperLAN/2 was standardized by the ETSI, the European Telecommunications Standards Institute. Close cooperation between ETSI and IEEE has ensured that there are similarities between the two standards although they remain very different in their implementation. Products based on HiperLAN/2 may start to appear on the U.S. market in 2003 or beyond. The protocol stack for the HiperLAN/2 has three basic layers: Physical Layer, Data Link Layer, and Convergence Layer.
- Whereas IEEE 802.11 networks can connect only to wired Ethernet networks, HiperLAN/2 offers high-speed wireless connectivity at up to 54 Mbps and seamless connectivity to cellular telephone systems and Asynchronous Transfer Mode (ATM), a wide-area network technology that uses fiber-optic media to transmit at 622 Mbps. HiperLAN/2 allows users to communicate over a high-speed external serial bus that can transmit at 400 Mbps known as IEEE 1394 (FireWire).

- When comparing WLANs, they should not all be considered as competing technologies, but instead should be looked at as complementary technologies.
- A WLAN's greatest strength—allowing users to roam freely without being connected to the network by wires—is also its weakness. Just as a roaming user can receive radio frequency signals anywhere in the building, an unauthorized user sitting in a parking lot outside the building can receive those same RF signals. Broadcasting network traffic over the airwaves has created an entire new set of issues for keeping the network secure. These issues have been heightened by studies that reveal that some of the security provisions in IEEE WLANs are flawed.
- WLANs can be protected through authentication and measures to ensure privacy. Authentication verifies that the user or device has permission to access the network. Privacy makes certain that transmissions themselves are not read by unauthorized persons. Researchers have raised questions about the security of IEEE authentication through Service Set Identifiers (SSIDs), and the Wired Equivalent Privacy (WEP) specification for data encryption to ensure privacy. Some vendors have added enhanced security features to their WLAN products.
- There are a variety of attacks that can be generated against WLANs. Due to the limitations of the IEEE WLAN security, enhanced security measures are considered important for wireless transmissions that require such protection.
- In order to increase the security of IEEE 802 WLANs, an IEEE task group is working on a draft known as IEEE 802.1x. This will allow WLANs to centralize the authentication of wireless clients. Other secure measures can be taken as necessary.

Key Terms

2X mode — See turbo mode.

16-level quadrature amplitude modulation (16-QAM) — A modulation technique used in 24 Mbps 802.11a transmissions that uses one signal to transmit 4 bits.

64-level quadrature amplitude modulation (64-QAM) — A modulation technique used in 54 Mbps 802.11a transmissions that uses 64 different signals.

access control list — A list of approved MAC addresses contained in an access point.

Asynchronous Transfer Mode (ATM) — A wide-area network technology that uses fiber-optic media to transmit at 622 Mbps.

authentication — A process that verifies that the user has permission to access the network.

CCK-OFDM — An optional transmit mode of the IEEE 802.11g draft.

digital certificates — Data files that are used for encrypted communication.

digital wrapper — A program that is wrapped around another program or file and acts as a gatekeeper to encrypt and secure data.

Dynamic Frequency Selection (DFS) — An appropriate radio channel that is selected to minimize interference.

Extensible Authentication Protocol (EAP) — A security protocol that allows a client to negotiate authentication with an external server.

FireWire — A high-speed external serial bus that can transmit at 400 Mbps, also known as IEEE 1394.

Forward Error Correction (FEC) — Error correction in an 802.11a WLAN.

HiperLAN/2 — A proposed high-speed WLAN that is similar to the IEEE 802.11a standard.

IEEE 802.11a — A standard for WLAN transmissions developed in 1999 for networks with speeds up to 54 Mbps and beyond.

IEEE 802.11e Task Group — A group working on incorporating QoS into 802.11 WLANs.

IEEE 802.11g — A draft for WLAN transmissions developed in 2001 for networks with speeds up to 54 Mbps using the ISM band.

IEEE 802.1x — A draft to increase the security of IEEE 802 WLANs.

IEEE 1394 — A high-speed external serial bus that can transmit at 400 Mbps, also known as FireWire.

MAC address — A unique 48-bit number that is burned into the network interface card when it is manufactured.

Orthogonal Frequency Division Multiplexing (OFDM) — A multiplexing technique used in 802.11a WLANs.

PBCC-22 (Packet Binary Convolutional Coding) — An optional transmit mode of the IEEE 802.11g draft.

privacy — Standards that assure that transmissions are not read by unauthorized users.

public key — Cryptography that uses matched public and private keys for encryption and decryption.

quadrature phase shift keying (QPSK) — A modulation technique used in 12 Mbps 802.11a transmissions that varies both the starting point and amplitude.

Remote Authentication Dial-In User Service (RADIUS) — A standard method for providing authentication services.

shared key — Cryptography that uses the same key to encrypt and decrypt a message.

subchannels — A division of a 20 MHz channel that carries data in an 802.lb WLAN.

turbo mode — An IEEE 802.11a option that permits increased speeds in excess of 54 Mbps.

Virtual Private Network (VPN) — A secure, encrypted connection between two points.

Wi-Fi5 — Another name for IEEE 802.11a.

Wired Equivalent Privacy (WEP) — The IEEE specification for data encryption between wireless devices.

Review Questions

1. The original IEEE 802.11 standard established in 1997 was for WLANs operating at what maximum speed?
   a. 1 Mbps
   b. 2 Mbps
   c. 3 Mbps
   d. 4 Mbps
2. The maximum mandatory speed of an IEEE 802.11a WLAN is ________________.
   a. 11 Mbps
   b. 33 Mbps
   c. 54 Mbps
   d. 108 Mbps

3. Another name for IEEE 802.11a is ________________.
   a. WECA
   b. Fast Ethernet
   c. Wi-Fi5
   d. 802.11g
4. IEEE 802.11a achieves its increase in speed and flexibility over 802.11b by each of the following except ________________.
   a. higher frequency
   b. lower bandwidth
   c. more transmission channels
   d. new multiplexing technique
5. The Unlicensed National Information Infrastructure (U-NII) band operates at the ________________ frequency.
   a. 2.4 GHz
   b. 33 MHz
   c. 5 GHz
   d. 16 KHz
6. The Federal Communications Commission (FCC) has segmented the 300 MHz of the U-NII spectrum into three segments or bands and each band has a maximum power limit. True or False?
7. The 5 GHz bands are available to WLANs worldwide. True or false?

8. Although other devices such as 2.4 GHz cordless phones, microwave ovens, and Bluetooth devices may cause interference problems with 802.11b networks in the 2.4 GHz ISM band, these devices are not a problem with 802.11a. True or false?
9. Within each frequency channel in an 802.11a WLAN there is a channel 20 MHz wide that supports 52 carrier signals. True or false?
10. A problem with 802.11a WLANs is the multipath distortion of the radio frequency (RF) signals that bounce off walls and furniture and are delayed reaching the receiver. True or false?
11. OFDM uses ________________ subchannels for data, and four are used for error correction.
12. Quadrature phase shift keying (QPSK) varies both the starting point and ________________.
13. Although 54 Mbps is the "official" top speed of 802.11a, the IEEE specification also allows for vendor-implemented higher speeds known as turbo or ________________.
14. The IEEE ________________ standard incorporates the stable and widely accepted features of 802.11b with the increased data transfer rates to those similar to 802.11a.
15. What is Dynamic Frequency Selection (DFS)?
16. What are the types of systems that HiperLAN/2 can connect with?
17. What are some advantages and disadvantages of IEEE 802.11a WLANs?
18. What are some advantages and disadvantages of HiperLAN/2?
19. What is authentication? Why is it important for WLANs?
20. List three shortcomings of WEP.

HANDS-ON PROJECTS

Setting Security on a WLAN

1. The Cisco Aironet 340 provides several different options for protecting the access point (AP) by using the Security Setup feature. The first and most important feature is to set up an account and password on the AP to prevent unauthorized users from gaining control.
   a. Open a browser and enter the IP number of the access point to display the Summary Status screen. Click **Setup** from the Summary Status page and then click **Security** under the Services heading. This will display the Security Setup page, as seen in Figure 7-16.

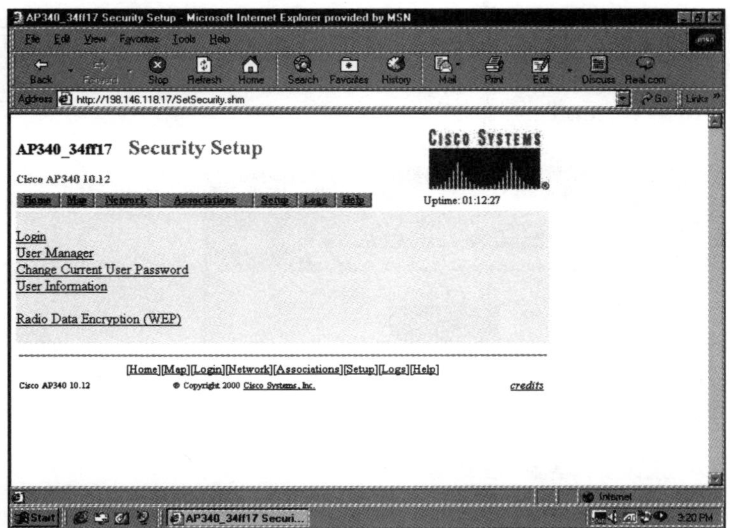

Figure 7-16 Security setup

b. To set up an account, click **User Information** to open the User Information screen. Click the **Add New User** button to open the User Management screen, as seen in Figure 7-17. Enter a username and password. Place a checkmark in the **Write**, **Ident**, and **Admin** boxes. This will give you full administrative privileges. Click **Apply** when finished entering the User Management information and you will be returned to the User Information screen.

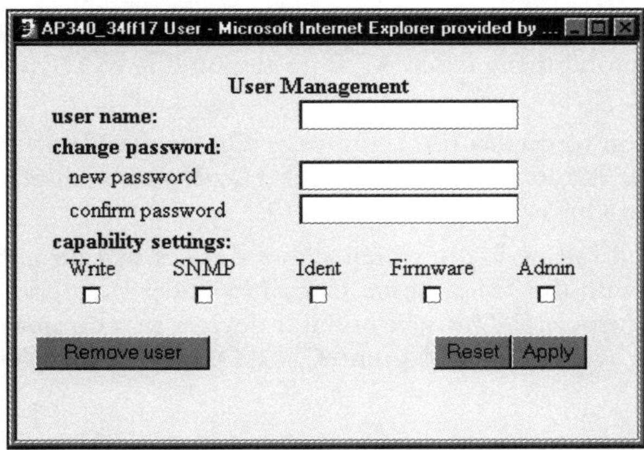

Figure 7-17 User management

c. The last step is to turn on the Cisco security features. Return to the Security Setup screen by pressing the **Back** button on the browser. Click **User Manager** to display the User Manager Setup screen, as seen in Figure 7-18. Click **Enabled** and then **OK** to turn on the system security.

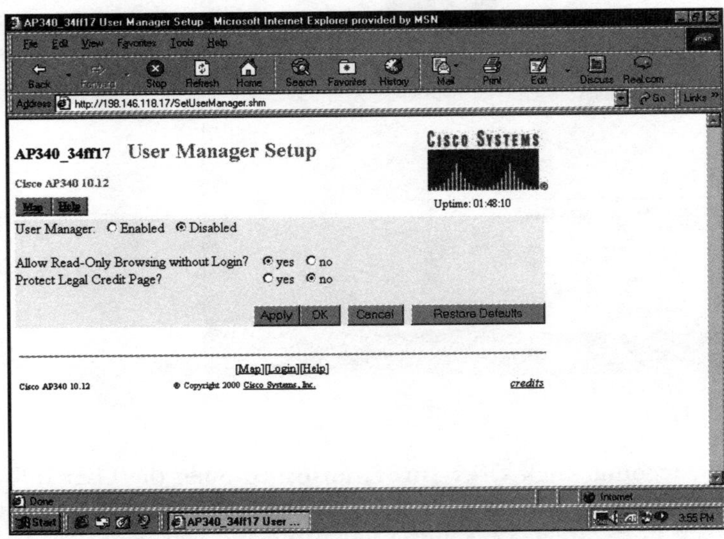

Figure 7-18 User Manager setup

d. Return to the Security Setup screen by clicking the **Back** button of the browser, then click **Login**. Log in using your username and password. Remain logged in for the next project.

2. In this project you will prohibit the Cisco AP from responding to active scanning requests.

   a. Click the **Setup** button to display the Setup page. Under the Network Ports heading, locate the AP Radio line and then click **Hardware** to display the AP Radio Hardware page. This is seen in Figure 7-19.

   b. With Cisco, the default setting is Yes, which allows devices that do not specify an SSID to associate with the access point. Click **No** under the option Allow "Broadcast" SSID to Associate? This will prohibit devices that do not specify an SSID from associating with this access point. Click **OK** when completed.

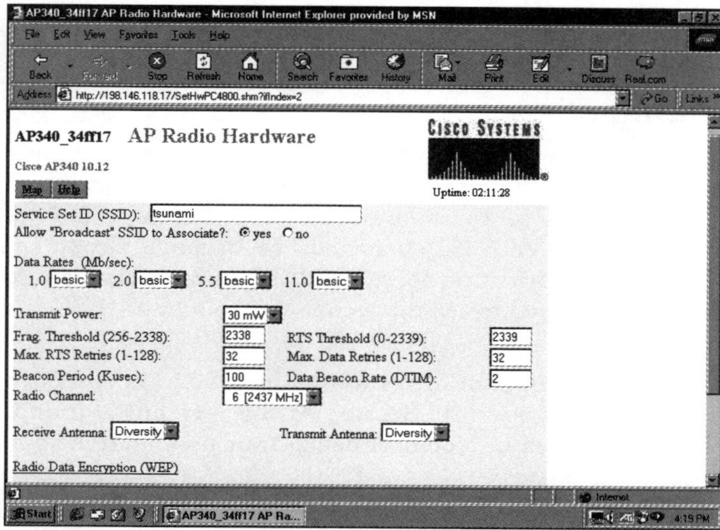

Figure 7-19 AP radio hardware

Researching IEEE

The Institute for Electrical and Electronic Engineers (IEEE) continues to play a critical role in establishing standards for networking as it has since the early 1980s. Using the Internet and other resources, research the IEEE organization. How did it start? Who makes up its membership? What are the advantages of being a member of this organization? What do the student chapters of the IEEE do? What is involved in the process for creating a standard? Write a one-page paper on the information that you find.

The Future of 802.11g

Much attention has been focused on the IEEE 802.11g standard and how it will fit with the 802.11a and 802.11b standards. Using the Internet and IT contacts that you may have, develop your own theory as to where the 802.11g standard will fit. Will it replace 802.11b? Will it co-exist with the other standards? Write a one-page paper on your opinion. Be sure to include materials that support your conclusion.

Researching VPNs

Industry experts agree that using a Virtual Private Network (VPN) to establish a secure, encrypted connection between two points is one of the best security steps that can be taken. Research and gather information about VPNs. How do they work? What are their advantages and disadvantages? What hardware and software is needed? Write a one-page paper on what you find.

CASE PROJECTS

The Baypoint Group

The Baypoint Group (TBG), a company that assists organizations and businesses with issues involving network planning and design, needs you as a consultant. Academic Computing Services (ACS) is a nation-wide organization that assists colleges and universities with technology issues. ACS has contacted The Baypoint Group and asked for their help. ACS needs more information about the IEEE 802.11a standard so that their salespeople will be better equipped to sell the technology to schools. TBG has asked you to help.

1. Prepare a PowerPoint presentation that outlines how 802.11a works and lists the advantages of 802.11a over 802.11b. Because ACS is a technical group, the presentation should have a level of technical detail. Your presentation should last 15-20 minutes.
2. ACS is pleased with your presentation, but they are concerned about security with WLANs. TBG has asked you to prepare another PowerPoint presentation that outlines the security strengths and weaknesses of a WLAN. Your presentation should consist of at least 15-20 slides.

OPTIONAL TEAM CASE PROJECT

Some of ACS' staff members have heard about the new HiperLAN/2 WLAN and think that it may become the worldwide standard instead of IEEE 802.11a WLANs. Form two teams of several individuals, with each team selecting one of these technologies. Research in depth the advantages and disadvantages of these respective technologies and how they work. Hold a debate in which each team presents a 10-minute talk about the advantages of their technology and the disadvantages of the opposing technology. After the talk allow time for questions.

CHAPTER

8

DIGITAL CELLULAR TELEPHONY

After reading this chapter and completing the exercises, you will be able to:

- Describe the applications that can be used on a digital cellular telephone
- Explain how cellular telephony functions
- List and describe the features of the generations of cellular telephony
- List and describe the four types of client software used on a digital cellular telephone
- Discuss the issues surrounding 3G implementation

Perhaps one of the most deceptive technologies in wireless communications is digital cellular telephony. From the user's perspective, digital cellular technology is commonplace. No matter where you travel, everyone seems to be using digital cellular phones to make and receive calls. And using a digital cellular telephone seems as easy as using any telephone. Yet from a technological view, there is nothing commonplace or simple about digital cellular telephony. It is probably the most competitive and complex of all wireless communication technologies. First, there is no single underlying digital cellular technology. There are a variety of competing technologies with such unfamiliar names as GSM and CDMA2000 1XEVDO, both across the U.S. and also around the world. Second, not only are there competing technologies, there are also xcompeting carriers, some of them among the largest corporations on the planet, each pushing a specific technology. Even governments have weighed in to the fray by auctioning off parts of the wireless spectrum to the highest bidder, earning billions of dollars in the process.

This chapter explores how cellular telephones work and looks at the complex technology behind digital cellular networks. We will also look at what can be done using digital cellular devices and view the various platforms and software that make these enhanced features work. Finally, we'll look at some of the issues surrounding implementation of digital cellular technology.

Applications

The rush to wireless digital cellular networks is being pushed by the new or expanded applications and features that it will provide to mobile users. The list of these features is impressive. Because the networks are based on digital instead of analog technology and can transmit at much higher speeds, they will not be limited to voice communications. Digital cellular telephones can be used to:

- Browse the Internet
- Access e-mail
- Participate in videoconferencing
- Receive travel, entertainment, and other types of information
- Run a variety of programs on the cellular devices

One of the most widely used applications in Europe and Japan is **Short Message Services (SMS)**. SMS allows for the delivery of short, text-based messages between wireless devices such as cellular telephones and pagers. SMS is not like two-way paging, which allows users to send many lines of text over data networks. The text messages of SMS are brief, limited to 160 characters in length (or 70 characters for non-Latin Arabic and Chinese characters). And SMS is not like text-message services that send messages over the Internet from a central site, such as an answering service sending a message to a physician. SMS lets users send messages directly from one device to another device without using the Internet.

Pagers work in a similar fashion to SMS. A user dials a phone number that is actually calling a device known as a paging terminal. Once the page is entered, the paging terminal converts it into a code and relays the code to transmitters, which send the code out as a radio signal throughout the coverage area.

SMS is used in several applications. These include:

- *Person-to-person:* This is the most common use of SMS, namely one user sending a text message to another user. It has been called the digital cellular equivalent to instant messaging.
- *Agent-to-person:* Automated agents can send notifications whenever an event occurs. These events are configured by the user. For example, an automated agent can send out an SMS message when a stock reaches a certain price or the user has received a voicemail message.
- *Information broadcast services:* These include news, weather, and sports scores sent on a regular basis or when a breaking story occurs.
- *Software configuration:* Changes to the software running on the cellular device can be performed by SMS.

- *Advertising:* Messages containing advertising can be sent to users over SMS.

Unsolicited advertising or "spam" over SMS is becoming a major issue. Although guidelines have been recommended for SMS advertising, such as limiting the message to 100 characters, mobile users still complain of receiving numerous unsolicited advertising messages daily on their mobile devices.

Although SMS is very popular in many countries, it has been slow to catch on in the U.S. Many industry experts attribute this to differences in culture and technology, namely:

- Most people in the U.S. who have wireless digital cellular technology also have fixed Internet access at home or work and send messages by e-mail. In Japan and Europe, where Internet access is much more limited because of its high cost, SMS has become a viable alternative to e-mail.
- In the U.S. the cost of making a wireless cellular telephone call is so inexpensive that it often makes more sense to pick up the phone and call someone than to type a text message. Overseas customers, on the other hand, pay much higher rates for wireless digital cellular telephone calls. Many of these users opt for using SMS, which is a cheaper way to communicate.
- U.S. consumers have a variety of alternatives to SMS, such as e-mail and two-way paging services.
- Cultural differences also have an impact. In many nations, small technological devices are viewed as being very popular and "trendy," whereas in the U.S. the overall emphasis is not focused on the device that sends the message but on the content of that message.

In spite of its slow start in the U.S., SMS is expected to become one of the major applications used on digital cellular telephones. With the average number of SMS messages sent annually worldwide in excess of 200 billion, many predict that it will be just a matter of time before SMS becomes popular in the U.S.

How Cellular Telephony Works

Cellular telephones work in a manner that is unlike wired telephones. There are two keys to cellular telephone networks. The first is that the coverage area is divided into smaller individual sections called **cells**, as seen in Figure 8-1. In a typical city the cells, which are hexagon-shaped, measure 10 square miles (26 square kilometers). At the center of each cell is a cell transmitter to which the mobile devices in that cell send and receive radio frequency (RF) signals. These transmitters are connected to a base station, and each base station is connected to a **mobile telecommunications switching office (MTSO)**. The MTSO is the link between the cellular network and the wired telephone world and controls all transmitters and base stations in the cellular network.

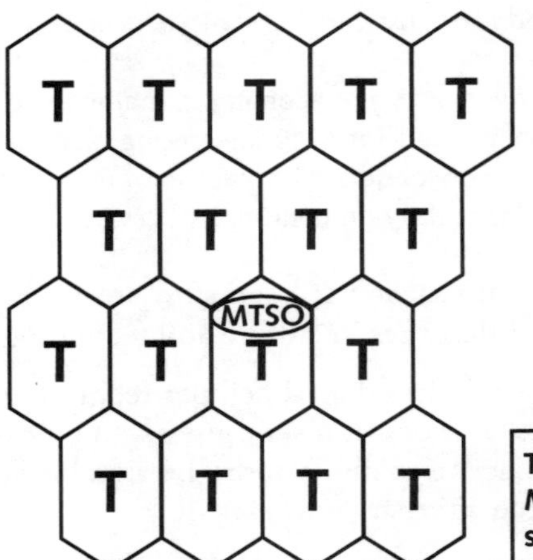

Figure 8-1 Cellular network

By the year 2004, it is estimated that there will be over 203 million cellular telephone subscribers in the U.S.

The second key to cellular telephone networks is that all of the transmitters and cell phones operate at a low power level. This enables the signal to stay confined to the cell and not interfere with any other cells. Because the signal at a specific frequency does not go outside of the cell area, that same frequency can be used in other cells at the same time. This is illustrated in Figure 8-2.

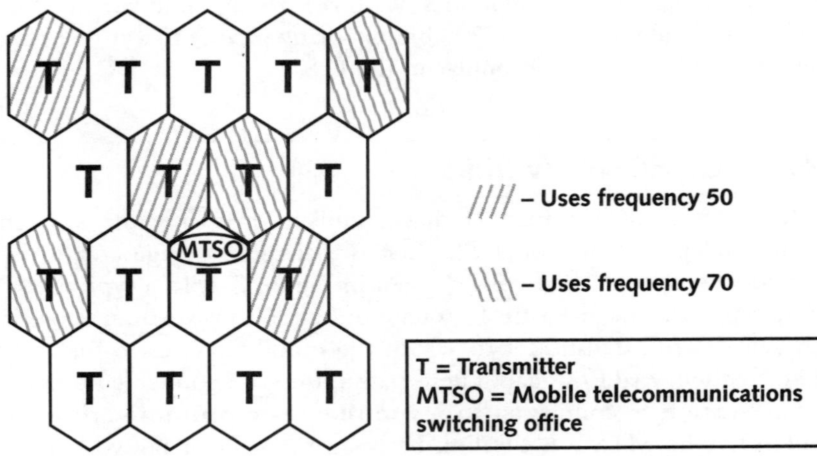

Figure 8-2 Frequency reuse

Because of frequency reuse, a typical cellular telephone network in one city uses only 830 frequencies to handle all callers.

All cell phones have special codes associated with them. These codes are used to identify the phone, the phone's owner, and the carrier or service provider (such as AT&T, Sprint, and many others). The codes that are used are summarized in Table 8-1.

Table 8-1 Cellular telephone codes

Code name	Size	Purpose
System Identification Code (SID)	5 digits	The carrier's unique identification number
Electronic Serial Number (ESN)	32 bits	The cellular phone's unique serial number
Mobile Identification Number (MIN)	10 digits	A unique number generated from the phone's telephone number

8

The ESN is permanently assigned to a specific cellular phone when it is manufactured. The MIN and SID codes are programmed into the phone when it is activated.

When a cellular telephone user moves around within the same cell, the transmitter and base station for that cell handle all of the transmissions. As the user moves toward the next cell, the cellular telephone will automatically associate with the base station of that cell. This is known as a **handoff**. However, what happens if a cellular user moves beyond the coverage area of the entire cellular network, for example, from Nashville to Boston? In this case the cellular telephone would automatically connect with whatever cellular network was in place in the remote area. The cellular network in the remote area (Boston) would communicate with the cellular network in the home area (Nashville) verifying that the user can make calls and also charge for the calls. This is known as **roaming**. Handoff and roaming are illustrated in Figure 8-3.

The steps that a cellular telephone uses to receive a call are as follows:

1. When the cell phone is turned on it listens for the SID being transmitted by the base station on the **control channel**, which is a special frequency that the phone and base station use for setup. If the phone cannot detect a control channel, it is out of range and displays a message to the user such as "No Service."

2. If the cell phone receives a SID, it compares it with the SID that was programmed into the phone. If they match, the cell phone is in a network owned by its carrier. The cell phone transmits a registration request number to the base station that the MTSO uses to track in which cell the phone is located.

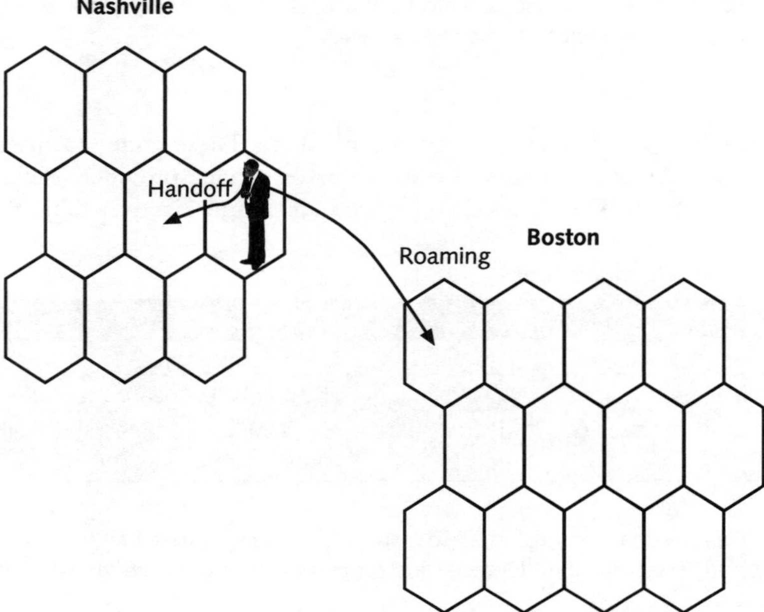

Figure 8-3 Handoff and roaming

3. If the SIDs do not match, then the cellular phone is roaming. The MTSO of the remote network contacts the MTSO of the home network, which confirms that the SID of the phone is valid. The MTSO of the remote network then tracks the phone and sends the information back to the home MTSO.
4. When a call comes in, the MTSO locates the phone through the registration request and then selects a frequency that will be used for communication. The MTSO sends the frequency information to the phone over the control channel. Both the phone and the transmitter switch to that frequency and the connection is then completed. This is illustrated in Figure 8-4.
5. As the user moves toward the edge of a cell, the base station notes that the signal strength is decreasing while the base station in the next cell determines that the phone's signal strength is increasing. The two base stations coordinate with each other through the MTSO. The cellular phone then gets a message on the control channel to change frequencies as it is handed off into another cell.

Although the Telecommunications Act of 1996 makes it illegal to intercept cellular transmissions, callers should remember that their conversations are being broadcast across the public airwaves and may not be as private as calls using the wired telephone network.

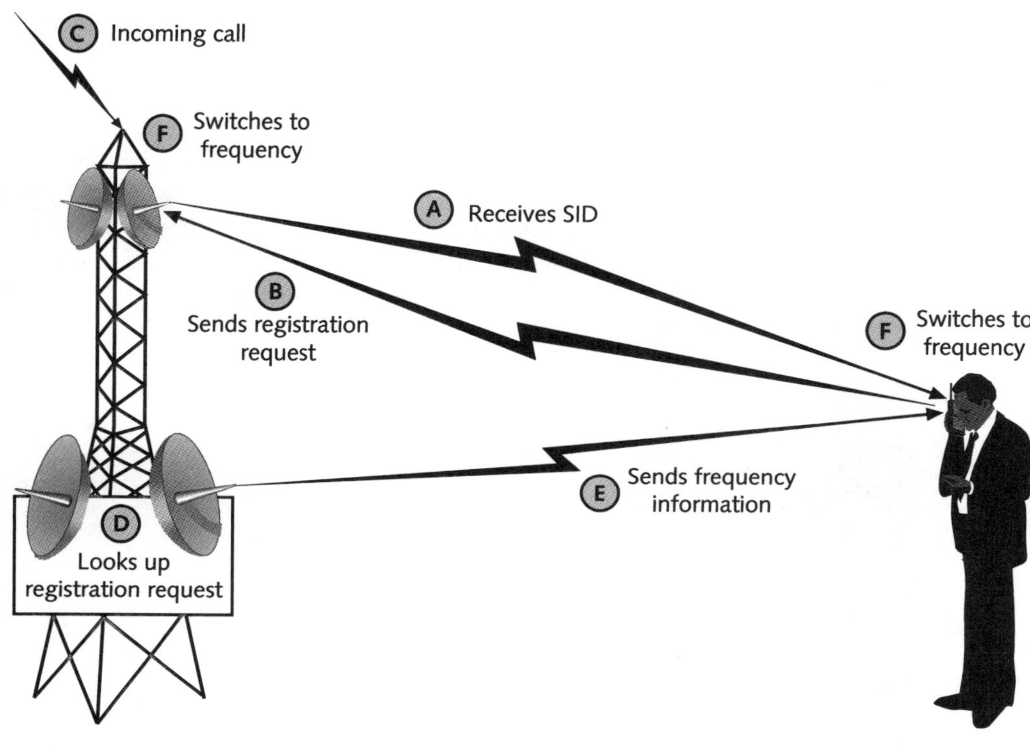

Figure 8-4 Receiving a call

8

Digital Cellular Technology

Cellular telephones have been available since the early 1980s in the United States. Since that time cell phone technology has changed dramatically. Most industry experts outline several generations of cellular telephony.

First Generation

The first generation of wireless cellular technology is known appropriately enough as **First Generation (1G)**. 1G uses analog signals, which are radio frequency (RF) transmissions sent in a wave-like form. The maximum transmission speed of a 1G network is 9.6 Kbps.

1G technology is based on the **Advanced Mobile Phone Service (AMPS)**. AMPS operates in the 800-900 MHz frequency spectrum. Each channel is 30 KHz wide with a 45 KHz passband (the additional space on each side of the transmission band). There are 832 frequencies available for transmission. For voice traffic there are 790 frequencies used and the remaining 42 are used for the control channel. However, because two frequencies are used for a cellular telephone conversation (one to transmit and one to receive), there are actually 395 voice channels and 21 are used for control channel functions.

The 30 KHz channels where chosen for AMPS because this gives a voice quality comparable to a standard wired telephone transmission.

AMPS uses Frequency Division Multiple Access (FDMA). See Chapter 3 for a review of FDMA. Recall that for RF systems there are two resources, frequency and time. Division by frequency, so that each caller is allocated part of the spectrum for all of the time, is the basis of FDMA. This is illustrated in Figure 8-5. FDMA allocates a single channel to one user at a time. If the channel deteriorates due to interference from other frequencies, the user is switched to another channel.

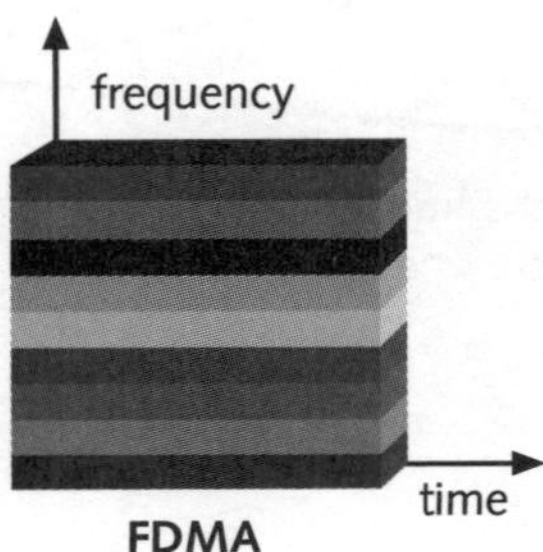

Figure 8-5 FDMA

AMPS was one of the first wireless communications systems to use FDMA. Although today AMPS is not commonly used, it still can be found in remote areas where digital service is difficult to support. This is because using AMPS, mobile devices can switch from a digital signal to an analog signal when necessary.

1G networks use circuit-switching technology. When a telephone call is made, a dedicated and direct physical connection is made between the caller and the recipient of the call through the telephone company's switch. While the telephone conversation is taking place, the connection remains open between only these two users. No other calls can be made from that phone while the first conversation is going on, and anyone who calls that phone will receive a busy signal. This direct connection lasts for the length of the call, at which time the switch drops the connection.

Analog signals, the basis for 1G cellular telephony, are prone to interference and do not have the same quality as a digital signal. In addition, sending data over an analog signal requires a modem or similar device to convert the signals from digital to analog and then back again. A 1G analog cellular telephone can only basically be used for voice communications. For these reasons 1G, although it was a pioneer in cellular telephony, was soon replaced with improved digital technology.

Second Generation

The next generation of cellular telephony is known as **Second Generation (2G)**, which started in the early 1990s and continues to the present. 2G networks transmit data between 9.6 Kbps and 14.4 Kbps in the 800 MHz and 1.9 GHz frequencies. The only major feature that 2G systems share with 1G is that they are circuit-switched networks.

2G systems use digital instead of analog transmissions. Digital transmissions provide several improvements over analog transmissions:

- Digital transmission uses the frequency spectrum more efficiently
- Over long distances the quality of the voice transmission does not degrade as with analog
- Digital transmissions are difficult to decode and offer better security
- On average, digital transmissions use less transmitter power
- Digital transmission enables smaller and less expensive individual receivers and transmitters

8

U.S. courts typically approve about 1,200 wiretaps each year, of which almost half are for wired telephone systems. About 40 percent of these wiretaps are for cellular transmissions and the rest are for pagers, faxes, and e-mail.

Another difference between 1G and 2G systems is that the carriers of 2G cellular networks build their cellular networks around different multiple access technologies. There are three different technologies that are used with 2G: TDMA, CDMA, and GSM. Time Division Multiple Access (TDMA) is used by AT&T networks. Whereas FDMA (used with AMPS) divides by frequency so that each caller is allocated part of the spectrum for all of the time, TDMA divides by time, so that each caller is allocated all of the spectrum for part of the time, as seen in Figure 8-6. TDMA divides a single 30 KHz radio frequency channel into 6 unique time slots, and each caller uses 2 time slots (one for transmitting and one for receiving). TDMA can send 3 times as many calls over a single channel than FDMA.

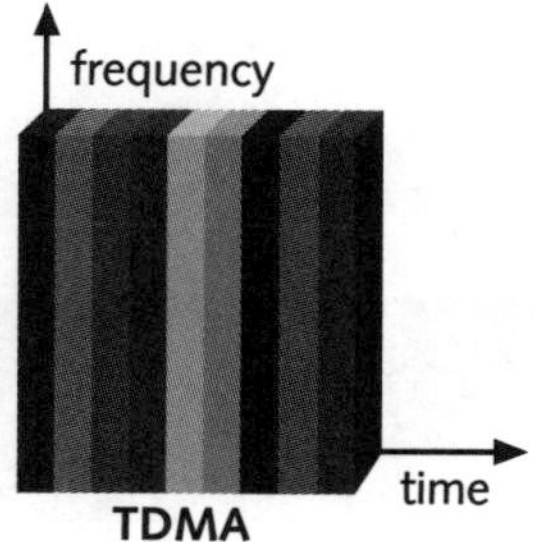

Figure 8-6 TDMA

Another multiple access technology, used by Sprint and other carriers, is Code Division Multiple Access (CDMA; introduced in Chapter 3). Whereas FDMA divides by frequency, so that each caller is allocated part of the spectrum for all of the time, and TDMA divides by time, so that each caller is allocated all of the spectrum for part of the time, with CDMA every caller is allocated the entire spectrum all of the time, as seen in Figure 8-7. CDMA uses unique digital codes, rather than separate RF frequencies, to differentiate between the different transmissions. A CDMA transmission is spread across the frequency and the digital codes are applied to the individual transmissions. When the signal is received, the codes are removed from the signal.

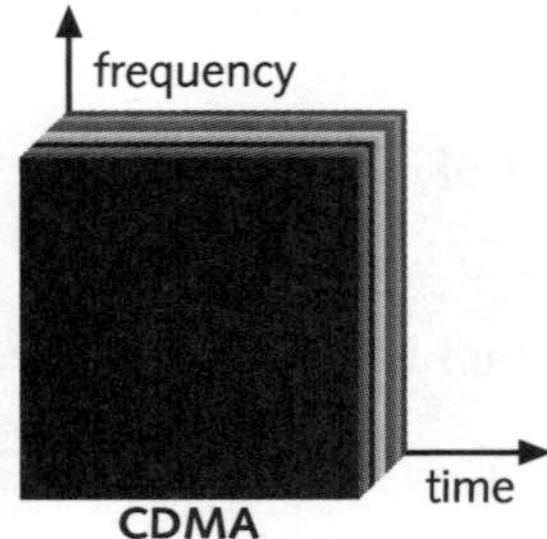

Figure 8-7 CDMA

The third multiple access technology used in 2G systems is **GSM (Global Systems for Mobile communications)**. GSM was developed in Europe as a standard for public mobile communications in the 1980s. VoiceStream is the primary GMS provider in the U.S. GSM uses a combination of FDMA and TDMA technologies. GSM divides a 25 MHz channel into 124 frequencies of 200 KHz each. Each 200 KHz channel is then divided into 8 time slots using TDMA. GSM systems can transmit at speeds up to 9.6 Kbps.

In 1989 the Cellular Telecommunications Industry Association (CTIA) chose TDMA over FDMA as the technology of choice for digital cellular networks. However, with the growing technology competition of CDMA and the fact that Europe was using GSM for mobile communications, the CTIA reconsidered and decided to let carriers make their own technology choices.

These three technologies—TDMA, CDMA, and GSM—make up the backbone of 2G digital cellular telephony. They are summarized in Table 8-2.

Table 8-2 2G technologies

2G name	Multiple access technology	U.S. carrier example
Time Division Multiple Access	TDMA	AT&T
Code Division Multiple Access	CDMA	Sprint
Global Systems for Mobile communications	GSM	VoiceStream

2.5 Generation

Digital cellular telephony today is largely considered to be somewhere in the later stages of 2G. Although the next big step will be to the Third Generation, getting there will not be an easy transition. There must be major changes to the network infrastructures as well as a completely new generation of mobile cellular devices deployed. It is expected that there will be an interim step known as the **2.5 Generation (2.5G)**. 2.5G networks operate at a maximum speed of 384 Kbps. At the present time 2.5G networks are sparsely deployed in only a handful nations, such as China, Japan, and Korea, along with a few cities in the U.S. and Europe.

The primary difference between 2G and 2.5G networks is that 2.5G networks are packet-switched instead of circuit-switched. Although circuit switching is ideal for voice communications, it is not efficient for transmitting data. This is because data transmissions occur in "bursts" with periods of delay in between. The delay results in time wasted while nothing is being transmitted. Packet switching requires that the data transmission be broken into smaller units or packets, and each packet is sent independently through the network to reach the destination.

Packet switching has two major advantages over circuit switching. First, packet switching is much more efficient because it can handle more transmissions over a given channel. Packet switching can increase the amount of traffic from 3 to 5 times over that of circuit switching. The second advantage is that packet switching permits an "always-on" connection. With a circuit-switched network, a connection between devices is dedicated only to those devices and it is not practical to keep that connection open when there is little or no traffic. This would be like calling a friend on the telephone and then laying the telephone down but not hanging up just in case you want to talk later. This prevents any other calls from coming in or going out. With packet switching it becomes practical to keep the connection up all the time.

The "always-on" feature, along with higher transmission speeds, were factors that have made cable modems and DSL connections so popular over dial-up connections for home use. With a cable or DSL connection the computer can always be connected to the network and there is never a wait for a connection to be established.

It is generally acknowledged that there will be three 2.5G network technologies. The migration from an existing 2G network to a 2.5G network depends on which 2G network technology is being used. For TDMA or GSM 2G networks, the next step would be to a 2.5G technology known as **General Packet Radio Service (GPRS)**. GPRS uses 8 time slots in a 200 KHz spectrum to transmit at a top speed of up to 114 Kbps. The next step beyond GPRS is **Enhanced Data Rates for Global Evolution (EDGE)**. EDGE is considered a "booster" for GPRS systems and can transmit up to 384 Kbps. EDGE, like GPRS, will be based on an entirely new modulation technique.

If the network transition is from a 2G CDMA network, instead of migrating to GPRS, the transition would be to **CDMA2000 1XRTT**. CDMA2000 1XRTT is designed to support 144 Kbps packet data transmission and to double the voice capacity of current generation CDMA networks.

Third Generation

Imagine videoconferencing with a friend in the U.S., using your cellular telephone while traveling on a train to Tokyo. That's the vision of **Third Generation (3G)**. 3G is intended to be a uniform and global worldwide standard for cellular wireless communication. The International Telecommunications Union (ITU) has outlined the standard data rates for a wireless cellular digital network. These rates are:

- 144 Kbps for a mobile user
- 386 Kbps for a slowly moving user
- 2 Mbps for a stationary user

As with 2.5G digital cellular networks, the technology of the 3G network depends upon the technology from which the transition is being made. If the technology is being made from CDMA2000 1XRTT, the next step would be to **CDMA2000 1XEVDO**. This technology can transmit at 2.4 Mbps. However, it can only send data and not voice. CDMA2000 1XEVDO must be coupled with CDMA2000 1XRTT if both types of data are needed to be transmitted. The successor to CDMA2000 1XEVDO will be **CDMA2000 1XEVDV**. Although it has no increase in speed over CDMA2000 1XEVDO, it can send both data and voice transmissions.

If the technology from which the transition is being made is EDGE, the next step technology to bring it up to 3G is **Wideband CDMA (WCDMA)**. WCDMA adds a packet-switched data channel to a circuit-switched voice channel. WCDMA can send at 2 Mbps in a fixed position and 300 Kbps when mobile.

The road to 3G digital cellular technology is currently very rough. Not everyone agrees which technologies will be players, and several of these technologies have not yet been fully tested. The actual technologies may be a variation of one or more of these mentioned above. Figure 8-8 illustrates the proposed technology paths to 3G.

Table 8-3 summarizes digital cellular technologies.

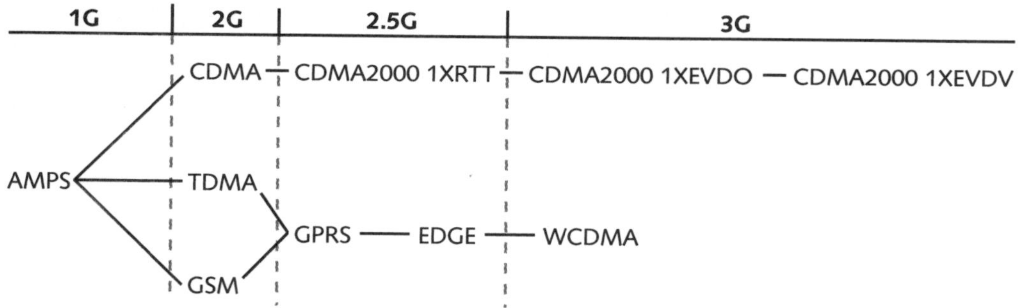

Figure 8-8 Digital wireless cellular migration path

Table 8-3 Digital cellular technologies

Name	Generation	Technology	Maximum Speed
AMPS	1G	Analog circuit-switched	9.6 Kbps
GSM	2G	Digital circuit-switched	9.6 Kbps
TDMA	2G	Digital circuit-switched	14.4 Kbps
CDMA	2G	Digital circuit-switched	14.4 Kbps
GPRS	2.5G	Digital packet-switched	114 Kbps
CDMA2000 1XRTT	2.5G	Digital packet-switched	144 Kbps
EDGE	2.5G	Digital packet-switched	384 Kbps
CDMA2000 1XEVDO and 1XEVDV	3G	Digital packet-switched	2 Mbps
WCDMA	3G	Digital packet-switched	2 Mbps

8

CLIENT SOFTWARE

In order for the various features, such as Internet surfing or videoconferencing, to operate on a wireless digital cellular device there must be client software that functions on the cell phone or device. The purpose of this software is to provide the functions and user interface so that data can be displayed or manipulated. Some client software is unique to cellular telephones while other software is used in a variety of different applications. This section looks at the most common types of digital cellular client software: WAP, i-mode, Java, and BREW.

Wireless Application Protocol (WAP)

As you learned in Chapter 1, the Wireless Application Protocol (WAP) provides a standard way to transmit, format, and display Internet data for devices like cell phones. WAP was developed in 1997 for Internet-enabled digital cellular phones, pagers, and other handheld devices to send and receive Internet text data. WAP-enabled devices do not display a rich user interface with graphics, images, and animation; only textual data is displayed. This limitation is due to the slower transmission speed and smaller viewing areas of cellular telephones. An example of a WAP display is seen in Figure 8-9.

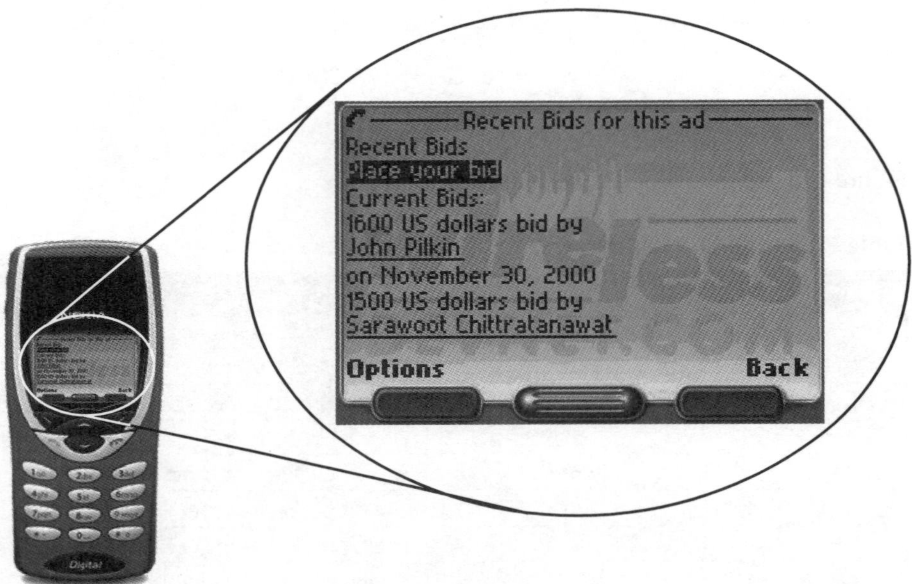

Figure 8-9 WAP display

With standard computers, Web browser software makes a request to the World Wide Web file server for a Web page. This page is transmitted back to the Web browser in Hypertext Markup Language (HTML), which is the standard language for displaying content on the Internet. When a Web server sends a Web page back to a computer, it is sending only HTML code. The Web browser is responsible for interpreting that code and displaying the results on the screen. A sample of HTML code is seen in Figure 8-10.

WAP follows this standard Internet model with a few variations. A WAP cell phone runs a tiny browser program called a microbrowser that uses Wireless Markup Language (WML) instead of HTML. WML is designed to display text-based Web content on the small screen of a cell phone. However, since the Internet standard is HTML, a WAP Gateway (sometimes called a WAP Proxy) must translate between WML and HTML. The WAP Gateway takes the Web page sent from the Web server in HTML code and changes it to WML language before forwarding it on to the cell phone. This is illustrated in Figure 8-11.

```
<html>

<head>
<meta http-equiv="Content-Type" content="text/html; charset=windows
-1252">
<meta name="GENERATOR" content="Microsoft FrontPage 5.0">
<meta name="ProgId" content="FrontPage.Editor.Document">
<title>Volenteer State Community College</title>
</head>

<body>

<div align="center">
  <center>
  <table border="0" cellpadding="0" cellspacing="0" width="709">
    <tr>
      <td width="240"> </td>
      <td width="469">
        <p align="left"><img border="0" src="vscc/VSCC01.jpg" width
="376" height="180"><b><i><font size="=1" color="#000080"><br>
        Volunteer State
        Community College is a public :<br>
        two-year institution of higher learning.  We are<br>
        located in beautiful Gallatin, Tennessee.<br>
        </font></i></b>
        <font size="+1"><i><font color="#000080"><b>
        <a href="http://www.tn.regentsdegrees.org/campus/vscc">
        <img border="0" src="vscc/TBRLogo.gif" align="left" width="
242" height="55"></a></b></font></i></font><b><i><font size="+1"><f
ont color="#000080"><br>
```

Figure 8-10 HTML code

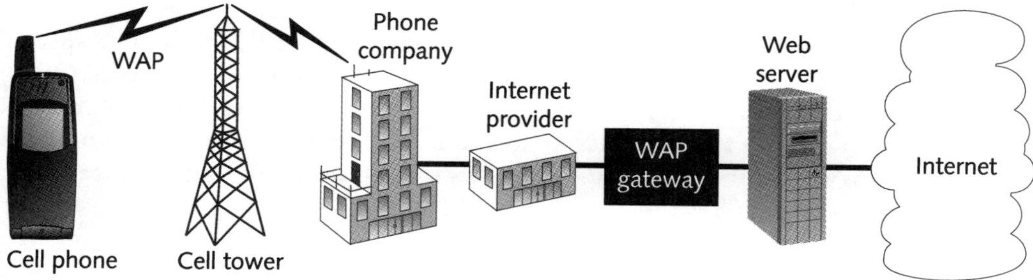

Figure 8-11 WAP

There several differences between HTML and WML. Many features of HTML do not exist in WML. For example, HTML can control the appearance of text in a browser by specifying the layout, the color, font, and styling. With WML the only changes available are the type of font to be used, instructions to make the text size larger or smaller, and basic formatting such underlining and bold. Figure 8-12 illustrates a simple WML document along with comments to display the words "Hello world" on a WAP cellular telephone.

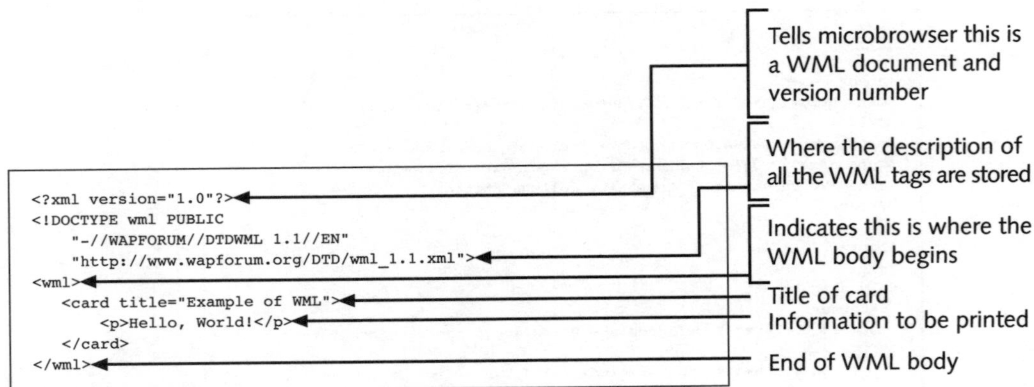
<?xml version="1.0"?>
<!DOCTYPE wml PUBLIC
"-//WAPFORUM//DTDWML 1.1//EN"
"http://www.wapforum.org/DTD/wml_1.1.xml">
<wml>
<card title="Example of WML">
<p>Hello, World!</p>
</card>
</wml>
Tells microbrowser this is a WML document and version number
Where the description of all the WML tags are stored
Indicates this is where the WML body begins
Title of card
Information to be printed
End of WML body

Figure 8-12 WML code

Tip

WML is case sensitive and all tags must be in lowercase.

WML is based on the **Extensible Markup Language (XML)**. XML uses indicators called "tags." Similar to HTML, which uses tags to describe how an item should be displayed on the screen, XML tags specify how the content should be formatted on the wireless device.

A WML document is called a **deck** that contains one or more blocks, known as **cards**. Most documents are too large to fit into the space of a cell phone display. To accommodate the small display, a document is divided into smaller pieces (cards) and displayed one at a time. Each card has text content and navigation controls. Although only one card can be displayed at a time on the cell phone, navigation between the cards is very fast because the entire deck is stored by the microbrowser. This is illustrated in Figure 8-13.

Tip

Because most cellular devices have limited storage space (1.4 Kb is typical), the number of cards in a deck should also be limited. Usually five or six cards per deck is optimum.

i-Mode

Another technology similar to WAP is known as **i-mode**. i-mode is an Internet access system owned by the Japanese corporation NTT DoCoMo, and it is based on **compact HTML (cHTML)**, a subset of HTML designed for mobile devices. cHTML has its own set of tags and attributes.

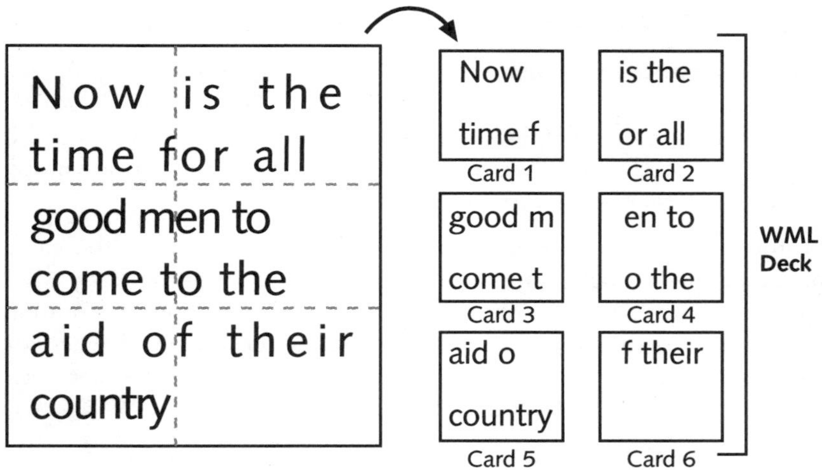

Figure 8-13 WML deck

In addition to cHTML tags, there are special i-mode tags, such us a tag to set up a link that dials a telephone number when pressed. There are also special DoCoMo character symbols for sadness, joy, and love.

Although i-mode is similar to WAP in terms of its functionality, there are several differences between them. i-mode uses cHTML instead of WML. Also, i-mode users are charged for the service by the amount of information downloaded plus a service charge, while WAP services are charged by the connection time. It is expected that i-mode and WAP will merge in the future into one technology.

Java

Java is a programming language that was developed by Sun Microsystems as an object-oriented language used for general-purpose business programming as well as interactive Web sites. Java is designed to run on almost any hardware platform. A subset of Java was specifically developed for programming wireless devices. This is known as **Java 2 Micro Edition (J2ME)**.

J2ME-enabled cellular telephones have more "intelligence" than basic digital cellular telephones that run a WAP microbrowser or i-mode. WAP and i-mode display only text and do not have the ability to manipulate data or perform applications. They also must always be connected to a server. J2ME, on the other hand, enables a cellular phone to access remote applications and e-mail as well as run programs on the cellular phone itself. These programs include voice-activated dialing, date books, and voice recorders. The cellular phone can actually be programmed to handle specific tasks. For example, a J2ME-enabled cellular phone can automatically turn off the ringer and forward any calls to voicemail whenever the user is in a meeting that has been entered into the phone's appointment book.

Binary Runtime Environment for Wireless (BREW)

The **Binary Runtime Environment for Wireless (BREW)** is different from the other digital cellular client software. Whereas WAP and i-mode are browsers and J2ME is a programming language, BREW is a runtime environment. This is a thin software interface layer that resides on a wireless device. It allows users to download programs over the air and run them on BREW-enabled devices.

BREW is noted as being efficient in its use of scarce memory on the cellular phone. BREW occupies only a small amount of flash memory and it dynamically allocates RAM for applications when they are running. BREW can also be used in combination with other applications and software elements that may reside on the device. For example, BREW can be installed on a device that already has an operating system installed. And any type of browser (HTML, WAP, cHTML, etc.) can run on BREW as an application.

Although WAP and i-mode do allow users remote access to the Internet, the fact that they do not support a rich set of graphics limits their popularity. Most industry experts predict that J2ME and BREW will be the major platforms for a variety of wireless devices even beyond digital cellular telephones.

Digital Cellular Issues and Outlook

Although some claim that digital cellular telephony is poised to sweep across the world and make major changes to the daily lives of its citizens, that optimism is far from unanimous. After years of promises, many industry experts are growing skeptical regarding some of the promises attributed to digital cellular telephony. Although everyone agrees that this technology will have an impact on how people work and play, the questions of when and how big a role digital cellular telephony will play are hotly debated.

There are several issues that face digital cellular telephony that prevent its rapid acceptance. These include competing technologies, limited spectrum availability, high infrastructure costs, and competition from other wireless options.

Competing Technologies

It is clear that there is no single road to 3G digital telephony. In Europe, it appears that WCDMA will become the standard, whereas in China and South Korea CDMA2000 seems to be the choice. Japan is leaning towards WCDMA. In the U.S., both 3G technologies, WCDMA and CDMA2000, are contenders.

Because these competing technologies are incompatible with each other, the goal of creating one global digital cellular network seems out of reach. And the competition between these technologies is only confusing consumers. The competition has also made consumers reluctant to pay for a technology that may not become the standard. In short, the competition between the different technologies has become a major hindrance to the acceptance of the next generation of digital cellular telephony.

Limited Spectrum

The single largest factor limiting the development of 3G is spectrum. This is especially apparent in the U.S., where a shortage of frequencies may seriously undermine 3G implementation. Although 3G can operate at almost any spectrum, an effort has been underway to designate the same part of the spectrum for 3G communications around the world. This would support using 3G from anywhere on the planet. Currently, 1.710 to 1.855 GHz and 2.520 to 2.670 GHz are designated as the worldwide spectrum to be used for 3G.

However, the U.S. Department of Defense currently uses the 1.7 GHz band for satellite control and military purposes. It is estimated that moving this to another part of the spectrum would cost billions of dollars and could take up to 15 years to complete. And sharing the spectrum between the carriers and the Department of Defense is not a viable option.

The FCC has started opening up other parts of the spectrum for 3G use. In late 2001, it determined that frequencies used by instructional television fixed services (ITFS) could also be used by 3G wireless carriers.

Another problem in addition to spectrum conflict is the need for additional spectrum. As more users began to use more 3G services, the amount of spectrum necessary to accommodate the users will increase. Even if the U.S. Department of Defense can move to another part of the spectrum, will that leave enough to meet the needs? It is unclear how this will be resolved.

Costs

The costs for 3G technology are also a drawback to its acceptance. It is estimated that 3G cellular telephones may cost as much as $300, in addition to the monthly service fees that could run as high as $90 per month. Compared with the very low costs of 2G digital cellular service and devices today, many are asking if that sharp price increase is worth the additional functionality that 3G provides.

The user's costs for 3G pales in comparison to the billions of dollars in costs for the carriers to build entire 3G networks. Just the cost of buying the spectrum itself for 3G networks is mind-boggling. In early 2001, carriers in Germany paid over $46 billion for licenses to use the spectrum. Carriers in other nations face similar costs. And that's just the starting point in building a 3G network. New base stations and transmitters must all be factored into the equation as well. Yet after investing huge sums into 3G, the carriers still face the question of consumer interest. What if they build it but nobody comes?

Other Wireless Options

Like Bluetooth and IrDA, 3G networks are faced with competition from other wireless technologies. The top speed for a 3G user is 2 Mbps when the user is standing still. However, 802.11a WLANs offer speeds of over 100 Mbps even when the user is mobile. Although the coverage area of a single WLAN is far less than a digital cellular network, deploying multiple access points can create large areas of coverage with high bandwidth and still provide mobility. And all of this is at a fraction of the cost of building a 3G network.

These other options have led several carriers to change their way of thinking. Some carriers are installing less-expensive WLANs in high-traffic "hot spots" in selected cities around the country as an alternative to investing in 3G. This permits them to provide mobile services today using a relatively inexpensive yet stable technology.

Some industry experts predict that mobile data access will be provided by WLAN networks that carriers build in high areas of concentrations, such as the downtown area of a city. The outlying areas and sparsely populated regions would be covered by 3G. Several cellular telephone vendors have already started developing mobile phones that support both 3G and IEEE WLANs.

Chapter Summary

- Cellular telephones work differently than wired telephones. There are two keys to cellular telephone networks. The first is that the coverage area is divided into smaller individual sections called cells. At the center of each cell is a cell transmitter to which the mobile devices in that cell send and receive radio frequency (RF) signals. The second key to cellular telephone networks is that all of the transmitters and cell phones operate at a low power level. This enables the signal to stay confined to the cell and not interfere with any other cells. Because the signal at a specific frequency does not go outside of the cell area, that same frequency can be used in other cells at the same time. All cell phones have special codes associated with them. These codes are used to identify the phone, the phone's owner and the carrier or service provider (such as AT&T, Sprint, and many others).
- When a cellular telephone user moves around within the same cell, the transmitter and base station for that cell handle all of the transmissions. As the user moves toward another cell, the cellular telephone will automatically associate with the base station of that cell. This is known as a handoff. If a cellular user moves beyond the coverage area of the entire cellular network, the cellular telephone would automatically connect with whatever cellular network was in place in the remote area. The cellular network in the remote area would communicate with that in the home area verifying that the user can make calls and also charge for the calls. This is known as roaming.
- The first generation of wireless cellular technology is known as 1G. 1G uses analog signals, which are radio frequency (RF) transmissions with a maximum transmission speed of 9.6 Kbps. 1G technology is based on the Advanced Mobile Phone Service (AMPS) standard. AMPS operates in the 800-900 MHz frequency spectrum and uses Frequency Division Multiple Access (FDMA). 1G networks use circuit-switching technology.
- The 2G generation of cellular telephony started in the early 1990s and continues to the present. 2G networks transmit data between 9.6 Kbps and 14.4 Kbps in the 800 MHz and 1.9 GHz frequencies. The only major feature that 2G systems share

with 1G is that they are circuit-switched networks. 2G systems use digital instead of analog transmissions. Another difference between 1G and 2G systems is that 2G systems use three different multiple access technologies: Time Division Multiple Access (TDMA), Code Division Multiple Access (CDMA), and GSM (Global Systems for Mobile communications). GSM was developed and is most popular in Europe. GSM uses a combination of FDMA and TDMA technologies.

- An interim generation, known as 2.5G, will serve as the stepping stone between 2G and the next full generation, 3G. 2.5G networks operate at a maximum speed of 384 Kbps. At the present time, 2.5G networks are sparsely deployed in only a handful nations.
- The primary difference between 2G and 2.5G networks is that 2.5G networks are packet-switched instead of circuit-switched. Although circuit switching is ideal for voice communications, it is not efficient for transmitting data.
- There are currently three different 2.5G network technologies. The migration from an existing 2G network to a 2.5G network depends on which 2G network technology is being used. For TDMA or GSM 2G networks, the next step would be to a 2.5G technology, known as General Packet Radio Service (GPRS). The next step beyond GPRS is Enhanced Data Rates for Global Evolution (EDGE). EDGE is considered a "booster" for GPRS systems and can transmit up to 384 Kbps. EDGE, like GPRS, will be based on an entirely new modulation technique. If the network transition is from a 2G CDMA network, instead of migrating to GPRS the transition instead would be to CDMA2000 1XRTT. CDMA2000 1XRTT is designed to support 144 Kbps packet data transmission and to double the voice capacity of current generation CDMA networks.
- 3G networks will provide new or expanded applications and features to mobile users. Because the networks are based on digital rather than analog technology and can transmit at much higher speeds, they will not be limited to voice communications. Before the next big step to 3G, there must be major changes to the network infrastructures as well as a new generation of mobile cellular devices.
- One of the most widely used applications in Europe and Japan is Short Message Services (SMS). SMS allows for the delivery of short, text-based messages between wireless devices such as cellular telephones and pagers.
- In order for the various features, such as Internet surfing or videoconferencing, to operate on a wireless digital cellular device, there must be client software that functions on the cell phone. Some of the client software that is used on digital cellular telephones is unique to cellular telephones while other software is used in a variety of different applications. Wireless Application Protocol (WAP) provides a standard way to transmit, format and display Internet data for devices like cell phones. WAP-enabled devices do not display a rich user interface with graphics, images, and animation; instead, only textual data is displayed. This limitation is due to the slower transmission speed and smaller viewing areas of cellular telephones. A WAP cell phone runs a tiny browser program called a microbrowser that uses Wireless Markup Language (WML) instead of HTML to display text-based Web content on the small screen of a cell phone. However, since the Internet standard is HTML, a WAP Gateway must translate between WML and HTML.

- Another client technology similar to WAP is known as i-mode. i-mode is based on compact HTML (cHTML), which is a subset of HTML designed for mobile devices. cHTML has its own set of tags and attributes. Although i-mode is similar to WAP in terms of its functionality, there are several differences between them. It is expected that i-mode and WAP will merge in the future into one technology.
- Java 2 Micro Edition (J2ME) is a subset of Java specifically developed for programming wireless devices. J2ME-enabled cellular telephones have more "intelligence" than basic digital cellular telephones that run a WAP microbrowser or i-mode. J2ME enables a cellular phone to access remote applications and e-mail as well as run programs on the cellular phone itself.
- Binary Runtime Environment for Wireless (BREW) is different from other digital cellular client software. Whereas WAP and i-mode are browsers and J2ME is a programming language, BREW is a runtime environment. This is a thin software interface layer that resides on a wireless device. It allows users to download programs over the air and run them on BREW-enabled devices.
- There are several issues that prevent the rapid acceptance of advanced generations of digital cellular telephony: competing cellular technologies and lack of standards, spectrum limitations, and the high costs of implementing 3G technology.
- 3G networks are also faced with competition from other wireless technologies. The top speed for a 3G user is 2 Mbps when the user is standing still. However, 802.11a WLANs offer speeds of over 100 Mbps even when the user is mobile. Some carriers are installing less-expensive WLANs in high-traffic "hot spots" in selected cities around the country as an alternative to investing in 3G. This permits them to provide mobile services today using a relatively inexpensive yet stable technology.

Key Terms

2.5 Generation (2.5G) — An interim step between 2G and 3G digital cellular networks.

Advanced Mobile Phone Service (AMPS) — The standard used for 1G analog cellular transmissions based on FDMA.

Binary Runtime Environment for Wireless (BREW) — This is a thin software interface layer that resides on a wireless device and creates a runtime environment.

cards — A smaller block of a WML document.

cells — A smaller area of a mobile network.

CDMA2000 1XEVDO — The 3G digital cellular technology that is a migration from CDMA2000 1XRTT.

CDMA2000 1XEVDV — The 3G digital cellular technology that is a migration from CDMA2000 1XEVDO.

CDMA2000 1XRTT — A 2.5G digital cellular network technology that is a migration from CDMA.

compact HTML (cHTML) — A subset of HTML that is designed for mobile devices

control channel — A special frequency cellular phones use for communication with a base station.

deck — A WML document.

Enhanced Data Rates for Global Evolution (EDGE) — A 2.5G digital cellular network technology that boosts GPRS transmissions.

Extensible Markup Language (XML) — A definition language that uses tags to describe the data.

First Generation (1G) — The first generation of wireless cellular telephony that transmitted at 9.6 Kbps using analog circuit-switched technology.

General Packet Radio Service (GPRS) — A 2.5G network technology that can transmit up to 40 Kbps.

GSM (Global Systems for Mobile communications) — One of three multiple access technologies that make up the 2G digital cellular system that uses a combination of FDMA and TDMA

handoff — The automatic transfer of the RF signal when moving from one cell to another cell within the same network.

i-mode — An Internet access system for digital cellular telephones.

Java — An object-oriented programming language used for general-purpose business programming and interactive Web sites.

Java 2 Micro Edition (J2ME) — A subset of Java specifically developed for programming wireless devices.

mobile telecommunications switching office (MTSO) — The connection between a cellular network and wired telephones.

roaming — The automatic transfer of the RF signal when moving from one cellular network to another network.

Second Generation (2G) — The second generation of cellular telephony that uses circuit-switched digital networks.

Short Message Services (SMS) — A delivery system for short, text-based messages sent between wireless devices such as cellular telephones and pagers.

Third Generation (3G) — Digital cellular wireless generation of cellular telephony with speeds up to 2 Mbps.

Wideband CDMA (WCDMA) — The 3G digital cellular technology that is a migration from EDGE.

Review Questions

1. The area of a cell is approximately how many square miles?
   a. 5
   b. 10
   c. 30
   d. 40

2. The device that connects the base stations with the wired telephone network is the ________________.
   a. transmitter
   b. cell phone
   c. MTSO
   d. CDMA
3. Each of the following is a valid cellular telephone code except ________________.
   a. System Identification Code (SID)
   b. Electronic Serial Number (ESN)
   c. Digital Serial Code (DSC)
   d. Mobile Identification Number (MIN)
4. ________________ occurs when a user begins moving towards another cell and the phone automatically associates with the base station of that cell.
   a. Roaming
   b. Handoff
   c. Hunting
   d. Multiplexing
5. The special frequency that a cellular phone and base station use for exchanging setup information is ________________.
   a. WCDMA
   b. cell tunnel
   c. control channel
   d. GB line
6. First Generation (1G) networks use analog signals and the maximum transmission speed is 9.6 Kbps. True or false?
7. 1G technology is based on Advanced Mobile Phone Service (AMPS). True or false?
8. Division by frequency, so that each caller is allocated part of the spectrum for all of the time, is the basis of TDMA. True or false?
9. 2G systems use digital instead of analog transmissions. True or false?
10. There are two different technologies that are used with 2G—WCDMA and CDMA2000. True or false?
11. The primary difference between 2G and 2.5G networks is that 2.5G networks are ________________ instead of circuit-switched networks.
12. When migrating from a TDMA or GSM network, the next step would be to a ________________.
13. ________________ is considered a "booster" for GPRS systems and can transmit up to 384 Kbps.

14. ________________ Generation is intended to be a uniform and global worldwide standard for cellular wireless communication.
15. What is Short Message Service (SMS)?
16. Explain how WAP works.
17. What are WML decks and cards?
18. What are differences between WAP and i-mode?
19. What are some advantages of Java 2 Micro Edition (J2ME)?
20. What is BREW? How is it different from other client software?

Hands-on Projects

1. Not all industry experts agree regarding the path to 3G. Using Figure 8-8 as the benchmark, conduct research to determine what other experts are predicting is the road to 3G. Based on your research, draw and label another alternative diagram entitled "The Road to 3G." Include updated dates regarding when these technologies are predicted to be in place.
2. Writing a WML application is not as difficult as it may seem. Using the Internet, find information about this new language for WAP-enabled devices. There are also several WAP emulators available on the Internet. Using one of these, write a short application that will display your name and today's date using WML. What problems did you encounter? How is it similar to other languages with which you may be familiar? What are the new features proposed for the next version of WML? Write a one-page paper on your research and include your WML application.
3. Extensive Markup Language (XML), which is the basis for WML, has become a key component in computers today. Even this textbook was written using XML. Using the Internet, research XML. What are its origins? How exactly does it differ from other descriptive languages? What are its strengths and weaknesses? Write a one-page paper on your findings. List five applications in which it is being used.
4. Just as the industry is divided regarding what digital cellular technologies will be found in the future, there is also concern about listed data rates. Several studies are revealing that there is a wide gap between the advertised data rates, such as 2 Mbps for a stationary user using 3G technology, and the actual rate, which may be much less. Using the Internet and other sources, find what the real speed of the 1G is through 3G technologies. Recreate Table 8-3 and add another column entitled "Actual Speed." Include a paragraph that explains why these speeds may actually be slower than the advertised speed. In your opinion, which figures should be used when comparing these technologies?
5. There are a variety of client software programs that can be used in addition to WAP, i-mode, J2ME, and BREW. These include Web Clipping, Microsoft.NET Mobile Internet Toolkit, Handheld Devices Markup Languages (HDML), and EPOC. Using the Internet and other sources, review three new client software

programs. Outline their strengths, weakness, and which applications they are most often found in. How do they compare against WAP, i-mode, J2ME, and BREW? Write a one-page paper on your findings.

CASE PROJECTS

The Baypoint Group

The Baypoint Group (TBG), a company of 50 consultants who assist organizations and businesses with issues involving network planning and design, has again requested your services as a consultant. Hunt Real Estate wants to supply all of its agents with WAP-enabled digital cellular telephones. The goal is to provide better support to agents who are showing houses to prospective buyers. The agents would be able to receive up-to-the-minute information about new listings, mortgage rates, and other vital information. However, not all of the agents are sold on the idea yet. TBG has asked you to help.

1. Create a presentation outlining the advantages of using a digital cellular telephone for Hunt Real Estate. Research the type of information that real estate agents need to know and show them how this could help them. Also, explain what WAP can do and how it works. Because this is not a highly technical group, be sure that your presentation is not too technical. Limit yourself to a maximum of 15 PowerPoint slides.
2. John Hunt, the president of Hunt Real Estate, was convinced by your presentation. However, John has heard about 3G and wants to know how this will affect their plans to purchase 2G equipment. TBG has asked you to create another presentation for John that explains the different generations of cellular technology. Create a PowerPoint presentation of 15–18 slides.

OPTIONAL TEAM CASE PROJECT

Hunt Real Estate is unsure if WAP is the technology they should invest in. They are considering i-mode, J2ME, and BREW as alternatives. Form a team of four individuals with each person selecting one of these technologies. Research in depth the advantages and disadvantages of these respective technologies and how they work. Hold a friendly debate in which each person presents a 5 minute talk about the advantages of his technology. After the talk allow time for the others to ask questions. Be prepared to defend your technology, knowing that the other individuals will be aware of its disadvantages.

CHAPTER

9

FIXED WIRELESS

After reading this chapter and completing the exercises, you will be able to:

- Define fixed wireless
- Explain the features of a remote wireless bridge
- List and describe three types of land-based fixed broadband wireless devices
- Tell how satellite transmissions work

Fixed broadband wireless, another wide area network (WAN) technology, is becoming a very popular choice today when transmissions must be sent over long distances but a wired option is either unavailable or is too expensive. In this chapter, we will explore the different types of fixed broadband wireless transmissions available today. These include remote wireless bridges, free space optics, Local Multipoint Distribution Service (LMDS), Multichannel Multipoint Distribution Service (MMDS), and satellite transmissions. First, we will define exactly what fixed wireless is.

What Is Fixed Wireless?

At first glance the expression *fixed wireless* seems to be puzzling. After all, mobility is the primary benefit of wireless devices. If a device is positioned or fixed in one location, couldn't it just as easily, and sometimes even more inexpensively, be connected by a wire to a network? Why would anyone need a "fixed wireless" device? The answer is that the term "fixed wireless" does not refer to mobile devices that can be *either* in a fixed location or be mobile. Instead, fixed wireless refers to wireless transmissions between devices that *cannot* be mobile. Fixed wireless typically refers to wireless communication between two or more office buildings.

Fixed wireless has become an extremely popular technology today for use in both home and business settings. The reason for its popularity is due to a major stumbling block with wired access to the Internet and other high-speed data networks, a problem known as the **last mile connection**. This refers to the connection that begins at a fast service provider, goes through the local neighborhood, and ends at the home or office. Whereas the connections that make up the nation's data transmission infrastructure are very fast and well established, the last mile connection that links these high-speed transmission lines to the home or office are much slower and not universally available. This is illustrated in Figure 9-1. These slow last mile connections are bottlenecks for users: any high-speed traffic must be throttled back to the slow speed of the last mile connection, which reduces the overall speed of the connection. Having the fastest last mile connection available is important because it provides the fastest total connection for the user. And a fast connection translates into saving time, and saving time means saving money.

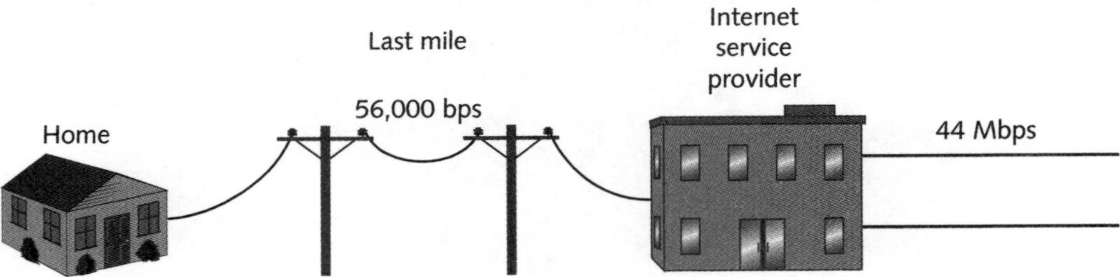

Figure 9-1 Last mile connection

Last Mile Wired Connections

There are a variety of last mile wired connections for home or office. For home users, there are currently three popular choices for the last mile wired connection between the home and an Internet service provider (ISP):

- A standard dial-up modem using telephone lines that can transmit at a top speed of 56 Kbps
- A cable modem, which can transmit up to 1.5 Mbps
- Digital Subscriber Line (DSL), which also can transmit up to 1.5 Mbps

However, these choices available to home users are generally not available or are unsuitable for business users in an office building setting. Connecting a dial-up modem to each user's computer in an office building for a 56 Kbps connection is simply out of the question. Almost no office buildings are wired for cable reception and thus cannot use a cable modem. DSL connections require that the building be within 12,000 feet (3.5 kilometers) of a telephone company's central office. Less than half of the office buildings in the U.S. meet that requirement.

Businesses in office buildings have taken a different route for their last mile connection. Some use **Integrated Services Digital Connection (ISDN)**, which is available from the local telephone carrier. ISDN can transmit on two channels at 64 Kbps or on four channels at 128 Kbps. Another option is to lease a special high-speed connection from the local telephone carrier, known as a **T1** connection (1.544 Mbps). Another leased option is a **T3** (44.736 Mbps) connection. Connections with even higher speeds usually require fiber optic cable, yet fewer than 10 percent of the buildings in the U.S. have fiber connected to them. Table 9-1 summarizes the connection options for homes and office buildings.

The T-carrier system, introduced by Bell Telephone in the U.S. in the 1960s, was the first successful system that supported digitized voice transmission.

9

Table 9-1 Connection options

Transmission Type	Speed	Typical Use	Time to transmit contents of one 680 MB CD-ROM (hours:minutes)
Dial-up modem	28 Kbps	Home	53:43
Dial-up modem	56 Kbps	Home	26:53
1 channel ISDN	64 Kbps	Home or office	24:10
2 channel ISDN	128 Kbps	Home or office	12:50
Cable modem	1 Mbps	Home	1:36
DSL	1.544 Mbps	Home	0:58
T1	1.544 Mbps	Office	0:58
T3	44.736 Mbps	Office, ISP	0:2
OC-12	622.08 Mbps	ISP	8 seconds
OC-256	13.271 Gbps	Internet backbone	Less than 1 second

Last Mile Wireless Connections

As an alternative to these last mile wired connections, many users and businesses have turned to wireless options. The advantages of last mile wireless connections are that they can cost less, can be installed faster, offer greater flexibility, and have better reliability. Using wireless as the last mile connection for buildings is called **fixed wireless**. It is *fixed* because the buildings are fixed in one position and are not mobile.

Although the term fixed wireless is fairly recent, the technology has been in use for several years. Fixed wireless networks have been used for both voice and data communications, generally in backhaul networks operated by telephone companies, cable TV companies, utilities, railways, paging companies, and government agencies. A **backhaul** connection is a company's internal infrastructure connection. For example, a phone company's backhaul network may be a connection from one telephone company central office to another. Today, fixed wireless broadband systems can be used to transmit almost anything that can be sent over any wired cable system, such as a T1 line, a cable television cable, a local area network connection, or a fiber optic cable.

Baseband vs. Broadband

There are two ways in which a signal can be transmitted. The first technique is called **broadband**. A broadband transmission sends multiple signals at different frequencies. This allows many different signals to be sent simultaneously. The second technique is called **baseband**. A baseband transmission treats the entire transmission medium as if it were only one channel. The signals are transmitted at one set frequency, allowing only one signal to be sent at a time. This is illustrated in Figure 9-2. By using broadband technology, fixed wireless systems can send and receive multiple signals simultaneously.

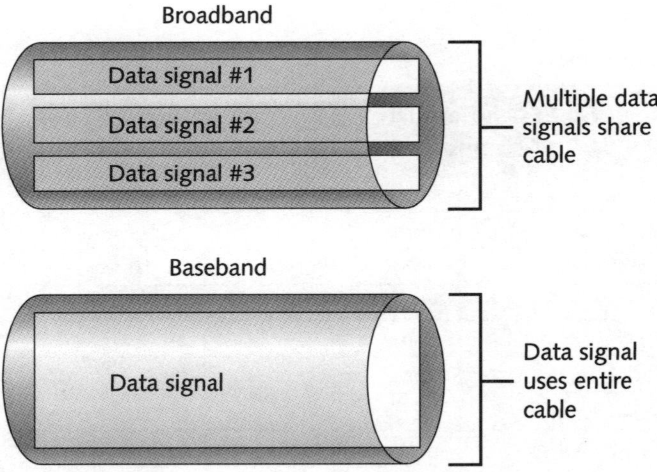

Figure 9-2 Baseband and broadband transmissions

Computer local area networks use baseband transmission. The names of some networks use the word "base," which stands for baseband. An example is Ethernet 100Base-T.

Providers

Fixed broadband wireless service can be obtained in two ways. First, it can be designed, installed, and managed by a private individual or owner of a building. A second method is to purchase the service from a wireless carrier. Some carriers install a fixed broadband wireless system on the roof of a building and then sell their communications services to the tenants of the building. These services are standard networking services and include network management, Internet access, Web hosting, and e-mail. The fact that these carriers use fixed broadband wireless technology is transparent to the user.

Frequency

Fixed broadband wireless systems use frequencies allocated for that specific use. These frequencies range from 900 MHz to 40 GHz. Improvements in technology over the years has had a major impact on fixed broadband wireless and this has been especially significant in the area of which frequencies can be used for transmissions. Today, higher frequencies can be used than those used in the past. This has resulted in two advantages. First, the use of a higher frequency requires a smaller antenna to send and receive signals. Use of a smaller antenna results in lower costs and wireless components that are easier to install and manage. A second advantage of higher frequencies is that more spectrum is available for all broadband use. Because users require less of a higher spectrum to send and receive, there is more spectrum available.

However, there are disadvantages to using higher frequencies. One disadvantage is that the components require more sophisticated technology and thus the systems are more expensive. Also, a higher-frequency signal may be more susceptible to weather conditions like rain and fog.

Not all parts of these frequencies are available to all users. Some frequency bands are assigned for private use while others are assigned for only carrier use. Within the private and carrier portions, some bands require a license to be obtained for use while other bands can be used without a license. This is illustrated in Figure 9-3.

Carrier Use		Private Use	
Licensed	Unlicensed	Licensed	Unlicensed

Figure 9-3 Frequency spectrum

Both private and carrier systems have a choice of using either a licensed or unlicensed spectrum. A private user could set up a fixed wireless system and use the private spectrum frequency without obtaining a license. Or, he could set up a system, obtain a license, and use a separate frequency. A carrier can do the same within the carrier frequency spectrum. The advantage of using the unlicensed spectrum is that it does not require a license from the FCC. The disadvantage is that the unlicensed spectrum is open to any user without a license. Interference from other systems on the unlicensed spectrum can be difficult to correct.

Limitations

There are three limitations of fixed broadband wireless. These are described below and illustrated in Figure 9-4.

- Fixed broadband wireless systems operate at frequencies that require line of sight. Unlike cellular wireless systems, fixed broadband wireless systems use stationary antennas with narrowly focused beams. Dish antennas that send and receive the signals are typically located at the top of buildings and towers to eliminate any interference from taller objects.
- The distance between devices is limited. Most fixed broadband wireless systems can transmit from a few miles up to 35 miles (56 kilometers).
- Fixed wireless broadband systems can only send from one device to one other device, unlike cellular wireless systems in which a single base station can communicate with many mobile devices.

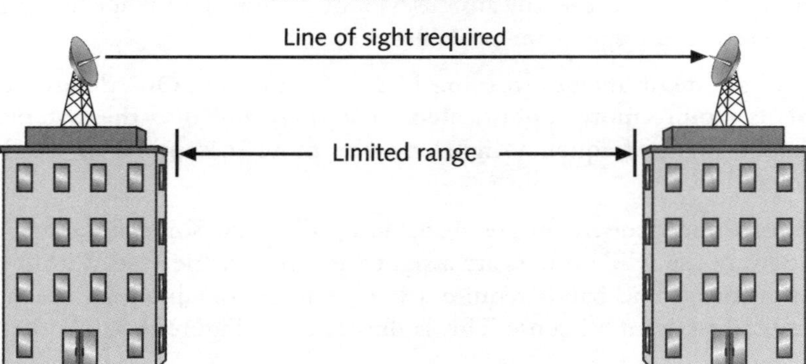

Figure 9-4 Fixed broadband wireless limitations

The IEEE committee 802.16 is currently working to develop standards for broadband wireless transmissions.

Land-Based Fixed Baseband Wireless

Of the available land-based systems, fixed wireless networks fall into two categories: baseband transmissions and broadband transmissions. In this section, the only current baseband transmission technology, remote wireless bridges, will be explored.

Remote Wireless Bridge

A **remote wireless bridge** is designed to connect two or more baseband networks that are located in different buildings. A **bridge** is a device that is used to connect two network segments even if those segments are using different types of physical media, such as wired and wireless connections. These remote wireless bridges are ideal solutions for connecting sites such as satellite offices, remote campus settings, or temporary office locations when the sites are separated by obstacles such as bodies of water, freeways, or railroads that make using a wired connection impractical or very expensive. The distance between buildings can be up to 18 miles (29 kilometers) transmitting at 11 Mbps or up to 25 miles (40 kilometers) when transmitting at 2 Mbps.

At 11 Mbps, remote wireless bridges are seven times faster than traditional T1 connections.

Remote wireless bridges have the same essential characteristics as IEEE 802.11b WLANs (see Table 9-2), with two important exceptions. First, remote wireless bridges transmit at a higher power than WLANs, typically 100 mW instead of the 30 mW used by 802.11b systems. Second, remote wireless bridges use directional antennas as well as the standard omnidirectional antennas. This allows the remote wireless bridge to focus its transmission in a single direction. Both of these differences are actually permitted within the IEEE 802.11b standards, so remote wireless bridges are correctly advertised as following the standard. However, an 802.11b access point could not be used in place of a remote wireless bridge. WLANs have a limited range due to the lower power level, and WLANs primarily communicate with mobile clients and not with another access point (AP) or similar device.

Table 9-2 Remote wireless bridge specifications

Characteristic	Specification
Data rates	1, 2, 5.5 and 11 Mbps
Wireless medium	Direct Sequence Spread Spectrum (DSSS)
Channel access method	CSMA/CD
Modulation	DBPSK (1 Mbps) DQPSK (2 Mbps) CCK (5.5 Mbps, 11 Mbps)
Security	WEP
Frequency	2.4 GHz
Channels	11 (U.S.) 13 (Europe)

As with a WLAN, the "heart" of a remote wireless bridge is a device that looks similar to an AP, as seen in Figure 9-5. This device, called a bridge instead of an AP, is responsible for sending and receiving the signals. Bridges typically have the same connections as an AP, which include a wired network connection to connect it to a standard wired Ethernet network and a serial port for configuring the bridge. However, some bridges may be accessed over the LAN connection for configuration. The bridge also contains special software for transmitting and receiving the signals. Most bridges have what is

9

known as delay spread that minimizes the spread of the signal so that it can reach farther distances. Bridges also have software that enables them to select the clearest transmission channel and avoid noise and interference.

Figure 9-5 Remote wireless bridge

Remote wireless bridges support two types of connections. The first is a point-to-point configuration. This configuration is used to connect two LAN segments over distance, as seen in Figure 9-6. The LAN segments can be either wired or wireless. The second configuration is a point-to-multipoint configuration. This is used to connect multiple LAN segments together, as seen in Figure 9-7. Remote wireless bridges can only communicate with other remote wireless bridges and cannot talk directly with the network clients. However, some bridge manufacturers allow the wireless bridge to also be configured as an AP. This allows the bridge to simultaneously communicate with other remote wireless bridges and to send and receive signals with the mobile clients in its area, as seen in Figure 9-8.

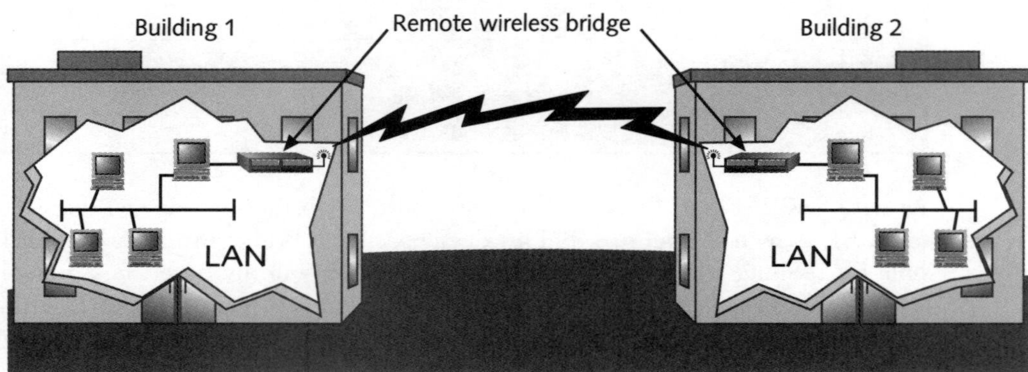

Figure 9-6 Point-to-point remote wireless bridge

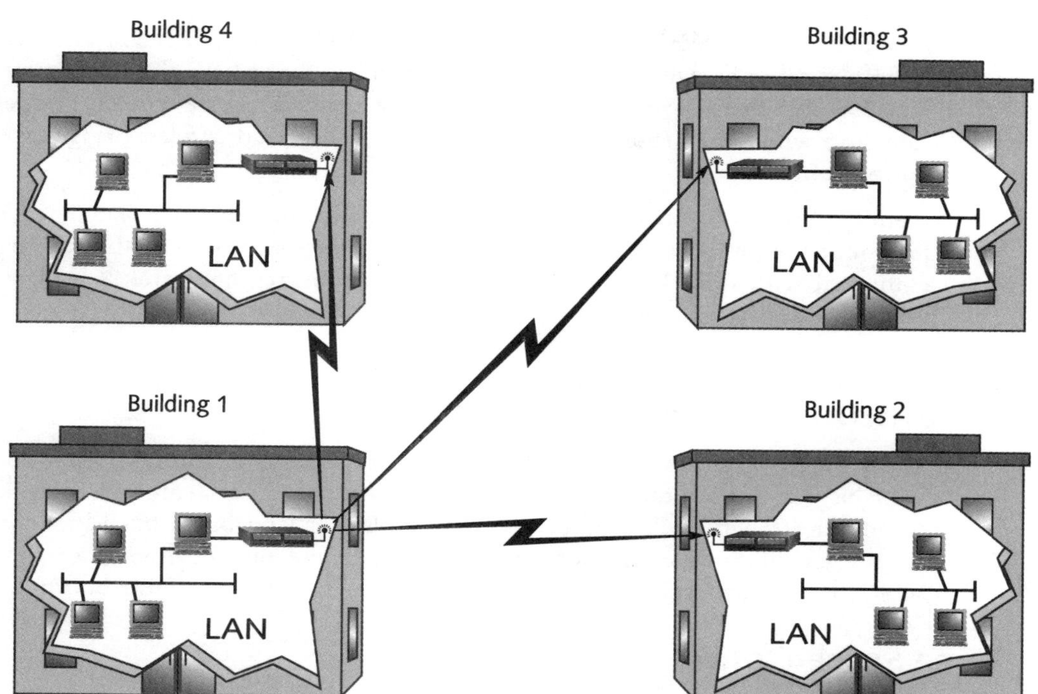

Figure 9-7 Point-to-multipoint remote wireless bridge

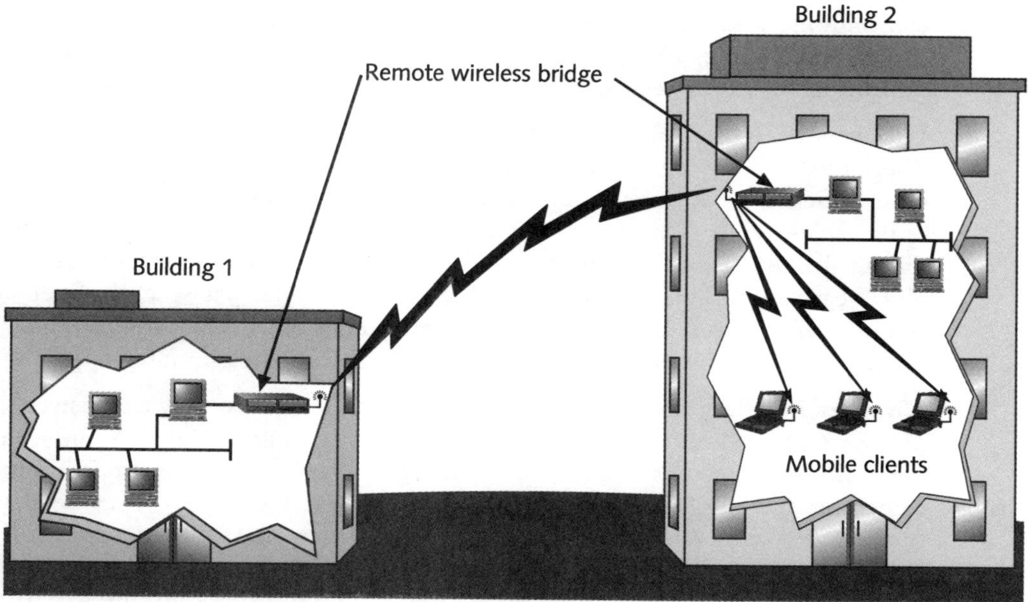

Figure 9-8 Wireless bridge as access point

9

In addition to radio frequency (RF) remote wireless bridges, there are also infrared (IR) remote wireless bridges. Because IR transmissions do not have the same security problems as RF, businesses and the military often use infrared remote wireless bridges in environments where the privacy of the data is essential. Infrared wireless bridges can transmit up to 10 Mbps.

Remote wireless bridges are an excellent alternative to expensive leased wired options for connecting remote buildings. With transmissions speeds of 11 Mbps up to 18 miles, compared with only 1.54 Mbps for T1 connections, remote wireless bridges are very popular in today's market.

LAND-BASED FIXED BROADBAND WIRELESS

You've seen how land-based fixed baseband systems are quite similar to 802.11b WLANs, except that they transmit at higher power and use remote wireless bridges to communicate between wired or wireless LANs. For land-based fixed broadband, there are several different transmission technologies. These include free space optics, Local Multipoint Distribution Service, and Multichannel Multipoint Distribution Service.

Free Space Optics

Free space optics (FSO) is an optical, wireless, point-to-point, line-of-sight broadband technology. Although it was originally developed over 30 years ago by the military, FSO has become an excellent alternative to high-speed fiber optic cable. Currently, FSO can transmit at speeds comparable to fiber optic transmissions of up to 1.25 Gbps at a distance of 4 miles (6.4 kilometers) in full-duplex mode. It is projected that future improvements in the technology will push the top speed to hundreds of Gbps.

FSO uses IR transmission instead of RF. FSO technology is similar to that used with a fiber optic cable system. A fiber optic cable contains a very thin strand of glass called the core, which is as thick as a human hair. Instead of transmitting electrical signals, fiber optic cables use light impulses. A light source, usually created by a laser or light emitting diodes (LEDs), flashes a light at one end of the cable that is detected at the receiving end. Because the light travels so quickly (186,000 miles per second), fiber optic cable systems can transmit large amounts of data at high speeds. In addition, these transmissions are immune to outside interference and cannot be easily intercepted.

However, installing fiber optic cables between buildings is a very expensive and lengthy process. Current costs to run a fiber optic cable can range as high as $3 million per mile, with almost 85 percent of that amount spent on digging trenches and installation. Street trenching and digging are not only expensive but they can also cause major traffic inconvenience, displace trees, and sometimes even mar or destroy historical areas. Because of these disruptions, some cities are even considering a moratorium on street trenching. And since laying fiber optic cable can be so time-consuming, with acquiring right-of-ways, moving existing buried utilities, and burying fiber optic cable, it is not uncommon for fiber optic installations to take six to eight months or more even between two buildings in close proximity.

FSO is an alternative to fiber optic cables. Sometimes called fiberless optical, FSO instead uses no medium like a fiber optic cable to send and receive signals. Instead, transmissions are sent by low-powered infrared beams through the open air. These beams, which do not harm the human eye, are transmitted by transceivers, as illustrated in Figure 9-9. Because FSO is a line-of-sight technology, the transceivers are mounted in the middle or upper floors of office buildings to provide a clear transmission path. However, unlike other technologies that require the units to be located on an open roof (which sometimes requires leasing roof space from the building's owner), FSO transceivers can be mounted behind a window in an existing office. FSO systems can carry full-duplex data at up to 1.25 Gbps over distances of several hundred meters to up to about 4 miles (6.4 kilometers).

Figure 9-9 FSO transceiver

Under perfect conditions FSO could transmit up to 6.2 miles (10 kilometers).

Recall that the lower-frequency portion of the electromagnetic spectrum is the area in which RF waves travel. The spectrum above 300 GHz is the area in which IR waves move. It is this part of the spectrum that FSO uses. This higher frequency is unlicensed worldwide, so it can be freely used without securing a license. The only limitation on its use is that the radiated power must not exceed specific limits in order to not harm the human eye.

FSO equipment works at either of two wavelengths. It is expected that there will be a single worldwide standard for these devices in the near future.

Advantages of FSO

There are several advantages of FSO:

- FSO installations cost significantly less than installing new fiber optic cables or even leasing lines from a local carrier. One recent project compared the costs of installing fiber optic cables to FSO in three buildings. The cost to install the fiber optic cables was almost $400,000, whereas the cost of FSO was less than $60,000.
- FSO can be installed in days or weeks compared to months or sometimes years for fiber optic cables. In some instances, FSO systems have been installed over a weekend in major office buildings with no disruption of service to the users.
- The transmission speed can be scaled to meet the user's needs, anywhere from 10 Mbps to 1.25 Gbps. If high speeds are not required, the user does not have to pay a premium for unused capacity but rather can have the FSO system designed to match the needs.
- Security is a key advantage in an FSO system. IR transmissions cannot be as easily intercepted and decoded as some RF transmissions.

Disadvantages of FSO

The primary disadvantage of FSO is that atmospheric conditions can have an impact on FSO transmissions. **Scintillation** is defined as the temporal and spatial variations in light intensity caused by atmospheric turbulence. Turbulence caused by wind and temperature variations can create pockets of air with rapidly changing densities. These air pockets can act like prisms and lenses to distort an FSO signal. Inclement weather is also a threat. Although rain and snow can distort a signal, fog does the most damage to transmissions. Fog is composed of extremely small moisture particles that act like prisms upon the light beam, scattering and breaking up the signal.

Scintillation is readily observed in the twinkling of stars in the night sky and the shimmering of the horizon on a hot day.

FSO overcomes scintillation by sending the data in parallel streams from several separate laser transmitters. These transmitters are all mounted in the same transceiver but separated from one another by distances of about 7.8 inches (200 mm). It is unlikely that while traveling to the receiver, all the parallel beams will encounter the same pocket of turbulence since the scintillation pockets are usually quite small. At least one of the beams will arrive at the target node with adequate strength to be properly received. This is called **spatial diversity**, because it exploits multiple regions of space. Spacial diversity is illustrated in Figure 9-10.

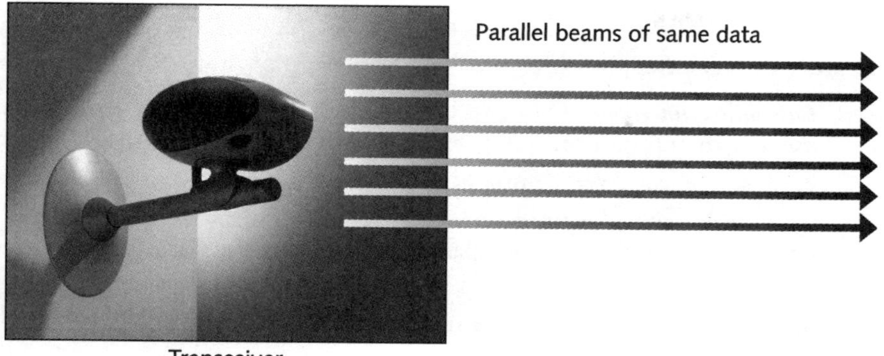

Figure 9-10 Spatial diversity

In dealing with fog, there are several potential solutions. One solution is to simply increase the transmitted power. In regions of heavy and frequent fogs, it may be necessary to choose FSOs that transmit at the highest available frequency because these devices can send at higher power levels. Several vendors also claim they customize their distance and product recommendations based on weather statistics for particular cities. Other FSO vendors use a backup system along with FSO to ensure that transmissions can go through in foggy weather.

In order to prove that FSO can send transmissions through fog, one vendor ran trials in some of the foggiest cities in the U.S.

Some experts recommend that the distance between FSO transceivers in regions of heavy and frequent fogs should be limited to 200 to 500 meters.

Signal interference can also be a potential problem for FSO, such as birds flying through the IR beam and blocking it. However, if the signal is temporarily blocked, the beam automatically reduces its power then raises itself to full power when the obstruction clears the beam's path.

Another problem is that tall buildings or towers can sway due to wind or seismic activity. Storms and earthquakes can also cause buildings to move enough to affect the aim of the beam. This problem can be handled in two ways. The first is known as beam divergence. With beam divergence, the transmitted beam is purposely allowed to spread or diverge so that by the time it arrives at the receiving device it forms a fairly large optical cone. If the receiver is initially positioned at the center of the beam, divergence can compensate for any movement of the buildings. The second method is through active tracking. Active tracking is based on movable mirrors that control the direction in which the beams are sent. A feedback mechanism continuously adjusts the mirrors so that the beams stay on target.

FSO Applications

There are a variety of applications for FSO. Some of the more common include:

- *Last mile connection*—FSO can be used in high-speed links that connect end-users with Internet service providers or other networks.
- *LAN connections*—Because of the ease with which FSO devices can be installed, they are a natural for interconnecting local area network segments that are housed in buildings yet are separated by public streets or other obstacles.
- *Fiber optic backup*—FSO can also be deployed in redundant links to back up fiber optic cables in case of a break in the cable.
- *Backhaul*—FSO can be used to carry cellular telephone traffic from antenna towers back to facilities wired into the public switched telephone network.

Most experts agree that FSO holds great potential for fixed wireless communications as well as for other wireless applications. It is predicted that FSO will start to become a major player in the wireless world within the next few years, particularly as technology improves to increase the transmission speed.

Local Multipoint Distribution Service (LMDS)

Local Multipoint Distribution Service (LMDS) is a fixed broadband technology that can provide a wide variety of wireless services. These services include high-speed Internet access, real-time multimedia file transfer, remote access to local area networks, interactive video, video-on-demand, video conferencing, and telephone service. LMDS can transmit from 51 to 155 Mbps downstream and 1.54 Mbps upstream over a distance of up to about 5 miles (8 kilometers).

Some industry experts predict that future speeds of LMDS may be as fast as 1.5 Gbps downstream and 200 Mbps upstream.

One of the best ways to describe LMDS is by examining each of the words that make up its name:

- *Local (L)* refers to the area of coverage of LMDS systems. Because it uses high frequency low-powered RF waves these have a limited range. The coverage area for LMDS is only between 2 to 5 miles (3.2 kilometers to 8 kilometers).

The U.S. Federal Communications Commission (FCC) grants LMDS licenses to carriers for a specific area.

- *Multipoint (M)* indicates that signals are transmitted out in a point-to-multipoint fashion. The signals that are transmitted back are point-to-point transmissions. This is illustrated in Figure 9-11.

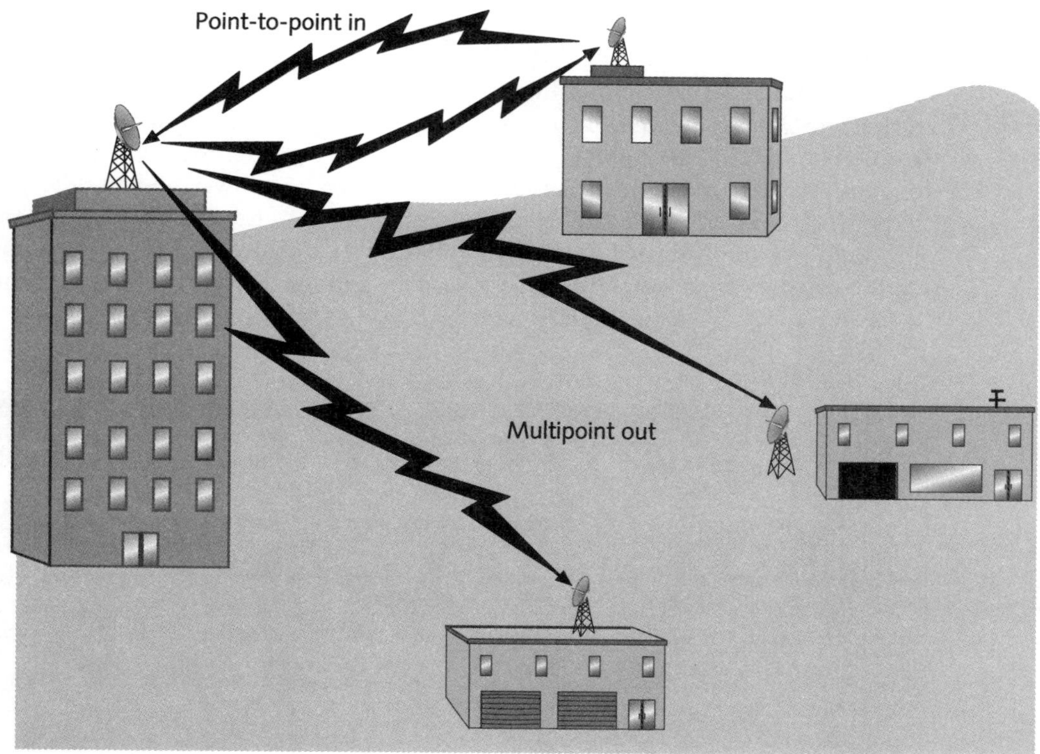

Figure 9-11 LMDS transmissions

- *Distribution (D)* refers to the distribution of the various types of information that can be transmitted. These include voice, data, Internet, and video traffic.
- *Service (S)* means that there are a variety of services available. However, the local carrier determines which services will be offered. Of all of the services that can be offered—voice, data, Internet, and video traffic—not all of them may be available to the local LMDS users. The services offered through an LMDS network are entirely dependent on the carrier.

LMDS is popular around the world. In Canada it is known as Local Multipoint Communication Systems (LMCS). Canada already has 3 GHz of spectrum set aside for LMDS and is actively setting up systems around the country. Many developing countries are using this technology as a way to bypass the expense of installing fiber optic cables.

9

Frequency

For many years communication technologies were focused on the lower part of the RF spectrum. This was because low frequency signals, when given enough power, can be sent long distances and penetrate even into buildings. Television and radio signals are examples of low frequency, high power signals.

Another type of RF wave is known as **microwaves**. Microwave transmissions take place in the 3 to 30 GHz range of the electromagnetic spectrum known as the **super high frequency (SHF)** band. This is illustrated in Table 9-3. Microwaves were originally used to transmit data in a point-to-point fashion, using the lower and middle part of the SHF band. The conventional thinking was that this low frequency, high-powered approach was the only way in which microwaves could be used for communication. High frequency microwave transmissions were ignored for many years and the section of the RF spectrum between 27.5 and 29.5 GHz went virtually unused.

Table 9-3 Frequency spectrum

Band	Frequency	Application
Very low frequency (VLF)	3 KHz – 30 KHz	Communication with submarines using telegraphy
Low frequency (LF)	30 KHz – 300 KHz	Marine navigation
Medium frequency (MF)	300 KHz – 3 MHz	AM radio
High frequency (HF)	3 MHz – 30 MHz	Ham radio
Very high frequency (VHF)	30 MHz – 300 MHz	FM radio
Ultra high frequency (UHF)	300 MHz – 3 GHz	Cellular telephone
Super high frequency (SHF)	3 GHz – 30 GHz	LMDS
Extremely high frequency (EHF)	30 GHz – 300 GHz	Advanced radio telecommunication
Light	300+ GHz	Visible, infrared, ultraviolet light

In the 1980s, research shifted from low frequency, high-powered microwaves to high frequency, low-powered signals over short distances. Engineers were interested in creating a point-to-multipoint video network in the high frequency band. This eventually became the technology behind LMDS, which uses high frequency, low-powered waves to send and receive signals over a shorter distance.

One of the early problems with the LMDS frequency spectrum was that this was the same spectrum used by certain satellite systems. In 1996 the FCC made initial spectrum allocations for LMDS. The spectrum between 27.5 MHz and 28.35 MHz (a total of 850 MHz worth of frequency) was allocated to LMDS systems on a primary basis. In addition, another 150 MHz of frequency, between 29.1 MHz and 29.25 MHz, was allocated to LMDS on a co-primary (shared) basis, along with 30 GHz and 31.075 GHz and 31.225 GHz.

Architecture

Because an LMDS signal can only travel up to 5 miles (8 kilometers), an LMDS network is composed of cells much like a cellular telephone system. A transmitter sends out signals to the fixed buildings within the cell, as seen in Figure 9-12. However, there are several differences between LMDS cells and a cellular telephone system. First, a cellular telephone system is intended for mobile users; LMDS is a fixed technology for buildings. Also, in a cellular telephone system the size of each cell is approximately the same and is based on to the distance the RF signal can travel from the tower to the user. That is not the case with LMDS. There are a variety of factors that can affect the size of the LMDS cell. Most of these are based on the fact that LMDS requires a direct line-of-sight. The main factors that determine the cell size are line-of-sight, antenna height, overlapping cells, and rainfall.

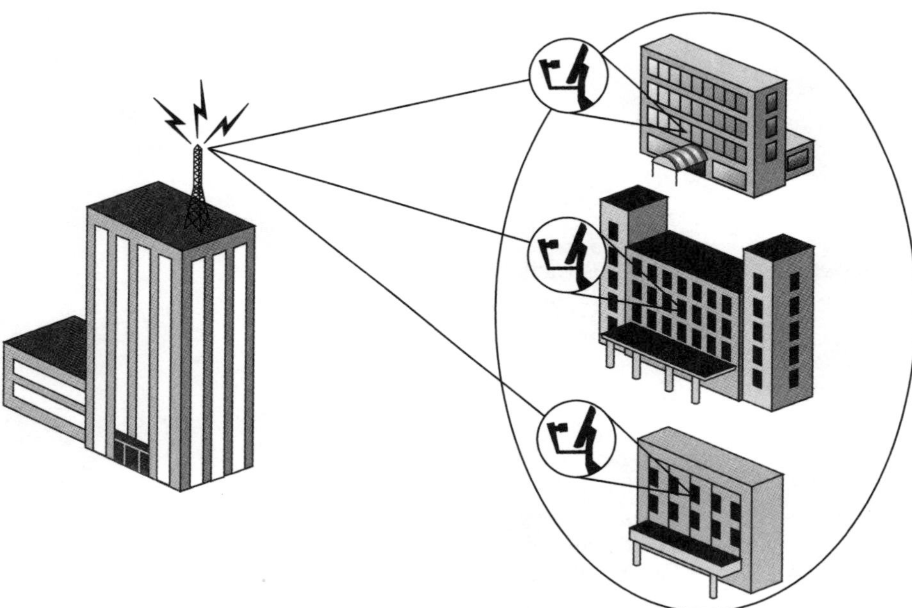

Figure 9-12 LMDS cell

- *Line-of-sight*—A direct line-of-sight between the transmitter and receiver is essential. In areas where there are tall buildings or other high obstructions, the cell size may need to be smaller to reach more customers. In Figure 9-13 a tall building obstructs the signal to other buildings. One solution is to divide the area into smaller cells, as seen in Figure 9-14.

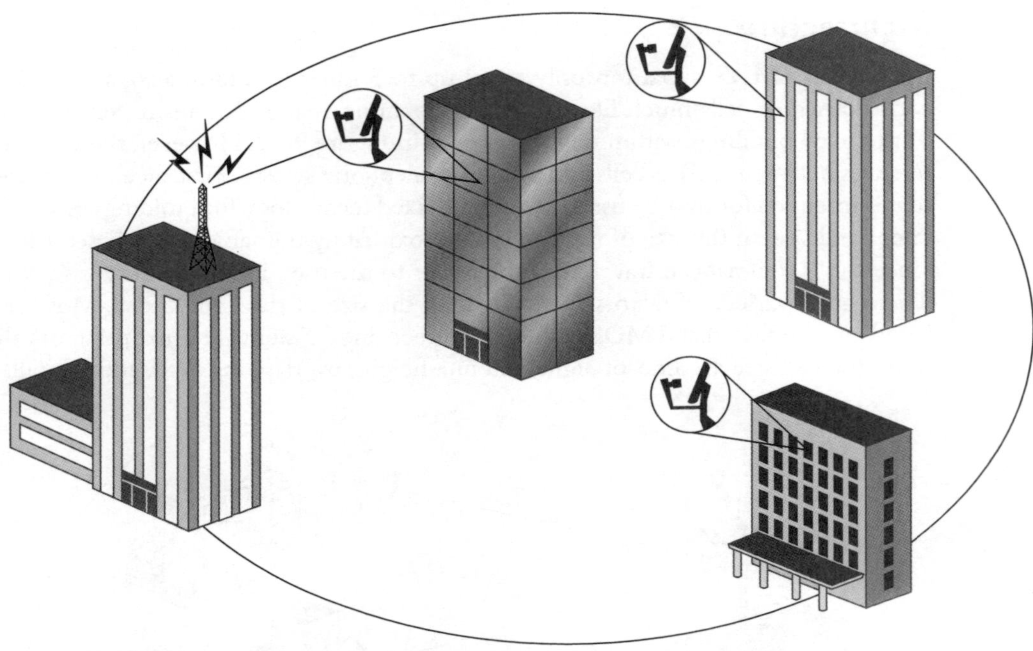

Figure 9-13 Tall building obstructs signal

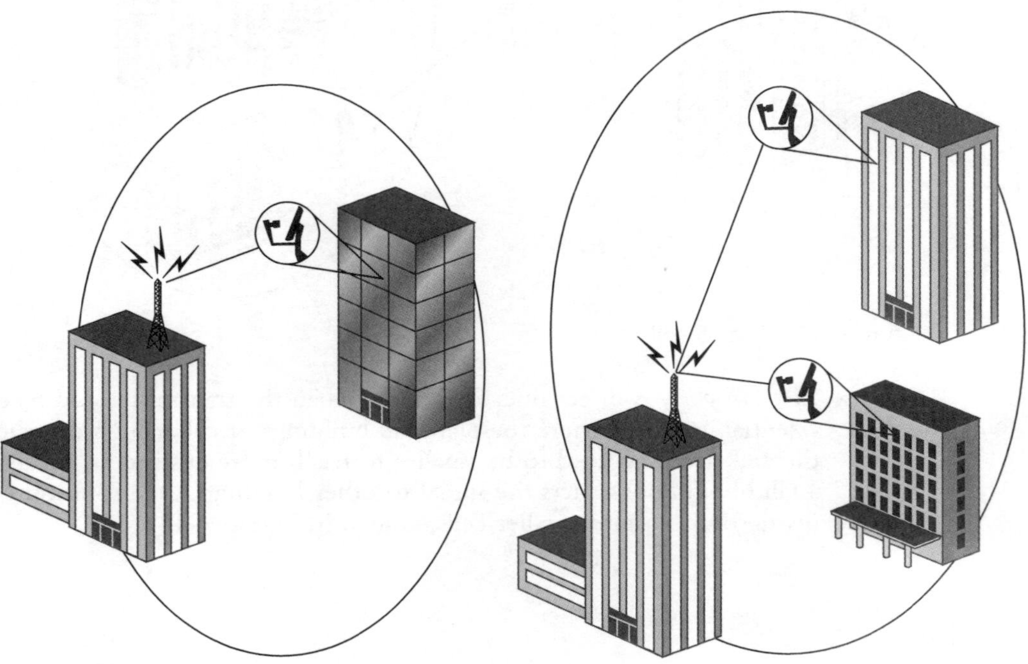

Figure 9-14 Divide into smaller cells

- *Antenna height*—Another factor to be considered is the height of the transmission and reception antennas. If the transmitting and receiving antennas can be placed on the rooftops of tall buildings, particularly those that are farthest away, then cells can typically be larger because the number of obstructions is reduced. This is seen in Figure 9-15.

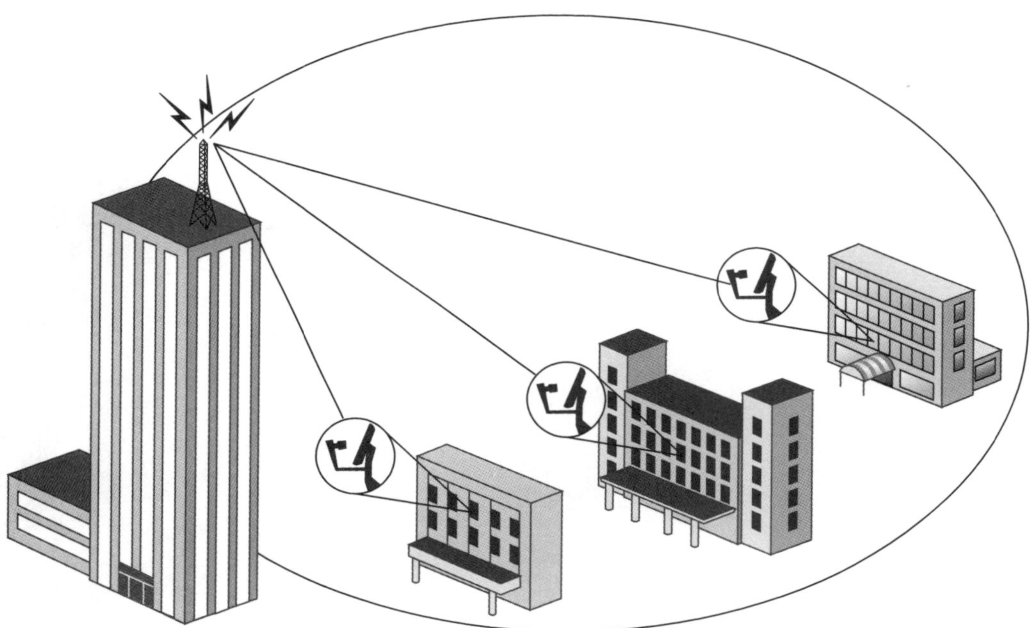

Figure 9-15 Antenna height

- *Overlapping cells*—Because LMDS is a line-of-sight technology, a signal sent from one tower may not reach all of the recipients. In one study, a single LMDS transmitter reached only slightly more than 60 percent of the buildings in an LMDS cell. With overlapping cells, however, that number increased to almost 85 percent of the buildings. The reason is that the second transmitter was able to reach buildings that the first one could not because the second had a better line-of-sight angle.
- *Rainfall*—Cell size is also determined by the amount of local rainfall. Because LMDS signals are microwaves, these signals react with water and lose strength. To correct this, LMDS can either increase the power of the transmissions when it rains, in an attempt to ensure a strong signal that reaches its destination, or reduce the cell size. Most LMDS cells are sized based on the average local annual rainfall. An LMDS cell, under ideal conditions, can be up to 5 miles (8 kilometers) across. However, most cells are between 2 to 5 miles (3.2 to 8 kilometers).

LMDS signals are broadcast from radio hubs that are deployed throughout the carrier's market. Each hub broadcasts signals to buildings within its cell. The radio hub connects to the service provider's central office, which in turn connects to other networks such as the Internet. This is seen in Figure 9-16.

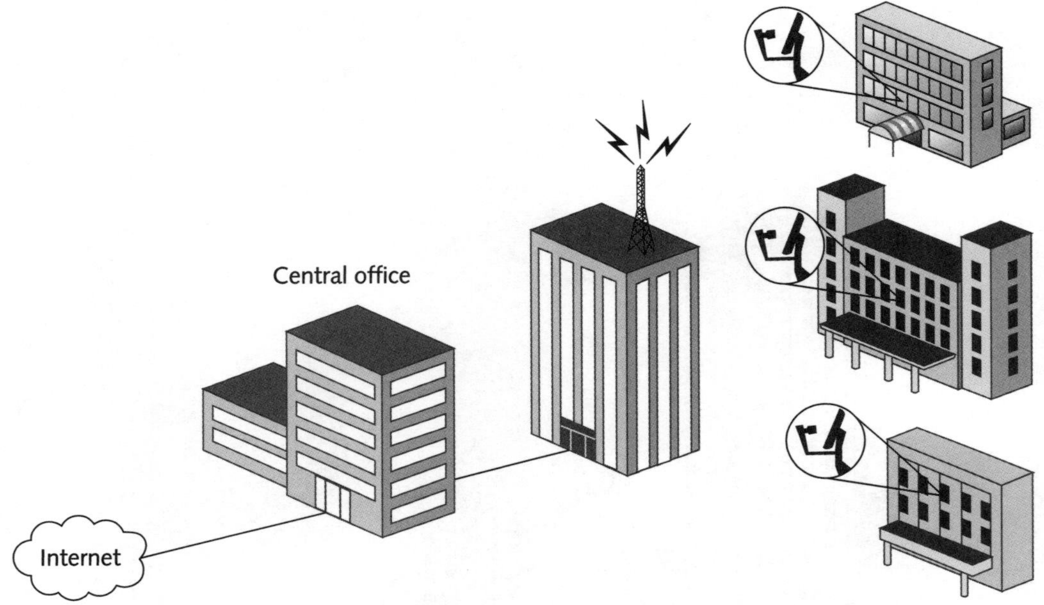

Figure 9-16 LMDS infrastructure

At the receiving site there are three pieces of equipment: a 12- to 15-inch diameter directional antenna, a digital radio modem, and a network interface unit. The antenna, which transmits and receives signals in a restricted direction, is usually installed on the roof of the building and must have a direct line of sight to a hub. The digital radio modem performs digital-to-analog and analog-to-digital conversions. The **network interface unit (NIU)** connects to other services, such as a local area network or telephone system. Rarely are individual telephones, computers, and video equipment connected directly to the NIU. This is illustrated in Figure 9-17.

LMDS systems can use either time division multiple access (TDMA) or frequency division multiple access (FDMA) to share the frequency spectrum among users. The modulation techniques can also vary among carriers. Most use a form of quadrature phase shift keying (QPSK) or quadrature amplitude modulation (QAM).

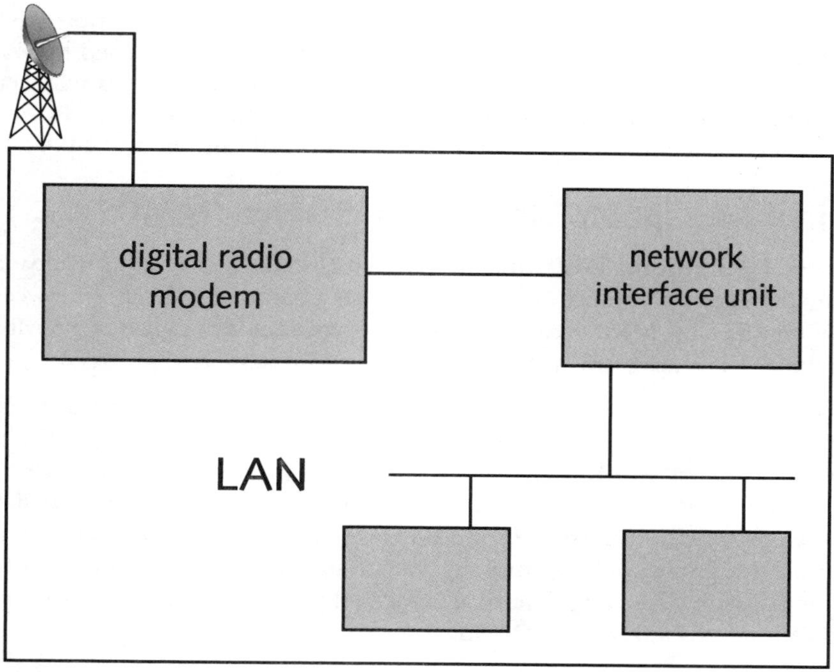

Figure 9-17 LMDS receiving equipment

Advantages and Disadvantages of LMDS

There are several advantages to LMDS:

- *Cost*—LMDS is a low-cost option to fiber optic cables. These costs are low for both the user and the carrier. For the user the cost is minimal to install the antenna, modem, and NIU compared to installing fiber optic cable. For the carrier, LMDS is an attractive last-mile solution because it allows large numbers of concentrated customers to be covered for a lower cost than wired alternatives.
- *Increased service area*—An LMDS network can be expanded one cell at a time. This means that an LMDS network can be installed selectively to cover the most profitable users first and later expanded as the customer base increases.
- *Capacity*—LMDS carriers can have as much as 1,300 MHz of spectrum in a local market. This spectrum can support simultaneously 16,000 telephone calls and 200 video channels.

There are also disadvantages to LMDS:

- *Requires line-of-sight*—LMDS requires a direct line-of-sight between buildings. Any object such as leaves, branches, trees, and buildings can block an LMDS signal. This means that the layout of an LMDS network can be limited by surrounding objects.

- *Affected by precipitation*—LMDS signals are susceptible to interference from rain and fog. Because high-frequency microwaves are absorbed by water, this reduces the strength of the signal during rain. LMDS systems may actually be better suited for regions with minimal rainfall, although carriers can use a variety of techniques to minimize the impact of rain on an LMDS signal.

Multichannel Multipoint Distribution Service (MMDS)

Multichannel Multipoint Distribution Service (MMDS) is a fixed broadband wireless technology that has many similarities to LMDS. One significant difference between them is the area of transmission. MMDS can transmit video, voice, or data signals at 1.5 Mbps downstream and 300 Kbps upstream at distances of up to 35 miles (56 kilometers).

The similarities between MMDS and LMDS can be seen by the fact that the last three words of each name (*Multipoint Distribution Service*) are the same and have the same definition. Only the first word in the name is different (*Multichannel* vs. *Local*). The word *Multichannel* goes back to the original use of this technology. MMDS was designed in the 1960s to provide transmission for 33 one-way analog television channels. This multiple-channel (multichannel) technology was designed for educational institutions to provide long-distance learning. The FCC allocated part of the frequency spectrum, from 2.5 GHz through 2.7 GHz, for MMDS.

However, the original vision for MMDS never fully materialized. Later, private companies purchased part of this spectrum to compete against wired cable television companies (MMDS is sometimes called wireless cable). Using MMDS, television signals could be wirelessly beamed into homes instead of delivered over a cable system. In the 1980s new digital technology allowed service providers to increase their capacity from 33 analog channels to 99 digital channels. Later improvements with compression and modulation techniques increased the capacity of MMDS to broadcast 300 channels.

A major change to MMDS came about in 1998. The FCC allowed service providers to use the 200 MHz of bandwidth in the MMDS frequency bands to provide two-way services such as wireless Internet access along with voice and video transmissions. Today MMDS is used as an option in both home and business settings. In the home, MMDS is an alternative to cable modems and DSL service, particularly in rural areas where cabling is scarce. It is also used to transmit over 300 channels of digital video. For businesses, MMDS is an alternative to T1 or expensive fiber optic connections. MMDS uses the 2.1 GHz and 2.5 GHz through 2.7 GHz bands to offer two-way service at speeds of up to 1.5 Mbps upstream and 300 Kbps downstream.

MMDS operates in many international markets at 3.5 GHz.

Layout

An MMDS hub is typically located on top of mountains, towers, buildings, or other high points. The hub uses a point-to-multipoint architecture that multiplexes communications to multiple users. The tower has a backhaul connection to the carrier's network, and the carrier network connects with the Internet.

Because they operate at a lower frequency than LMDS, MMDS signals can travel longer distances. This means that MMDS can provide service to an entire area with only a few radio transmitters compared to LMDS. MMDS uses cells like LMDS. However, an MMDS cell size can be up to 35 miles (56 kilometers) across, which covers 3,800 square miles (6,080 square kilometers) in area. A similar area would require over 100 LMDS cells.

On the receiving location, a directional antenna approximately 13 by 13 inches (33 cm) is aimed to receive the MMDS signal, as seen in Figure 9-18. This antenna, sometimes called a **pizza box antenna** for obvious reasons, is usually installed on the roof of a building so that it has a direct line-of-sight to a radio transmitter. A cable runs from the antenna to an MMDS wireless modem, which converts the transmitted analog signal to digital. The modem then can connect to a single computer or a LAN, as seen in Figure 9-19.

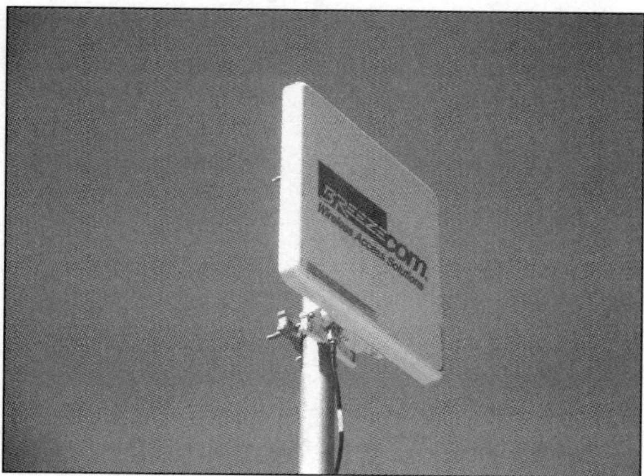

Figure 9-18 Pizza box antenna

Work is already underway for **Second Generation MMDS**. Unlike current MMDS that uses standard multiplexing techniques like PSK and that requires line-of-sight, Second Generation MMDS will use Orthogonal Frequency Division Multiplexing (OFDM). This will create a stronger signal as well as eliminate the line-of-sight requirement, which increases coverage to buildings in the cell and simplifies antenna installation. It is projected that Second Generation MMDS speeds may reach up to 9 Mbps downstream and 2.0 Mbps upstream.

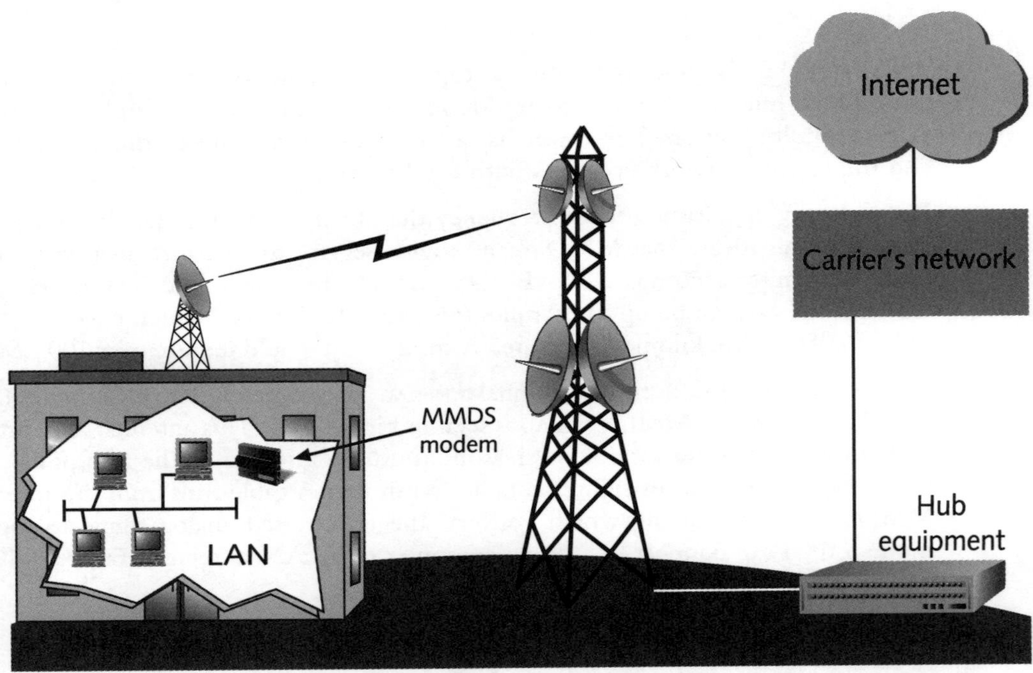

Figure 9-19 MMDS infrastructure

Advantages and Disadvantages of MMDS

There are several advantages to MMDS. These include:

- *Signal strength*—Low-frequency MMDS RF signals can travel farther, generally are less susceptible to interference from rain or fog, and are better able to penetrate buildings than high-frequency LMDS RF signals.
- *Cell size*—Because MMDS signals carry farther and are less susceptible to interference, MMDS transmitters can cover areas seven times larger than LMDS transmitters.
- *Cost*—As a rule, the cost of electronic equipment is linked to the frequency used to transmit: the higher the frequency, the higher the cost of the equipment. Because MMDS uses a lower frequency in comparison to LMDS, MMDS equipment is less expensive.

The disadvantages to MMDS include:

- *Requires direct line of sight*—Current generation MMDS still requires a direct line-of-sight between the tower and the buildings. This not only makes installation more difficult but it eliminates a large number of buildings in a given cell simply because they are blocked by taller obstructions.

- *Shared signals*—An MMDS cell can cover a large area of all users within a 35 mile (56 kilometer) radius. However, these large numbers of users all share the same radio channels. As a result, data throughputs and speed is decreased as more users are added. Although providers sometimes quote transmission rates of up to 10 Mbps, because it is shared the actual speed may be closer to 1.5 Mbps.
- *Security*—Carriers do not encrypt the wireless MMDS transmissions. Although only a highly sophisticated user could intercept and read the transmissions, many business users may need to add security to their transmissions to keep them safe.
- *Limited markets*—Currently, MMDS is available in only a limited number of areas across the U.S. Broad deployment of this technology may not occur until Second Generation MMDS, which does not require a direct line-of-sight, becomes available.

With the anticipated growth of 3G digital cellular service, the FCC was asked to relocate users in the 2.5 GHz spectrum, including MMDS, to another band to free up this spectrum for 3G service. However, in late 2001 the FCC issued a decision that it will not relocate these license-holders. This solidifies the future of MMDS and will increase the number of carriers offering this service.

SATELLITE FIXED BROADBAND WIRELESS

Although the use of satellites for personal wireless communication is fairly recent, satellites themselves have been used for worldwide communications for over 40 years. Satellite use falls into three broad categories. First, some satellites are used to acquire scientific data and perform research in space. The second category of satellites looks at earth from space. These include weather satellites and military satellites. The third category of satellites are those devices that are simply "reflectors"; that is, they are used to bounce or relay signals from one point on earth to another point. These satellites include communications satellites that reflect telephone and data transmissions, broadcast satellites that reflect television signals, and navigational satellites. These are illustrated in Figure 9-20. Wireless communications uses the third category of satellites, as objects to bounce signals from one point on earth to another.

Satellites generally send and receive on one of three frequency bands, known as the L-band, Ku-band, and the Ka-band. These are summarized in Table 9-4. Satellite systems are classified according to the type of orbit that they use. The three orbits are low earth orbiting (LEO), medium earth orbiting (MEO), and geosynchronous earth orbiting (GEO).

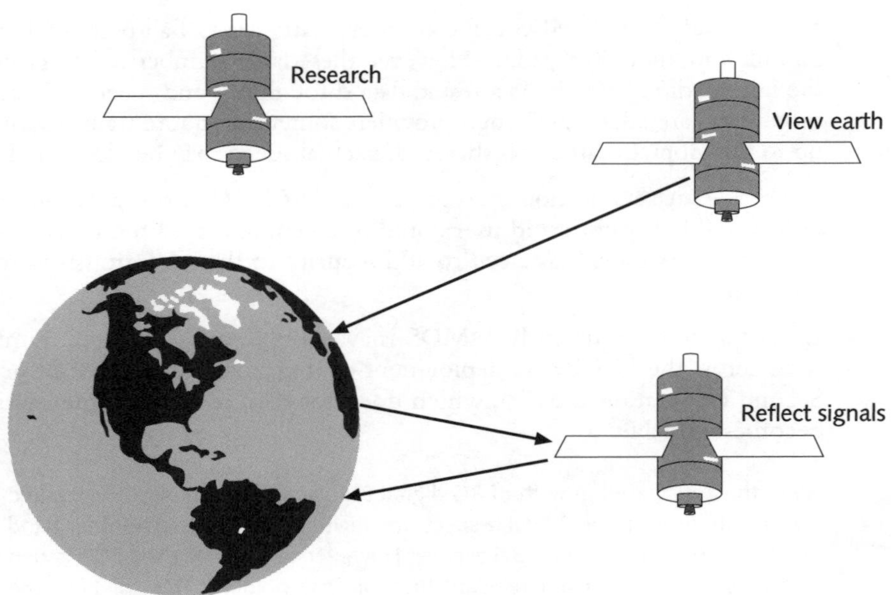

Figure 9-20 Three types of satellites

Table 9-4 Satellite frequencies

Band	Frequency
L-band	1.53–2.7GHz
Ku-band	11.7–12.7 GHz download; 14–17.8 GHz uplink
Ka-band	18–31 GHz

Low Earth Orbiting (LEO)

Low earth orbiting (LEO) satellites orbit the earth at an altitude of just 200 to 900 miles (321 to 1,448 kilometers). Because they orbit so close to earth, LEO satellites must travel at high speeds so that the earth's gravity will not pull them back into the atmosphere. Satellites in LEO travel at 17,000 miles (27,359 kilometers) per hour, circling the earth in about 90 minutes.

Because LEOs are in such a low orbit, their area of earth coverage (called the footprint) is small, as seen in Figure 9-21. This means that more LEO satellites are needed to provide coverage, compared to MEO and GEO satellites. One LEO system calls for over 225 satellites for total coverage of the earth.

LEO systems have a low **latency** (delays caused by signals that must travel over a long distance) and use low-powered terrestrial devices. It takes about 20 to 40 milliseconds for a signal to bounce from an earth-bound station to a LEO then back to an earth station again.

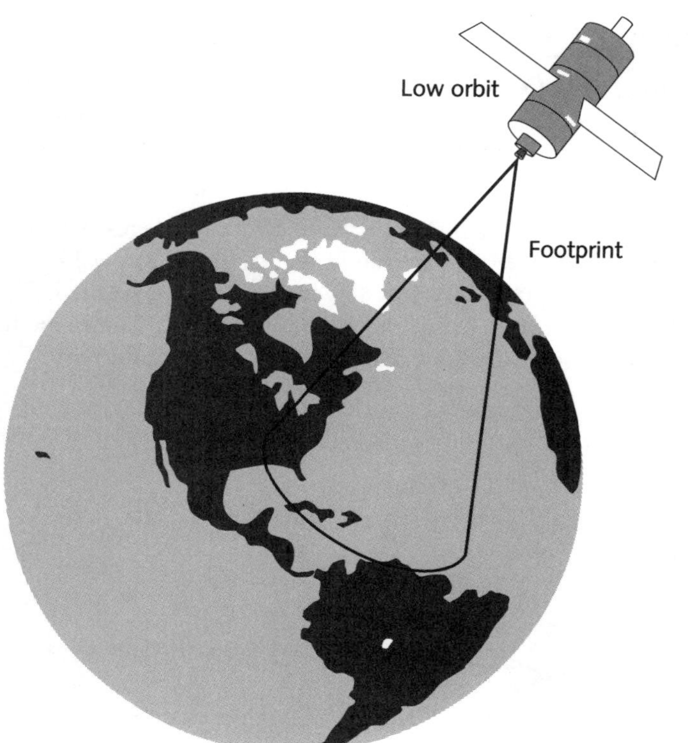

Figure 9-21 LEO footprint

LEO satellites can be divided into "Big LEOs" and "Little LEOs." Little LEOs provide pager, cellular telephone, and location services. Using a Little LEO satellite, a user can make a phone call from anywhere on earth. This compares to cellular telephone service that requires the user to be in a specific area of coverage. Big LEOs carry voice and data broadband services, such as wireless Internet access. One current wireless Internet service provides shared downstream data rates of up to 400 Kbps but depends on a telephone line for upstream data to an ISP. Another LEO wireless Internet service provides two-way data services with speeds of up to 500 Kbps. Two-way satellite Internet users need a two-foot by three-foot dish antenna and two modems (one each for uplink and downlink).

When using LEO for wireless Internet access, there must be a clear view in the direction of the equator. This is because LEO satellites orbit over the equator area. Foliage from trees and heavy rains can affect reception of signals.

In the future LEOs are expected to be in demand for three markets: rural conventional telephone service, global mobile digital cellular service, and international broadband service. The speeds for wireless access are expected to exceed 100 Mbps.

Medium Earth Orbiting (MEO)

Medium earth orbiting (MEO) satellites orbit the earth at altitudes between 1,500 and 10,000 miles (2,413 to 16,090 kilometers). Some MEO satellites orbit in near perfect circles, have a constant altitude, and travel at a constant speed. Other MEO satellites revolve in elongated orbits.

Because they are farther from the earth, MEOs have two advantages over LEOs. First, they do not have to travel as fast; a MEO can circle the earth in up to 12 hours. Second, MEOs have a bigger earth footprint and thus fewer satellites are needed. This is illustrated in Figure 9-22. On the other hand, the higher orbit also increases the latency. A MEO signal takes from 50 to 150 milliseconds to make the round trip.

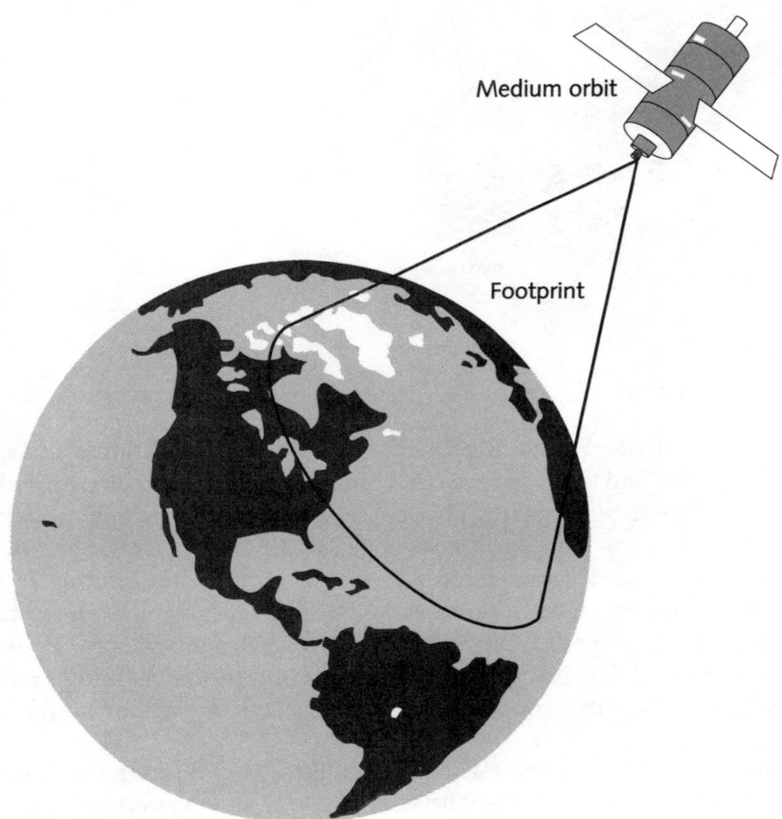

Figure 9-22 MEO footprint

Geosynchronous Earth Orbiting (GEO)

Geosynchronous earth orbiting (GEO) satellites are stationed at an altitude of 22,282 miles (35,860 kilometers). A GEO satellite orbit matches the rotation of the earth and moves as the earth moves. This means that it remains "fixed" over a given location on the earth and seems to hang motionless in space. Because of its high altitude, a GEO satellite can provide continuous service to a very large footprint because it is so far from earth. In fact, only three GEO satellites are needed to cover the entire earth except for the polar regions. Yet the high altitude also causes GEO satellites to have high latencies of about 250 milliseconds and require high-powered terrestrial sending devices. GEO satellites are used for world-wide communications and typically not fixed broadband wireless.

Although it is much more expensive to launch a GEO satellite, it has a lifespan of 12 to 15 years. The average lifespan of a LEO satellite is only five years. Because the footprint of a GEO is so large, GEO satellites are much more efficient compared to LEO satellites. LEO satellites spend a portion of their orbit over areas where coverage may not be needed, such as the oceans.

The International Telecommunications Union (ITU) regulates GEO usage.

Chapter Summary

- One of the problems for both home and office users who need to access the Internet or other high-speed data networks is known as the last mile connection, which is the connection that begins at a fast service provider, goes through the local neighborhood, and ends at the home or office. Whereas the connections that make up the nation's data transmission infrastructure are very fast and are well established, the last mile connection that links these high-speed transmission lines to the home or office are much slower and not universally available.
- For home users there are currently three popular choices for the last mile wired connection: a standard dial-up modem using telephone lines, a cable modem, and Digital Subscriber Line (DSL). For a business user located in an office building, the same choices for home users are generally not available or are unsuitable. As an alternative to these last mile wired connections, many users have turned to wireless options. Last mile wireless connections can cost less, can be installed faster, offer greater flexibility, and have better reliability. Using wireless as the last mile connection for buildings is called fixed wireless. It is fixed because the buildings are fixed in one position.
- There are two ways in which a signal can be sent. The first technique is called broadband, which sends multiple signals at different frequencies. This allows many different signals to be sent simultaneously. The second technique is called baseband, which treats the entire transmission medium as if it were only one channel.

- Fixed broadband wireless service can be obtained in one of two ways. First, they can be designed, installed, and managed by a private individual or owner of a building. A second method is to purchase the service from a wireless carrier.
- Fixed broadband wireless systems use frequencies allocated for that specific use. These frequencies range from 900 MHz to 40 GHz. Both private and carrier systems have a choice of using either a licensed or unlicensed spectrum.
- There are three limitations of fixed broadband wireless. The first is that these systems operate at frequencies that require line of sight. A second limitation is that the distance between devices is limited. A third limitation is that fixed wireless broadband systems can only send from one device to one other device.
- A remote wireless bridge is designed to connect two or more baseband networks that are located in different buildings. The distance between buildings can be up to 18 miles (29 kilometers), transmitting at 11 Mbps or up to 25 miles (40 kilometers) when transmitting at 2 Mbps. Remote wireless bridges are essentially identical to IEEE 802.11b WLAN systems, except that remote wireless bridges transmit at a higher power than WLANs, and remote wireless bridges use directional antennas as well as the standard omnidirectional antennas.
- Remote wireless bridges support two types of connections. The first is a point-to-point configuration. This configuration is used to connect two LAN segments over distance. The LAN segments can be either wired or wireless. The second configuration is a point-to-multipoint configuration. This is used to connect multiple LAN segments together.
- Free Space Optics (FSO) is an optical, wireless, point-to-point, line-of-sight broadband technology. Although it was originally developed over 30 years ago by the military, FSO has become today an excellent alternative to high-speed fiber optic cable. Currently, FSO can transmit at speeds comparable to fiber optic transmissions of up to 1.25 Gbps at a distance of 2.5 miles (4 kilometers). It is projected that future improvements in the technology will push the top speed to the hundreds of Gbps. Sometimes called fiberless optical, FSO transmissions are sent by low-powered infrared beams through the open air. These beams, which do not harm the human eye, are transmitted by transceivers. Because FSO is a line-of-sight technology, the transceivers must be mounted high in office buildings to provide a clear transmission path.
- Local Multipoint Distribution Service (LMDS) is a fixed broadband technology that can provide a wide variety of wireless services. These services include: high-speed Internet access, real-time multimedia file transfer, remote access to LANs, interactive video, video-on-demand, video conferencing, and telephone service. LMDS can transmit from 51 to 155 Mbps downstream and 1.54 Mbps upstream over a distance of up to about 5 miles (8 kilometers).
- Because an LMDS signal can only travel up to 5 miles, an LMDS network is composed of cells much like a cellular telephone system. A transmitter sends out signals to the fixed buildings within the cell. However, there are several differences

between LMDS cells and a cellular telephone system. First, a cellular telephone system is intended for mobile users; LMDS is a fixed technology for buildings. Also, in a cellular telephone system the size of each cell is approximately the same and is based on the distance the RF signal can travel from the tower to the user. That is not the case with LMDS. There are a variety of factors that can affect the size of the LMDS cell. Most of these are based upon the fact that LMDS requires a direct line-of-sight. The main factors that determine the cell size are line-of-sight, antenna height, overlapping cells, and rainfall.

- Multichannel Multipoint Distribution Service (MMDS) is a fixed broadband wireless technology. MMDS shares similarities with LMDS. However, one significant difference between them is the area of transmission. MMDS can transmit video, voice, or data signals at distances of up to 35 miles (56 kilometers). Because it operates at a lower frequency, MMDS signals can travel longer distances. This means that MMDS can provide service to an entire area with only a few radio transmitters compared to LMDS. Today MMDS is used as an option in both home and business settings. In the home, MMDS is an alternative to cable modems and DSL service, particularly in rural areas where cabling is scarce. It is also used to transmit over 300 channels of digital video. For businesses, MMDS is an alternative to T1 or expensive fiber optic connections. MMDS uses the 2.1 GHz and 2.5 GHz through 2.7 GHz bands to offer two-way service at speeds of up to 1.5 Mbps upstream and 300 Kbps downstream.

- Although the use of satellites for personal wireless communication is fairly recent, satellites themselves have been used for worldwide communications for over 40 years. Many satellites are used as “reflectors”; that is, they are used to bounce or relay signals from one point on earth to another point. These satellites include communications satellites that reflect telephone and data transmissions, broadcast satellites that reflect television signals, and navigational satellites. This is the way in which wireless communications uses satellites: as an object to bounce a signal from one point on earth to another.

- Low Earth Orbiting (LEO) satellites orbit the earth at a low altitude of just 200 to 900 miles (321 to 1,448 kilometers). Because they orbit so close to earth, LEO satellites must travel at high speeds so that the earth’s gravity will not pull them back into the atmosphere. Satellites in LEO travel at 17,000 miles (27,359 kilometers) per hour, circling the earth in about 90 minutes. Because LEOs are in such a low orbit, their footprint is small. This means that more LEO satellites are needed to provide coverage. LEO systems have a low latency and use low-powered terrestrial devices. It takes about 20 to 40 milliseconds for a signal to bounce from an earth bound station to a LEO then back to an earth station again.

- Medium Earth Orbiting (MEO) satellites orbit the earth at altitudes between 1,500 and 10,000 miles (2,413 to 16,090 kilometers). Because they are farther from the earth MEOs have two advantages over LEOs. First, they do not have to travel as fast; a MEO can circle the earth in up to 12 hours. Second, MEOs have a bigger earth footprint and thus fewer satellites are needed. On the other hand, the higher orbit also increases the latency. A MEO signal takes from 50 to 150 milliseconds to make the round trip.

- Geosynchronous Earth Orbiting (GEO) satellites are stationed at an altitude of 22,282 miles (35,860 kilometers). A GEO satellite orbit matches the rotation of the earth and moves as the earth moves. This means that it remains "fixed" over a given location on the earth and seems to hang motionless in space. Because of its high altitude a GEO satellite can provide continuous service to cover the entire earth by only three satellites. Yet the high altitude also causes GEO satellites to have high latencies of about of 250 milliseconds and require high-powered terrestrial sending devices. GEO satellites are used for world-wide communications and typically not for fixed broadband wireless.

Key Terms

backhaul — A company's internal infrastructure connection.

baseband — A transmission technique that treats the entire transmission medium as only one channel.

bridge — A device to connect two network segments.

broadband — A transmission technique that sends multiple signals at different frequencies.

fixed wireless — A wireless last mile connection.

free space optics (FSO) — An optical, wireless, point-to-point, line-of-sight broadband technology.

geosynchronous earth orbiting (GEO) satellites — Satellites that are stationed at an altitude of 22,282 miles (35,860 kilometers).

Integrated Services Digital Connection (ISDN) — A last mile connection that can transmit at 64 Kbps (2 channels) or 128 Kbps (4 channels).

last mile connection — The actual connection that reaches the home or office.

latency — Delays caused by signals that must travel over a long distance.

Local Multipoint Distribution Service (LMDS) — A fixed broadband technology that can provide a wide variety of wireless services.

low earth orbiting (LEO) satellites — Satellites that orbit the earth at an altitude of 200 to 900 miles (321 to 1,448 kilometers).

medium earth orbiting (MEO) satellites — Satellites that orbit the earth at altitudes between 1,500 and 10,000 miles (2,413 to 16,090 kilometers).

microwaves — Part of the spectrum from 3 to 30 GHz.

Multichannel Multipoint Distribution Service (MMDS) — A fixed broadband wireless technology that transmits at 1.5 Mbps over distances of 35 miles (56 kilometers).

network interface unit (NIU) — A device that connects an LMDS modem to a LAN or telephone system.

pizza box antenna — A small antenna used for MMDS systems.

remote wireless bridge — A system designed to connect two or more baseband networks together that are located in different buildings.

scintillation — The temporal and spatial variations in light intensity caused by atmospheric turbulence.

Second Generation MMDS — The successor to MMDS that uses OFDM and eliminates direct line-of-sight requirements.

spatial diversity — The sending of parallel beams during free space optical transmissions.

super high frequency (SHF) — Part of the frequency spectrum from 3 to 30 GHz.

T1 — A special high-speed connection leased from the local telephone system that transmits at 1.544 Mbps.

T3 — A special high-speed connection leased from the local telephone system that transmits at 44.736 Mbps.

Review Questions

1. The term fixed wireless is generally used to refer to ________.
   a. buildings
   b. cars
   c. satellites
   d. cell phones
2. What is the connection that begins at a fast service provider, goes through the local neighborhood, and ends at the home or office?
   a. 1 mile
   b. last mile
   c. OSP
   d. Linksys
3. Each of the following are last mile connections for home users except ________.
   a. satellite
   b. dial-up modem
   c. DSL
   d. baseband
4. A leased special high-speed connection from the local telephone carrier for business users that transmits at 1.544 Mbps is ________.
   a. T1
   b. T2
   c. T3
   d. T11

5. The transmission that treats the entire transmission medium as if it were only one channel is ________________.
   a. broadband
   b. analog
   c. baseband
   d. line
6. Fixed broadband wireless service can be obtained in one of two ways: they can be installed and managed by a private individual or purchased from a wireless carrier. True or false?
7. The use of a higher frequency requires a larger antenna to send and receive signals. True or false?
8. Both private and carrier systems have a choice of using either a licensed or unlicensed spectrum. True or false?
9. One of the limitations of fixed broadband wireless is that these systems operate at frequencies that require line of sight. True or false?
10. A remote wireless bridge is designed to connect two or more broadband networks together that are located in different buildings. True or false?
11. A device called a ________________ is used instead of an access point (AP) in a remote wireless bridge network.
12. Sometimes called fiberless optical, ________________ uses no medium like a fiber optic cable to send and receive signals; instead, transmissions are sent by low-powered infrared beams through the open air.
13. The maximum coverage area for a Local Multipoint Distribution Service (LMDS) network is ________________ miles.
14. LMDS uses ________________ frequency low-powered waves to send and receive signals over a shorter distance.
15. Define each of the words in Local Multipoint Distribution Service (LMDS).
16. List five factors that can determine the cell size of a Local Multipoint Distribution Service (LMDS) cell.
17. What was Multichannel Multipoint Distribution Service (MMDS) originally designed for? How is it used today?
18. List the three major ways in which satellites are used. Which is used for fixed broadband wireless?
19. Describe Low Earth Orbiting (LEO) satellites.
20. How can the Geosynchronous Earth Orbiting (GEO) satellite system cover the earth with only three satellites?

HANDS-ON PROJECTS

1. Integrated Services Digital Network (ISDN) and T1 lines are still used for wired office connections today. Using the Internet, research these two technologies. How long have they been used? What are their advantages? What are their disadvantages? How much longer will they be used? Write a one-page paper on your findings.
2. What wireless services do the local carriers offer in your area? What are the costs? What are their plans for future services? Create a chart that outlines your findings.
3. Free space optics have been used extensively in emergency situations where wired communications were destroyed or failed. Using the Internet and other sources, research an instance when remote wireless bridges saved the day. How long did the installation take? Why was it chosen? What problems had to be overcome? Write a one-page paper on your research.
4. Remote wireless bridges are based on the WLAN 802.11b standard. Is it possible to use the new 802.11a standard or HiperLAN/2? Using the Internet and other sources, determine if these other technologies can be used for remote wireless bridges. Write a paper on your conclusion.
5. Create a table that lists the differences between LMDS and MMDS. Use the Internet or other printed sources to locate additional information for your table.

CASE PROJECTS

The Baypoint Group

Your services as a consultant have been requested by The Baypoint Group (TBG), a company that assists organizations and businesses with issues involving network planning and design. Performance Air is a passenger charter airline that operates out of an airport on the west side of the city. Currently, Performance Air is paying $2,000 per month for a T1 line but wants to reduce its costs. It has asked TBG for assistance in making a decision, and TBG has turned to you.

1. Create a presentation for Performance Air outlining the advantages and disadvantages of each of the following types of wireless access: cable modem, DSL, T1, T3, free space optics, LMDS, MMDS, and LEO. Because the audience listening to your presentation includes their IT staff, your presentation should be technical in nature. Limit yourself to a presentation that will not exceed 15 minutes worth of PowerPoint slides.
2. Greg Charles, the president of Performance Air, is interested by your presentation. However, Brian Marcs, the IT Director, thinks that they can set up their own wireless system using 802.11a equipment and save even more money. Greg has asked you to create an executive summary paper regarding your opinion on the appropriateness of this technology. Create a one-page document that outlines the advantages and disadvantages of this approach.

OPTIONAL TEAM CASE PROJECT

Performance Air has spoken with the local telephone carrier and two private companies. Each organization is promoting a different service to Performance Air: LEO, LMDS, and MMDS. Performance Air wants to first connect their terminal with an office building located about half a mile away. However, they are unsure which technology would best suit their needs. Form three teams, with each team selecting one of these technologies. Research in depth the advantages and disadvantages of these respective technologies and how they work. Hold a friendly debate in which each person presents a 5-minute talk about the advantages of his technology. After the talk allow time for the others to ask questions. Be prepared to defend your technology, knowing that the other individuals will be aware of its disadvantages.

CHAPTER

10

WIRELESS COMMUNICATIONS IN BUSINESS

After reading this chapter and completing the exercises, you will be able to:

- List the advantages of wireless communications
- Discuss the challenges of wireless communications
- Explain the steps needed to build a wireless infrastructure

In the early 1930s a mathematician developed a formula that could be used to make accurate weather forecasts, which was something that was unheard of at that time. However, because this was before the time of computers and calculators, it took almost three months of hand calculations in order to come up with the next day's forecast. This obviously was far too late to be of any use, and many individuals scoffed at such a preposterous solution to weather forecasting. However, with the introduction of computers 15 years later, the amount of time needed for the calculations was dramatically decreased. Suddenly this model for weather forecasting became very popular, and is the basis of today's weather forecasting.

The point is that with any new idea or technology, sometimes you have to "think outside of the box." It requires vision to see how an idea or technology could be used. This also applies to new technologies like wireless communications. Some users question why we should consider wireless technology when the existing wired system seems to work just fine. This again may be a lack of vision to look beyond the current setting to consider how wireless could improve things today as well as provide innovative functions for tomorrow.

In this chapter, we'll consider what it takes to make the vision of wireless technology into a successful business reality. We'll look at the steps to incorporate wireless technology into a business, and at the advantages and challenges that face business users who consider adopting this new technology. We will then explore the steps that can be taken to move from a totally wired infrastructure to one that incorporates wireless technology.

ADVANTAGES OF WIRELESS TECHNOLOGY FOR BUSINESS

The advantages of incorporating wireless technology into a business are far-reaching and can positively impact an organization in many ways. These advantages include universal access to corporate data, increased productivity, increased customer access to their own data, data availability around the clock, and improved information technology (IT) support.

Universal Access to Corporate Data

The first advantage of wireless technology is that it provides access to corporate data from almost any location. This universal access can help a business generate more revenue. For example, a traveling sales representative calling on a customer needs the most current information at his fingertips before he walks in the door. He could review printouts in his hotel room the night before, but these are only as recent as the day they were printed. He could access the company's corporate database from his hotel room that morning, but changes in inventory and sales will occur before he has his 2:00 P.M. appointment.

However, wireless technology can provide access to corporate data from almost anywhere. A sales representative can use WAP on his digital cellular telephone to access data such as the status of the customer's most recent order, view past buying history, current inventory, and review an up-to-the-minute competitor's price list just before he steps out of his car for his meeting. By having universal access to the latest data, the sales representative will be well prepared to make the sale.

Traveling sales representatives are not the only users who can benefit from universal access to corporate data. Anyone who needs to be mobile but needs access to data can benefit from it. Physicians who move around a hospital can have current data at their fingertips to make decisions that result in lower costs and improved care for patients. Factory managers likewise can access data as they walk through the warehouse viewing available storage space for arriving inventory. Wireless technology can also be important when all parties are in one location. For example, during an intense negotiation session attorneys, bankers, and clients can all use wireless notebooks to access data or receive SMS messages on their cellular phones that would help them make the best decision.

Industry experts agree that access to corporate data from almost anywhere is the greatest advantage of wireless technology. This allows decisions to be made quickly from any location with the most up-to-date information. For a business this translates into increased revenue.

Increased Productivity

Having universal access to corporate data leads to increased productivity by employees. In a survey by Cisco in 2001, users reported that when using a wireless LAN (WLAN) they can access data almost two hours more each day than if they were only using a wired network. This is because when they are away from the computer in their office for meetings, conferences, and sales calls, they can still access the network through wireless technology. If the additional two hours of connection time translated into 70 minutes of increased productivity (a standard ratio), this means the average user could be 22 percent more productive. For a worker with a salary of $64,000 this means that the annual productivity improvement per wireless user could be worth as much as $7,000 each year to the business. In addition, almost two-thirds of WLAN users reported that the wireless connection improved the accuracy of their everyday tasks.

Almost 87 percent of the WLAN users surveyed reported that the wireless technology even improved their quality of life because it provided them increased flexibility, productivity, and time savings.

Increased Access to the Customer's Own Data

A key factor in reducing business costs is to shift the burden of accessing a customer's data from the business to the customer. If customers can see data about themselves on the business' computer system, they can make better and more informed decisions. This decreases the use of the business' human resources, which in turn reduces costs for the business and increases revenue.

An example of customer access to their data can be seen in the airline industry. Most airlines have Web sites where customers can view schedules, make reservations, and check on the current status of their frequent flier miles. This results in a cost savings to the airlines because they can hire fewer telephone reservation clerks. Some airlines are adding wireless technology in the airports themselves. Customers can view their flight information once they enter the terminal to find out their gate number and when they should check in. Personal check-in is available for those who have a wireless PDA, which allows customers to print their own boarding tickets and check in their baggage at curbside (though they still must pass through the standard security procedures). This helps the airline make better use of their staff or even reduce staffing. In addition, customer satisfaction is increased because the wait in lines is reduced, and increased satisfaction means a repeat customer. All of this is a result of wireless technology that makes the customer's data available from more locations, which reduces the burden on the business and thus increases revenue.

Data Availability 24/7

Leaving work at 5:00 P.M.—and leaving the work behind—is a thing of the past. Business professionals regularly work evenings, nights, weekends, and holidays to catch up and stay ahead. This means that business users need access to corporate data 24 hours a day, 7 days a week. In the past this required a trip back to the office on weekends or staying late at night to finish that report. Wireless technology, however, can help make data available from almost anywhere at any time. This means that a business user can still catch her son's soccer match or daughter's music performance without being tied to the office.

Improved IT Support

Wireless technology can help improve the support that IT departments provide to users. Two of the most significant advantages to IT departments are easier setup and decreased cabling costs compared to wired systems. Other improvements include easier and less time-consuming moves of equipment, more efficient use of office space, and lower support and maintenance costs. This translates to lower costs for the business and more time to the IT staff to provide improved support to the users.

Challenges of Using Wireless Technology

Just as there are distinct advantages for a business to use wireless technology, there are challenges as well. These challenges include a reliance on new technology, competing technologies, data security and privacy, user reluctance, and a shortage of qualified staff.

New Technology

Any new technology faces glitches and problems simply because it has not been as thoroughly tested as a mature technology. Being an early adopter of a new technology can sometimes place a heavy burden on a business. Frequently, early adopters are the ones who discover the bugs in a technology. There may be few experts to turn to in order to answer questions or solve problems. On occasions, support from the vendor itself may be spotty because the product is new and the support team does not have the experience needed to solve problems.

Businesses that elect to become early adopters face the problem of being on the "bleeding edge" of the cutting edge technology. They may end up investing many hours trying to solve problems so the new system will work.

Competing Technologies

Some wireless technologies are clearly based on approved industry standards, such as WLANs following the IEEE 802.11b and 802.11a standards. A business that uses an IEEE standard WLAN is assured that they are investing in a technology that will be the standard for several years to come.

Yet with other wireless technologies, such as digital cellular telephony, there is no clear indication which competing technology will become the standard and which ones will fade away. This poses a critical decision for businesses. Selecting the wrong technology may mean investing hundreds of thousands of dollars in a technology that may be "orphaned" in a few years with dwindling users and support. Not only would this result in a loss of money but it also means that instead of being an industry leader, that business is now running to catch up with the rest.

As long as technologies continue to compete before one becomes the standard, businesses face a tremendous risk in selecting the right wireless technology. Businesses must not only determine which technology is best for them, but also which technology will be viable into the future.

Data Security and Privacy

Wireless technology's greatest strength—allowing users to roam freely without being connected to the network by wires—is also its greatest weakness. Just as a roaming user can receive radio frequency (RF) signals anywhere within a building, so too can an unauthorized user outside the building receive those same RF signals. Broadcasting network traffic over the airwaves has created a concern for keeping that data secure. Most industry experts agree that opening up a corporate network by adding a wireless component without considering security is simply asking for serious problems.

User Reluctance

Change can be painful because it takes time and energy to learn a new system. Unless users can see an immediate benefit to changing, they will be reluctant to do so. And some users, no matter how much the new technology promises to be beneficial, simply don't want to change at all; they are too comfortable with the old way. Requiring users to adapt to new technology and new procedures using wireless communications can sometimes be difficult.

Shortage of Qualified Staff

Wireless communications technology has in some way touched almost all industries, including manufacturing, health care, telecommunications, retail, and others. As the technology continues to infiltrate these businesses, the need for information technology (IT) professionals to develop and implement wireless applications and provide support is skyrocketing. However, many schools and training facilities have not yet caught up with the demand for wireless IT workers. This has resulted in a shortage of qualified IT professionals to install, support, and maintain wireless systems.

The advantages and challenges of wireless technology are summarized in Table 10-1. Before embarking on building a wireless infrastructure in a business, it is critical that the advantages and challenges be considered carefully. Starting out on a journey without knowing the dangers that may lie ahead could be a recipe for failure.

Table 10-1 Wireless advantages and challenges

Advantages	Challenges
Universal access to corporate data	New technology
Increased productivity	Competing technologies
Increased access by customers to their own data	Data security and privacy
Data availability 24/7	User reluctance
Improved IT support	Shortage of qualified staff

Building a Wireless Infrastructure

Once a business has decided to invest in wireless technology, it faces the task of building a new wireless infrastructure. This is much like adding a new network to the organization. In fact, several of the steps necessary to build this new infrastructure are similar to those needed when adding a new wired network.

Evaluate Needs

"Do we really need it?" is a question that must be asked first when adding a wireless infrastructure to a business. Sadly, this question is often asked too late in the process. Sometimes a change in a procedure or additional personnel may solve the problem instead of investing in wireless technology.

Evaluating the need for wireless technology is a time–consuming process, but it is the essential first step. Evaluating needs involves looking at the organization and the current network, gathering basic information, and determining costs.

Look at the Organization

The first step in assessing the need is to step back and look at the organization or business as a whole. Sometimes users fall into the trap of viewing only their department or unit instead of seeing the big picture of the entire organization. There are a series of basic yet vital questions that need to be asked. These questions include:

- What is the purpose or mission of the organization?
- Is the current mission expected to change in the future?
- What is the current size of the organization?
- How much growth is anticipated?
- Who are our closest competitors?
- What is the outlook for this industry as a whole?

Although these questions may seem very basic, they can help to refocus the thinking back onto the organization as a whole and away from one part of it. In addition, questions like these can often reveal a great deal in terms of assessing needs. For example, a business that has lost 20 percent of its market share and is facing financial difficulties may not be in a position to invest heavily in new wireless technologies. On the other hand, a business that has captured a niche in the marketplace and currently has no serious competitors may be poised for rapid growth and wireless technology may help keep them in the lead for years to come. Obtaining a firm grip on the organization as a whole and its current status will reveal if an investment today in wireless technology is the right step.

Assess the Current Network

The next step is to look at how the organization or business actually uses its current network. For example:

- How does the current network support the organization's mission?
- What are the strengths and weaknesses of the current network?
- How many users does it support?
- What essential applications run on the network?

How the network supports the organization is an important consideration. Examining the current status of the network, such as the applications that run on the network and the number of users, can reveal much of this information.

Different industries often have different network requirements. The banking industry must have networks that have a very high degree of security. The manufacturing industry may have networks that must be completely fault-tolerant and cannot afford any downtime. Educational institutions may be able to tolerate a small amount of downtime but are faced with authenticating thousands of new users every few months. Each segment is different and has different network requirements. These should be taken into consideration when viewing the current network.

Assessing the current network can help to identify why a new technology may be needed. If the current network can be upgraded or adapted to meet the current needs, then wireless technology may not be necessary at this time. However, if the current network cannot support the anticipated future growth of the business or there is a clear indication that wireless technology can help the business grow, then investing in it may be the answer.

The task of assessing the current network can be helped by documenting the current network in detail. Because networks tend to grow in an unplanned fashion as new users or equipment are suddenly needed, it is sometimes surprising to see just exactly what the current network does.

A table like Table 10-2 that summarizes the network can be helpful. If the network is complex, a diagram or layout of the network can also help. An example of a diagram is seen in Figure 10-1.

Table 10-2 Sample current network table

Number of clients	55
Types of clients	35 — Windows XP 20 — Windows 2000
Number of servers	1 — Windows 2000
Type of network	Ethernet 100Base-T Switched
Type of cable medium	Category 5e
Types of devices	5 laser printers 1 scanner Connects to Gigabit campus backbone

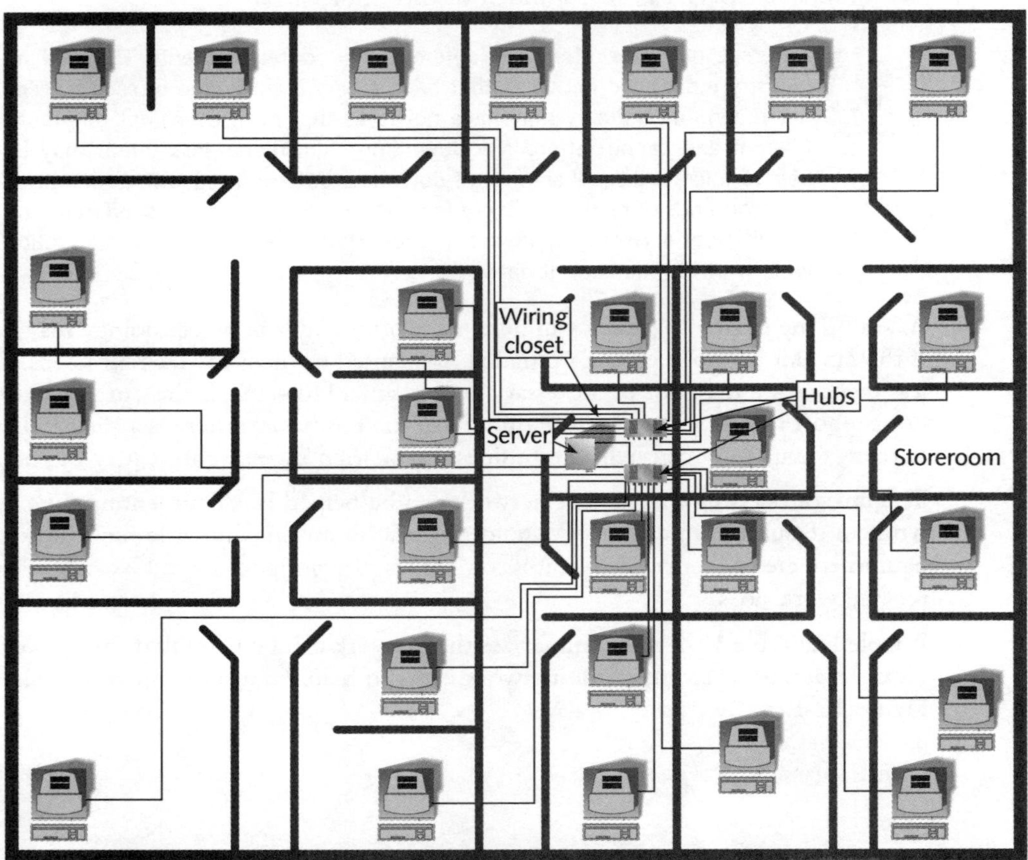

Figure 10-1 Sample network diagram

Gather Information

After the organization and the current network have been evaluated and it is determined that wireless technology can fit into the current business strategy, the next step is to gather information. With all of the different wireless technologies available and with the constant changes taking place in this area, the expertise to gather the information may be beyond that of the current IT staff. Many organizations turn to outside consultants and vendors to help provide information at this point. Some organizations may send out a **request for information (RFI)**. An RFI seeks to gain information about what vendors may have to offer. RFIs are general in scope. For example, a broad statement such as, "The vendor will install a wireless network on the second floor of the building to accommodate 45 users" may be enough to start things rolling. Several different vendors are encouraged to respond with information about the particular products that they sell that will meet those needs.

Once all of the RFIs have been returned, the organization can examine each of them in detail. Generally a pattern will emerge from the RFIs returned from the different vendors. For example, if four vendors recommend a radio frequency (RF) IEEE 802.11a wireless WLAN while one vendor recommends using Bluetooth, the direction to take begins to become clear. However, caution should be taken regarding RFIs. Vendors want to sell a product or service to the business and may sometimes overemphasize the strength of their product while minimizing its weaknesses. Independent research is still needed after the RFIs have been received.

Return on Investment

After potential solutions have been suggested by vendor RFIs and independent research has been conducted, a determination of the costs of the project is necessary. However, the cost by itself cannot be the sole basis of the decision. Rather, the cost has to be taken in light of the benefit that the project will provide. It may cost $50,000 to implement wireless technology, which might seem like a high cost. However, if the new technology will increase revenue by $250,000, then the cost seems very reasonable.

Determining the cost in relationship to the benefits is known as calculating **return on investment (ROI)**. In strict accounting terms, ROI is the profit divided by the investment. ROI projections are useful when considering the purchase of products or services needed for a business. ROI is best expressed over a specific period of time. For example, you might project that a $50,000 wireless network will save a total of $75,000 in 18 months. The trick with ROIs is to determine all of the costs as well as all of the projected savings.

When determining costs, it is important to consider all costs involved. **Upfront costs** are costs that are necessary to start a project, such as installing the wireless technology in order to start using it. For example, upfront costs for a WLAN include purchasing access points and wireless NICs for all devices and computers. The number of access points depends on the coverage area, number of users, and types of services needed. Hardware costs may vary depending on such factors as performance requirements, coverage requirements, and bandwidth.

Yet upfront costs are not the only costs to be considered. Beyond these basic equipment costs, it is important to take into account other costs as well. **Recurring costs** are often overlooked when determining costs. A recurring cost is a cost that may continue to be paid over an extended period of time. For example, if a free space optics transceiver is to be leased from a local carrier, that annual lease is a recurring cost and should be considered as part of the total cost for the technology. Other costs such as installation, projected maintenance, hardware or software maintenance contracts, IT staff training, and user training should all be factored into the total cost.

A much more difficult task is to determine the savings that can be accumulated. Because the system is obviously not already in place, it may be very difficult to decide what savings or increased revenue can be accrued. The key here is to be as realistic as possible. Gathering information from other users of the technology can be very helpful.

One study conducted by Cisco in 2001 concluded that savings for wireless technology would save the average college almost $57,000 per year and save a hospital $130,000 annually.

Although ROI studies are considered very important, they still are not conducted as frequently as they should be. In a recent survey only 26 percent of those responding said that they conducted an ROI analysis prior to installing a WLAN system. Almost 25 percent indicated there was "simply no need to" while 16 percent said that cost was simply not an issue.

Develop a Plan

Once it has been determined that a real need exists that can be solved by implementing wireless technology, and the ROI is positive, the next step is to create a plan. The adage that "those who fail to plan, plan to fail" is never more true than when considering a new technology. The landscape is littered with projects that were poorly planned at the beginning, and after watching "cost overruns" escalate astromonically the project was finally abandoned. Developing a sensible, workable plan is perhaps the most critical piece of the entire process. Planning should never be done in a vacuum; instead, the IT staff, users, and consultants may all be asked for their input. Once the plan has been completed, a request for proposal is sent out to vendors for them to respond with a formal cost for the project or equipment.

Who To Involve

Making an investment in wireless technology involves the efforts of many different people. One of the most important groups is the IT staff and IT professionals of the organization. The purpose of using the IT staff is twofold. First, they have a broad background in technology and can contribute much to the dialog regarding their experiences and knowledge base. They are the most trained technologists for that organization, and they need to be treated as such. Nothing alienates an IT staff more quickly than to arbitrarily hire an outside consultant without first tapping the expertise in house.

A second reason for involving the IT staff at this point is to make them aware of the proposed project, since they will be the ones who will be providing technical support and training. This group will be the strongest "cheerleaders" of the new technology to the users. If the IT staff is alienated from the planning process, the project is very like to be slow to take off or even fail.

Another important group to involve in planning are the users themselves, since they will be the ones who are actually using the new wireless technology. Generally it is not practical to involve all users at this stage. Instead, a representative group can be selected to participate. However, the group should represent a true cross-section of the user base. Too often the most technological users who are enthusiastic about any new technology are the only ones chosen to participate. These users will enthusiastically support any new technology project, especially if they get to be among the first to test it. The representative group should not just include these types of users. Instead, it should also include the "average" user as well as those who have a reputation of being negative toward change and new technology. Not only will this allow for impartial input to the planning process, but it may also serve to get a better cross-section of users "on board" when the new technology rolls out.

Because they work with customers on a daily basis, the IT staff can provide names of positive, negative, and neutral users to help in the planning process.

External consultants are generally the third group that participate in the planing process. They have the advantage of being outside the organization and can view the organization and its needs from an unbiased perspective.

A common mistake is to turn an entire project over to consultants and allow them to create the plan. This approach results in a plan that does not benefit from the expertise of the local users and IT staff, and may in fact antagonize them. Instead, consultants should be used as one source of input, but not the sole source. It is important to schedule regular meetings with consultants and ask them for detailed explanations as the project moves forward. Consultants should provide in the plan a schedule of activities, a list of proposed technology, and a phased implementation plan. This permits responses from the other participants in the planning process as well as ensures that the planning phase stays on target.

Request for Proposal

Once a plan for wireless technology has been designed, the next step is for the organization to submit a **request for proposal (RFP)**. An RFP is a detailed planning document that is sent to vendors with precise specifications for the products and services that the organization intends to buy. RFPs are much more detailed than RFIs. An RFP may start with, "The vendor will install an 802.11b WLAN network for 45 users in an area in which users are no more than 275 feet from the access point," and should include more detailed information such as a proposed schedule, known issues (such as a building that contains asbestos), and any other information that would assist the vendor in creating his response. Some of the key elements to be contained in an RFP include:

- *Statement of values*—A statement of values helps the vendors see the "philosophy" of the business and what is important. For example, is network performance more important than the average response time that it takes the vendor to respond to a problem? Or, is the immediate availability of the hardware and software more important than price? A statement of values assists the vendor in developing their response RFP.
- *Description of operations*—A description of the business itself is also helpful for the vendors. This would include any future business plans that might affect the RFP, such as an expansion in a branch office building.
- *Current network and applications*—The RFP should describe the current network, such as the number of sites, the current configuration, along with the applications that are currently being used and the planned additions.
- *Timetable*—The RFP should include a timetable that lists specific dates. An example is shown in Table 10-3.

Table 10-3 Sample RFP timetable

Proposed Date	Activity
May 1	Date RFP is issued
May 15	Last date that written questions may be submitted by vendors
May 30	Date RFP responses are due
June 15	The week that initial cuts will be made
July 1	The week that presentations by the finalists will be made
July 15	Date the contract will be awarded
August 15	Date the contract will be finalized
September 10	Date work is to begin
February 12	Date work is to be completed

Vendors will respond to the RFP with their solution for the project. The vendor's response should contain detailed information regarding what will be installed, timelines, and how much it will cost. Once all of the RFPs have been received and analyzed, a final decision can then be made regarding which vendor will be selected. Choosing a vendor should be done carefully by checking the vendor's background and references. Selecting a vendor who submits the lowest cost RFP can often turn out to be a very costly decision.

One of the responses that may appear in the RFPs could be from a **wireless application service provider (WASP)**. A WASP can design and create a wireless application and even deliver the software, hardware, security, and networks as one complete package. Because many of the wireless devices, languages, and applications are so new and diverse, a WASP may have the expertise needed to get the project up and running quickly. Many WASPs will even host the application on their own wireless network, in which case the services are subscribed to rather than purchased.

Perform a Limited Trial

After the RFPs have been received and the vendor has been selected, it is important to perform a limited trial. It is usually possible to borrow sample hardware and software from the vendor who won the bid. The IT staff should be thoroughly involved in the trial, along with a select group of users. Those users who were involved in the planning process are good candidates.

The new wireless technology should be "put through the paces." Devices should be connected and then taken offline, the base stations should disconnected, and other similar activities should be performed to see how the technology reacts under both normal and unusual circumstances. This is a time in which the IT department can be introduced to the technology and start learning troubleshooting techniques while dealing with the trial group of users. The security of the new technology should also be thoroughly tested at this point. It is also an opportunity for managers to see the technology in action so that they can begin to understand how it will impact the business.

Begin Training

After the technology has been tested thoroughly, the next step is to begin training. Training provides all users as well as support specialists with the knowledge to effectively operate and support the new wireless technology. Users need to know how to use the new hardware and software, and the support staff needs to know how to manage the network and diagnose problems. Training will increase the effectiveness of the new technology once it is installed because users will have less of a learning curve. This, in turn, will minimize the drop in productivity that is normally associated with the installation of a new system. Also, well-trained users will have fewer questions and require less IT support after they start using the new system.

The IT staff must be trained first. This may include on-site training from the vendor, if it was included as part of the RFP, or attending workshops or specialized classes that cover the technology. Once the staff has been trained then they in turn can train the users. Because all users learn differently, a variety of training sessions should be offered to accommodate them. The different types of training include:

- Small group sessions
- Detailed written manual

- Web-based training
- One-on-one sessions

Roll Out to All Users

As the training moves towards completion, the final rollout to all users can begin. The most efficient way to do a widespread rollout of a wireless technology is to do it in phases. If possible, start with just one department or unit of the business. The IT staff will be able to deal with problems more easily if they only have to deal with one department or unit at a time. This also allows for any problems to be solved that only affect one department instead of the entire community of users.

On occasion, a project may need to go "live" before it is entirely debugged and before every feature is added due to time considerations. If this is the case, it is important that the key users understand this and feel comfortable with the temporary state of the new technology. Their leadership among the other users can make or break the project.

Once the system is installed and running in a unit, it is a good idea for the vendor and the IT staff to confer and identify any problems that may have arisen before additional units are brought on. IT staff members can also compare notes to determine if the training sessions meet the needs of the users based on the number of questions they received. The training can then be "tweaked" as the remaining users are trained.

Provide Support

Whereas training is primarily done before the new system is turned on, support is the continued follow-up for answering questions and assisting users. User support functions can be organized in a variety of different ways. These include:

- Establish informal peer-to-peer support groups
- Create formal user support groups
- Maintain a help desk center
- Assign support to the IT department

Each of these has its own set of strengths and weaknesses. However, establishing and staffing an internal help desk is one of the most effective means of support. A **help desk** is a central point of contact for users who need assistance using technology. The help desk manages customer problems and requests, and also provides support services to solve the problem. The help desk can provide basic information to users, such as why an FSO connection is slower in the rain. The help desk can also be a good source of identifying areas, based on user responses, where improved technology can save the company money. Some suggestions regarding a help desk include:

- Have one telephone number for the help desk
- Plan for increased call volume after the new network is installed

- Create a method to effectively track problems
- Use surveys to determine user satisfaction
- Periodically rotate network personnel into the help desk
- Use information from the help desk to organize follow-up training

Chapter Summary

- The advantages of incorporating wireless technology into a business are far-reaching and can positively impact an organization in many ways. Industry experts agree that access to corporate data from almost anywhere is the greatest advantage of wireless technology. This allows decisions to be made quickly from any location with the most up-to-date information. A second advantage is that universal access to corporate data leads to increased productivity and accuracy by employees. Wireless technology can also reduce business costs by shifting the burden of accessing a customer's data away from the business to the customer. Wireless technology can also help make data available from almost anywhere at any time. Finally, wireless technology can help improve the support that IT departments provide to users.
- Just as there are distinct advantages for a business to use wireless technology, there are also challenges. Any new technology faces glitches and problems simply because it has not been as thoroughly tested as a mature technology. Being an early adopter of a new technology can sometimes place a heavy burden on a business. Secondly, with some wireless technologies, such as digital cellular telephony, there is no clear indication which competing technology will become the standard and which ones will never be heard from again. This poses a critical decision for businesses to be sure that they invest in the correct technology. Thirdly, wireless technology's greatest strength—allowing users to roam freely without being connected to the network by wires—is also its greatest weakness. Just as a roaming user can receive radio frequency (RF) signals anywhere within a building, so too can an unauthorized user outside the building receive those same RF signals. In addition, some users are reluctant to change to a new technology. Finally, the need for information technology (IT) professionals to develop and implement wireless applications and provide support is skyrocketing. This has resulted in a shortage of qualified IT professionals to install, support, and maintain wireless systems.
- Once a business has decided to invest in wireless technology, it faces the task of building a new wireless infrastructure. This is much like adding a new network to the organization. The first step is to evaluate the need for wireless technology. The entire organization should be looked at as a whole. Sometimes users fall into the trap of viewing only their department or unit instead of seeing the big picture of the entire organization. The next step is to look at how the organization or business actually uses its current network. Assessing the current network can help to identify why a new technology may be needed. If the current network can be upgraded or adapted to meet the current needs, then wireless technology may not be necessary at this time. However, if the current network cannot support the anticipated future growth

of the business or there is a clear indication that wireless technology can help the business grow, then investing in it may be the answer. After the organization and the current network have been evaluated and it is determined that wireless technology can fit into the current business strategy, the next step is to gather information. Some organizations may send out a Request for Information (RFI). After potential solutions have been suggested by vendor RFIs and independent research has been conducted, a determination of the costs of the project is necessary. However, the cost by itself cannot be the sole determination. Rather, the cost has to be taken in light of the benefit that the project will provide. Determining the cost in relationship to the benefits is known as the Return on Investment (ROI).

- Once it has been determined that a real need exists that can be solved by implementing wireless technology and the ROI is positive, the next step is to create a plan. Developing a sensible, workable plan is perhaps the most critical piece of the entire process. Planning should include the IT staff, users, and consultants. Once a plan has been designed, the next step is for the organization to submit a Request for Proposal (RFP). An RFP is a detailed planning document that is sent to vendors with precise specifications for the products and services that the organization intends to buy. RFPs are much more detailed than RFIs.

- After the RFPs have been received and the vendor has been selected, it is important to perform a limited trial. It is usually possible to borrow sample hardware and software from the vendor who won the bid. The IT staff should be thoroughly involved in the trial, along with a select group of users. Those users who were involved in the planning process are good candidates. The new wireless technology should be tested to see how the technology reacts under both normal as well as unusual circumstances. This is a time in which the IT department can be introduced to the technology and start learning troubleshooting techniques while dealing with the trial group of users.

- After the technology has been tested thoroughly, the next step is to begin training. Training provides all users as well as support specialists the knowledge to effectively operate and support the new wireless technology. Users need to know how to use the new hardware and software, and the support staff needs to know how to manage the network and diagnose problems. Training will increase the effectiveness of the new technology once it is installed because users will have less of a learning curve. This, in turn, will minimize the drop in productivity that is normally associated with the installation of a new system. Also, well-trained users will have fewer questions and require less IT support after they start using the new system.

- As the training is moving toward completion, the final rollout to all users can begin. The most efficient way to do a widespread rollout of a wireless technology is to do it in phases. It should start with just one department or unit of the business. The IT staff will be able to deal with problems more easily if they only have to deal with one department or unit at a time. This also allows for any problems to be solved that only affect one department instead of the entire community of users.

- Support is the continued follow-up for answering questions and assisting users. User support functions can be organized in a variety of different ways. Establishing and staffing an internal help desk has shown to be one of the most effective means of support. A help desk is a central point of contact for users who need assistance using the network. The help desk manages customer problems and requests, and then provides support services to solve the problem.

KEY TERMS

help desk — A central point of contact for users who need assistance using technology.

recurring costs — Costs that continue to be paid over a period of time.

request for information (RFI) — A document sent to a vendor to gain general information about a vendor's products or solutions to a problem.

request for proposal (RFP) — A detailed planning document with precise specifications for the products and services.

return on investment (ROI) — The profit or advantage of an action.

upfront costs — Costs that are necessary to start a project.

wireless application service provider (WASP) — An organization that can design, create, and deliver a complete wireless application.

REVIEW QUESTIONS

1. The primary advantage of wireless technology is ________________.
   a. universal access to corporate data
   b. lower cost
   c. newer technology
   d. reduced bandwidth
2. Each of the following can be used by a help desk to provide service to the users except:
   a. Have one telephone number.
   b. Create a method to effectively track problems.
   c. Report users' questions to their supervisor.
   d. Use surveys to determine user satisfaction.
3. If customers can see data about themselves on the business' computer system, it will enable them to ________________.
   a. gain access to secret corporate data
   b. sell this data to other people
   c. reduce the amount of bandwidth needed for their home computer
   d. make better and more informed decisions

4. Each of the following is an advantage to the IT department for adopting wireless technology except ________________.
   a. easier setup
   b. less time-consuming moves of equipment
   c. higher maintenance costs
   d. decreased cabling costs
5. Any new technology faces problems simply because ________________.
   a. it has not been used and thoroughly tested as a mature technology
   b. it is based on a weaker standard
   c. managers are unfamiliar with it
   d. old technology is always slower
6. All wireless technologies are clearly based on approved industry standards. True or false?
7. Wireless technology's greatest strength, allowing access without being connected to the network by wires, is also its greatest weakness. True or false?
8. There is a shortage of qualified IT professionals to install, support, and maintain wireless systems. True or false?
9. "Do we really need it?" is a question that must be asked first when adding a wireless infrastructure to a business. True or false?
10. Sometimes users fall into the trap of viewing only their department or unit instead of seeing the big picture of the entire organization. True or false?
11. The banking industry must have networks that have a ________________ degree of security.
12. The task of assessing the current network can be helped by documenting the ________________ network in detail.
13. A(n) ________________ seeks to gain information about what vendors may have to offer and are general in their scope.
14. Determining the cost in relationship to the benefits is known as ________________.
15. A ________________ cost is a cost that may continue to be paid over an extended period of time.
16. List the three groups that should be involved in developing a plan and why they should be involved.
17. Why is it a mistake to turn the entire planning process over to external consultants? What is a better approach instead of this?

18. Describe a request for purchase (RFP).
19. What is a wireless access service provider (WASP), and what services can a WASP provide?
20. What is the advantage of a limited trial? What are some steps that should be taken during a trial?

HANDS-ON PROJECTS

1. Because everyone learns differently, it is important to provide a variety of different types of training sessions for the users of new technology. Research the different types of learning styles that are common among most people and make a list of them. Then, write a one-paragraph description of the type of training that you believe would go best with that type of learning style.
2. A help desk is a vital tool for providing continued maintenance and support for users of IT. Using a variety of sources, such as textbooks and the Internet, write a one-page paper about the type of help desk that you would set up for a business. Include times of operation, number of support staff needed, and how the help desk would contact the technicians with a problem and continue to track that problem until it is resolved.
3. A shortage of qualified IT staff is a critical area of concern. Use the Internet to research this problem and describe what is being done about it at the national and state levels. What are your suggestions for addressing this problem?
4. What are some ways to overcome user reluctance to adopt a new technology? What techniques would work for those who are opposed to any technology? What techniques would work for those who are just opposed to any change? Write a one-page paper on your findings.
5. Using the network at your school as a model, draw a diagram and complete a table like Table 10-2 that describes that network. Include a narrative of its history and what changes are anticipated in the next 12 months.
6. Locate and identify four organizations in your area that install and service WLANs. Find out as much as you can about these organizations, and make a recommendation regarding which one you would hire. What were their strengths and weaknesses? How did they compare with one another? Write a one-page paper on your conclusions.

CASE PROJECTS

The Baypoint Group

The Baypoint Group (TBG), a company that assists organizations and businesses with issues involving network planning and design, has hired you as a consultant once again. GHS is a chain of sporting good stores that cater to the sport of soccer. Because GHS has grown in popularity, it now has nine stores in the area. GHS is considering implementing a wireless technology that will link all of its stores through wireless broadband service, installing WLANs in each store, and providing its employees with PDAs for better customer service. GHS is unsure how to start this process. They have asked TGB for help, and TGB has turned to you.

1. Create a presentation for GHS that explains the steps necessary to implement a wireless technology infrastructure from evaluating the needs through providing support. Your presentation should last about 20–25 minutes. Use PowerPoint to create your slides.
2. The GHS management is ready to start the process after hearing your presentation. They feel that one of the barriers they must overcome is providing support for their users. GHS does not have a centralized help desk; instead employees help each other and the IT staff does a limited amount of instruction, just enough to get the user through his or her problem. GHS would like your opinion on how to set up a help desk and what services it should provide. Create a short (10-minute) PowerPoint presentation about what a help desk does, its advantages and disadvantages, and some tips on using a help desk for GHS.

Optional Team Case Project

The decision by GHS to move to a wireless infrastructure has met with some resistance from a few employees who either do not understand the advantages of the technology or who simply don't want to change. Form two teams, with each team selecting either the advantages or disadvantages of wireless technologies. Hold a friendly debate in which each person presents a 3–5 minute talk about the advantages of his technology. After the talk allow time for the others to ask questions. Be prepared to defend your technology.

APPENDIX

A

History of Wireless Communications

Studying the history of a topic does not always evoke thrills and excitement. In fact, the question "Who cares about the past?" is often asked when studying history is even mentioned. However, there are several benefits to studying the history of a technology such as wireless communications. First, our current technology wasn't discovered overnight, like stumbling upon a previously unknown island in the ocean. There are always several smaller steps that take place to lead up to the development of the new technology. Tracing the development of these earlier discoveries can help us better understand how the final technology actually functions. Being able to see how a technology was created piece-by-piece, just as the early inventors did, can help us see how each piece fits with the next development and to understand how the technology actually works.

Another advantage of studying the historical development of technology is that it reveals how the device was accepted and used by society. This shows what value society placed on that technology and is a good predictor how it will be used in the future. In short, studying the past helps us understand where we are headed.

Finally, historical study helps us better appreciate the technology. Some of today's great technological marvels were the result of years of painstaking trial and effort by some of the great minds of earlier days. How they persevered as early trailblazers without knowing exactly where they would end up is a testimony to their character and helps us better appreciate what we have before us today.

Early Developments

The word *telegraphy* comes from a Greek word that means "writing in distance." Telegraphy is a system of communication that is able to transmit signals that represent coded letters and numbers or other signs of writing over long distances. Telegraphy can be divided in acoustic (sound), optical (sight), and electrical transmissions.

Acoustic telegraphy has very ancient origins. Greek historians tell how the Persian king Darius I in 500 BC could send news from the capital city to the outlying provinces of the empire by means of a line of shouting men positioned on hills. This kind of transmission was determined to be 30 times faster than normal couriers carrying the information. Julius Caesar in 50 BC said that the nation of the Gauls could call to war their entire army in only three days just by using the human voice.

Early optical telegraphy consisted of fire at night and smoke or reflections from shiny objects during the day to transmit signals. A device called a hydraulic telegraph was used by the Caraginese around 500 BC. It consisted of two large vases placed on distant hills. The vases were filled with water and had a floating vertical pole at the center with coded letters attached to it. Messages were sent by rising or lowering the pole (by emptying or adding water to the vases) to move the coded letter to a certain point.

An optical telegraph was developed by Claude Chappe in 1792. Coded signals were based on the different positions of three wooden interlinked arms that rotated at the top of a fixed vertical pole. The central arm (called a regulator) was longer than the other two arms (called indicators). The indicator arms could rotate freely around a center and be positioned at 45 degree angles. A book 92 pages long contained 92 different words on each page (for a total of almost 8,500 words). The arms of the optical telegraph were moved to indicate the page number and the word number of the particular word that was to be transmitted. The optical telegraph was officially adopted by the French government and several other European states.

The discovery of electrical current led to the introduction of electrical telegraphy in the early 1880s. Samuel Morse toured Italy in 1830 as a well-known painter. When he was sailing back to the United States, the concept of a telegraph based on *electromagnetism* came to him. Electromagnetism is a magnetic force created by a current of electricity. His first telegraph receiving instrument was constructed from a wooden clock motor that provided the power to move a paper tape under a pen. The pen was moved by an electromagnet that was driven from a telegraph line. A canvas stretcher from his painting supplies was used as a frame to support the device. He received a patent for his telegraph invention in 1838, the same year he completed his last two paintings. In 1844 Morse sent the famous words from the Bible, "What hath God wrought!" on his telegraph from the U.S. Capitol Building in Washington, DC, to Baltimore.

Morse tried without success to obtain European patents for his telegraph. In addition, he invented a code now known as the Morse code for use with his telegraph instrument.

James Maxwell, a Scottish physicist, was also very interested in electromagnetism. In 1861 he developed a mathematical model for a hypothetical medium that consisted of a fluid that could carry electric and magnetic effects. Maxwell theorized that if the fluid became elastic and a charge was applied to it, this would set up a disturbance in the fluid, which would produce waves that would travel through the medium. It was calculated that these waves would travel at the speed of light. Maxwell published his work in 1873.

In 1888 the German physicist Heinrich Hertz made the discovery of radio waves, which are a form of electromagnetic radiation. This confirmed Maxwell's theory. He devised a transmitter that radiated radio waves, and detected them across the length of his laboratory using a metal loop with a gap at one side. When the loop was placed within the transmitter's electromagnetic field, sparks were produced across the gap. This proved that electromagnetic waves could be sent out into space and could be remotely detected. Although people had seen the effects of radio waves before, nobody had realized what they were.

Radio waves were originally called "Hertzian waves."

RADIO

Guglielmo Marconi was born in Bologna, Italy, in 1874. By age 21 he had already performed simple experiments that had convinced him it was possible to send signals by using electromagnetic waves. His first successes were at short distances, only about 330 feet (100 meters) between his house and the end of the garden.

Scientists and other experts at that time believed that electromagnetic waves could only be transmitted in a straight line, and then only if there was nothing in the way. They thought that the main obstacle to radio transmission was the curvature of the earth's surface. Marconi was convinced that transmission was possible between two distant points even if they were separated by an obstacle. He placed his transmitter near his house and the receiver almost 2 miles (3 kilometers) away behind a hill. Overseeing the receiver was the Marconi's servant, Mignani, who was holding a rifle. His responsibility was to fire a rifle shot when the signal was received. From his house, Marconi pushed the key of the transmitter three times and then heard the answer of a distant gunshot. His experiment proved that electromagnetic waves had traveled a distance and overcome an obstacle. With the completion of his experiment in 1895, Marconi had demonstrated that wireless telegraphy, also known as radio communications, was possible.

The word *radio* comes from the term *radiated energy.*

Marconi found little enthusiasm for his invention in Italy. He presented his device to the Italian government, only to be told by an Italian minister that it was "not suitable for telecommunications"! However, in England, where his mother was born, Marconi received support and financial backing and was able to patent his invention. In 1897, the British Ministry of Posts gave him money and technicians to continue his experiments and the transmission distances gradually became longer, up to 60 miles (100 kilometers).

In 1901, Marconi set up a transmitting station in England, and a receiving station was built on the other side of the Atlantic Ocean on the island of Newfoundland. For three hours every day, a signal was transmitted while Marconi experimented with newer and larger types of antennas suspended from light kites. On December 12, 1901, a signal was received at Newfoundland. For the first time electromagnetic waves had crossed the Atlantic Ocean, traveling a distance of 2,175 miles (3,500 kilometers). Although Marconi did not know it at the time, the success of his experiment was due to the presence of the *ionosphere*. The ionosphere, a layer of the upper atmosphere (between 40 to 310 miles or 60 to 500 kilometers), plays a fundamental role in all radio communications. The ionosphere reflects electromagnetic waves like a mirror and allows a radio signal to travel far distances.

The ionosphere was discovered by an English physicist in 1924.

Marconi quickly put his work on wireless telegraphy to practical use. In 1899 for the first time a distress signal was sent from a shipwrecked boat to a station on land using wireless telegraphy, enabling its passengers to be rescued. Marconi also visited the United States and helped the U.S. Navy set up communications between its cruisers. In 1903, while sailing from England to the U.S., Marconi established the first press agency. News information was flashed to the ship via wireless transmissions. This information was then printed onboard the ship as part of a newspaper.

Marconi continued to refine his wireless telegraphy devices. In 1904 he built a rotating device that led to the development of horizontal antennas, which permitted a tremendous increase in the strength of received signals. He later patented this device. In 1934 he demonstrated how a ship, in case of fog and in total blindness, could safely find the entrance of a harbor using wireless signals. In 1935 he performed distant search experiments that would eventually lead to the invention of radar.

Marconi also studied microwaves, early television technology, and started research on the therapeutic use of radio waves called Marconitherapy.

Marconi died in Rome in 1937. To remember his great contribution to wireless telegraphy, radios all around the world observed a long minute of silence on that date.

In 1909 Marconi was awarded the Nobel prize for Physics.

TELEVISION

The idea of transmitting pictures and sound over distance occupied the minds of dreamers for centuries. Yet unlike radio, television was not created by one individual at one specific point in time. Instead, television evolved over a period of 50 years based on the discoveries and efforts of many scientists and visionaries.

The basic process of television involves transmitting images by converting light to electrical signals. This is known as *photoelectric technology*. Early attempts to send still images down a telegraph wire in the mid 1800s were based on *electrochemical technology*. In 1842 Alexander Bain proposed a facsimile telegraph transmission system based on electrochemical technology. Bain proposed that metallic letters of the alphabet could be transmitted chemically. Electrified metal letters could be scanned by a pendulum device and reproduced at the other end of the telegraph wire by a synchronized pendulum contacting a piece of chemical paper.

Historians normally associate Bain's ideas with the modern day facsimile (fax) machine.

Bain's proposal was improved upon in 1847 when F. Bakewell of Great Britain patented a chemical telegraph. Bakewell replaced the pendulums with synchronized rotating cylinders. By 1861, handwritten messages and photographs could be sent over telegraph lines.

In 1873, Louis May, a British telegrapher, discovered the basics of photoconductivity. He found that selenium bars, when exposed to light, were a strong conductor of electricity. He also found that the conduction of electrical current would vary depending on the amount of light hitting the bars. A later discovery revealed that changes in electrical voltage produced by selenium when scanning a document could magnetically control a pencil at the receiving end of the transmission. By 1881, Shelford Bidwell successfully transmitted silhouettes using both selenium and a scanning system. He called the device the scanning phototelegraph.

The first working device for analyzing a scene to generate electrical signals suitable for transmission was a scanning system proposed and built by Paul Nipkow in 1884. The scanner consisted of a rotating disc with a number of small holes (*apertures*) arranged in a spiral in front of light sensitive selenium. As the disc rotated, the spiral of 18 holes swept across the image of the scene from top to bottom in a pattern of 18 parallel horizontal lines. This had the effect of dividing the picture into 18 lines of dots or picture elements (*pixels*). For reproduction of the scene, a light source, controlled in intensity by the detected electrical signal, was projected on a screen through a similar Nipkow disc that rotated in synch with the pickup disc.

The Nipkow disc device was capable of transmitting about 4,000 pixels per second.

This was known as the world's first electromechanical television system. However, Nipkow could not build a reliable working system because he was unable to amplify the electric current created by the selenium to drive a receiver. Nevertheless, Nipkow demonstrated a scanning process for the analysis of images by dissecting a complete scene into an orderly pattern of pixels that could be transmitted by an electrical signal and reproduced as a visual image. This became the basis for present-day television.

With improvements in technology mechanical television later became practical. In 1928 television signals were being sent from London to New York. By 1932 the first home mechanical television sets were available and over 10,000 sets were sold. These first sets delivered a crude picture consisting of a cloudy 40-line image (compared to 525 lines on today's televisions) on a six-inch square mirror. The sets cost between $85 and $135.

North America's first television station, W3XK in Wheaton, Maryland, was started in the 1930s.

Most historians generally credit Vladimir Zworykin as the "father of television." A Russian immigrant, Zworykin came to the United States after World War I and went to work for Westinghouse. From 1920 until 1929 Zworykin performed some of his early experiments in television. He developed the first practical TV camera tube known as the *iconoscope* in 1923. Zworkin's iconoscope (from the Greek for "image" and "to see") consisted of a thin film coated with a photosensitive layer of potassium hydride. His kinescope picture tube formed the basis for subsequent advances in the field. With this crude camera tube and a kinescope as the picture reproducer, he had the essential elements for electronic television. By 1931, with the iconoscope and kinescope well-developed, electronic television was ready to be launched.

A lesser-know early electronic television pioneer was Philo Farnsworth. At age 19 Farnsworth persuaded an investor to secure venture capital for an all-electronic television system. Farnsworth established his laboratory first in Los Angeles and later in San Francisco. It was there in 1927 that Farnsworth gave the first public demonstration of the television system he had dreamed of for six years. He was not yet 21 years old. Farnsworth was quick to develop several of the basic concepts of an electronic television system and was granted many patents.

By 1939 widespread commercial electronic television broadcasting started in the U.S. The National Broadcasting Company (NBC) started regularly scheduled broadcasts in the New York area to only 400 sets. In 1941, the American Federal Communications Authority set the standards for broadcast television. With the start of World War II, however, television production stopped in the U.S.

At the end of the war, there was a two-year delay in the development of television as the Federal Communications Authority considered proposals for color television systems. In 1947, all proposals for color television were rejected. Black and white sets, however, were manufactured in large quantities. In 1946 there were only 7,000 televisions in the U.S. By 1950 there were over 10 million sets.

It took until 1954 for the National Television System Committee (NTSC) to set the standard for color broadcast television. They settled on a system that was compatible with existing black and white TV sets. Color was achieved by inserting the color information inside the black and white signal. The color standard specified 625 lines at 25 frames per second.

By 1970, television had become the primary information and entertainment medium in the world. Today it is estimated that there are 605 million television sets worldwide. However, the standards for television broadcasting are not universal. There are 15 different variations of broadcasting standards used around the world.

RADAR

Radar has been hailed as one of the greatest scientific developments of the first half of the 20th century. Although radar is usually associated with detecting airplanes in the sky, or ships on the ocean, it actually is used in a variety of different ways. Some of these include:

- Radar is used extensively in weather forecasting and to provide early warning for severe weather. A radar system known as NEXRAD (NEXt Generation Weather RADar) can gauge the size, intensity, wind speed, and direction of storms, the amount of water vapor in clouds, and can detect high-level circular wind patterns that cause tornadoes.
- Radar is used to help archaeologists excavate ancient sites. Radar can be used from space satellites and airplanes to scan entire regions for possible archaeological sites. The radar waves can penetrate earth, sand, and volcanic ash that cover ancient sites. When the waves strike rock or metal the echo is reflected back. This helps archeologists determine the best location to dig.
- Radar helps engineers study highway tunnels for potential hidden dangers. Radar can be mounted on a truck and driven through a tunnel that is built under a body of water. Radar can quickly and accurately scan the tunnel for any leaks.
- Located on a space shuttle, radar can be used to locate stagnant pools of water in areas of dense foliage on earth. With this information, the stagnant water, which can harbor insects carrying disease, can be located and drained.
- Radar has also helped provide information about the universe. It is used to locate comets, map stars, and probe planets that cannot be seen with a regular telescope.

"Radar" is an acronym for *RA*dio *D*etection *A*nd *R*anging.

Radar is an active remote sensing system that operates on the principle of echoes. When a person in a room yells out, her voice is sent out as sound waves and is reflected back by the walls to the ears of the listener. Instead of sound waves, radars use radio waves because radio waves travel faster, further, and are reflected better than sound waves. Radio waves travel at the speed of light (186,000 miles or 300,000 kilometers per second).

Radar performs three primary functions:

- It transmits microwave signals (called the *pulse*) toward a target.
- After reaching an object it is reflected back and the radar receives a return portion of the transmitted signal (called the *backscatter*), as seen in Figure A-1.
- It observes the strength, behavior, and the time delay of the returned signals and produces a "blip" on a screen, as seen in Figure A-2.

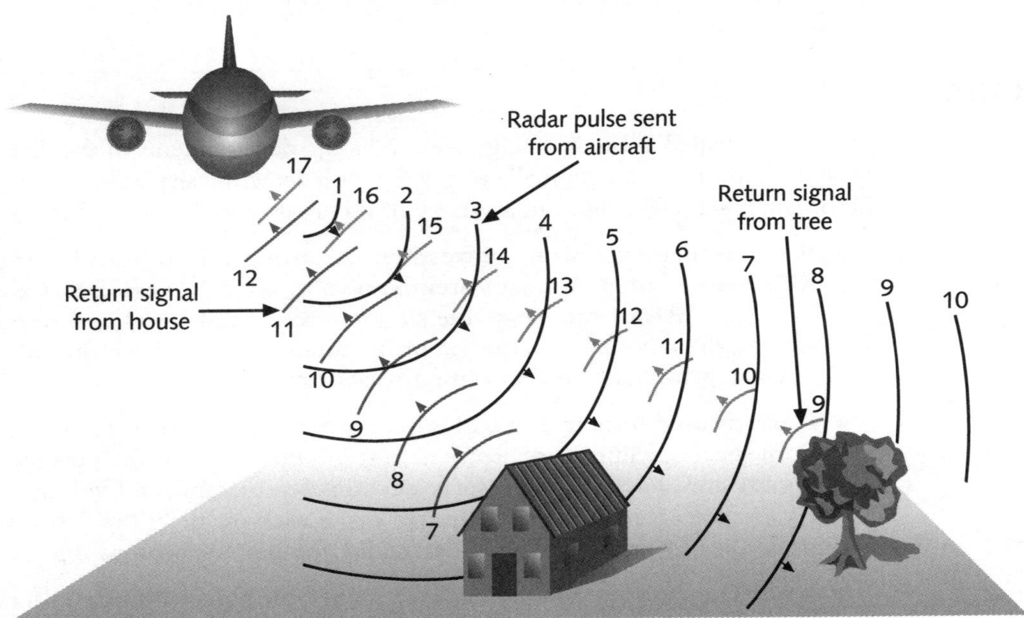

Figure A-1 Radar pulse and backscatter

A radar display shows a map-like picture of the area being scanned. The center of the picture responds to the radar antenna and the radar echoes are shown as bright spots on the screen. The distance of the spot from the center of the screen indicates how far away the object is.

The "blips" produced on a screen will vary depending upon the object reflecting the waves. Sophisticated radar can identify not only an airplane in the sky but also its type, manufacturer, and whether it is friend or foe.

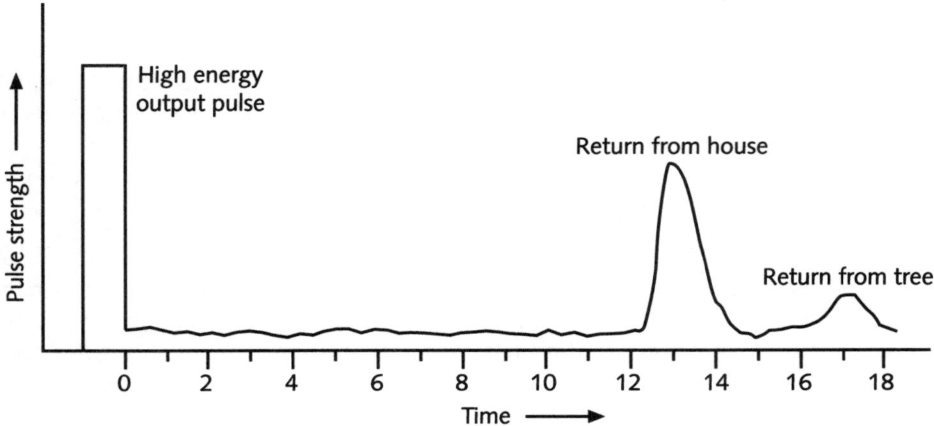

Figure A-2 Radar blips

A special type of radar known as Doppler radar is frequently used today by meteorologists to locate tornados and microbursts, which are downdrafts of air traveling at very high speeds. Doppler radar takes advantage of the *Doppler Effect*. The Doppler Effect is when the frequency of an electromagnetic wave is changed as the wave hits a moving object. Unlike regular radar, Doppler radar sends out waves at multiple sets of frequencies. Upon striking the target, the wave is reflected back at a different frequency than the transmitted wave. The radar compares the frequency of the returned echo with that of the transmitted wave. When the difference is calculated, the speed of the object, which caused the shift in frequency, can be calculated. Wind patterns are shown on the radar display in different colors. The faster a wind is moving the brighter its color.

Doppler radar is also used by law enforcement agencies to locate speeding motorists. Most police radar guns have a split-screen display window, which shows both the speed of the target and the speed of the patrol vehicle.

The development of radar dates back to the discoveries of the 1860s and 1870s, when James Maxwell developed the equations that outlined the behavior of electromagnetic waves, and Heinrich Hertz discovered radio waves. Several years later, a German engineer named Christian Huelsmeyer proposed the use of radio echoes to avoid collisions in marine navigation. The first successful radio range-finding experiment occurred in 1924, when the British scientist Edward Appleton used radio echoes to determine the height of the ionosphere.

The first practical radar system was produced in 1935 by the British physicist Robert Watson-Watt. By 1939 England had established a chain of radar stations along its southern and eastern coasts to detect aggressors in the air or on the sea. About the same time two British scientists were responsible for the most important advance made in the technology of radar during World War II. Henry Boot and John Randall invented an electron tube that was capable of generating high-frequency radio pulses with large amounts of power.

SATELLITES

A *satellite* is any object that orbits or revolves around another object. For example, the moon is a satellite of the earth, and the earth is a satellite of the sun. Man-made satellites provide communications capabilities around the world, transmitting television signals, telephone calls, faxes, computer communications, and weather information. Satellites can be sent into space through a variety of launch vehicles.

The theory of satellites dates back to 325 years before the first man-made satellite was ever launched. Sir Isaac Newton in the 1720s was probably the first person to conceive the idea of a satellite. Newton illustrated how an artificial satellite could be launched from the earth. He pictured the earth with a high mountain and a cannon on top of the mountain firing shots parallel to the ground. Each time the cannon was fired more gunpowder was used and the shot went farther before striking the ground. Because the earth is round, the shots would curve around it. According to Newton's theory, with enough gunpowder, a shot could eventually go fast enough to circle the earth completely and come back to the mountaintop.

During the Second World War, the German military made great strides in the development of rocket technology. However, even the best rocket technology of that day could not achieve an earth orbit. In 1945 Arthur C. Clarke, a science fiction author, wrote an article that envisioned a network of communications satellites. Three satellites could be placed into space at 22,000 miles (35,400 kilometers) so as to orbit the planet every 24 hours. These satellites would be able to transmit signals around the world by transmitting in a "line of sight" with other orbiting satellites. At the time of his writing, the idea was not well received.

Satellites of today that follow this same orbit are said to reside in the "Clarke Belt."

The economic feasibility of satellites in the early days was hotly debated. At a cost of over one billion dollars for a satellite, there were serious questions regarding its return on investment.

On October 4, 1957, the Soviet Union launched Sputnik 1. Sputnik 1 was described as "a radio transmitter in a 23-inch polished aluminum ball." Sputnik was equipped with transmitters to broadcast on two different frequencies, and it circled the globe every 90 minutes. After 18 days its battery was exhausted and the transmitting ceased, and almost three months later Sputnik 1 was incinerated as it fell from orbit back into earth's atmosphere. A month after Sputnik 1 the Soviets launched Sputnik 2 and its passenger, Laika, a dog who has the distinction of being the first living creature to enter outer space.

The U.S. followed with its own launch of Explorer 1 in early 1958. The first communications satellite was launched later that same year. The Signal Communication by Orbital Relay

(SCORE) satellite broadcasted a Christmas message from President Dwight Eisenhower of "Peace on earth, good will toward men" as it orbited the earth for 12 days until its batteries failed. A succession of Soviet and American launches resulted in larger and more sophisticated satellites reaching orbit. In 1961Yuri Gegarin became the first man in orbit.

The U.S. and Soviet Union launched six satellites in 1958, 14 in 1959, 19 in 1960, and 35 satellites in 1961. In 1962, the United Kingdom and Canada launched satellites of their own, along with the 70 satellites launched by the U.S. and Soviet Union.

After the initial launches, the benefits and prestige associated with satellite communications made satellites a popular item. The National Aeronautic and Space Administration (NASA) confined itself to experiments with "mirrors" or passive communications satellites while the U.S. Department of Defense was responsible for "repeater" or active satellites which amplified the received signal at the satellite and provided a much higher quality of communications. In 1960, NASA launched Echo 1, a passive reflector satellite with no amplification possibilities. The Echo satellites were basically large metallicized balloons that served as passive reflectors of radio signals. At the time of its launch, it was thought that passive reflector satellites could serve a purpose in communications, but the technology was soon abandoned because the reflected signal was so weak.

In 1960 the American Telephone and Telegraph Company (AT&T) filed a request with the Federal Communications Commission (FCC) for permission to launch an experimental communications satellite. The U.S. government reacted with surprise because there had never been such a request and there was no policy in place to regulate satellites. AT&T designed, built, and even paid for the launches with its own funds, reimbursing NASA for its use of the rockets. The Telstar I and II spacecraft were prototypes for a constellation of 50 medium earth orbit (MEO) satellites that AT&T was working to put in place. Telstar was the first modern communications satellite to be placed in orbit. However, when the U.S. government later decided to give the monopoly on satellite communications to a consortium, AT&T's satellite project was halted.

The first words transmitted over satellite were not as memorable as Alexander Bell's "Watson, come here I need you!" or Samuel Morse's "What hath God wrought?" The first transmitted words were, "Will everybody please get off this line?" So many people were trying to be the first to hear the transmission that the circuit was being overloaded!

In 1964 an international organization known as INTELSAT (INternational TELecommunications SATellite Organization) was formed. Intelsat was a consortium of over 130 governments and organizations. Intelsat launched a series of satellites with the goal of providing total earth coverage (excluding the North and South Poles) by satellite transmission. This was achieved by 1969. Today Intelsat has 19 satellites in orbit that are open to use by all nations. The Intelsat consortium owns the satellites, but each nation owns their own earth receiving stations.

INTELSAT completed its global coverage just days before the first men walked on the moon in 1969, enabling one half billion people around the world to watch the landmark event.

NASA led the next new wave of communications satellite technology with the launch of Advanced Communications Technology Satellites (ACTS) in 1993. ACTS pioneered the use of several new developments, such as on-board storage and processing and all digital transmission, which make satellite transmission more reliable.

The explosive popularity of cellular telephones advanced the idea of always being connected no matter where you were located on earth. Several companies committed themselves to providing a solution by using satellites in low earth orbit (LEO). The most ambitious of these LEO systems was Iridium, sponsored by Motorola. Iridium planned to launch 66 satellites into polar orbit at altitudes of about 400 miles (650 kilometers). Iridium's goal was to provide communications services to hand-held telephones around the world in 1998. However, Iridium declared bankruptcy in 1999. The total cost of the Iridium system was in excess of three billion dollars.

Iridium originally planned to have 77 satellites, and thus was named after the 77th element in the periodic charts. However, when the plans were scaled back to only 66 satellites, the name Iridium continued to be used because Element 66 has the less pleasant name Dysprosium.

CELLULAR TELEPHONES

In the 1930s and 1940s two-way car radios were installed and used by police, utility companies, government agencies, and emergency services. However, these two-way car radios had several disadvantages and were not very convenient to use. In 1946 in St. Louis, AT&T and Southwestern Bell introduced the first American commercial mobile radio-telephone service to private customers. "Mobiles," as they were called, used the newly issued vehicle radio-telephone licenses granted to Southwestern Bell by the FCC. They operated on six channels. However, interference soon forced Bell to use only three channels.

In a rare exception to the Bell System common practice, subscribers to this first system could actually buy their own radio sets and not use AT&T's equipment.

With two-way car radios a central transmitter with one antenna could serve a wide area. This is illustrated in Figure A-3. However, this system could not be used with mobiles. The reason is that car-mounted transmitters were not as powerful as the central antenna and thus their signals could not always be transmitted all the way back. To overcome this limitation, smaller receivers with antennas were placed on top of buildings and on poles around the city, creating smaller *cells*, or ranges of service areas. When someone was using their mobile the conversation that they heard was transmitted on one frequency by the central transmitter to their moving car. When they spoke on their mobile, however, that transmission was sent on a separate frequency that the nearest receiver antenna picked up. In other words, messages were received on one frequency from the central transmitter but messages were sent to the nearest receiver on a separate frequency. When the car moved from one cell to another that was served by a different receiver, the switch between cells was known as a *handoff.* This is illustrated in Figure A-4.

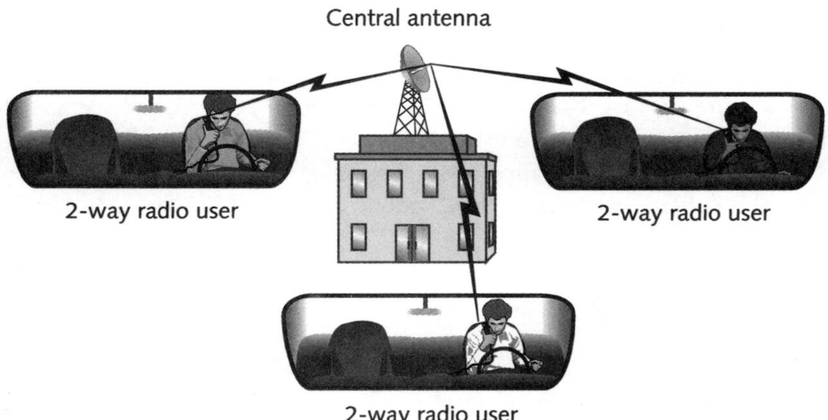

Figure A-3 2-way car radios

Figure A-4 Mobiles using cells

As innovative as mobiles were, there were still several serious limitations. The first limitation was a lack of available frequencies. Mobiles required two frequencies to make a transmission, one frequency to transmit on and one to receive. A single radio-telephone call took up as much frequency space as a radio broadcast station. In the late 1940s there was very little unused transmission space available. And because the FCC gave priority to emergency services, government agencies, utility companies, and services it thought helped the most people, this left only a tiny amount of frequencies available for mobiles. Most mobile telephone systems could not accommodate more than a total of 250 users, with only a handful actually being able to transmit at one time.

At this time the technology for the mobiles was not refined and they actually required six times the amount of frequency that would be needed today.

The second limitation was that waves at lower frequencies travel great distances, sometimes hundreds of miles when they skip across the atmosphere. Although high-powered transmitters gave mobiles a wide operating range the signals could also be detected in adjacent cities. Telephone companies could not reuse their channels in nearby cities due to this potential interference; they required at least 75 miles between mobile systems.

Despite the limitations, mobile service was highly desired. Every city that offered mobiles had lengthy waiting lists. By 1976 only 545 customers in New York City had Bell System mobiles but 3,700 customers were on the waiting list. Some individuals were on waiting lists for up to 10 years. Although allocating more frequency would have solved the problem, the FCC did not do so. Even as late as 1978 all mobile carriers nationwide had just 54 channels.

The first modern cellular telephone systems in the early 1980s used 666 channels.

Although mobiles had limitations and were only used by very few people, they nevertheless launched the basic concept of cellular phones. Designers realized that by using small cells they could use lower-powered transmitters. They also determined that if they could have each cell use a different frequency, then by reusing these frequencies they could substantially increase the traffic capacity of mobile phones. At that time, however, the technology to do so did not exist. Nevertheless the concepts of using cells and of frequency reuse laid the foundation for cellular telephones 50 years later.

In 1969 the Bell System developed a commercial cellular radio operation using frequency reuse. The unusual setting for this venture was on trains running from New York City to Washington, DC, using pay telephones. Passengers could make telephone calls onboard while the trains were moving at 100 miles an hour. Six channels were reused in nine zones along the 225 mile route. A computerized control center in Philadelphia managed the system. Thus the first cell phone was a pay phone.

In July of 1978 AT&T and Illinois Bell started a pilot project in Chicago of analog-based cellular telephone service. Ten cells covering 21,000 square miles made up the Chicago system. This first equipment test began using 90 Bell System employees, and after six months it was opened to the general public. This early cellular telephone proved that a large cellular system could work.

Advanced Mobile Phone Service (AMPS) began setting up analog cellular telephone operations in other parts of the world. An 88-cell system in Tokyo began in December 1979, and a system in Mexico City with one cell started in August 1981. Europe saw cellular service introduced in 1981, when the Nordic Mobile Telephone System began operating in Denmark, Sweden, Finland, and Norway. This was the first multinational cellular system.

Initially U.S. cellular telephone development did not keep up with the rest of the world. The most significant reason was the breakup of the Bell System by the U.S. federal court system and the FCC's 1981 regulations that required the Bell System or a regional operating company, such as Bell Atlantic, to have competition in every cellular market. However, the popularity of cellular soon began to spread across the nation along with the development of an analog cellular infrastructure. The American cellular phone industry grew from less than 204,000 subscribers in 1985 to 1,600,000 in 1988.

Roaming from one city or state in the U.S. was easy because the U.S. system was based on an analog cellular system. In contrast, it was almost impossible to roam in Europe. During the 1980s a plan was launched to create a single Europe-wide digital mobile service with advanced features and easy roaming. This network started operating in 1991. In the U.S. there was no such movement because the analog system was working well.

Today cellular telephone deployment is worldwide, but development remains concentrated in three areas: Scandinavia, the United States, and Japan. There are over 60 million cellular phone users, creating about $30 billion in annual revenues.

APPENDIX

B

TECHNICAL SUMMARIES

This appendix contains summaries of wireless communications technical data and additional information.

GENERAL INFORMATION

ASCII Codes

The American Standard Code for Information Interchange (ASCII) character set defines 256 characters. The first 32 values (0–31) are non-printing control characters such as *Return* and *Line feed*, while the next 96 values (32–127) are printing characters. The remaining 128 values (128–256) represent special non-printing characters that are used for display purposes.

Table B-1 ASCII control characters

Character	Decimal Value	Binary Value	Description
NUL	0	00000000	Null character
SOH	1	00000001	Start of heading
STX	2	00000010	Start of text
ETX	3	00000011	End of text
EOT	4	00000100	End of transmission
ENQ	5	00000101	Enquiry
ACK	6	00000110	Acknowledge
BEL	7	00000111	Bell
BS	8	00001000	Backspace
HT	9	00001001	Horizontal tab
LF	10	00001010	Line feed
VT	11	00001011	Vertical tab
FF	12	00001100	Form feed
CR	13	00001101	Carriage return
SO	14	00001110	Shift out
SI	15	00001111	Shift in
DLE	16	00010000	Data link escape
DC1	17	00010001	Device control 1 (XON)

Table B-1 ASCII control characters (continued)

Character	Decimal Value	Binary Value	Description
DC2	18	00010010	Device control 2
DC3	19	00010011	Device control 3 (XOFF)
DC4	20	00010100	Device control 4
NAK	21	00010101	Negative acknowledge
SYN	22	00010110	Synchronous idle
ETB	23	00010111	End of transmission block
CAN	24	00011000	Cancel line
EM	25	00011001	End of medium
SUB	26	00011010	Substitute
ESC	27	00011011	Escape
FS	28	00011100	File separator
GS	29	00011101	Group separator
RS	30	00011110	Record separator, block-mode terminator
US	31	00011111	Unit separator

Table B-2 ASCII printing characters

Character	Decimal Value	Binary Value	Description
SP	32	00100000	Space
!	33	00100001	Exclamation mark
"	34	00100010	Quotation mark
#	35	00100011	Cross hatch (number sign)
$	36	00100100	Dollar sign
%	37	00100101	Percent sign
&	38	00100110	Ampersand
'	39	00100111	Closing single quote (apostrophe)
(	40	00101000	Opening parentheses
)	41	00101001	Closing parentheses
*	42	00101010	Asterisk
+	43	00101011	Plus
,	44	00101100	Comma
-	45	00101101	Hyphen
.	46	00101110	Period
/	47	00101111	Slant
0	48	00110000	Zero
1	49	00110001	One

Table B-2 ASCII printing characters (continued)

Character	Decimal Value	Binary Value	Description
2	50	00110010	Two
3	51	00110011	Three
4	52	00110100	Four
5	53	00110101	Five
6	54	00110110	Six
7	55	00110111	Seven
8	56	00111000	Eight
9	57	00111001	Nine
:	58	00111010	Colon
;	59	00111011	Semicolon
<	60	00111100	Less than sign
=	61	00111101	Equals sign
>	62	00111110	Greater than sign
?	63	00111111	Question mark
@	64	01000000	At-sign
A	65	01000001	Uppercase A
B	66	01000010	Uppercase B
C	67	01000011	Uppercase C
D	68	01000100	Uppercase D
E	69	01000101	Uppercase E
F	70	01000110	Uppercase F
G	71	01000111	Uppercase G
H	72	01001000	Uppercase H
I	73	01001001	Uppercase I
J	74	01001010	Uppercase J
K	75	01001011	Uppercase K
L	76	01001100	Uppercase L
M	77	01001101	Uppercase M
N	78	01001110	Uppercase N
O	79	01001111	Uppercase O
P	80	01010000	Uppercase P
Q	81	01010001	Uppercase Q
R	82	01010010	Uppercase R
S	83	01010011	Uppercase S
T	84	01010100	Uppercase T
U	85	01010101	Uppercase U

Table B-2 ASCII printing characters (continued)

Character	Decimal Value	Binary Value	Description
V	86	01010110	Uppercase V
W	87	01010111	Uppercase W
X	88	01011000	Uppercase X
Y	89	01011001	Uppercase Y
Z	90	01011010	Uppercase Z
[	91	01011011	Opening square bracket
\	92	01011100	Backslash
]	93	01011101	Closing square bracket
^	94	01011110	Caret
_	95	01011111	Underscore
`	96	01100000	Opening single quote
a	97	01100001	Lowercase a
b	98	01100010	Lowercase b
c	99	01100011	Lowercase c
d	100	01100100	Lowercase d
e	101	01100101	Lowercase e
f	102	01100110	Lowercase f
g	103	01100111	Lowercase g
h	104	01101000	Lowercase h
i	105	01101001	Lowercase i
j	106	01101010	Lowercase j
k	107	01101011	Lowercase k
l	108	01101100	Lowercase l
m	109	01101101	Lowercase m
n	110	01101110	Lowercase n
o	111	01101111	Lowercase o
p	112	01110000	Lowercase p
q	113	01110001	Lowercase q
r	114	01110010	Lowercase r
s	115	01110011	Lowercase s
t	116	01110100	Lowercase t
u	117	01110101	Lowercase u
v	118	01110110	Lowercase v
w	119	01110111	Lowercase w
x	120	01111000	Lowercase x
y	121	01111001	Lowercase y

Table B-2 ASCII printing characters (continued)

Character	Decimal Value	Binary Value	Description
z	122	01111010	Lowercase z
{	123	01111011	Opening curly brace
|	124	01111100	Vertical line
}	125	01111101	Closing curly brace
~	126	01111110	Tilde
DEL	127	01111111	Delete

Table B-3 Telecommunications standards organizations

Organization Name	Jurisdiction
American National Standards Institute (ANSI)	National
Electronic Industries Association (EIA)	National
Telecommunications Industries Association (TIA)	National
Internet Engineering Task Force (IETF)	National
Institute of Electrical and Electronics Engineers (IEEE)	National
European Telecommunications Standards Institute (ETSI)	Multinational
European Committee for Electrotechnical Standardization/European Committee for Standardization (CEN/CENELEC)	Multinational
International Telecommunications Union (ITU)	International
The International Standards Organization (ISO)	International

Table B-4 Open system interconnect layers

Layer	Function
Application (Layer 7)	Provides the user interface to allow communications services. These services may include such things as e-mail and transferring files.
Presentation (Layer 6)	Handles how the data is represented and formatted for the user.
Session (Layer 5)	Permits the devices to hold ongoing communications across the network. Handles session setup, data or message exchanges, and tear-down when the session ends.
Transport (Layer 4)	Ensures that error-free data is given to the user.
Network (Layer 3)	Picks the route the transmissions take and handles addressing for delivery.
Data Link (Layer 2)	Detects and corrects errors. If data is not received properly, the Data Link Layer would request it to be retransmitted.
Physical (Layer 1)	Sends signals or receives signals.

Table B-5 Comparison of speeds for Internet connections

Transmission Type	Speed	Typical Use	Time to transmit contents of one 680 MB CD-ROM (hours:minutes)
Dial-up modem	28 Kbps	Home	53:43
Dial-up modem	56 Kbps	Home	26:53
1 channel ISDN	64 Kbps	Home or office	24:10
2 channel ISDN	128 Kbps	Home or office	12:5
Cable modem	1 Mbps	Home	1:36
DSL	1.544 Mbps	Home	0:58
T1	1.544 Mbps	Home	0:58
T3	44.736 Mbps	Office, ISP	0:2
OC-12	622.08 Mbps	ISP	8 seconds
OC-256	13.271 Gbps	Internet backbone	Less than 1 second

Table B-6 Comparison of speeds for computer and LAN connections

Connection Name	Speed	Common Uses
Serial (RS232c)	115 Kbps	External modems
Parallel (IEEE 1284)	500 Kbps – 2 Mbps	Printers
Bluetooth (1.1)	1 Mbps	Cell phones, PDAs
Small Computer System Interface (SCSI-2)	5 Mbps – 10 Mbps	External scanners
Universal Serial Bus (USB)	12 Mbps	Digital cameras
IrDA (VFIR)	16 Mbps	Notebooks
FireWire (IEEE 1394)	50 Mbps	Digital video
Ultra ATA/100	100 Mbps	Internal hard drives
Peripheral Component Interface (PCI)	132 Mbps (33 MHz)	Internal expansion cards
Ultra-3 SCSI	160 Mbps	Internal hard drives
Fibre Channel (ISO 1496-1)	1 Gbps	Server farms

Radio Frequencies

Table B-7 Common radio frequency bands and uses

Band	Frequency	Common Uses
Very Low Frequency (VLF)	10 KHz to 30 KHz	Maritime ship-to-shore
Low Frequency (LF)	30 KHz to 300 KHz	Cordless telephones
Medium Frequency (MF)	300 KHz to 3 MHz	AM radio
High Frequency (HF)	3 MHz to 30 MHz	Short wave radio, CB radio
Very High Frequency (VHF)	30 MHz to 144 MHz 144 MHz to 174 MHz 174 MHz to 328.6 MHz	TV stations 2-6, FM radio Taxi radios TV stations 7-13
Ultra High Frequency (UHF)	328.6 MHz to 806 MHz 806 MHz to 960 MHz 960 MHz to 2.3 GHz 2.3 GHz to 2.9 GHz	Public safety Cellular telephones Air traffic control radar WLANs (802.11b)
Super High Frequency (SHF)	2.9 GHz to 30 GHz	WLANs (802.11a)

Table B-8 Unregulated frequency bands

Unlicensed Band	Frequency	Total Bandwidth	Common Uses
Industrial, Scientific, and Medical (ISM)	902–928 MHz 2.4–2.4835 GHz 5.725–5.85 GHz	234.5 MHz	Cordless phones, WLANs, Wireless Public Branch Exchanges
Unlicensed Personal Communications Systems	1910–1930 MHz 2390–2400 MHz	30 MHz	WLANs, Wireless Public Branch Exchanges
Unlicensed National Information Infrastructure (U-NII)	5.15–5.25 GHz 5.25–5.35 GHz 5.725–5.825 GHz	300 MHz	WLANs, Wireless Public Branch Exchanges, Campus applications, long outdoor links
Millimeter Wave	59–64 GHz	5 GHz	Home networking applications

Table B-9 Unlicensed National Information Infrastructure (U-NII) spectrum

U-NII Band	Frequency (GHz)	Maximum Power Output (mW)
U-NII Lower Band	5.15–5.25	40
U-NII Middle Band	5.25–5.35	200
U-NII Upper Band	5.725–5.825	800

Table B-10 Comparison of ISM and U-NII

Unlicensed Band	Frequency	Total Bandwidth
Industrial, Scientific, and Medical (ISM)	902–928 MHz 2.4–2.4835 GHz 5.725–5.85 GHz	234.5 MHz
Unlicensed National Information Infrastructure (U-NII)	5.15–5.25 GHz 5.25–5.35 GHz 5.725–5.825 GHz	300 MHz

Personal Area Network Information

Table B-11 IrDA Versions

IrDA Version	Speed
Serial Infrared (SIR)	9,600-115,200 bps
Fast Infrared (FIR)	4 Mbps
Very Fast Infrared (VFIR)	16 Mbps

Table B-12 Bluetooth power classes

Name	Power Level	Distance
Power Class 1	100 mW	330 feet (100 meters)
Power Class 2	2.5 mW	33 feet (10 meters)
Power Class 3	1 mW	3 inches (10 centimeters)

Local Area Network Information

Table B-13 802.11b ISM Channels

Channel Number	Frequency (GHz)	Channel Number	Frequency (GHz)
1	2.412	8	2.447
2	2.417	9	2.452
3	2.422	10	2.457
4	2.427	11	2.462
5	2.432	12	2.467
6	2.437	13	2.472
7	2.442	14	2.484

B

Table B-14 WLAN comparison

WLAN	802.11	802.11b	802.11g	802.11a	HiperLAN/2
Spectrum	2.4 GHz	2.4 GHz	2.4 GHz	5 GHz	5 GHz
Standard maximum speed	2 Mbps	11 Mbps	54 Mbps	54 Mbps	54 Mbps
Optional maximum speed				108 Mbps	
Medium access control	CSMA/CA	CSMA/CA	CSMA/CA, ODFM	ODFM	TDMA
Frequency selection	FHSS or DSSS	DSSS	DSSS, single carrier	Single carrier	Dynamic Frequency Selection
QoS	No	No	No	No	Yes
Radio link quality control	No	No	No	No	Yes

Wide Area Network Information

Table B-15 Digital wireless cellular migration path

Name	Generation	Technology	Maximum Speed
AMPS	1G	Analog circuit-switched	9.6 Kbps
GSM	2G	Digital circuit-switched	9.6 Kbps
TDMA	2G	Digital circuit-switched	14.4 Kbps
CDMA	2G	Digital circuit-switched	14.4 Kbps
GPRS	2.5G	Digital packet-switched	114 Kbps
CDMA2000 1XRTT	2.5	Digital packet-switched	144 Kbps
EDGE	2.5G	Digital packet-switched	384 Kbps
CDMA2000 1XEVDO and 1XEVDV	3G	Digital packet-switched	2 Mbps
WCDMA	3G	Digital packet-switched	2 Mbps

Table B-16 Remote wireless bridge specifications

Characteristic	Specifications
Data Rates	1, 2, 5.5 and 11 Mbps
Wireless Medium	Direct Sequence Spread Spectrum
Channel Access Method	CSMA/CD
Modulation	DBPSK (1 Mbps) DQPSK (2 Mbps) CCK (5.5 Mbps, 11 Mbps)
Security	WEP
Frequency	2.4 GHz
Channels	11 (US) 13 (Europe)

Glossary

1/3 rate Forward Error Correction (FEC) — An error correction scheme that repeats each bit three times for redundancy.

16-level quadrature amplitude modulation (16-QAM) — A modulation technique used in 24 Mbps 802.11a transmissions that uses one signal to transmit 4 bits.

16-pulse position modulation (16-PPM) — A modulation technique that translates four data bits into 16 light impulses.

2.5 Generation (2.5G) — An interim step between 2G and 3G digital cellular networks.

2.5G — A digital cellular technology that sends data at a maximum of 384 Kbps.

2/3 rate Forward Error Correction (FEC) — An error correction scheme that uses a mathematical formula to add extra error correction bits to the data sent.

2G (second generation) — A digital cellular techno-logy that sends data at up to 14 Kbps.

2X mode — *See* turbo mode.

3G (third generation) — A digital cellular technology that sends data at up to 2 Mbps and will harmonize all of the different specifications used around the world into one universal standard.

4-pulse position modulation (4-PPM) — A modulation technique that translates two data bits into 4 light impulses.

64-level quadrature amplitude modulation (64-QAM) — A modulation technique used in 54 Mbps 802.11a transmissions that uses 64 different signals.

802.11 standard — An IEEE standard released in 1990 that defines wireless local area networks at a rate of either 1 Mpbs or 2 Mpbs. All WLAN features are contained in the PHY and MAC layers.

802.11b standard — A 1999 addition to the IEEE 802.11 standard for WLANs that added two higher speeds, 5.5 Mbps and 11 Mbps. Also known as Wi-Fi.

access control list — A list of approved MAC addresses contained in an access point.

access point (AP) — A device connected to the wired local area network that receives signals and transmits signals back to wireless clients.

access point (AP) — A device that receives the signals and transmits signals back to wireless network interface cards (NICs).

active mode — A state in which the Bluetooth device actively participates on the channel.

active scanning — The process of sending frames to gather information.

active slaves — Slave devices that are connected to the piconet and are sending transmissions.

ad hoc mode — A WLAN mode in which wireless clients communicate directly among themselves without using an access point.

adaptive array processing — A radio transmission technique that replaces a traditional antenna with an array of antenna elements.

Advanced Mobile Phone Service (AMPS) — The standard used for 1G analog cellular transmissions based on FDMA.

ambient light — Bright surrounding light.

American National Standards Institute (ANSI) — A clearinghouse for standards development in the United States.

American Standard Code for Information Interchange (ASCII) — An arbitrary coding scheme that uses the numbers from 0 to 255.

ampere — Measure of the number of electrons that move through a conductor.

amplifier — A component that increases a signal's intensity.

amplitude — The height of a carrier wave.

amplitude modulation (AM) — A change in the height of the cycle.

amplitude shift keying (ASK) — A binary modulation technique whereby 1 bit has a carrier signal while a 0 bit has no signal.

analog signal — A continuous signal.

antenna — A copper wire, rod, or similar device that has one end up in the air and the other end connected to the ground through a receiver.

AppleTalk — A network protocol stack used by Apple for its Macintosh computers.

associate request frame — A frame sent by a client to an access point that contains the client's capabilities and supported rates.

associate response frame — A frame returned to a client from the access point that contains a status code and client ID number.

association — The process of communicating with other wireless clients or the access point so that the client can become accepted as part of the network.

asynchronous connection-less (ACL) link — A packet-switched link that is used for data transmissions.

Asynchronous Transfer Mode (ATM) — A wide-area network technology that uses fiber-optic media to transmit at 622 Mbps.

attenuation — A loss of signal strength.

authentication — A process that verifies that the user has permission to access the network.

authentication — The process of verifying that the device asking to join the piconet should be allowed to join.

automatic retransmission query (ARQ) — An error correction scheme that continuously retransmits until an acknowledgement is received or timeout value is exceeded.

backhaul — A company's internal infrastructure connection.

backoff interval — A random amount of time that two computers wait before attempting to resend.

bandpass — A filter that passes all signals that are between the maximum and minimum threshold.

bands — Sections of the radio frequency spectrum.

bandwidth — The range of frequencies that can be transmitted.

Base 2 number system — *See* binary number system.

Base 10 number system — *See* decimal number system.

baseband — A transmission technique that treats the entire transmission medium as only one channel.

Basic Service Set (BSS) — A WLAN mode that consists of wireless clients and one access point.

baud — A change in a carrier signal.

baud rate — The number of times that a carrier signal changes per second.

beacon frame — A frame sent from the access point to all stations.

binary number system — A numbering system commonly used by computers that has a base number of 2 and uses the digits 0 and 1.

Binary Runtime Environment for Wireless (BREW) — This is a thin software interface layer that resides on a wireless device and creates a runtime environment.

bit — A binary digit; an electronic 0 or a 1 based on the binary number system.

bits per second (bps) — The number of bits that can be transmitted per second.

Bluetooth — A wireless standard for devices to transmit data at up to 1 Mbps over a distance of 33 feet.

Bluetooth radio module — A single radio transmitter/receiver (transceiver) that performs all of the necessary transmission functions.

bridge — A device to connect two network segments.

broadband — A transmission technique that sends multiple signals at different frequencies.

buffering — The process that the access point uses to temporarily store frames for clients that are in sleep mode.

byte — Eight binary digits (bits).

cable modems — A technology used to transmit data over a television cable connection.

cards — A smaller block of a WML document.

carrier sense — The process of listening before sending in order to detect other traffic.

Carrier Sense Multiple Access with Collision Avoidance (CSMA/CA) — The IEEE 802.11 standard procedure used by WLANs to avoid packet collisions.

Carrier Sense Multiple Access with Collision Detection (CSMA/CD) — The IEEE 802.3 Ethernet standard that specifies contention with a backoff interval if a collision occurs.

carrier signal — A transmission over a radio frequency that carries no useful information.

CCK-OFDM — An optional transmit mode of the IEEE 802.11g draft.

CDMA2000 1XEVDO — The 3G digital cellular technology that is a migration from CDMA2000 1XRTT.

CDMA2000 1XEVDV — The 3G digital cellular technology that is a migration from CDMA2000 1XEVDO.

CDMA2000 1XRTT — A 2.5G digital cellular network technology that is a migration from CDMA.

cells — A smaller area of a mobile network.

challenge-response strategy — A process used to check if the other device knows a shared identical secret key.

channel access methods — The different ways of sharing in a network environment.

channels — Another name for frequencies.

chipping code — A bit pattern used in a DSSS transmission. The term "chipping code" is used because a single radio bit is commonly referred to as a "chip."

circuit switching — A dedicated and direct physical connection is made between two transmitting devices.

Code Division Multiple Access (CDMA) — A technique that uses spread spectrum technology and unique digital codes to send and receive radio transmissions.

collision — A conflict between packets sent by two computers that transmit packets at the same time.

compact flash (CF) card — An expansion card that is used with PDA devices.

compact HTML (cHTML) — A subset of HTML that is designed for mobile devices.

Complementary Code Keying (CCK) — A code of a set of 64 8-bit code words used for transmitting at speeds above 2 Mbps.

connected mode — A state when a device is either an active slave or a master.

consortia — Industry-sponsored organizations that have the goal of promoting a specific technology.

contention — One type of channel access method in which computers compete with each other for the use of the network.

control channel — A special frequency cellular phones use for communication with a base station.

control frames — MAC frames that assist in delivering the frames that contain data.

crosstalk — Signals from close frequencies that may interfere with other signals.

cycle — An oscillating sine wave that completes one full series of movements.

data frames — MAC frames that carry the information to be transmitted to the destination clients.

de facto standards — Common practices that the industry follows for various reasons.

de jure standards — Standards are those that are controlled by an organization or body.

decimal number system — A numbering system that has a base number of 10 and uses the digits 0-9.

deck — A WML document.

deflection angle — The off-alignment angle between two IrDA devices.

detector — A diode that receives a light-based transmission signal.

dibit — A signal that represents two bits.

diffused transmission — A light-based transmission that relies on reflected light.

digital certificates — Data files that are used for encrypted communication.

digital signal — Data that is discrete or separate.

digital subscriber lines (DSL) — A technology used to transmit data over a telephone line.

digital wrapper — A program that is wrapped around another program or file and acts as a gatekeeper to encrypt and secure data.

direct sequence spread spectrum (DSSS) — A spread spectrum technique that uses an expanded, redundant code to transmit each data bit.

directed transmission — A light-based transmission that requires the emitter and detector to be directly aimed at one another.

directional antenna — An antenna that sends the signal in one direction.

disassociation frame — A frame sent by the new access point to the old access point to terminate the old access point's association with the client.

Distributed Coordination Function (DCF) — The default access method for WLANs.

Distributed Coordination Function IFS (DIFS) — The standard interval between the transmission of data frames.

Dynamic Frequency Selection (DFS) — An appropriate radio channel that is selected to minimize interference.

dynamic range — The amount by which a signal's maximum intensity exceeds its minimum detectable level.

electromagnetic interference (EMI) — Interference with a radio signal; also called noise.

Electronic Industries Association (EIA) — U.S. industry vendors from four areas: electronic components, consumer electronics, electronic information, and telecommunications.

emitter — A laser diode or a light-emitting diode that transmits a light-based signal.

encryption — The process of encoding communications and ensures that the transmissions cannot be easily intercepted and decoded.

Enhanced Data Rates for Global Evolution (EDGE) — A 2.5G digital cellular network technology that boosts GPRS transmissions.

European Committee for Electrotechnical Standardization/European Committee for Standardization (CEN/CENELEC) — A multinational standards organization whose role is to set standards regarding environmental and electromechanical issues.

European Telecommunications Standards Institute (ETSI) — A standards body that is designed to develop telecommunications standards for use throughout Europe.

Extended Service Set (ESS) — A WLAN mode that consists of wireless clients and multiple access points.

Extensible Authentication Protocol (EAP) — A security protocol that allows a client to negotiate authentication with an external server.

Extensible Markup Language (XML) — A definition language that uses tags to describe the data.

filter — A component that is used to either accept or to block a radio frequency signal.

firewall — A device that prevents unauthorized access of a network.

FireWire — A high-speed external serial bus that can transmit at 400 Mbps, also known as IEEE 1394.

First Generation (1G) — The first generation of wireless cellular telephony that transmitted at 9.6 Kbps using analog circuit-switched technology.

fixed broadband wireless — Data transmissions that use antennas between sites up to 35 miles apart.

fixed wireless — A wireless last mile connection.

flash memory — Solid-state technology memory that contains no moving parts.

Forward Error Correction (FEC) — Error correction in an 802.11a WLAN.

fragmentation — The division of data to be transmitted from one large frame into several smaller frames.

frame — Another name for a packet.

free space optics (FSO) — An optical, wireless, point-to-point, line-of-sight broadband technology.

frequency — A measurement of radio waves that is determined by how frequently a cycle changes.

Frequency Division Multiple Access (FDMA) — A radio transmission technique that divides the bandwidth of the frequency into several smaller frequency bands.

frequency hopping spread spectrum (FHSS) — A spread spectrum technique that uses a range of frequencies and changes frequencies during the transmission.

frequency modulation (FM) — A change of the number of waves used to represent one cycle.

frequency shift keying (FSK) — A binary modulation technique that changes the frequency of the carrier signal.

full-duplex transmission — Transmissions that enable data to flow in either direction simultaneously.

gain — The measure of the directional intensity of an antenna pattern.

General Packet Radio Service (GPRS) — A 2.5G network technology that can transmit up to 40 Kbps.

geosynchronous earth orbiting (GEO) satellites — Satellites that are stationed at an altitude of 22,282 miles (35,860 kilometers).

gigahertz (GHz) — One billion hertz.

GSM (Global Systems for Mobile communications)— One of three multiple access technologies that make up the 2G digital cellular system that uses a combination of FDMA and TDMA.

half-duplex transmission — Transmission that occurs in both directions but only one way at a time.

handoff — The automatic transfer of the RF signal when moving from one cell to another cell within the same network.

help desk — A central point of contact for users who need assistance using technology.

hertz (Hz) — The number of cycles per second.

high-pass filter — A filter that passes all signals that are above a maximum threshold.

HiperLAN/2 — A proposed high-speed WLAN that is similar to the IEEE 802.11a standard.

hold mode — A state in which the Bluetooth device can put slave units into hold mode where only the slave's internal timer is running.

HomeRF Working Group — A group of over 50 different companies from the personal computer, consumer electronics, communications, and software industries that established the SWAP standard.

hopping code — The sequence of changing frequencies used in FHSS.

Hypertext Markup Language (HTML) — The standard language for displaying content on the World Wide Web.

i-mode — An Internet access system for digital cellular telephones.

IEEE 1394 — A high-speed external serial bus that can transmit at 400 Mbps, also known as FireWire.

IEEE 802.11a — A standard for WLAN transmissions developed in 1999 for networks with speeds up to 54 Mbps and beyond.

IEEE 802.11e Task Group — A group working on incorporating QoS into 802.11 WLANs.

IEEE 802.11g — A draft for WLAN transmissions developed in 2001 for networks with speeds up to 54 Mbps using the ISM band.

IEEE 802.1x — A draft to increase the security of IEEE 802 WLANs.

Independent Basic Service Set (IBSS) — A WLAN mode in which wireless clients communicate directly among themselves without using an access point.

Industrial, Scientific and Medical (ISM) band — An unregulated radio frequency band approved by the FCC in 1985.

infrared light — Light that is next to visible light on the light spectrum that has many of the same characteristics as visible light.

infrastructure mode — A WLAN mode that consists of wireless clients and one access point.

inquire mode — A state when a device is looking for other devices with which to connect.

inquiry procedure — A process that enables a device to discover which devices are in range and determine the addresses and clocks for the devices.

Institute of Electrical and Electronic Engineers (IEEE) 802.11a — A standard that allows WLAN computers to transmit up to 54 Mbps.

Institute of Electrical and Electronic Engineers (IEEE) 802.11b — A standard that allows WLAN computers to transmit up to 11 Mbps over a distance of 375 feet.

Institute of Electrical and Electronics Engineers (IEEE) — A standards body that establishes standards for telecommunications.

Integrated Services Digital Connection (ISDN) — A last mile connection that can transmit at 64 Kbps (2 channels) or 128 Kbps (4 channels).

Integrated Services Digital Networks (ISDN) — A technology that transmits data over telephone lines at a maximum of 256 Kbps.

interframe spaces (IFS) — Time gaps used for special types of transmissions.

intermediate frequency (IF) — The output signal from the modulation process that is between 10 MHz and 100 MHz.

International Organization for Standardization (ISO) — An organization to promote international cooperation and standards in the areas of science, technology, and economics.

International Telecommunications Union (ITU) — An agency of the United Nations that sets international telecommunications standards and coordinates global telecommunications networks and services.

Internet Engineering Task Force (IETF) — A standards body that focuses on the lower levels of telecommunications technologies.

Internetwork Packet eXchange/Sequenced Packet eXchange (IPX/SPX) — A network protocol stack found on Novell NetWare LANs.

IrDA — An acronym for the **I**nfrared **D**ata **A**ssociation and also a standard for wireless infrared communications.

Java — An object-oriented programming language used for general-purpose business programming and interactive Web sites.

Java 2 Micro Edition (J2ME) — A subset of Java specifically developed for programming wireless devices.

kilohertz (KHz) — One thousand hertz.

kilowatts (kW) — Thousands of watts.

last mile connection — The actual connection that reaches the home or office.

latency — A time delay from when a device stops transmitting until it is be ready to receive.

latency — Delays caused by signals that must travel over a long distance.

license exempt spectrum — Unregulated radio frequency bands that are available in the U.S. to any users without a license.

light spectrum — All the different types of light that travel from the sun to the earth.

line of sight — The direct alignment as required in a directed transmission.

link manager — Special software in Bluetooth devices that helps identify other Bluetooth devices, creates the links between them, and sends and receives data.

Local Multipoint Distribution Service (LMDS) — A fixed broadband technology that can provide a wide variety of wireless services.

Logical Link Control (LLC) — One of the two sublayers of the IEEE Project 802 Data Link layer.

low earth orbiting (LEO) satellites — Satellites that orbit the earth at an altitude of 200 to 900 miles (321 to 1,448 kilometers).

low-pass filter — A filter that passes all signals that are below a maximum threshold.

lux — A photometric measurement of light intensity.

MAC address — A unique 48-bit number that is burned into the network interface card when it is manufactured.

management frames — MAC frames that are used to set up the initial communications between a client and the access point.

master — A device on a Bluetooth piconet that controls all of the wireless traffic.

Media Access Control (MAC) — One of the two sublayers of the IEEE Project 802 Data Link layer.

medium earth orbiting (MEO) satellites — Satellites that orbit the earth at altitudes between 1,500 and 10,000 miles (2,413 to 16,090 kilometers).

megahertz (MHz) — One million hertz.

microbrowser — A tiny browser program that runs on a WAP cell phone.

microwaves — Part of the spectrum from 3 to 30 GHz.

milliamps (mA) — Thousandths of an amp.

milliwatt (mW) — One thousandths of a watt.

Mini PCI — A small card that is functionally equivalent to a standard PCI expansion card used for integrating communications peripherals onto a notebook computer.

mixer — A component to combine two inputs to create a single output.

mobile telecommunications switching office (MTSO) — The connection between a cellular network and wired telephones.

modem (MOdulator/DEModulator) — A device used to convert digital signals into an analog format, and vice versa.

modulation — The process of changing a carrier signal.

modulation index — The amount that the frequency varies.

Multichannel Multipoint Distribution Service (MMDS) — A fixed broadband wireless technology that transmits at 1.5 Mbps over distances of 35 miles (56 kilometers).

multipath distortion — The same signal being received not only from several different directions but also at different times.

nanosecond (ns) — One billionth of a second.

narrow-band transmissions — Transmissions that send on one radio frequency or a very narrow portion of the frequencies.

network adapter — A hardware device that connects a computer to the network.

Network Address Translator (NAT) — A router that hides the internal network addresses from the outside world for security.

network interface card (NIC) — A hardware device that connects a computer to the network.

network interface unit (NIU) — A device that connects an LMDS modem to a LAN or telephone system.

network protocol — The format and order of the messages exchanged between two or more communication devices based on standards.

network protocol stack — A set of network protocols taken together as a whole.

noise — Interference with a signal.

non-return-to-zero (NRZ) — A binary signaling technique that increases the voltage to represent a 1 bit, but provides no voltage for a 0 bit.

null data frame — The response that a client sends back to the access point to indicate that the client has no transmissions to make.

official standards — *See* de jure standards.

omnidirectional antenna — An antenna that sends out the signal in a uniform pattern in all directions.

Open System Interconnect (OSI) model — A seven-layer abstract model of networking developed by the ISO (International Organization for Standardization).

Orthogonal Frequency Division Multiplexing (OFDM) — A multiplexing technique used in 802.11a WLANs.

oscillating signal — A wave that illustrates the change in a carrier signal.

packet — A smaller segment of the transmitted signal.

packet acknowledgment (ACK) — A procedure for reducing collisions by requiring the receiving station to send an explicit packet back to the sending station.

packet switching — Data transmission that is broken into smaller units.

page mode — A state when a master device is asking to connect to a specific slave.

paging procedure — A process that enables a device to make an actual connection to a piconet.

parity bit — An optional bit that is used for error checking.

park mode — A state in which the Bluetooth device is still synchronized to the piconet but it does not participate in the traffic.

park/hold mode — A state when a device is in part of the piconet but is in a low-power mode.

parked slaves — Slave devices that are connected to the piconet but are not actively participating.

passband — A minimum and maximum threshold.

passive scanning — The process of listening to each available channel for a set period of time.

PBCC-22 (Packet Binary Convolutional Coding) — An optional transmit mode of the IEEE 802.11g draft.

peer-to-peer mode — A WLAN mode in which wireless clients communicate directly among themselves without using an access point.

Peripheral Component Interface (PCI) — The standard 32-bit PC bus architecture.

personal area network (PAN) — *See* piconet.

Personal Digital Assistant (PDA) — A hand-held computer device often used for taking notes, making records, and communicating with other devices.

phase modulation (PM) — A change in the starting point of a cycle.

phase shift keying (PSK) — A binary modulation technique that changes the starting point of the cycle.

Physical Layer Convergence Procedure (PLCP) sublayer — One of the two sublayers of the IEEE Project 802 PHY layer that reformats the data received from the MAC layer into a packet and determines when the data can be sent.

Physical Medium Dependent (PMD) sublayer — One of the two sublayers of the IEEE Project 802 PHY layer that includes standards for the characteristics of the wireless medium (IR and RF) and defines the method for transmitting and receiving data through that medium.

piconet — A Bluetooth network that contains one master and at least one slave that use the same channel.

piconet — Two or more Bluetooth devices that are sending and receiving data with each other.

pizza box antenna — A small antenna used for MMDS systems.

Point Coordination Function (PCF) — The 802.11 optional polling function.

Point Coordination Function IFS (PIFS) — A time gap interval that clients use when polling nodes that have a specific time requirement.

polar non-return-to-zero (Polar NRZ) — A binary signaling technique that increases the voltage to represent a 1 bit, but drops to negative voltage to represent a 0 bit.

polling — A channel access method in which each computer is asked in sequence whether it wants to transmit.

power management — An 802.11 standard that allows the mobile client to be off as much as possible to conserve battery life but still not miss out on data transmissions.

power over Ethernet — A technology that provides power over an Ethernet cable.

privacy — Standards that assure that transmissions are not read by unauthorized users.

probe — A frame sent by a client when performing active scanning.

probe response — A frame sent by an access point when responding to a client's active scanning probe.

Project 802 — A set of specifications developed by the Institute of Electrical and Electronics Engineers (IEEE) to ensure interoperability among network devices.

proprietary — A created device that is owned by a specific vendor.

public key — Cryptography that uses matched public and private keys for encryption and decryption.

quadbit — A signal that represents four bits.

quadrature amplitude modulation (QAM) — A combination of phase modulation with amplitude modulation to produce 16 different signals.

quadrature phase shift keying (QPSK) — A modulation technique used in 12 Mbps 802.11a transmissions that varies both the starting point and amplitude.

quality-of-service (QoS) — A technology that allows transmissions to be prioritized.

radio frequency spectrum — The entire range of all radio frequencies that exist.

radio module — A small radio transceiver built onto microprocessor chips that are embedded into Bluetooth devices and enable them to communicate.

radio wave (radiotelephony) — An electromagnetic wave created when an electric current passes through a wire and creates a magnetic field in the space around the wire.

reassociation — The process of a client dropping the connection with one access point and reestablishing the connection with another.

reassociation request frame — A frame sent from a client to a new access point asking whether it can associate with the access point.

reassociation response frame — A frame sent by an access point to a station indicating that it will accept its reassociation with that access point.

recurring costs — Costs that continue to be paid over a period of time.

Remote Authentication Dial-In User Service (RADIUS) — A standard method for providing authentication services.

remote wireless bridge — A system designed to connect two or more baseband networks together that are located in different buildings.

repeater — A device commonly used in satellite communications that simply "repeats" the signal to another location.

request for information (RFI) — A document sent to a vendor to gain general information about a vendor's products or solutions to a problem.

request for proposal (RFP) — A detailed planning document with precise specifications for the products and services.

Request to Send/Clear to Send (RTS/CTS) — An 802.11 option that allows a station to reserve the network for transmissions.

return on investment (ROI) — The profit or advantage of an action.

return-to-zero (RZ) — A binary signaling technique that increases the voltage to represent a 1 bit, but the voltage is reduced to zero before the end of the period for transmitting the 1 bit, and there is no voltage for a 0 bit.

roaming — The automatic transfer of the RF signal when moving from one cellular network to another network.

RZI (return to zero, inverted) — A modified binary signaling technique in that the voltage to represent a 0 bit is increased.

scanning — The process that a client uses to examine the airwaves for information that it needs in order to begin the association process.

scatternet — A group of piconets in which connections exist between different piconets.

scintillation — The temporal and spatial variations in light intensity caused by atmospheric turbulence.

Second Generation (2G) — The second generation of cellular telephony that uses circuit-switched digital networks.

Second Generation MMDS — The successor to MMDS that uses OFDM and eliminates direct line-of-sight requirements.

Service Set Identifier (SSID) — A unique identifier assigned to an access point.

shared key — Cryptography that uses the same key to encrypt and decrypt a message.

Shared Wireless Access Protocol (SWAP) — A set of specifications for wireless data and voice communications around the home that can include computer equipment, cordless telephones, and home entertainment equipment.

Short IFS (SIFS) — A time gap used for immediate response actions such as ACK.

Short Message Services (SMS) — A delivery system for short, text-based messages sent between wireless devices such as cellular telephones and pagers.

sidebands — The sum and the differences of the frequency carrier that serve as buffer space around the frequency of the transmitted signal.

signal-to-noise ratio (SNR) — The measure of signal strength relative to the background noise.

simplex transmission — Transmission that occurs in only one direction.

sine wave — A wave that illustrates the change in a carrier signal.

slave — A device on a Bluetooth piconet that takes commands from the master.

sled — An external attachment known for a PDA that permits external cards to attach to the device.

sleep mode — A power-conserving mode used by notebook computers.

slot time — The amount of time that a station must wait after the medium is clear.

sniff mode — A state in which the Bluetooth device listens to the piconet master at a reduced rate so that it uses less power.

spatial diversity — The sending of parallel beams during free space optical transmissions.

spread spectrum transmission — A technique that takes a narrow signal and spreads it over a broader portion of the radio frequency band.

standby mode — A state when a device waiting to join a piconet.

start bit — An optional bit used as a delineator that indicates when the transmitted byte starts.

stop bit — An optional bit used as a delineator that indicates when the transmitted byte stops.

subchannels — A division of a 20 MHz channel that carries data in an 802.lb WLAN.

subnets — A smaller unit of a network.

super high frequency (SHF) — Part of the frequency spectrum from 3 to 30 GHz.

SWAP — *See* Shared Wireless Access Protocol.

switching — Moving a signal from one wire or frequency to another.

synchronous connection-oriented (SCO) link — A symmetric point-to-point link between a master and a single slave in the piconet that functions like a circuit-switched link by using reserved slots at regular intervals.

T-1 — A technology to transmit data over special telephone lines at 1.544 Mbps.

T1 — A special high-speed connection leased from the local telephone system that transmits at 1.544 Mbps.

T3 — A special high-speed connection leased from the local telephone system that transmits at 44.736 Mbps.

Telecommunications Industries Association (TIA) — Over 1,100 members that manufacture or supply the products and services used in global communications.

Third Generation (3G) — Digital cellular wireless generation of cellular telephony with speeds up to 2 Mbps.

Time Division Multiple Access (TDMA) — A transmission technique that divides the bandwidth into several time slots.

time slots — The measurement of a PLCP frame.

traffic indication map (TIM) — A list of the stations that have buffered frames waiting at the access point.

Transmission Control Protocol/Internet Protocol (TCP/IP) — The standard network protocol stack used on the Internet.

tribit — A signal that represents three bits.

turbo mode — An IEEE 802.11a option that permits increased speeds in excess of 54 Mbps.

two-level Gaussian frequency shift keying (2-GFSK) — A binary signaling technique that uses two different frequencies to indicate whether a 1 or a 0 is being transmitted in addition to varying the number of waves.

UART (Universal Asynchronous Receiver/Transmitter) — A microchip that controls a computer's interface to its attached serial devices through a serial port or IrDA port.

ultra-wideband transmission (UWB) — Low-power, precisely timed pulses of energy that operate in the same frequency spectrum as low-end noise, such as that emitted by computer chips and TV monitors.

Universal Asynchronous Receiver/Transmitter (UART) — A microchip that controls a computer's interface to its attached serial devices through a serial port or IrDA port.

Universal Serial Bus (USB) — A low-speed serial interface that operates at a maximum speed of 12 Mbps.

Unlicensed National Information Infrastructure (U-NII) — An unregulated band approved by the FCC in 1996 to provide for short-range, high-speed wireless digital communications.

unregulated bands — *See* license exempt spectrum.

upfront costs — Costs that are necessary to start a project.

virtual carrier sensing — An 802.11 option that allows a station to reserve the network for transmissions.

Virtual Private Network (VPN) — A secure, encrypted connection between two points.

voltage — Electrical pressure.

WAP — *See* Wireless Application Protocol.

WAP gateway — A device that translates HTML to WML so that it can be displayed on a WAP cell phone; also called a WAP proxy.

WAP proxy — A device that translates HTML to WML so that it can be displayed on a WAP cell phone; also called a WAP gateway.

watt — A single unit of electrical power.

Web browser — Software that runs on a local PC and makes a request from the World Wide Web file server for a Web page.

Wi-Fi — Another name for the IEEE 802.11b standard.

Wi-Fi5 — Another name for IEEE 802.11a.

Wideband CDMA (WCDMA) — The 3G digital cellular technology that is a migration from EDGE.

Wired Equivalent Privacy (WEP) — The IEEE specification for data encryption between wireless devices.

Wireless Application Protocol (WAP) — A standard for transmitting, formatting, and displaying Internet data for devices like cell phones.

wireless application service provider (WASP) — An organization that can design, create, and deliver a complete wireless application.

wireless communications — The transmission of user data without the use of wires.

wireless gateway — A combination of several technologies that permits a home user to have wireless capabilities.

wireless home networking adapter — A device that connects to a home computer to transmit and receive data over radio waves.

wireless local area network (WLAN) — A local area network that is not connected by wires but instead uses wireless technology.

Wireless Markup Language (WML) — A language for displaying Internet content on WAP cell phones.

wireless network interface card — A network interface card (NIC) installed in a computer that performs the same functions as a standard NIC, except that it does not have a cable that connects it to the network, and it includes an antenna for wireless communication.

WML — *See* Wireless Markup Language.

Index

A

B

G

H

I